WARRIOR
POET

ALSO BY ALEXIS DE VEAUX

Na-ni
Spring in the Street
Don't Explain: A Song of Billie Holiday
An Enchanted Hair Tale

WARRIOR POET

A Biography of

Audre Lorde

Alexis De Veaux

W. W. Norton & Company
New York   London

Excerpts of poems from *Collected Poems* by Audre Lorde.
Copyright © 1997 by the Estate of Audre Lorde. Used by the
permission of W. W. Norton & Company, Inc.

For information about permission to reproduce
selections from this book, write to Permissions, W. W. Norton &
Company, Inc., 500 Fifth Avenue, New York, NY 10110

Book design by Brooke Koven
Production manager: Julia Druskin
Manufacturing by The Maple-Vail Book Manufacturing Group

Library of Congress Cataloging-in-Publication Data

De Veaux, Alexis, 1948–
Warrior poet : a biography of Audre Lorde / Alexis De Veaux.—1st ed.
p. ; cm.
Includes bibliographical references and index.
ISBN 0-393-01954-3
1. Lorde, Audre. 2. Poets, American—20th century—Biography. 3. Feminists—
United States—Biography. 4. Lesbians—United States—Biography. 5. African
American lesbians—Biography. 6. African American poets—Biography.
7. African American women—Biography. I. Title.
PS3562.O75 Z66 2004
811'.54—dc22

2003023349

W. W. Norton & Company, Inc., 500 Fifth Avenue, New York, N.Y. 10110
www.wwnorton.com

W. W. Norton & Company, Ltd., Castle House, 75/76 Wells Street, London W1T 3QT

1 2 3 4 5 6 7 8 9 0

To my dear L

CONTENTS

INTRODUCTION

Audre Lorde lived two lives. As this biography proposes, in her first life the three themes of escape, freedom, and self-actualization were crucial determinants. The theme of escape was central to Lorde's childhood and teenage years. As a young woman, the overarching theme of freedom provided both problematic and imaginative constructs for Lorde's lesbianism, structuring her identities as poet, mother, teacher. These multiple identities evolved, defined by her identity as lesbian, and by the development of a black lesbian eroticism within and without her work. Her eroticism became essential to Audre Lorde's self-actualization most specifically when, in November 1977, she confronted the possibility of cancer in her life.

Lorde's second life began after she was diagnosed with breast cancer and underwent a mastectomy in 1978. That life was defined by four related themes: her experiences with breast cancer; fear of a cancer recurrence; denial of the diagnosis of secondary liver cancer; and finally acceptance that she had metastatic cancer of the liver and that it was incurable. The impact of cancer performed a transfiguration not only of Lorde's physicality but of her personality, creativity, and social activism.

Crucial to understanding Lorde's two lives was coming to terms with how to write her biography. Since this was to be the first biography of Audre Lorde, there were no models; no one else's book about her to use as a measure. With that in mind, I interviewed her children, one of her sisters, her ex-husband, many of her lifelong friends, former students, other artists who were her peers, and several feminist activists. Not only did I have access to the interviews Gloria Joseph conducted with Lorde prior to Lorde's death, I also had access to Joseph's interviews of Lorde's sisters, Phyllis and Helen. I had many conversations with Gloria Joseph, from whom I learned important insights. I took trips to Grenada, Carriacou, and St. Croix, and walked around the Harlem neighborhood where Lorde grew up, as well as St. Paul's Avenue on Staten Island, where she'd lived with Frances Clayton and her children.

The artifacts of Lorde's life informed my approach. The executors of her estate permitted me sole access to the contents of the thirty-odd boxes of her papers and memorabilia officially archived at Spelman College, in Atlanta, Georgia. The Lesbian Herstory Archives in Brooklyn, New York; the Caribbean Cultural Center in Manhattan; and the Schomburg Center for Research in Black Culture in Harlem provided additional materials. Lorde left over sixty unpublished journals, and they are a primary source for examining her interior life. Along with her published writings, these journals are crucial to a portrait of who she was. In addition, I read and made use of numerous critical articles about her and reviews of her work. I also taught her work in undergraduate and graduate Women's Studies seminars as a way of examining aspects of her biography. Lorde's letters, speeches, copies of audio- and videotapes, medical records, photographs, wedding dress, divorce papers, passports, lists of things to do, and prescription medicines were further invaluable sources of information.

There were constant decisions to be taken, sentence by sentence, about how to make use of the interstices between "private," "unpublished," "published," and "public" data. How to overcome the struggle between justice to Audre Lorde and justice to the historical record. And how to write of an Audre Lorde who was brilliant, intimidating, visionary: a woman who was creatively ambitious; financially generous toward other women writers, though she was often barely solvent herself; competitive with respect to her peers; sexually aggressive; vulnerable to any real or perceived racial slight; and at once intensely public and intensely private. How to write of her rage and oftentimes violent temper; to present her as real rather than as monstrous. How to walk the bridges of her life, to become—and not become—her. How to write of "the difficult miracle"[1] of being human.

Initially, searching for *the* truth seemed central to making these decisions. In time, I remembered what my mother used to say: "There are three sides to every story. Your side, my side, and the truth." That is what she would say whenever she doubted the explanations my siblings and I gave for our behavior, when her perception of the truth differed from ours. The truth, my mother explained, is unknown and resides within the unknown because every storyteller performs two acts: telling some things and leaving out other things. Thus, we all tell the stories we want to tell truths about. Recalling my mother's triangulated construct of arriving at—or not arriving at—the truth released me from looking for one truth. I began to accept seemingly differing scripts, differing artifacts, as competing truths.

In Audre Lorde's life, there were many moments shaped by such truths. Like individual portraits taken over a lifetime, they were true in the moment and co-existed, much as the double gaze of the subject at the camera's lens and the eye behind it. However much that double gaze might be read as contradictory—either by the subject or the photographer—after the fact, contradiction alone does not define truth. In short, competing truths, or "facts," are useful to shaping complexities rather than absolutes.

Deciding when or whether to make distinction between the "real" and the "fictive" Audre Lorde raised its own issues. Lorde's highly stylized literary imagination blended facts with fiction in her poetry, interviews, published journal entries, and prose, and framed much of what was publicly known about her childhood and life. Discursive interpretations of Lorde's life, and much of the theory about her life and work, were dependent upon her published versions. Without the advantage of access to her unpublished journals, manuscripts, correspondence, to the private perspectives of family, friends, and associates, such readings of Lorde were valid as discourse, if not truth. Thus, verifying events, dates, relationships, and other "facts" often necessitated taking a subjective rather than objective position as biographer[2] and seeing "all facts as artifacts, and context and argument as copartners of fact."[3] Of course, the danger here rests within my subjectivity and in an interpretive voice that sees Lorde through her eyes and mine. This in turn produces "an uncomfortable sort of double vision,"[4] in which my own critical imagination projects an essential but inherently dangerous landscape[5] upon which Lorde's lives are reconstructed and upon which I have told truths about the story I wanted to tell.

A story of the story of her life, then, this biography begins by situating Lorde's development within the context of her parents' migration from the Caribbean to America and ends with Lorde's return to the Caribbean—to St. Croix, specifically, two years after she was diagnosed with metastasized liver cancer. She lived for six years beyond the end of her work as social activist. Although her activism was far from over once she took up residence in St. Croix, the pace of living there provided a needed respite from the warrior life she'd led on the activist front lines of America. I conclude the biography in 1986 rather than in 1992, when she died, for significant reasons. Chief among these was my sense of Lorde's spiritual homelessness for much of her life. A self-described "black, lesbian, feminist, mother, poet warrior," she entered many "homes," or social movements, throughout her life; and yet, until she relocated to the Caribbean, she remained searching, each time, for a more perfect, more fully accepting homeland.

Another primary reason for ending the biography in 1986 was because I did not want to overemphasize the cancer. Beyond what was necessary to explicate her two lives up until that time, I had no wish to chronicle the prognostics of a terminal disease. In her final years, Audre Lorde managed complex medical realities with each new bout of hope, despair, emergency, prescription for medication, appointment, surge or absence of energy; refusing all the while to live without art, peace, a political life, the women she loved.

ACKNOWLEDGMENTS

THERE ARE SO many I wish to thank. Without this vast community of resources, I could not have withstood the demands of this project.

I thank Audre Lorde. She left behind an extraordinary legacy, and the opportunity to contribute to an understanding of it is an honor. Along with her published work, her journals were foundational to a portrait of who she was. I thank her children, Elizabeth Lorde-Rollins and Jonathan Rollins. Lorde's ex-husband, Edwin Rollins, broke a silence he'd maintained some twenty years after their divorce. I am grateful he was willing, and trusting enough to do so. Lorde's sisters, Helen Lorde, Phyllis Lorde Blackwell, and Mavis Jones, were generous beyond expectation, as was her cousin, Hilda Wells. I thank Frances Clayton, Lorde's partner in life for some seventeen years. Although Ms. Clayton did not respond to my efforts to interview her and to include her perspectives on their life together, her silence challenged me even more.

As Lorde's companion, Gloria Joseph was exceptionally generous. She gave me the tapes and transcripts representing months of interviews that Lorde directed, before her death, were to be used in constructing her biography. She also provided me with boxes of Lorde's papers, video-tapes, journals, photographs, unpublished work, and other memorabilia. A witness to the event, it was Joseph who offered the details shaping the story of Lorde's meeting with one of the twin sisters she did not know she had, which I use in the Epilogue. Our conversations, in person, by mail, and by telephone, were crucially important; as was her support, despite our often differing interpretations of Audre Lorde's life.

Of the intimate friends Lorde was known to, I thank Adrienne Rich and Michelle Cliff who, in addition to allowing extensive interviews, gave me access to their private correspondence. I also thank Diane di Prima, Joan Sandler, Ruth Baharas Gollobin, Blanche Cook, Clare Coss, Barbara Smith, Margaret Randall, Jewelle Gomez, Cheryl Clarke, Yolanda Rios Butts, Melinda Goodman, Neal and Martha Einson, Judith McDaniel, Nancy Bereano, and Joan Nestle, and Ada Gay Griffin and Michelle Parkerson for their film, *A Litany for Survival: The Life and Work of Audre Lorde.*

I am indebted to the following individuals and institutions for their invaluable research assistance and support: Glendora Johnson-Cooper, Associate Librarian, State University of New York at Buffalo; Tom Taylor, English Department, Hunter College; Tracy Flaum, Assistant Counsel, Office of Legal Affairs, Hunter College; the Lesbian Herstory Archives, Brooklyn, New York; Mora Byrd, Caribbean Cultural Center, New York City; Dr. Harold P. Freeman, Director, Department of Surgery, Harlem Hospital Center, New York City, and former national president of the American Cancer Society; the communications office of John Jay College of Criminal Justice, New York City; Mrs. Nin, secretary, St. Catherine of Genoa School, New York City; Sharon Howard, librarian, the Schomburg Center for Research in Black Culture, New York City; Sister Luann Carmon, St. Mark's School, New York City; Federal Bureau of Investigation, Freedom of Information-Privacy Acts Section, U.S. Department of Justice; Dr. Angela Bowen, formerly of the University of Massachusetts; the staff and faculty of the Department of African American Studies, SUNY at Buffalo; Dr. Bahati Kuumba, Women's Resource Center, Spelman College, Atlanta; Maida Tilden; Mary Van Vorst, WBFO, Buffalo, New York; Cindy Ehlers and Mary Soom, reference librarians, Lockwood Library, State University of New York at Buffalo;

the information specialists at Roswell Park Cancer Institute, Buffalo, New York; Bev Harrison, a former staff member of the Department of American Studies, SUNY at Buffalo, for transcribing my interviews; Spelman College, for housing Lorde's papers; and the estate of Audre Lorde.

I owe an enormous debt to my research assistants, Anne Borden (Department of Women's Studies, SUNY at Buffalo), Michelin Gooden (Department of African American Studies, SUNY at Buffalo), Aprille Charity Nace (Undergraduate Library, SUNY at Buffalo), and Ayanna Blake (Ronald E. McNair Baccalaureate Program, SUNY at Buffalo); without them I could not have tracked down essential materials from national and international sources. In particular, Shelby Crosby, a doctoral student in the English Department, SUNY at Buffalo, was an extraordinary assistant and friend whose faith in me was a light in the dark. She taught me how to access and use on-line databases; I owe her a debt I can never repay. I also owe an enormous debt to Taronda Spencer, Archivist at Spelman College for her generosity, dedication, and willingness to respond to my cries for help.

My colleagues and friends at the State University of New York at Buffalo deserve particular mention. I am deeply grateful to my colleague in Women's Studies, Professor Monica Jardine, who mentored much of my thinking on Caribbean history, inspiring and challenging me through countless hours of conversation and debate. I thank Professor Judy Scales-Trent, School of Law; Professor Stephanie Phillips, School of Law; Kerry Grant, Dean of the Graduate School (former Dean, College of Arts and Sciences); Professor Isabel Marcus, School of Law; former Associate Professor Carlene Polite, Department of English; Professor Nathan Grant, Department of English; Professor Deidre Lynch, Department of English; Professor Stephen Henderson, Department of Theatre and Dance; Professor Peter Ekeh, Department of African American Studies; Professor John Mohawk, Center for the Americas; Professor Michael Frisch, Department of History; and colleagues who are no longer on the faculty of the Department of American Studies, including Professors Francisco Pabon, Elizabeth Kennedy, Hester Eisenstein, and the late Professors Alfredo Matilla and Lawrence Chisolm. I thank Professor Chisolm's partner, Pat Shelly, who, in the midst of her grief, guided me through Larry's vast library, carrying out his wish that his books be given to his friends, colleagues, and former students. Thus I inherited a number of books on black history and cultural studies that have enriched me immensely. I appreciate and thank the staffs of the Departments of Women's Studies and American Studies, including Iris Cintron, Kathy Kosinski, and June License.

I thank all of my undergraduate and graduate students for participating in and helping me to promote the first seminars solely devoted to Audre Lorde's work to be taught at SUNY at Buffalo.

For their faith in me, I am grateful, beyond words, to the following writers: Elaine Brown, Wesley Brown, Abena Busia, Jayne Cortez, Jimmie Gilliam, Calvin Hernton, June Jordan, Catherine McKinley, Toni Morrison, Aisha Rahman, Sonia Sanchez, Alice Walker, Michele Wallace, Mary Helen Washington, and Evelyn C. White.

I am especially thankful to my agent Charlotte Sheedy, and her associates at the Charlotte Sheedy Literary Agency, Inc. Also to Jill Bialosky, vice president and senior editor at W. W. Norton, for her faith in this project. Her assistant editor, Deirdre O'Dwyer, deserves a special thank you here for her patience and editorial skills, which guided me through the tedious task of revising a lengthy manuscript.

I thank my family, the De Veaux clan, and other very special people in my life, including Marie Dutton Brown, Carole Byard, Kathy Engel, Cheryll Greene, Gwendolen Hardwick, Evelyn M. Harris, Sheila Lloyd, Valerie Maynard, Kathryn Neeson, Debora Ott, Ted Pearson, Jonathan Snow, Susan L. Taylor, my gardening mentors Catherine and Jeff of All Seasons Lawn Care, my accountant Linda Rader, my "intellectual son" Dr. Mark Anthony Neal, and Dr. Safoura Boukari, who taught me about sisterhood the African way.

I thank Cande, my cocker spaniel and constant companion, for teaching me how to communicate in other tongues.

I thank all who've ever touched my life and are too numerous to name here.

Finally, but first and foremost, I thank Loyce Stewart, without whom I could not rise above the clouds.

the first life

PART ONE

"The Transformation of Silence . . ."
(1934–54)

ONE

AUDRE LORDE's birthplace, Harlem, New York City, became known in the decade before she was born as the "Negro capital of the world." The most vibrant urban community of its time, black Harlem was a symbol of "Negro" success.[1] It had birthed the Harlem Renaissance, which brought to its neighborhoods writers, artists, and cultural powerbrokers the likes of Alain Locke, Langston Hughes, Ale'lia Walker, Countee Cullen, Zora Neale Hurston, Charles Johnson, and Jessie Fauset, among the scores of known and lesser known artists. Harlem had been synonymous with W. E. B. Du Bois's "Talented Tenth" and the "New Negro" movement, and later, with Marcus Garvey's United Negro Improvement Association (UNIA), and his ill-fated "Back to Africa" movement.[2] The neighborhood became a hotbed of unprecedented black artistic and cultural life, underwritten by white patrons eager to experience "the souls of black folk" at the same time they manipulated, censored, and capitalized upon them financially.[3] By the mid-1920s, natives of Harlem were real estate brokers, racketeers, an educated elite, semiskilled and unskilled laborers, entertainers, bootleggers, religious and quasi-religious leaders. It also drew to its teeming streets and tree-lined boulevards thousands of southern, working-class black migrants in search of better economic opportunities.

At the same time, Harlem had become home to black immigrants from West Africa, South America, and several Caribbean island-nations. In the first three decades of the twentieth century, an estimated forty thousand Caribbean immigrants, hailing largely from islands colonized by the British and also in search of better economic conditions, settled in Harlem.[4] This mixture of native-born and foreign-born blacks created a community in which an interplay of multiple ethnicities, languages, social customs, and shifting identities informed the dynamics of an area shaped by intraracial cooperation and conflict.[5]

It was no coincidence that the historic migration of southern blacks to the North and Caribbean immigrants to America would happen at the same time. Both migratory movements were influenced and affected by changing labor conditions, the growth patterns and needs of industry in both geographic locations, and by expanding transportation networks which made access to northern cities more possible.[6]

Like their southern counterparts, most Caribbean immigrants were young and single. Once in the States, they moved in with relatives already established or with someone from their home island, and into established or emerging black communities—a pattern enforced by racist housing practices, which limited the general pool of housing prospects for native- and foreign-born blacks alike.[7] They relied on extended kinship networks to provide jobs, a social life, and a sense of home. As was the case with most native-born families who migrated intact, theirs were two-parent households.[8]

Despite misperceptions of these migrants as peasants from rural areas, many who settled in Harlem came from small towns and cities; many had migrated from one Caribbean island to another before immigrating to the States. Although the vast majority were working class, a small percentage were skilled tradespeople who found jobs in industry and commerce.[9] Others were educated professionals who made up a Caribbean Talented Tenth,[10] and were vital members of Harlem's renaissance, its radical political circles, and fledgling professional and business classes. Caribbean immigration might be viewed as male-led, since men outnumbered women; but women played an important role in shaping the flow of migration from region to region, within their own families, and in maintaining social networks between home and New York City. Caribbean women sent clothes, money, and news back to the islands.[11]

Two of Linda Belmar Lorde's sisters, Henrietta and Lila, had already come to America; Lila worked at Sak's Fifth Avenue. They encouraged Audre's parents to come to the States. From all accounts, Linda and Frederick Byron Lorde arrived in Harlem sometime in 1924, the date that would end a thirteen-year period, beginning in 1911, of heavy black immigration.[12] They traveled by steamer in steerage. Like the millions of European immigrants flocking to the United States in search of better economic opportunities as they disembarked in New York Harbor and passed through Ellis Island, the Lordes were young (she twenty-seven years old, he twenty-six, married only a year), poor, and determined to make their fortunes in "the land of opportunity."

One of the many survival strategies Linda Belmar Lorde brought with her from Grenada was a strong work ethic, inculcated by the women on her mother's side of the family. Her mother, Elizabeth Noel (known as "Ma-Liz"), had an older sister, Annie. The Noel sisters lived on Noel's Hill in Grenville. They were hardworking tenders of the soil, fruit harvesters, and goat and pig farmers; their mother, Ma-Mariah, taught them the healing properties of common herbs. They also had a brother, Matthew, of which little is known. Their neighbors knew the Noel sisters as haughty women who, convinced of the privileged status of their lighter skin, looked down upon darker-skinned Grenadians. The caste system of color hierarchy they internalized had been around since the French first subdued and then intermixed with the island's Carib Indians in 1650; and had persisted as Grenada was alternately colonized by the French and British empires. In 1783, Grenada passed into British hands solely, and the British imported African slaves to work their sugar plantations.[13] Generations later, miscegenation borne out of slavery and colonialism produced the culture of the color-conscious Noel sisters.

Liz and Annie led typical, uncomplicated lives; their routines were disturbed only now and then by the sight and sounds of young men from nearby islands whose interisland voyages in search of work and lives at sea brought them to the coastal shores of Grenville town. Two such men were the Belmar brothers, Portuguese seamen who'd settled in Carriacou, a small island just off Grenada.

Like other men from Carriacou, the Belmar brothers often docked there, to replenish their supplies and to find work or rest, before setting out to sea again. Although Grenville town was home to many young, unmarried women, it was the refined, intriguing Noel sisters who caught their eyes. Once smitten, the Belmars courted and then married the two sisters. While Annie returned to Carriacou with her husband to live in a house in the hills between L'Esterre and Harvey Vale, Liz stayed on in Grenada with her sailor-husband, Peter. Each time Liz gave birth, she shuttled on one of the interisland ferries to Carriacou and the comfort of her sister's midwifery skills.[14]

When Ma-Liz was pregnant with the last of her seven daughters, Lila, Peter Belmar died at sea. With no job and no money coming in and head of the family now, Ma-Liz hired herself out to other families in need of child care, augmenting a meager income with her abilities as a seamstress. She made clothes for richer people, and designed outfits for entire wedding parties. Despite the trials of being the family's primary financial provider—a new role thrust on her by widowhood—she held her head high, proudly determined to accept neither charity nor defeat. She was to pass the example of her own womanhood on to her second youngest, Linda, and to her other daughters.

With Ma-Liz working away from home, Sister Lou (as she was called), the third and oldest daughter still living at home at the time, mothered her younger sisters. She cultivated in them the Belmars' sense of superiority as a family of light-skinned women and their ingrained dislike for the cheap habits of "common" (meaning darker-skinned) people who drank in public, put their business in the street, and otherwise carried themselves without comportment.

As the years went by, Linda internalized the Belmars' prejudices toward black people who were darker than them. Gray-eyed and light enough to be white herself, she was "extremely fair"-skinned and developed into a woman who "set a great store by the shade of people's color," demonstrating "intense prejudice" toward "dark black people," of whom she was as deeply mistrustful as she was of whites. Racially black but white in looks, and suffering the burden of being "somewhere in between," Linda Belmar developed an intense dislike of both dark black and white people—a self-loathing which had its roots in the sexual history between the Portuguese, Carib, and British vividly present in the rainbow of shadings, hair, eye color, and social attitudes of her own family members.[15]

The courtship between Linda Belmar and Byron Lorde began almost immediately after Linda finished the seventh grade, the Grenadian equivalent of junior high school, at age seventeen. It was to last almost ten years, during which parental control, the Belmars' high social standards, and an overprotective sense of what was "proper" made it difficult for Linda's admirers. Ma-Liz raised some objection to Byron because he'd had children previously and was "too black."[16] Although not a dark-skinned black man, Byron was certainly darker than the Belmars; but he was a charming, handsome, ambitious six-footer who would become first a police constable, then the owner of a general store. His persistence would eventually win over Linda's family.

The son of an unmarried woman, Byron had been left at age seven in the care of a father he did not know.[17] At fifteen, an apprentice in his father's tailoring business, he ran away to sea. He lived as a drifter, and searched for his mother. He found her years later: she was married, had new sons, and didn't want Byron around.[18] Unwilling to divulge anything about his childhood and adolescent years, little else is known of Byron Lorde's early life.

Byron and Linda were married in 1923, in what was then called the Main Church, which was Catholic. The almost fairy-talelike wedding was a huge family affair and the wedding party's outfits were handmade by Ma-Liz. Nearly six feet tall herself, buxom, and a considered beauty (who later developed bad teeth that caused her not to like to smile), Linda stood at the altar in a gown made of orange blossoms and lace her father bought in Trinidad because there was no fabric in the stores in Grenville back then. Horse-drawn carriages transported the bridal party and wedding guests to the reception in Soubise, a town not far from Grenville, where an enormous cake, a three-piece band, and tables of food awaited them.

After the Lordes were married, they lived above the store in Grenville that Byron owned. As the store's manager and the wife of a respectable civil servant, Linda maintained her social distance from her less fortunate customers—some of whom could read neither the store's name nor the romance magazines she'd peruse in her spare time, musing over stories rife with fantasies of true love, fictional sex, images of dashing men and beautiful but sexually submissive women.

About a year after they were married, the Lordes sold off everything they had to pay for their passage to the United States. Once there, they made their way to Harlem, moved in with Linda's sisters, and began looking for work.

But the realities of American racism and xenophobia limited their access to job opportunities. Despite his experience as a policeman back home, Byron Lorde had no chance of gaining employment with New York City's segregated police department, whose ranks locked out native- and foreign-born blacks alike, but swelled with white ethnics. Nor would he find the road paved with gold as an entrepreneur. While Caribbean-owned businesses found something of a niche in Harlem, they were more often than not the outgrowth of immigrants with skilled trades who could not find employment; import-export businesses catering to black immigrant populations, like African American businesses, faced extreme disadvantages in a Harlem economy dominated by first- and second-generation Europeans.[19] In America, Byron Lorde was just another unskilled black man in competition with other blacks for the few available jobs open to "coloreds."

Similarly, Linda Lorde had no employable skills. For the vast majority of working-class black American and Caribbean immigrant women, domestic work and low-paying, non-union service jobs were the chief means by which they contributed financially to the survival of their households. Her options thus limited, Linda sought work suited to the "household" skills she had.

After landing several menial but short-term jobs, Byron secured one loading and unloading trucks at the old Waldorf-Astoria Hotel and Linda also got a job there as a chambermaid.[20] At the time, jobs as chambermaids in a prestigious hotel like the Waldorf were reserved for white working-class women, most of whom were Irish. But Linda was able to get the job because she could pass for white.[21] The Lordes had never planned to stay in the States permanently. Still, the young couple worked hard for three years, dreaming of the day they would return home with the smell of success reeking from fine clothes, money in their pockets, and enviable tales of America.

When the Waldorf-Astoria's owners announced that the luxurious hotel would soon close and be demolished to make way for the Empire State Building, the Lordes had to find other work. Still holding onto their dream, caught amid heightening competition for jobs[22] and desperate for work, Byron took a job peddling an apple pushcart on Broadway. And Linda, mindful of the prevailing racist attitudes of white employers, stepped over the color line, passing once again, in order to secure a job as a scullery maid in a teashop on Columbus Avenue and 99th Street. There, she worked twelve hours a day seven days a week, washing and scrubbing kitchen utensils in the back of an all-white establishment. The proprietor thought she was Spanish, and Linda Lorde astutely let him think so.

White Americans were often more tolerant of light-skinned, Spanish-speaking and Spanish-looking immigrants, in spite of their general suspicions about "foreigners." Indeed, the presence of significant numbers of dark-skinned immigrants who spoke European languages in a variety of accents redefined white and black American notions of race in the early decades of the twentieth century.[23] Foreign-born blacks were more often able to secure better jobs, and were treated with greater respect than American-born blacks—especially once their foreign blackness could be established.[24] Ideas about racial solidarity initially underlay the support of black Americans for their Caribbean sisters and brothers. But the competition for jobs and the ability of black immigrants seemingly to transcend race by constructing new, racially acceptable identities fueled intraracial tensions. In the 1920s, black civic leaders encouraged black Americans who could pass as Spanish to do so in order to gain employment.[25]

The history of fair-to-white-skinned African Americans passing between the racial corridors of "blackness" and "whiteness," and their reasons for doing so, is well documented in African American literature.[26] Early notable examples include the narrative of Ellen and William Craft, *Running a Thousand Miles to Freedom* (1860) and Nella Larsen's two novels, *Quicksand* (1928) and *Passing* (1929). As a way of assimilating, members of racially white ethnic groups (such as Jews) and homo-

sexuals have also "passed" in order to gain social acceptance, employment, housing, and education. John Howard Griffin, whose best-selling
Black Like Me (1959) told the story of a white man who applied black
shoe polish to his skin and then traveled throughout the South to learn
what it felt like to be black, appropriated the passing phenomenon in
reverse,[27] largely out of curiosity. For blacks who've had to pass, however,
it is a painful way to survive and has nothing to do with curiosity.

Linda kept her job at the Columbus Avenue teashop until the winter
of 1928, when she was stricken with a near-fatal case of pleurisy, an
infection in the lungs she'd never suffered before in experiencing New
York's winters. Bedridden, she stayed home one day while Byron went to
the teashop to retrieve her paycheck and soiled uniforms. When the
comely, darker-skinned man identified himself as Linda's husband, the
owner—realizing that she was probably black too, and worse, that he'd
been duped into allowing a black woman to work for him—fired her on
the spot.

By now, the glitter that was Harlem's renaissance had begun to fade.
With its best years on the wane, the flurry of artistic and cultural production[28] that was to define its eruption slowed, as the stock market
crash of 1929 and the Great Depression of the 1930s ravaged the nation.
Caught in the economic collapse laying waste to Harlem and the rest of
the country, the Lordes' dream of returning home crumbled.

Harlem remained a haven for the black intelligentsia and social elite
who were at the center of its cultural movement, as well as for a continuing stream of voyeuristic whites, now with decreasing disposable
incomes. Although its educated, middle-class blacks could, and did,
find economic refuge in jobs as well-paid civil servants (particularly as
postal workers and public school teachers), its poor and working class
suffered an encroaching poverty. The situation worsened with diminish-
ing family incomes, and economic exploitation by absentee whites who
hired black managers to collect spiraling rents while still controlling
most of Harlem's real estate.[29]

In 1929, the Lordes lived at 108 West 142nd Street, in a section of Harlem with a concentration of Caribbean residents. With the birth of their
first daughter, Phyllis, they turned their attention toward their new roles
as parents. Byron assumed the role of family breadwinner and patriarch

typical of the island culture from which they'd come, while it fell to Linda to be wife and homemaker. Two years later, in 1931, a second daughter, Helen, was born. Byron then enrolled in night school, eventually finishing high school and taking college-level courses in real estate management, which paved the way for him to obtain a real estate broker's license. He had a new dream now: he would make his fortune at the head of a real estate empire modeled on the legendary success of Harlem's black real estate agent, Philip Payton.[30] Shortly thereafter, he opened an office at 357 Lenox Avenue and 128th Street and began his fledgling business, first by managing apartment buildings and rooming houses owned by whites, and later, properties he'd lease or buy.

Though Harlem was to stumble to its feet, a specter of its former self, it was now cast in the shadow of a mid-1930s America defined by President Franklin Delano Roosevelt's promise of a "New Deal." Audre Lorde was born into this Harlem. However ghostlike its post-depression scene, Harlem was still alive in Langston Hughes's brownstone on 127th Street, and in Countee Cullen's public school classrooms. Its community pride was still evident in the raucous street corner gatherings of political orators, the pulpits of the likes of Father Divine,[31] and the emerging literary imagination of James Baldwin.

The third and youngest sister, Audrey Geraldine Lorde, was born in Sloane Hospital, now Harlem's Columbia Presbyterian Medical Center, on February 18, 1934. She was a post-depression baby and "a product of migration and mixture, of the synthesis and clash of black cultures in urban America."[32] What is known about Audre's childhood comes chiefly from Audre herself. Filtered through a highly stylized, literary imagination, certain "facts" and "events" are played, replayed, and edited in the corpus of her work, published interviews, and literary memory.

A WRITER WHO wrote extensively about herself in "mixed" genres, Lorde would emerge as an "expert on her own life and as the maker of a life on paper." She remembered what she wanted or needed to, as artist and historian.[33] Thus, her narratives were self-conscious, literary, performances;[34] an excavation, and synthesis, of memory, imagination, and truth.[35]

As a writer, Audre Lorde detailed a childhood at the hands of a Roman Catholic, emotionally distant mother by whom she was both intimidated and erotically fascinated. She depicted her father as a hard-working, silent, and shadowy figure, who shared little intimacy with his daughters, save for the evening ritual of greeting him with a kiss when he returned from work. In recalling her older sisters, she remembered their cruelty toward her and her exclusion from their girlish intimacies.[36]

Her memories of her childhood became almost mythic constructions of an ugly duckling[37] who was legally blind before age five, clumsy, inarticulate, born left-handed, a stutterer (who got whipped repeatedly), fat and black. Recalling the abuses encumbered by fate, and reinventing them, she rendered her childhood as literature, coming close to "the precincts of classical tragedy."[38] By her own accounts, she was lonely, unwanted, and unloved.

But Audre was the baby and favored, her sisters thought, by their mother. In their memories, she was a precocious, demanding child—a pest, who, alone among them, dared to defy their parents' authority.[39] At age three, she was willful. Often, she'd collapse into tantrums and refuse to go out when her mother dressed her so the two of them could pick up Phyllis and Helen from school at noon, then escort them back after a home-cooked lunch. The school, St. Mark's Academy, a Catholic elementary school, was only four blocks away, on 138th Street off Lenox Avenue.[40] Mrs. Lorde was obsessively fearful of letting the children out of her sight; it was her daily routine to escort them back and forth at lunchtime and pick them up again at day's end.[41] At times, Audre would talk back to her mother, enraging Mrs. Lorde, who abhorred any disrespect and beat the willful Audre almost daily for her insolence. While Phyllis, and Helen to a lesser extent, would never openly defy their parents, Audre "broke all the rules."[42]

Typically, jealousy, position in the family, and sibling rivalry tempered the sisters' relationships with one another. As the baby, Audre was "special."[43] She was exempt from household chores and later, when she went to school, even from homework sometimes. Audre's specialness as youngest and last child extended to her physical problems: she needed glasses (which when broken or lost were expensive to replace, and Phyllis and Helen were charged with seeing to it Audre kept track of them) and her bad feet required corrective shoes. Phyllis was their father's favorite, most like him in temperament. She'd escaped his disappointment at not having a son when two more daughters were born. But Helen, the middle child, had neither Phyllis nor Audre's status and suffered emotionally in ways different from the other two. She became emotionally needy, trading perfect behavior for a chance at her parents' affection and attention. Only three years older than Audre, she felt emotionally incapable of caring for a baby (among other things, it was her job, at age five, to take down Audre's trundle bed at night and to wash Audre's socks). This burden resulted in Helen resenting Audre's expectations for love and attention from her—love and attention Audre should have received from their hardworking but almost never affectionate parents.[44]

When Mrs. Lorde left the three of them alone in order to go to work at their father's real estate office, helping him manage the responsibilities of overseeing rooming houses and tenants,[45] Phyllis and Helen resented having to care for this bratty child. They often allied against her, excluding Audre from their conversations and activities. Closer in age, they shared a bedroom and school rituals, an intimacy Audre resented. In retaliation, Audre resisted Phyllis's authority as the oldest and had physical scuffles with Helen. She would grow up to be jealous of her sisters' assumed closeness.[46] In truth, as children in a household where intimacy was discouraged, Phyllis and Helen were neither overfriendly nor particularly affectionate with each other;[47] excluding Audre was payback for all the trouble she caused them.

As a young child, Audre was never allowed out to play alone and therefore came to have limited knowledge of a Harlem other girls her age knew from sharing such rituals as double-dutch, and from socializing freely in its streets. For much of her childhood, Harlem imprinted itself on Lorde in half-seen, fleeting images. Her sense of Harlem came largely from looking out through the windows of their apartment, from going back and forth the few blocks to church and school. It came in snatches on hurried errands with her mother and on those Sundays after church when her father took the family out sightseeing on one of the double-decker buses that ran downtown and back. As such, Harlem was simultaneously real and imagined, solid and fluid, for Audre. Not allowed wholly to enter it, she experienced the neighborhood partly as a voyeur, a voyeurism coded within her parents' voyeurism as black immigrants who—by racial and social condition and personal choices they made—would never fully enter American society.[48]

Harlem was never "home" to Mrs. Lorde. She was as intimidated by Harlem as she was formidable walking its streets. She made no intimate friends there and did not socialize outside of family gatherings at the homes of her relatives. Mrs. Lorde longed for her real, Grenadian home, speaking of it often. She would become lost in reveries of the "safety" of home and how nice "home" was; rhapsodizing about its foods and fruit trees, its royal blue hills, the surrounding sea. She'd recall for her daughters tales of a lost paradise, embroidered with select bits of family history, childhood memories, and "the way things were done at home," her memories challenged by the psychic and physical trauma of mediating a new terrain, cultural dislocation, and the trauma of migration itself.[49] Of the three girls, Audre was the most interested in her mother's stories of home. Beyond their seductive lure, it is fair to say that Audre identified with Mrs. Lorde's deep sense of feeling out of place, of not belonging to the home she lived in, and with her desire to reify an imagined home. As Audre grew older, she came to dislike living in her parents' household and even felt a stranger within it.

Mrs. Lorde's imagined "home" had no stories of its socioeconomic underpinnings, or of the institutionalized poverty of the colonized. But her stories, which conjured up a paradise of lime trees and sea foam, were the family's roots in a place where, she let them know, they had none. Here, they were outsiders who would one day return to their real home.

Mr. Lorde, on the other hand, never talked of home, at least not in front of his daughters. Not even when Audre, curious and eager to hear, would try to get him to, as she often did. For Audre and her sisters, their father's home was something whispered about behind their parents' bedroom door. Unlike their mother's vividly painted past, his consisted of dark, abstract, disconnected bits and pieces they'd sometimes overhear. His silence was deafening and obtuse; wedged, like an emotional live wire, between the dissipating dream of a prodigal son returning home and his dissociation from its ambiguities. Although Audre was to say her parents did not directly encourage her to write poetry, she would also say that "Poetry was something I learned from my mother's strangenesses and my father's silences."[50]

The post-depression years of relative economic prosperity were soon followed by America's entry into World War II. An able-bodied man in his later thirties by then, Byron feared the draft. As the demand for troops increased, even men in their thirties faced that possibility. Byron avoided the draft by taking a job working the night shift at Maxin Manufacturing, a war plant in Queens that made aluminum fittings for airplanes. All the while, he kept his ambitious real estate ventures afloat both as rental agent and handyman when repairs were necessary to the properties he managed. Working day and night, his enterprise prospered as the war lengthened. Working-class black Harlemites, benefitting from an increasing availability of war-related jobs, could now afford the rents associated with better housing.

During the war, as afterwards, Linda was indispensable to his ambitions. To her domestic and maternal obligations were added civic responsibilities: assisting in the distribution of ration books in Harlem and joining other mothers at St. Mark's Academy, who kept regular watch for enemy airplanes in the skies. She managed the office whenever Mr. Lorde had to be away showing a property, or to catch a few hours of sleep. She took care of the books, interviewed prospective tenants, collected rents, cleaned rooms, and waited for deliveries of the second-grade coal, unused by the war effort, which provided heat to their rooming house tenants. Like many immigrant women who became unofficial partners in their husbands' entrepreneurial efforts, she was Byron Lorde's staunchest supporter; without her input, the business could not have had the longevity and relative success it did.

By the time Audre entered school, in September 1939, she could read and write well above the expectations of the nuns at St. Mark's Academy Elementary School. At St. Mark's, Helen and Phyllis were obedient Catholic girls. They learned their catechisms inside out, never questioned the nuns, and did what they were told. Audre was, on the other hand, recalcitrant, refusing to fit into the mold. She argued and reasoned with the nuns. She questioned religious ideas and practice her older sisters and other students accepted as gospel truth. The Sisters of the

Blessed Sacrament found it hard to believe she belonged to the Lorde family. They openly compared her behavior to that of her older sisters, sending notes home to her parents, and beating her when she disobeyed.

At school as at home, Audre was the antithesis of the proper, submissive "young lady" the Lordes expected and demanded of their daughters. Where Phyllis and Helen were graceful, Audre, who could not see, except in amorphous shapes, was clumsy. Where they were acquiescent and well behaved, she was stubborn (during penmanship practice she'd drop the "y" from her first name because it was neither a neat letter nor aesthetically pleasing to her). A's and B's were expected of the Lorde girls. A bright student academically, Audre met those expectations, but her grades for conduct were frequently lower than her academic scores.[51]

To her parents, especially her mother, Audre was "wildish."[52] Neither parent understood her. She was not like them. But she was, after all, "a Lorde," whose pride presumed her "special and particular above anybody else in the world."[53] Thus they attempted to remake her, using beatings, disapproval, and manipulative language they hoped would perform on her a corrective, psychic surgery.[54] Compared to them, she was not their kind of Lorde, and they demanded she "straighten up and act right."[55]

Audre had her own painfully wrought comparisons. She was the chubbiest sister and the darkest daughter of a white-looking black woman who made it known that "you didn't trust anybody whose face is black because their heart is black."[56] Recognizing herself as the darkest child, Audre interpreted her mother's constant denigration of dark black people and their implicit evil as a comment on her own propensity for evil. Not pretty, not light-skinned, she was the outsider in a family of outsiders. The one always in trouble at school, which kept her in trouble at home; where her mother beat her again, for defying the nuns' authority and for being indifferent to the expected code of behavior. Later, as an adult, she would delight in this "bad girl image," reinventing and further institutionalizing her outsider status.[57]

In some respects, Audre grew up in a typical Caribbean immigrant household in which upward mobility, proper behavior, good morals, an emphasis on education, and a strong work ethic were stressed. Never relinquishing their Caribbean identity, Linda and Byron Lorde strove to subvert the veil of the foreigner hanging over them—the racial, social, and class subtexts that impeded the assimilation strategies of so many foreign-born blacks. Struggling to rise out of the poverty of "newcomers," they focused on becoming legitimate Americans by earning their U.S. citizenship. As immigrants who rose to the position of lower-middle-class blacks, they insisted on making something of themselves, and their daughters.

In other respects, Audre grew up in a household run by parents who erected emotional walls between themselves and their children. Good people but emotionally distant,[58] the Lordes insisted on discipline and restraint. They had rigid, inhibitive ideas about child rearing. Obedience was the rule and good behavior expected, never rewarded. Love was expressed through material security—a roof over the head, food on the table, the yearly tuition for Catholic school. Both the Lordes expected their children to stay in their place, "to be seen and not heard." They were intolerant of natural curiosity, sheltering their daughters from, and explaining little of, the adult world they would inherit.[59] As the girls grew older, sex and anything related to the body were never openly discussed. Friendships with other children were frowned upon and the Lordes disallowed having company at home. To the extent that they could, they kept the outside world outside.[60]

Audre's youthful self-analysis had roots in other psychic issues. She suffered from terrible, inexplicable nightmares (which were to haunt her throughout her life), the terrors of which went unattended, if not ignored, by her parents. Mrs. Lorde was a disciplinarian but never a confidante or friend. As such, the mother-daughter bond was marred by the verbal and physical violence of her mother's disapprovals. Audre loved her mother but could not please her. She needed and demanded a show of affection, which was physically and emotionally denied. She responded to her parents' lack of money and frugality by stealing from them. Once, when her father suspected her of stealing money from his pocket, he grilled her for hours at the kitchen table, his revolver on the table between them—an act and show of force which sealed her fear of him. Although she'd stolen the money, she fiercely lied about doing so, fearful that he might shoot her.

Not only was Audre fearful of both her parents, she believed they did not love her. A bright child (a characteristic that appealed to her parents), she was sensitive and creative, but she was reared by hardened realists with a pragmatic approach to life.

Mrs. Lorde was an austere woman, who rarely touched or comforted her daughters physically. Although she was a dutiful mother, and in her own way, loving, what maternal love she dispensed came across as tough love. The parent whose authoritative hand they usually felt when they disobeyed, she was their principal disciplinarian, "fathering" them in a reversal of roles that was inconsistent with the gender-specific roles their parents otherwise performed.[61]

While Mr. Lorde often accompanied his daughters to school in the mornings on his way to work, he was emotionally absent, cultivating his distance in a gender-defined fatherhood. As patriarch, he was the provider and spent most of his time at work. He expected his wife to see to the children. In the evenings when he came home, he and Mrs. Lorde ritually disappeared into their bedroom or into the kitchen, for at least an hour, where they discussed in private any decisions to be made regarding the children and the family's well-being; often they spoke to each other in a West Indian patois so as not to be understood, if overheard, by their daughters. Once those decisions were made, the Lordes reappeared, handing down their non-negotiable, parental law. Afterwards, Mr. Lorde would have dinner and read *The New York Times*, silent and even less approachable.

As parents, the Lordes exercised conflicting views on religion and complicated views on color and race. A staunch Roman Catholic, it was Mrs. Lorde who escorted the girls to church every Sunday. Mr. Lorde never accompanied them, preferring to stay at home while they were gone and cook for them his "special" breakfasts of scrambled eggs, chicken livers, and onions. Once they were home and the meal consumed, he'd retire to the living room and preoccupy himself with the *Sunday Times*. While both parents associated certain culturalisms with being black American and poor (foods like black-eye peas and rice, and hog-head cheese) and forbade these things in their home, Mr. Lorde identified himself as "a race man" and supported the precepts behind Marcus Garvey's "Back to Africa" movement. He was a regular at political meetings in Harlem attended by Caribbean and black Americans.

In contrast, Mrs. Lorde would have nothing to do with politics and remained peculiarly color-conscious, expressing deep-seated, negative racial feelings toward darker-skinned black people. Even when circumstance made it necessary for her to rely on a black person, she did so with the deepest suspicions. Once, when a fishbone caught in her throat and she had to be hospitalized for a day or two, she paid a neighbor across the street to watch the girls. Mrs. Hogan, a single parent and incidentally dark-skinned, adored the Lorde girls and was happy to help out, treating them like her own. A sweet and generous woman, she certainly would have watched the girls for nothing,[62] but paying her was a way Mrs. Lorde kept friendship, and therefore intimacy with darker-skinned black people, at a distance.

Nor did she trust any association between black and white people which hinted of sexual relations. Once, while interviewing a prospective interracial couple who wanted to rent a room in one of the rooming houses she and her husband managed, Mrs. Lorde openly discouraged them from doing so, speaking to them in negative, disapproving tones; and indicating afterwards, to her daughters, that she'd wanted "none of that kind of stuff in her house."[63]

Strict to a fault, the Lordes discouraged individuality and self-expression, except when those qualities were indications of their own success as good parents. Despite the financial hardship any extras meant, the Lordes acquired a piano, insisting Phyllis and Helen both take piano lessons at the home of Mrs. Hanley, a piano teacher in Harlem, and that they practice daily. That Helen enjoyed playing the piano more than Phyllis did and became a better than average pianist was considered a sign of "good breeding" and an acceptable creative expression the Lordes cultivated in their daughters. In public, Mr. and Mrs. Lorde treated their daughters like trophies.[64] Mr. Lorde was particularly fond of parading the quieter, more acquiescent Phyllis before his friends at neighborhood political gatherings. At the homes of their aunts, Phyllis or Helen might be asked to play the piano. Audre would be asked to stand and recite one of the poems (usually something by Edna St. Vincent Millay) she was fond of reciting at home, where her spontaneous recitations were normally discouraged. Even so, she was writing her own poems, in secret.

By age twelve, Audre's head was full of poems she'd memorized. It was also full of words she'd never heard used but was seduced by. "Words had an energy and power and I came to respect that power early," she once remarked.[65] Her parents' words were laced with cadences of the Caribbean. They were also laced with rigid, working-class values. As immigrants to Harlem and outsiders in America, the Lordes used a language they believed necessary to their own and their daughters' survival. In doing so, they marked Audre's journey into language as she began to negotiate the world beyond Harlem.

TWO

M Y FATHER leaves his psychic print upon me," Audre began the meditative Introduction to *Zami*, "silent, intense, and unforgiving. But his is a distant lightning. Images of women flaming like torches adorn and define the borders of my journey."[1] Audre grew up in an insular, largely female environment where her mother, her two sisters, her maternal aunts and her mother's stories of Grenadian female kin formed a prototypical women's community, culturally and spiritually. The insular, black female world in which she grew up at home both collided and intersected with the predominantly white female world at St. Mark's Academy where, typically, the culture of Catholic school barely masked a paternalistic racism, and nuns lived and worked in a gendered subculture isolated from intimate association with men.[2] She would be transferred to another Catholic school where, from the sixth to eighth grades, girls were separated from boys, and where she would interact exclusively in another prototypical community of peers who were white females. These early experiences would define and shape her later ideas about women, community, and difference.

In the summer of 1945, the Lorde family moved further uptown, to a Washington Heights apartment on West 152nd Street between Amsterdam and Broadway. A section of Upper Harlem known for its spacious, prewar apartment buildings, Washington Heights was then largely populated by working- and lower-middle-class subcommunities of white ethnics, such as the Irish; an encroaching black presence, beginning at the turn of the century, pushed white Manhattanites living in Harlem further north.[3] At the time, few blacks were allowed to live in the well-kept neighborhood. Most of those who did were segregated to the east of Broadway, the street that marked the racial divide between blacks and whites.

The Lordes were the first black family to move onto that block. For Audre, it was the beginning of some personal freedom. She was now allowed out of the house alone, to play and jump rope. With Phyllis and Helen in high school, Mrs. Lorde also allowed Audre to go back and forth to school on her own, relinquishing, to some extent, her fears of the dangers inherent in urban American life. The move signaled the family's upward mobility; but simultaneously, it divested them of the racial comforts of the predominantly black, increasingly overpopulated, deteriorating central Harlem neighborhood they'd established themselves in for years. A week after they moved in, the landlord of the building committed suicide, despondent over the fact that he'd been forced to rent to colored people.

That September, Audre's parents enrolled her in St. Catherine's School, located at 508 West 153rd Street, one block from their new home. They hoped the new school would instill in her more discipline, and that they'd find themselves less embarrassed by her temperamental behavior.

At St. Catherine's, Audre was an immediate outsider. Whereas St. Mark's Academy had an all-black student population, the student body at St. Catherine's was all-white. As its first black student, Audre began her association with white peers, and soon came to see that association as racially problematic. She was ill-prepared for this new reality. Neither of her parents openly discussed their own experiences with American racism. When "problems" arose, Linda and Byron ignored them—avoiding confrontations and forging ahead—largely because their pride would not allow them to do otherwise. But Audre complained the white students made fun of her braids and secretly left notes in her desk telling her she stank. Once when Audre showed these notes to one of the Sisters, she was informed black people did smell different than whites, though it was cruel of the other children to point out something Audre could not help.[4] Mrs. Lorde dismissed Audre's complaints as a lack of personal fortitude, an unwillingness to submit to authority, and an inability to absorb whatever life dished out with a stiff West Indian upper lip. In time, though, the Lordes reluctantly agreed to allow Audre to take the entrance exam for Hunter High School, on 68th Street and Park Avenue, by which she was accepted and which she entered in September 1947.

At Hunter, Lorde was in an academic, if not racial, milieu to which she was better suited. It was a small girls' school, with small classes and no nuns. Its students were considered the brightest in the city, admitted only after ranking in the highest percentile on math and English entrance exams. The majority of students came from white middle- and upper-middle-class families.

Her four years spent there were marked by Audre's formal baptism into poetry. She was fascinated by the British Romantic poets Keats, Byron, and Shelley,[5] by the works of T. S. Eliot and the American poets Elinor Wylie and Edna St. Vincent Millay. The "emotional complexity" and intensity of feeling in their words captured and inflamed her imagination.[6] By the time she was fourteen, she was trying to imitate that complexity and intensity.

THE TRIUMPH

Up from the cool and soothing earth
Into the great unheard
Into the fire of new rebirth,
Flew man, the sea venger bird . . .[7]

Audre also came to admire the work of a relatively lesser known poet, Helene Magaret. Magaret was a Catholic, and her poetry appeared in leading literary publications in the late 1930s and the 1940s.

She was the author of *The Trumpeting Crane* (1934), *I See the Great Horse* (1937), and *Change of Season* (1941), all published by Farrar & Rinehart in New York. Her poems explored a range of themes: the mystery of life; the joys and sorrows of friendship, love, and religion; the silences of the heart. Audre later credited Helene Magaret with helping her "not to be afraid of my unacceptable feelings"[8]—feelings for the beauty of everyday things, friendship, and love that were unacceptable at home. At Hunter, Audre found a spiritual, if not racially perfect, home—"a space of recovery, a place where there is finally a connection between tongue and spirit."[9]

She also made her first real friends there, in a small, inner circle of young women who called themselves "The Branded" (although the name was more a private designation and came later).[10] "The Branded" wrote poetry and skipped classes to wander the city's streets and bookstores. They held séances, burned candles, and "called up poets." "The Branded" practiced magic, mental telepathy, and various occult arts with each other, testing their curiosity about mysticism and other non-conventional spiritual practices. They were girls mostly from lower- and lower-middle-class families, "who got into the school by dint of being smart."[11] They had names like Gloria Pages, Joan O'Malley, Diane di Prima, Gabriel Bernhard. Some were the daughters of immigrants and thus understood a similar socioeconomic, if not racial and ethnic, reality. All were the daughters of an America that was segregated, anti-Communist, and whose World War II bombs launched the Atomic Age. They were growing up at the dawn of the Cold War. To them, their parents had conformed to Harry Truman's America and to a bland, unquestioning life they rebelled against. Diane di Prima was one friend who would remain significant in Audre's life after Hunter. Entering Hunter a semester after Audre, in the winter of 1948, born into a working-class Italian family, di Prima was also writing poems.[12] Although slightly younger than Audre, the two became quick friends in a school where like-minded mavericks easily found each other.

Throughout high school, in the mornings before classes, "The Branded" would arrive at Hunter early, gathering in an empty classroom to read their poems to each other. They were Audre's first literary support group, the vehicle for her shift from writing poetry in secret to reading her poems in public. These early poems imitated the linguistic styles of Millay, Eliot, Wylie, Magaret, and others;[13] they expressed Audre's "love for the blind beauty of words."[14] While a member of "The Branded," Audre also became excited about and involved with the school's literary magazine, *Argus*, for which she enthusiastically did the grunt work of typing and editing.

As an exclusively female, intensely loyal community,[15] "The Branded" fulfilled Audre's emotional need for acceptance, despite being its only black member. Yet she was conscious of the unspoken subtext of race.[16] She felt alone in a way they were not. As the only Caribbean member of the group, she grew practiced at suffocating her Caribbean background; choosing and allowing herself to be known as black, and therefore shifting toward identification with the black Americans that her parents disdained. Audre came to see herself, both in the group and in American society, as "a black girl in a society that was basically white."[17]

She witnessed overt racism. The same year she entered Hunter, her family took a sightseeing trip to Washington, D.C., for the Fourth of July, stopping during their tour of historical landmarks for ice cream at a nearby parlor. At the time, D.C.'s restaurants were segregated, and the white waitress refused to serve them. The Lordes left, stoically silent. Audre was never to forget the anger and fury of that rejection and humiliation. Nor would any of "The Branded" have to experience it. Still, race was the only barrier to their sisterhood: she found in them female affirmation, and the acceptance, attention, and love she craved.

AUDRE WAS READING voraciously. She possessed an impressive bank of knowledge on a range of subjects by the time she entered Hunter.[18] She was a girl to whom di Prima and others could openly talk, but who didn't talk much about herself. A quick-witted facility with words masked "depths of sadness, a lot of secrets, and a lot of reserve."[19]

Audre kept the words for life at home to herself, writing them down in her private journal. There she described her adolescent longings to leave ("If they only knew. I'm just counting time til I'm eighteen. Then they'll see")[20] and to escape the constant tension, especially between herself and her mother.[21] In the journal, Audre's teenaged angst focused on her feeling that her mother hated her and on a compelling loneliness borne of an irrational but deeply rooted sense that she was unloved:[22] "Last year was rotten. Maybe this year I'll get along a little better with them—my family. Particularly that woman my mother. I wonder why she hates me so?"[23] She did not write of her parents' disapproval of friends and white people, both of which defined her life outside of home. But she did write, often, of her intense attraction to one of her teachers, Miriam Burstein:[24] "Sometimes when I think of Miriam I wish I had never met her. I would never have known the wonderful days of happiness, but I would never have experienced the pain I know. But looking at it detached, she's helped me so much, and I'll always have those talks & that June day in the park with her. Oh Miriam. . . ."[25]

As a teenager, Audre also had a circle of black female friends, for the first time; but she generally kept those friendships separate from the friendships with white schoolmates she cultivated at Hunter. Whenever the two circles overlapped, it was at her initiation. Her black friends all lived in Harlem and were, like Audre, attending predominantly white schools for bright and talented students. There was Joan Alexander, a dancer, who went to the High School of Music and Art, and whose family lived near Eighth Avenue and Morningside Park at the time. Joan was friends with Frances Goings, a schoolmate who lived on 113th Street and Seventh Avenue. Having gone to the same modeling school, Frances was friends with Genevieve Johnson, who went to Hunter and lived on 119th Street.[26] Genevieve studied ballet and modern dance and was a bright, talented dancer who should have been a student at Music and Art, not Hunter.[27] After Genevieve met Audre, she introduced Audre to Joan, who thought of Audre as a bright, lonely girl and socially reserved until she was sure she had control. Yet Audre appeared proper, intimidating, and dignified in carriage; she was, in spite of herself, very much like her mother.

Audre's teenaged friendships with other girls, her feelings toward female teachers, were unquestionably homoerotic, and raised "mixed feelings"[28] in her about her own sexuality. With little attention to the boy or two she had a crush on at the time, her journal records an eroticized fascination with her friends' hair, clothing, and bodies; longings for their approval; her unrequited crushes on the teachers to whom she gave flowers and cards on their birthdays, bought with money stolen from her parents; and her anger and sense of rejection when her affections were not returned, particularly by Burstein.[29] The most homoerotic of her friendships was with Genevieve. The two became friends in 1947, Audre's freshman year at Hunter.

Genevieve—"Genny"—was Audre's first love. Although theirs wasn't a sexual relationship (which Lorde later regretted, noting they were lovers "in all but the physical"),[30] Audre's love for Genny was heightened by her envy of Genevieve's physical grace as a dancer, her thin body and "very fair" skin.[31] From the beginning, the attraction was intense. She spent as much time with Genevieve as she could negotiate with her parents, or steal by cutting school, acting out girlish, sexualized postures and scenarios in the streets and at Genevieve's house. They had an intimate, physical relationship as confidantes—one that bore the stamp of mutual erotic need.

Audre adored Genny. Indeed, Genevieve was Audre's alter ego. A maverick personality, she had the daring Audre did not, more personal freedom and responsibility for herself. Genevieve was truly a free spirit, whereas Audre was trying to become one.[32] Genevieve was the daughter of a divorced, working mother who encouraged creativity (enrolling Genevieve in ballet and modern dance classes) rather than selectively ignoring it. Unlike Audre, who belonged to "The Branded," Genevieve didn't need a group to belong to and "was not a member of anything."[33] At the same time, Audre was extremely sympathetic to Genevieve as an only child. At home, she felt like "an only," too, and their friendship mirrored a longing for an ideal sister neither one had.

Underneath a "sassy" exterior,[34] however, Genevieve Johnson was a sensitive, troubled girl. Unsettled by her parents' separation (which happened before she was born), she longed for the whole family her father's presence would provide, blaming her mother for his absence and, therefore, his rejection of her. By at least one account, Phillip Johnson was a handsome, fascinating man; an intellectual who, like so many black men of his time, had been hampered and soured by lack of opportunity.[35] Genevieve looked for her father for years before she found him. But when she chose to move in with him and his new wife, she was unhappy with them. Ella treated Genevieve as if she didn't want her around;[36] both of them shattered Genevieve's yearnings for a "whole" family.

Genevieve was also "compulsive" about committing suicide[37] by the time she was fifteen, having already slashed her wrists in one failed attempt. She was sent back to school in the telltale bandages.[38] What made her try again? Was it a sexually abusive father, as Audre and others speculated?[39] Was it loneliness, despair, a disturbed mind, a broken heart? The fear of being sexually "abnormal" at a time when blackness itself was abnormal?[40] The exact reasons are not known. Two months short of her sixteenth birthday, Genevieve died on March 27, 1950, in Harlem Hospital after swallowing fifteen capsules of rat poisoning. Ironically, it was one capsule for every year of her life.

Audre was traumatized by Genny's suicide. She had been baptized in the Roman Catholic Church.[41] In spite of her attempts at rebellion, she was raised to believe and practice the tenets of Catholicism, as her mother insisted. She'd been taught to feel guilty for a myriad of "sins" and knew well that the act, even the idea, of suicide was a sin that damned the spirit eternally to Purgatory.[42]

Psychologically, Audre felt guilty for not preventing Genevieve's death. As the months went by, her grief was palpable. "Grass has grown and withered over the grave where my darling is buried,"[43] she wrote in her journal that December. In her dreams, she saw her "beautiful lovely Genevieve"[44] alive and then dead. She dreamt of her own death by poison and was so haunted by these visions she was "almost afraid to go to sleep."[45] Audre believed she had participated in killing Genevieve—by letting her "swallow poison and never raising a finger to stop her."[46] She carried that guilt into adulthood.

Six months after Genevieve Johnson's death, Audre attempted to create distance from her grief and guilt. Writing of Genny in a brief remembrance, "Impressions of a friend,"[47] she reflected on her friend's "personality, many-sided as it was," seeing beneath Genevieve's hard sense of humor "a certain cynical truth that was in everything she said or did. She was, in reality, laughing at herself and the world in general,—contemptuous even of the things she herself believed." On two pieces of paper torn from a notebook, Audre detailed Genevieve's contradictions (she was "devoid of personal prejudices or emotion" at the same time as

"she was also capable of the deepest feeling"); as well as her own realization that there was a "strange bitterness" to everything Genevieve did, an
"uncaring manner" at the core of her that was "more than a jibe at conventional things." Audre questioned what drew her to Genevieve, posit-
ing an answer in "the innate longing in me to do some of the things she
did,—be able to see things and people with the same startling clarity she
had, & to dismiss them in the next breath."

Audre now thought that Genny's "way of seeing was curiously
warped—not inwardly, like some, nor yet in an outward direction,—but
in a subtle mixture of both that made her see almost instantly into the
core of things and people." Yet she could identify in Genevieve an
absence of depth and a detachment toward others countered only by her
"passion for dancing," which was "the only thing that merited more than
a cursory glance from her."

With striking clarity, Audre analyzed the impact of their "short and
bitter-sweet" relationship, recognizing that it "formed a thick and indeli-
ble line across the emotional background of my adolescence," which
she saw as inseparable from her own growing up. Thus in her attempt
to take some emotional distance, she discovered a lifelong connection to
Genevieve.

That momentary distancing was revelatory: though she was Genevieve's constant companion and believed she knew better than anyone
else how Genevieve felt, Audre was "painfully aware, at times," that even
she knew very little about her friend. Audre may have come to this conclusion as a way of reconciling with an unknowable Genevieve, and with
the silence that ultimately engulfed her. Genevieve's death may have
come to symbolize for Audre, later in life, "what women lose when they
don't speak their truths."[48] But at sixteen, she had neither answers nor
language for what telling or surviving those truths would entail.

Except for Genevieve, Audre's early homoerotic attractions were to
white females with whom, more often than not, she found acceptance,
recognition, and intellectual parity. By and large, her social interactions
were predominantly with whites. When she began to date men, she dated
white males. As such, she rebelled against and rejected the racially segregated world of social relations constructed at home by her parents and in
outer society. By the time she was seventeen, she'd met Gerry Levine at a

party given by friends involved with the Labor Youth League. Levine was white, amiable, "and intelligent."[49] They began to date, going to concerts, the theatre, the beach, and for walks—much to her parents' displeasure.

By now, life at Hunter seemed to have lost some of its luster. Deeply hurt over not being elected editor in chief of *Argus*, Audre focused on passing her exams and graduating, assiduously recording in her journal the days going by. She also detailed her frustration with Miriam Burstein, to whose persona[50] she was deeply attracted, and who remained the focus of erotic fantasy and a crush that was unrequited.[51]

At this point, Audre was preoccupied with closing the chapter on her adolescence, anxious to be free of her parents and to begin life on her own. According to her journal, she wrote fewer poems during this period. However, once when she submitted a poem to *Argus*, the magazine's literary editor rejected it for publication on the grounds Audre should not aspire to become "a sensualist poet."[52] The criticism pointed to Audre's nascent imitations of the Romantics. The rejection angered though it did not defeat her. She sent the unsolicited poem, "Spring," to *Seventeen* magazine, which paid her for it and published it in April 1951. The publication vindicated Audre, confirming the potential commercial value of her "sensuous" literary style. Although it marked the beginning of her publishing career, Audre did not record this seminal event in her journal until several months afterwards, noting the poem's publication as probably the nearest she would get to fame.[53] "Fame" connoted adoration and attention, both of which Audre felt deeply bereft of. It would come, of course, in its many disguises, over the years; but for now it was as shadowy as life after high school.

Graduation exercises were held on the evening of June 26, 1951. Cornelia Newton, who taught English and poetry, praised Audre before the assembly as "one of her future poets."[54] But Audre saw that recognition as a hollow victory. Though she'd won a scholarship worth $1,400, her parents could not afford the additional monies needed to attend Sarah Lawrence College, an expensive private college for young women then, in Bronxville, New York, where she "wanted so badly to go."[55] Thus Audre left Hunter deeply disappointed, and even more angered by what she continued to see as her parents' deliberate lack of support.

After years of working long hours, Byron Lorde's health began to suffer, as first high blood pressure, then a series of heart attacks plagued him. Audre seemed to take little notice of this; she was furious at her parents and intent on gaining her freedom. Unable to attend Sarah Lawrence, she set her sights on getting into Hunter College, the affiliate of Hunter High School. She then turned her attention toward finding a job that would help pay for school.

Finding a job was harder work than she had foreseen. As the summer drew on, Audre wanted out of her parents' home now more than ever and became increasingly frustrated by a fruitless search for employment. She was still dating Levine, growing "extremely fond of him."[56] But she was ambivalent about having sex with him. According to her journal, although she was not a virgin then, she was sexually inexperienced and knew little, if anything, about men.[57]

During a chance encounter on the street while looking for work, she made the acquaintance of Ida Cullen, the widow of Countee Cullen. Introducing herself as a poet, Audre was pleased to meet Mrs. Cullen, whom she described as "a very nice person."[58] Mrs. Cullen invited Audre to the Countee Cullen Writers' Workshop, which met regularly then in Harlem. An admirer of Countee Cullen's poetry,[59] Audre attended a session of the workshop the evening of July 12, but never returned. Still, it was the first literary group she would connect with—aside from her association with "The Branded"—and the connection would prove significant later, when she attempted a more formal connection to Harlem's literary traditions via the Harlem Writers Guild.

By mid-July, she'd found a job at Beth David Hospital in downtown Manhattan. Lorde worked the night shift there as a nurse's aide, earning $25 a week. Her plan was to begin at Hunter in September and move out into an apartment of her own.

According to her journal, she plotted her escape for more than a month.[60] When a nasty fight erupted between Audre and her sister Helen one day, Mrs. Lorde threatened to call the police, which Audre reasoned was further evidence of her mother's hatred for her. She seized upon the moment for a precipitous break with her family—in particular, her mother—and announced she was moving out. "My way," she recorded in her journal that night, "must be always forward from now on—I've burnt all of my bridges behind me."[61] The following day, July 31,

1951, she moved in with a friend, Iris, who had an apartment on Rivington Street on the Lower East Side.

She had, she felt, closed the chapter at last; she could live her own free life (however fearful of the unknown) rather than a prescribed one, as her mother had.[62] But Audre's desire for distance from her mother would prove ultimately impossible. She was bound to her mother in a "ruthless intimacy"[63] defined as much by pain and rage as it was by love.

For the balance of the summer, Audre lived on the Lower East Side. Peopled by generations of working-class Polish, Jewish, and other Eastern European immigrants who had settled its neighborhoods, the Lower East Side was a mixture of established and fluctuating communities. With its Old World values still as palpable as the transplanted faces once peering from windows in the tenements of sprawling slums, it had been left a legacy of progressive social reform by women like Emma Goldman and Lillian D. Wald.[64] Life on the Lower East Side—with its bustling food shops mirroring the Park Avenue Market under the New York Central train tracks from 110th to 116th Streets in East Harlem (today known as La Marqueta) where, as a girl, she accompanied her mother to shop for Caribbean produce—provided a comforting and stabilizing, if not culturally familiar connection to her own immigrant roots. Whether or not Audre knew the history of progressive social reform on the Lower East Side, she connected with the tenacious ways in which its residents held onto their traditions and past.

In the meantime, her relationship with Gerry Levine continued; her feelings for him had now evolved from fondness to love. Audre's journal entry vowing she "would never have sex with any man" contradicted the earlier one in which she'd noted she was not a virgin. She remained deeply ambivalent about sex with Levine, preferring the physical closeness of kissing and petting to genital contact. Over the course of the summer, however, she had sex with Levine often, privately taking herself to task for being a "liar" and a "coward."[65] By the beginning of September, they were having their "usual misunderstandings in bed" and she noted that she could not "accept and conform to the sexual side"[66] of their relationship; she was clearly uncomfortable with any dynamic that presupposed her submissiveness and an absence of control. In her journal, she was still obsessing over Miriam Burstein.

Desiring a place of her own, Audre moved to Brighton Beach, a community on the outskirts of Brooklyn populated mostly by Germans and Russian Jews. She rented a room in an apartment building, 3238 Brighton and Seventh Streets, sharing a kitchen and bathroom with an elderly German woman whose loneliness and racist utterings she could hear through their common walls at night. Audre's own loneliness was exacerbated by the break with her family and by living so far out of the city. The only thing good about living in Brighton Beach for her was the smell of the Atlantic Ocean and the long stretch of boardwalk to Coney Island.

Audre registered for classes at Hunter College on September 14, 1951. The following evening, alone and deep in thought while walking the boardwalk, she ran into the Robinsons, a couple who'd been tenants in a building her father managed. Mrs. Robinson informed Audre her father was ill and encouraged her to go see him.[67] She was still ambivalent toward her father, fearful of his rejection and of his lingering authority over her. In spite of her determined efforts at independence, she was hurt that her parents had not tried to find her. Contacting them now would mean crossing back over the charred, splintered bridge of the past, the pain of which she had medicated, she'd thought, with doses of Gerry Levine and freedom.

But her chance meeting with the Robinsons brought home the realization that she'd "forgotten, almost, the pain and fear of the everyday world." Although she visited regularly with her older sister Phyllis, who was married by now and with whom she'd grown closer since moving out of their parents' home, Audre wanted little to do with the past. She wrote in her journal: "if I go to see him [Byron] now, I will be renewing my part as Audrey the Lorde daughter, with the difference from before that I will now be trying to live the part of Audrey the individual, also." Deeply conflicted, Audre realized that, "on the other hand, he's dying, I know. And he is my father, despite all which has passed between us."[68] She called home the next day and spoke to her father. And yet, given her apprehensions, Audre's journal is curiously silent as to how the conversation between them went.

Carrying a full course load at Hunter, Audre continued her literary studies, majoring in English and minoring in philosophy. One of the people she studied with was Hoxie Fairchild, an elderly British scholar who came to Hunter one semester. Fairchild taught a course in the Romantics and had a tremendous influence on Audre, furthering her interests in the poetry of Byron, Keats, Shelley, and Wordsworth, and guiding her work on the connections between the Beat poets and the Romantics.[69] Happily ensconced at Hunter, she commuted back and forth, juggling the demands of school and working nights at Beth David, consuming amphetamines to stay awake during her shifts.

However much she tried to concentrate on school, Audre was suffering from depression brought on by the break with her family and the souring relationship between herself and Levine. She wanted him to love her; but his interest in her seemed more sexual than anything else. Audre blamed herself, citing her emotional demands and inability to perform according to sexual expectation as the reasons for their problems.[70] She continued to see him, but remained ambivalent about their sexual relationship, reluctantly agreeing they should see each other less.

Audre's ambivalence about having sex with Levine, however, did not indicate a general distaste for sex with men but rather an ambivalent sexual curiosity. A week before she broke up with Levine, she was propositioned by the driver of the cab in which she was riding home. To Audre, the cab driver's request was "clear and natural like asking for a dance." Buoyed by "a feeling of curiosity more than want or desire,"[71] and by the driver's insistence that sex without attachment was fun, she agreed. The cab driver shut off the meter and pulled over on the Brooklyn Expressway. But once he entered her, Audre found herself withdrawing, hesitant, tense, and unable to go through with it, in spite of his physical likeness to Levine and the sexual excitement of a promiscuous moment.[72] The lure of sex without attachment, of sexual experimentation without emotional commitment, would become an incentive in future relationships with men and women, as she developed a sense both of the distinction between love and sexual expression, and of love tied to sexual expression.

Audre's relationship with Levine steadily unraveled. Symbolic of both her sexual and personal freedom, it illuminated a consistent, nightmarish loneliness. She became even more depressed. "I was alone," she wrote in her journal, "more alone than I ever thought possible. So alone that I felt mad. If I continue like this I'll be a psycho within a year."[73] Though she kept up with her studies, she was too depressed to show up for work and was fired from Beth David in mid-October 1951. With no job and her last paycheck spent, she pawned her typewriter and sold her blood to a blood bank for money. Her financial desperation was relieved when, through the Student Employment Office at Hunter, she found another job, this time as a medical receptionist. She began working afternoons in the office of a Dr. Stall. Around the same time, her father's health worsened, and on October 28, she received a telegram from Phyllis notifying her that he was seriously ill. He'd had another, more damaging heart attack. Audre went to see him at Columbia Presbyterian Medical Center. He was in an oxygen tent, and she wondered if he would die.[74]

As the relationship with Levine drew to a close, Audre considered going to a psychiatrist. She approached the mother of a friend, Crystal Field—a dancer and former schoolmate of Joan Alexander's and founder of the Theater for a New City—who recommended one. "If I can straighten myself out," she wrote in her journal in November, "I'll be able to cope with almost anything."[75] Crystal's mother gave Audre the name of a Dr. Papanek. Audre called and made an appointment.

On the day of the appointment, she took a friend, Mephi, with her for support. A former student at Hunter and a lesbian, Mephi was still close to Audre. At Hunter, she'd been known for wearing tuxedos, which she sported with great style. She'd fallen in love with her teacher, Cornelia Newton, and the two were now living together.[76] Audre spent a good deal of time visiting with them and going to parties at their Greenwich Village apartment. She envied the relationship Mephi and Newton had and that she and Miriam Burstein did not.[77] But she kept her association with them separate from her association with Gerry Levine, whom she still saw occasionally.

Audre was to have several therapists during her life. She saw Dr. Papanek at least three times that November,[78] paying eight dollars a visit. Other than noting the days of her appointments, Audre's journal is curiously short on descriptions of their sessions, recording scant details of their time together or how long after the first three visits she continued to be Papanek's patient.

Equally curious is the omission in her journal of the discovery that she was pregnant, presumably by Levine, sometime early in January

1952; and her subsequent illegal abortion the day before her eighteenth birthday, in February.[79] She'd thought about terminating the pregnancy herself but realized that was impossible. In an undated, handwritten paragraph on a piece of paper, she recorded her fears: "For a few nights I'd had livid nightmares of myself upon the table, & the doctor's hand being bitten off by a razor-sharp pair of infant wolf-like teeth that reached out from my womb, & I knew I couldn't do it."[80]

In time, Audre became disenchanted with the atmosphere at Hunter. Gone was the smaller, more pampered, all-female environment she'd come to associate with its name. She'd expected to find at Hunter College the sense of community and congeniality she'd had at Hunter High, and was dissatisfied with the absence of camaraderie, political awareness, and rebelliousness among this more conventional student body. During this time, she moved from her room in Brighton Beach to an apartment she sublet from a friend of Joan Alexander's. The apartment was on Spring Street on the Lower East Side. Lorde returned there like a homing pigeon.

A tiny three-room walk-up with a bathtub in the kitchen, it became a haven for an odd assortment of friends: left-wing sympathizers; interracial couples like Joan Alexander and her fiancé, Al Sandler; those of "The Branded" she was still close to; and a host of young white lesbian women for whom she became, alternately, a big sister and a mother figure.[81]

Audre's analysis of the dynamics underlying her friendships with these young women conveniently excluded a racial one as she focused primarily, and voyeuristically, on the eroticized presence of "all the beautiful young women" she was "sheltering."[82] Indeed, this may have been "the genesis of Audre's later . . . role as the God/Mother: a creative, divine, nurturer open-breasted to the needing many."[83] But the constant presence of these young women, especially those who were lesbians, was both sexually stimulating and sexually frustrating. By the summer of 1952, she made a conscious decision to have a lesbian relationship.

That spring, Audre returned to Harlem as a source of literary connection. Every Thursday night, she took the train uptown to the weekly meetings of the Harlem Writers Guild. The Guild was the brainchild of four writers: Rosa Guy, John Oliver Killens, Walter Christmas, and John Henrik Clarke. It began in the late 1940s as a storefront workshop for young black writers seeking to express their creativity and promote social change. The Guild created an alternative to the white literary world that was largely inaccessible to them as black writers. By the early 1950s, the workshop became formally known as the Harlem Writers Guild and later influenced generations of black writers, including Maya Angelou, Paule Marshall, Julian Mayfield, Louise Meriwether, among others. Although primarily a literary association, the Guild also promoted political activism. Some of its participants were union organizers, Progressive Party members, and contributors to Communist periodicals and publications. The Guild's most active members shared a Pan-African ideological perspective.[84]

The weekly meetings of the Harlem Writers Guild put Audre in touch with an organized black consciousness, afforded her an opportunity to have her poems heard, and was where the writer and scholar of African Studies, John Henrik Clarke, mentored her. Clarke taught Audre "wonderful things about Africa." He became a father figure, admiring and encouraging her poetry. But Audre felt that an "uneasy dialogue" existed between herself, Clarke, and the largely black male, heterosexual group, whom she suspected "tolerated but never really accepted"[85] her. That assessment was based on several factors: rumors that, downtown, Audre was sexually involved with white women; the male-centered, heterosexist bent in the Guild; and Audre's own insecurity. Though from Harlem originally, she was deliberately estranged from the daily life there. She was not active in the black nationalist struggle as it was then defined, especially by the Guild's members. At the time, she had neither an articulated black identity nor a firm sense of her own sexuality, which contributed to a sense of feeling out of place. In the end, the Harlem Writers Guild would prove a temporary literary home. But Audre's association with it was the vehicle for the publication of one of her poems in the Spring 1952 issue of the *Harlem Writers Quarterly*, which Clarke edited.

IN THE FALL OF 1952, Audre moved to Stamford, Connecticut, after dropping out of Hunter. She'd heard jobs were plentiful there, and moved into a room with a shared bathroom in a private house on Mill

River Road. She found a job at the Crystal Ribbon factory, from which she was summarily dismissed after just three weeks. Audre knew no one in Stamford; her poems and her typewriter became her companions.

She soon found another job at Keystone Electronics. It was a small factory in which quartz crystals, imported from Brazil and used in radio and radar machinery, were cut, ground, refined, and classified according to the degree of electrical charge they emitted. As an assembly-line worker at Keystone, along with other black and Puerto Rican women who labored under horrific work conditions, Audre was constantly exposed to carbon tetrachloride—overexposure can destroy the liver and cause cancer of the kidneys. She was also exposed to X-ray machines used to read the charges from the crystals. When these machines were used without shields, workers faced doses of constant low radiation well above acceptable safety levels.[86] Anyone who worked with the X-ray machines at one of the coveted jobs in the "Reading Room" and logged in a certain amount of crystals above the expected base count was "rewarded" with a bonus. It was dirty, low-wage work, a health risk which many of the workers, poor women without other options, succumbed to as they rationalized about the seconds they saved by not pulling down the shields over the X-ray machines. That way, they could work faster to earn meager bonuses in their weekly paychecks.

While at Keystone, Audre met Virginia "Ginger" Thurman, a divorcée slightly older than herself. This became Audre's first significant sexual relationship with a black woman. It was also the first time she admitted, however tentatively, to being gay. To Audre, Ginger was a "gorgeously fat"[87] femme. When Audre introduced Ginger to Joan Alexander once, Joan found Ginger to be "very sweet" but huge."[88] But Audre found in Ginger an appealing quality: she was physically graceful in spite of her large size, and Audre still struggled with her own lack of physical grace. Further, Ginger was, like herself, interested in a sexual relationship more than emotional attachment and knew well what it meant to protect the private world of homosexual desire.[89]

Right before Christmas 1952, Audre's father suffered a severe stroke. Sometimes accompanied by Ginger, she commuted back and forth to the Columbia Presbyterian Medical Center to visit him as he lay in the terminal ward, coming face to face again with the estranged relationship between herself and her mother. When Byron Lorde died early in 1953, Audre attended the funeral, staying in New York several days afterwards to be with her family. The death of Byron Lorde devastated his wife and daughters and left Audre numb. She would be unable to begin to come to terms with his death or her grief until several years afterwards.

Back in Connecticut, she was given one of Keystone's coveted jobs in the Reading Room. In order to increase her weekly bonuses, she began cheating on her count by hiding handfuls of crystals in her socks, chewing them up and spitting them into the toilet on her breaks. How much of those "little shards of rock"[90] did she inadvertently swallow? How long do carbon tetrachloride and low doses of radiation linger, undetected and parasitic, in the human body, before the cells of the body turn upon themselves, cancerous and outraged? Was this experience the medical root of Audre's cancer?[91]

The factory's forewoman soon began to suspect Audre's increasing ability to "slot" more crystals than anybody else. In March 1953, Audre was given two weeks' pay and fired. In the spring of that year, she left Stamford and returned to New York City, moving in with Joan Alexander.

Joan was sharing what was then considered an expensive apartment with another friend, Crystal Field. The furnished brownstone apartment at 141 West 87th Street, between Columbus and Amsterdam Avenues, was at garden level. It had a fireplace and a backyard, which Audre loved to spend time in. She also loved the big, old-fashioned kitchen, in which she would whip up inventive, spicy, Caribbean-style dishes with peas, codfish, mint, and other savory ingredients. After Audre got a job in a health center, they split the $100-a-month rent three ways. As young working women, they didn't have much money, but they gave lots of parties, and their apartment overflowed with an interracial crowd of artistic and bohemian types.

During this period, Audre and Joan's friendship deepened. For Joan, Audre was a willing confidante whom she trusted and turned to for advice, particularly when it came to Joan's affairs. Although Audre's reactions were somewhat prudish, as a friend she was remarkably pragmatic and loyal. Audre also supported Joan's desire to tease out a more androgynous persona. With Audre's approval, Joan experimented with dress and hairstyles that were decidedly boyish.[92] For Audre, Joan's friendship helped to counter her ever present sadness, the rootlessness she now experienced. Even so, Audre remained guarded and private, taking in more than she gave out.

Often, after work, in late spring, they'd rendezvous in the Village, walking along McDougal Street, sitting in Washington Square Park, soaking up its bohemian flavor. Or they'd find themselves a table at the Waldorf Café, one of the popular cafés where the likes of LeRoi Jones (now Amiri Baraka), James Earl Jones, Sr., and James Baldwin often hung out. In the evenings, they'd sometimes attend one of the loft parties or clubs peopled by an assortment of jazz musicians, poets, interracial couples, and black intellectuals who were more at home in the freer, social climate of the Village than they were uptown in Harlem.[93]

When Joan's fiancé, Al, returned from living and painting in Mexico, he was full of stories of expatriated writers and artists living more freely there, unbridled by the fevered, anti-Communist hysteria of McCarthyism. Her interest piqued by Al's stories of artistic freedom, as well as by Mexico's geographic proximity and its tropical culture, Audre decided on a trip there and began taking Spanish classes at Berlitz in preparation.

Life at the apartment came to an end. Crystal, who could no longer afford her share of the rent, moved home to her mother's house in Queens; then Joan moved out, marrying Al and resettling in Brooklyn. Unable to afford the rent alone, Audre had to move but still couldn't afford a place of her own.

Through Joan, she met Ruth Baharas. Joan and Ruth were friends who worked in the International Workers Organization (IWO), a fraternal organization that consisted of ten different societies organized along racial and ethnic lines—including the Frederick Douglass Society, whose members were black. The IWO was active on the political left, had a membership of over 180,000 and provided low-cost insurance for its constituents.[94] By 1953, it was on the U.S. Attorney General's list of subversive organizations. A stenographer working for the Jewish Society of the IWO, Ruth Baharas (now Gollobin) was ten years Audre's senior, Jewish, and had an apartment at 61 East Seventh Street and Second Avenue in a section of the Lower East Side that was fast becoming known as the East Village.

Audre moved into Ruth's East Village apartment that May—1953—

grateful for a place to stay until she left for Mexico. Joan had informed Ruth—who was straight—that Audre was a lesbian. Ruth was less fazed by Audre's lesbianism than she was curious. But Audre was adept now at intimacy without self-revelation and she was characteristically guarded about the details of her private life, communicating to Ruth only the vaguest sense of her "problems." To Ruth, Audre seemed young, unhappy, indecisive, and yet "a very determined person," in spite of "an air of sadness"[95] cocooning her.

Ruth Baharas was no stranger to the sadness that accompanied being "other."[96] She was a political leftist at a time when the U.S. government demanded nationalist loyalty, and legislated against dissent. She was intimate with the particular realities of anti-Semitism; and she well understood a sense of isolation that was both personal and historic. Her mother, a Russian-Ukrainian, had come to the United States in 1907 before the Bolshevik Revolution. When the Union of Soviet Socialist Republics (USSR) was formed, the Ukraine became one of those republics; the Ukrainian people no longer had autonomous citizenship. This left Ruth's mother to feel she had no country. Ruth lived with the constant threat of her mother being deported at any time because of her status in America as a "non-citizen" for nearly fifty years. Not long after Audre moved in, Ruth's mother was arrested under the McCarran Act and eventually deported, having freely admitted, while filling out a questionnaire, to her previous membership in the Communist Party despite the fact she was not a member of the party at the time of her arrest.[97] In the anti-Communist national mood which fueled suspicions of the foreign-born, Ruth's advocacy on behalf of her mother was not lost on Audre, and she provided a sympathetic ear.

By midsummer, public outcry against the prosecution of Julius and Ethel Rosenberg reached fever level. Arrested in the summer of 1950, the Rosenbergs had been charged with espionage—passing vital information on the atomic bomb to the USSR between 1944 and 1945. They were both U.S. citizens. Much of the evidence against the Rosenbergs was supplied by Mrs. Rosenberg's brother, David Greenglass, a machinist who was himself under indictment, and by Harry Gold, a confessed spy.[98] Publicized accounts of the trial and the government's suspicious case against them mobilized the left in protest. Many claimed the Cold

War political climate made a fair trial impossible, as did anti-Semitic reactions to the Rosenbergs. Others questioned the value of the materials they'd allegedly passed to the USSR. A member of the Committee in Defense of the Rosenbergs, Ruth Baharas encouraged Audre's growing sympathy toward the Rosenbergs and her participation in the committee's activities.

After the Rosenbergs were found guilty of espionage and sentenced to death, Audre, Ruth, and Joan boarded a bus in early June bound for Washington, D.C., where a large contingent of women planned to march in front of the White House and appeal for a stay of execution.[99] Despite an international campaign for clemency, the Rosenbergs were executed at Sing Sing Prison on June 19, 1953. Like others who'd rallied to the cause, Audre was demoralized by their execution. Disillusioned, fearful of an odious political climate, she wondered now if "there was any place in the world that was different from here, anywhere that could be safe and free, not really even sure of what being safe and free could mean."[100] In the coming trip to Mexico, she saw an escape.

Privately now, Joan and Al Sandler began to express concern to Audre about her openly lesbian relationships.[101] While interracial heterosexual relationships, such as theirs, were considered politically correct within the left-wing movement, homosexuals and homosexual relationships, interracial or not, were highly problematic; the left had no analysis then of interlocking racial and sexual oppressions. The Sandlers worried that being gay would lead to a stereotypical life of misery for Audre, and as her friends, they also wanted to protect themselves from the stain of homosexuality Audre's friendship might bleed on them politically. They informed Audre they couldn't remain friends with her if she continued having relationships with women. Joan, at least, had had no problems with Audre's lesbian connections previously. She'd accompanied Audre to several parties at Cornelia and Mephi's Village apartment. Audre had introduced her to a number of lesbian women she liked, and she'd found the whole scene "interesting, at the time." But she agreed with Al to discontinue their friendship; much later, she would acknowledge that decision as infantile, motivated by politics, and very hurtful to Audre.[102] In truth, Audre wasn't out as a lesbian at the time. What the Sandlers knew of her personally was not a publicly articulated identity, and their reasoning had more to do with their own homophobia and the homophobia of the left. That homophobia made the left wing a problematic political home for Audre.

Feeling isolated and alone, she left for Mexico. Disgusted by the country's swing to the right, Audre imagined a future scenario in which the language of McCarthyism could be easily appropriated by her comrades on the left to target homosexuals.[103] In the airport, she felt as if she were boarding the plane with her "coat tails on fire."[104] Over time, the rupture with the Sandlers would heal and the conversation that caused it was never spoken of. However "silent, intense and unforgiving" her father had been, his identity as a "race man" had imprinted upon Audre's psyche a heightened social conscience. But she hadn't yet found a female-centered community in which she could express her convictions.

PART TWO

"Poetry Is Not a Luxury"
(1954–69)

THREE

A UDRE ARRIVED in Mexico City with the names of a few contacts, some savings, and a rudimentary understanding of Spanish.[1] She was twenty years old and it was 1954. She checked into the Formos, a third-rate hotel in the heart of the Distrito Federal. The following day she moved into the Hotel Fortin, an affordable though not inexpensive hotel Al Sandler had recommended.[2] From the first days of her arrival, Mexico cast light upon Lorde's relationship to her poetry and to herself as lesbian.

Mexico City seemed to her "a teeming mess,"[3] "fantastically big and disordered,"[4] and the thinner air made her dizzy initially. She moved about the city that first week adventurous yet "terrified,"[5] having never lived so far from New York before. Taken in by new sights and smells, "the feeling of color and light,"[6] she toured the streets, old museums, shops, and parks. At times, she was mistaken for Cuban by Mexicans and for Mexican by Americans, a confusion she attributed to her skin coloring and natural hairstyle (which she'd worn since leaving high school), as well as to the fact she was a *turista*, an obvious outsider.[7] She found Mexicans friendly, and she was in awe of seeing brown-skinned people, of every hue, wherever she went. In a letter to Ruth Baharas, Audre wrote that she felt "like an onion,"[8] peeled of layers of its own smothering skins. She was elated at being out of the United States, away from the political despair of her comrades; away from her own rootless life. But by the end of the first week, she was suffering her "first real bout of homesickness."[9] She felt "terribly lonely for people to make friends with,"[10] and anxiously awaited the start of classes at the Cuidad Universitaria, where by the second week she'd registered for courses in Mexican history, ethnology, and folk song at the National University of Mexico. For the most part, she entertained herself by exploring Mexico City alone, feeling "more and more at home."[11]

By now, Audre's sense of home was fluid, defined by her mother's portable sense of "home"—a reconstruction of longings and reality. Home, she'd learned from her mother, signified "a place of deep spiritual connection."[12] Having fled a sense of rootlessness, Audre arrived in Mexico spiritually disconnected and was, at this point in her life, spiritually homeless. But she was to find in Mexico "an affirmation,"[13] a spiritual connection, as she now felt herself "unfolding like some large flower."[14]

Anxious for classes to begin, she took a day trip to Cuernavaca, a suburb on the outskirts of Mexico City, to visit with Frieda "Freddi" Mathews, whose name had been given to her by a friend of Ruth Baharas. Freddi was living there with her daughter, Tobi, in an apartment duplex off the main market.

While visiting with Freddi, Audre got a taste of Cuernavaca's bohemian life. The area was populated with expatriates from abroad. She later described it as "a haven for political and spiritual refugees"[15] from the States, including Agnes Kaufman, Hope Faye (an active member of the Communist Workers Association), Albert and Margaret Maltz (who'd fled to Mexico with their family as a result of the McCarthy purge in Hollywood), Agnes Bolton (Eugene O'Neill's first wife), and numerous other mostly older, white middle-class leftists who were or felt they were political outlaws in McCarthy's America. Some of the women were lesbian or bisexual. Audre was enchanted by the friendly stream of people Freddi introduced her to as they sat talking at a café table in the square, which she imagined was like being in Paris, only it was Mexico.[16]

She was even more enchanted by the conversation, the easy laughter over cups of *cafe con leche*, and the sense of community. By evening's end, she felt accepted by Freddi's crowd, and had several invitations to stay at people's houses for a weekend.[17] She was struck by the magical quality of Cuernavaca's beauty and quiet, by the easy life of its residents; she immediately liked it more than she liked the overcrowded grittiness of Mexico City. Shortly thereafter, she made the decision to move to Cuernavaca in search of cheaper housing and the glimpse of community she'd seen there.

With Freddi's help, by the beginning of April Audre had rented an inexpensive house that was quiet, sunny, and private, part of a compound shared by several other women who were friends and looked out for each other. The house came with a garden and pool. Audre settled in, ecstatic.[18] Living in Cuernavaca now meant a commute back and forth to Mexico City and to her classes.

In the light of Cuernavaca, both natural and spiritual, Audre underwent an epiphany that changed and deepened her ideas about poetry. One day, while walking down a hill at dawn on her way to the square for the bus that would take her to the Cuidad Universitaria, she realized there was a connection between the "quality of light"[19] in Mexico, what she felt deeply, and words.[20] For the first time in her life, she "had an insight into what poetry could be."[21] Where once she'd thought of her poems as "love for the blind beauty of words",[22] she now saw in them the possibility to "*re*-create"[23] a feeling, like the one she was having on that hill, rather than the dreamlike imitation of feeling she felt so much of her writing had been.[24] In draft after draft of poems in her journal, Audre struggled now for a poetic language closer to re-creation of feeling:

> Spring comes like a kiss to Mexico
> A land where winter's claws
> Are filed to ineffectual blows
> That do not last a chilly day . . .
>
> And I have known an eastern spring
> The cruel, unharnessed, harsh

Big-city spring.
The lonely morning's binding
misty fingers—
And the sun, long tired
Of fighting winter snow,
Breaking forth with fury
We are ill-prepared to meet,
Tempting us with wild &
                    witching promises
She cannot fulfill.[25]

In Cuernavaca, Audre met her future lover, Eudora Garrett. Garrett was a journalist, lesbian, at least twenty-seven years older than Audre, and prone to alcoholic bouts.[26] Lorde publicly made much of her affair with Garrett,[27] but an explicit sexual relationship between the two of them is unsubstantiated by her journal at the time.[28] She did write about meeting Eudora in April. The two were friendly, at the least, until Lorde left Mexico for the States, in July 1954. The significance of their affair is mired in competing truths. But with Lorde, the truth was as complex as it was convenient.

It was Garrett who "totally engaged"[29] Audre in the erotic, psychic, and physical aspects of lesbian loving for the first time, embodying Audre's deepest desires for a sister–confidante–teacher–loving mother figure. Fluent in Spanish and in Mexican culture, Garrett showed Audre "the way to the Mexico" she'd "come looking for, that nourishing land of light and color"[30] where she found a sense of home. Eudora Garrett was both racial and sexual other, a combination Lorde found increasingly attractive in the social and political circles she inhabited. Theirs was an affair of limited potential, with an implicit understanding of the temporary, fleeting nature of what was between them. Significantly, their brief affair had a prescient aspect: Eudora Garrett was the first woman Lorde knew who'd had a mastectomy as a result of breast cancer, and she did not wear a prosthesis to camouflage the fact that she had only one breast.[31]

Lorde hoped to find a job which would support an extended stay in Mexico, but was unable to do so by the beginning of June. Packing her things and closing up the house she'd rented, she decided to travel on to Oaxaca and its surrounds.

One evening in Oaxaca, she met George Lepere, an American mill magnet salesman with permanent Mexican residency who was traveling south on business.[32] More experienced traveling in Mexico, he made a "wonderful companion"[33] as the two of them left Oaxaca on June 17[34] and traveled in each other's company over the next six days. With Lepere as her guide, Audre saw more of the country, making stops in Tehuantepec and San Cristóbal in Chiapas state.[35]

Back in Cuernavaca by June 25, she immediately went to see Eudora Garrett. Garrett had decided by then to move to Mexico City and was packing up to do so when Audre returned.[36] With no place of her own now, Audre stayed at Agnes Kaufman's. The prospect of returning to New York City loomed, but Audre was not looking forward to leaving Mexico and Garrett, who was in the throes of an alcoholic bout. Between the end of June and the beginning of July, Audre spent as much time as she could with Garrett.

Audre left for New York on July 5, 1954. In Cuernavaca, she'd gotten a brief glimpse of a community of women, and of how a shared sense of being outsiders shaped that community. She had a new understanding of the potential of poetry to connect her feelings with words. She also had a deeper sense of herself as lesbian. These experiences defined a spiritual connection to aspects of herself she hadn't felt before.

FOUR

"I HAVE ALWAYS wanted to be both man and woman," Lorde declares in her Prologue to *Zami*. "I would like to enter a woman the way any man can, and to be entered—to leave and to be left— to be hot and hard and soft all at the same time in the cause of our loving."[1] It was a statement embodying a complex sexuality she would initially act out in the predominantly, but not exclusively, white lesbian bar culture of the mid- to later 1950s.

Lorde moved back to Ruth Baharas's East Village apartment. Before Mexico, Baharas's home and friendship had been a safehouse for her; a stop on her escape to freedom. When she came back to it, she had been invested with a new spirit. She was daily challenging herself to practice the freedoms she had defined. What was she to make of being woman, black, a writer? At her core, still, was an excruciating loneliness. Alternately named and unnamed in years before, when it was "a dark and empty cavern where sometime shrieking howling winds ravened back and forth, and a sometime vacuum strangled all into silence," loneliness was "an endless death" now; but she could "survive, a new and wandering, wondering stranger free of dark in a new nameless country—better only perhaps because it too is undefined, and when it becomes bounded, another, and yet another."[2] This new, nameless, undefined country would house Lorde's desire to be linked with other women erotically. During this period her poetry was shaped by that desire and an attendant loneliness.

In 1955, she returned to Hunter College—and to the world of intellectual engagement. Her studies in literature and philosophy, the world of books and ideas, fed Lorde's foundational identity, fueled, as it were, by an insatiable intellect and fascination with minutiae. Though she did not think of herself as a scholar, Lorde was to become "a living philosopher,"[3] whose social consciousness was articulated through constant, intellectual shape-shifting as she came to view herself as representative of multiple oppressed communities. In resuming her studies as an English major, she studied Euro-American literary traditions. She continued shifting between her identities as student and as black—identities that were at once externally static and internally fluid.

Emboldened by her affair with Eudora Garrett, Lorde now understood a deepened intimacy with her own lesbian eroticism, one that engaged altering masculine ("to leave") and feminine ("to be left") desires within her. But like many homosexuals then, Lorde generally kept closeted her lesbianism at Hunter College.

Hunter was a microcosm of 1950s America, a decade characterized by rigid gender roles, the rise of the nuclear family as critical to social harmony, laws against "sexual psychopaths," and state-sanctioned harassment of homosexuals. Cold War America nurtured an antihomosexual culture in which "deviance" was suppressed.[4] As in preceding decades, the 1950s saw the continuation of a climate in which homosexuals were generally ostracized, and homosexuality was both implicitly and explicitly outlawed. Resisting social pressures to stay closeted, a homosexual subculture flourished in the gay bars, where intimacy, desire, and likeness were openly expressed.[5]

Searching for a lesbian scene that was different from the bleak, doomed narratives painted in such popular books as Radclyffe Hall's *The Well of Loneliness* (1928) and Ann Bannon's *Odd Girl Out* (1957), Audre embraced the gay-girls bar scene at night and on the weekends; there she was lesbian, but black. The bars she frequented had names like Page Three, Laurel's, The Sea Colony, The Swing, and The Bagatelle (The Bag); most were located on recessed streets of the East and West Village.

Black lesbians who frequented bars owned by whites, and patronized largely by white working-class lesbians, were sexual outsiders in New York's black communities. Although black lesbians could, and did, patronize straight black bars, they often did so at the cost of comfort. The white-owned lesbian bars offered a more inviting community. In the late 1960s, these bars became focal points for articulating lesbian resistance. Even so, they offered complicated arenas, in which black women who were lesbians traded sexual ease with other lesbians for racial solidarity with each other. As Lorde was to discover, the few black lesbians she encountered in white bars rarely related to each other on the level of their shared racial reality;[6] and they subsumed their identities as black women within their identities as "gay-girls." Though increasingly racially mixed, such bars were not free of racist practices. Many black lesbians knew well the spoken and unspoken racial tension their presence created, even as interracial couples and expressions of interracial desire were common. Still, black and white lesbians associated here across racial barriers in ways most straight women (black or white) did not before the civil rights and contemporary feminist movements of the 1960s and the 1970s.

Lorde's membership in the circle of white lesbian lovers and friends who became her community underscored a complicated reality: gayness was one bond of difference connecting them, but race was *a* difference separating them. Without the benefit of, or personal necessity for, a political analysis of race and racism, white lesbians were often uncomfortable with race-centered conversation; and they protected the fragile bond created by a one-dimensional community based on sexuality.

Lorde's analyses of the sexual and racial contours of difference and social oppression, as a black woman, were unpopular with some white lesbians she associated with at the time. The home she found in community with them was a precarious shelter in which she was deeply conflicted by her compartmentalization as either silenced black or colorless lesbian. Lorde both enjoyed her exotic position and resented the isolation of being an outsider in this newfound "community." Thus, her bonds with white lesbian women were troubled, insufficient as definitions of community.[7] Just as the bond of gayness was insufficient for her, so too was the concept of gayness performed in the bars.

As public spaces, the bars were intense, complex sexual theatres in which lesbians were no longer alone and had the chance to develop ideas about community and act out desire. Most lesbians who frequented the bars identified as butch or femme and were, in the fifties, exclusively one or the other.[8] Lesbians who switched roles, or who were neither exclusively butch nor femme, were snidely labeled "ky-ky" and "AC/DC," and were seen as sexually ambiguous to lesbians with more boundaried sexual identities and reputations. They upset the bars' social order.[9]

In appearance, at least, Lorde was neither exclusively butch nor exclusively femme. She danced between wardrobes and personas, shifting between the more feminine attire she reserved for her straight persona and the world of work, and her bar costumes of blue jeans and pin-striped shirts, which were not as butch as the more rigid persona of some other lesbians, nor distinctively femme. Lorde was not into the rigid definition of "dyke chic," with its constant presentations of an either/or. Nor was she into the rigid role-playing performed by most lesbians in and outside the bars, earning a reputation for herself as "ky-ky."[10] Lorde could be both "masculine" and "feminine" at once. She let free and experimented with a flirtatious (femme) and sexually an aggressive (butch) lesbian eroticism, which was not—and would never be—bound by others' expectations of monogamy.

Lorde wanted to believe in, and practice, loving without boundaries—a philosophy and behavior she found consistent with rebellion against heterosexually scripted models of monogamy. Her choice represented the uncharted landscape, the "new nameless country," of loving women without becoming imprisoned by those very models. Ideologically, at least, she was free then to be sexual with whomever she wanted, whenever she wanted. She began to experiment with having one loving relationship with a specific partner, and separating that relationship from sexual intimacy with friends.[11]

Not long after she returned from Mexico, Lorde became involved with Marion Masone. When they met, Masone was living in Stamford, Connecticut, but traveled down to New York on occasion and liked to frequent the bars. Something of a loner herself, Marion was white, an aspiring printmaker, close to Audre in age and affecting an androgynous, beatniklike persona. With Marion, Lorde could share poetry, conversation about art, and outsider identity. As their affair continued, Audre became more enamored, exchanging her social shyness for Marion's constant companionship.

Lorde also got bolder about bringing women home to Ruth Baharas's apartment, although she and Ruth did not ever openly discuss her lesbianism. The fact that they never did so had as much to do with Baharas's unwillingness to pry as it had with a complicated sense of privacy and self-reserve on Lorde's part, which allowed her to appear open even when she was not. The living arrangements between them gave Audre increasingly more space in which to entertain, as Ruth spent more time away from the apartment in pursuit of her own love affairs.

Lorde's memory as to how Ruth's apartment eventually became hers differs from Ruth's. In Lorde's version, Ruth had been outed by "a visiting higher-up in progressive circles" who'd discovered, on a visit to the apartment one night while Audre was home, that Ruth was sharing an apartment with a lesbian. Thus challenged, Ruth was forced to choose between maintaining an unblemished reputation with other progressives or disassociating from them and the political work that meant so much to her.[12] In her version, Ruth claimed to be centered on efforts to keep her mother from being deported, the loss of her job with the International Workers Organization, and a new job working for the Committee to Protect the Foreign Born—which had an office in Chicago.[13] Whatever the case, Baharas moved to Chicago in 1956, leaving her apartment to Lorde. After two years in Chicago, she left for Poland in 1958; the two women would not see each other again until 1964, when Ruth returned to the States. With the apartment to herself now, Audre asked Marion Masone to move in.

Marion did move in, eventually, setting up household with Audre and sharing their lives together. While Audre reestablished a niche as a student, Marion took a string of jobs less suited to her aspirations as an artist. They spent less time in the bars, staying at home and entertaining friends there. Life with Marion eased her loneliness, and Audre found her first experiment in living with a lover erotic, meaningful, and satisfying.

She was terrified of her own emotional vulnerability. The freedom to love without boundaries masked a "deeply rooted mechanism" in Lorde, which kept her emotionally safe, "untouchable," and protected. In that sense, she allowed herself to give "freely in areas not commonly given yet holding tight the door to a more essential self." Lorde required commitment from others and needed an "intensity" to match her own that was real and necessary for emotional and sexual satisfaction, but she understood well that what she demanded of others was something she herself could not truly, easily, give—even as she felt she wanted to, had to, believed that she should. She understood this double standard as "cruelty in its essence."[14] The mental doors she slammed on others frightened her when they did the same; this made her emotionally uneasy with anyone who practiced their self-preservation on her.

By the latter half of the fifties, Audre Lorde's life was a puzzle of oscillating subcurrents. There was that recurring, maddening loneliness of the soul. The sexual gratification she felt in the company and arms of white women, which inevitably led to racial self-loathing. The still unresolved separation from her mother. Being a black lesbian in the mostly white, gay environs of the Village. The "deep suspicion" with which she and too many other black lesbians viewed each other; and the fear of her own blackness mirrored in their eyes.[15] There was her life as a student working odd jobs to put herself through. Typical of the lives she and her friends led as social outlaws, she began smoking marijuana socially. And she returned to taking the amphetamines she periodically relied on, especially during times of competing stresses. Taking "speed" boosted her physical stamina and enabled her to study after working late shifts.

Between the latter months of 1957 and early 1958, Lorde became a patient of Clement Staff, a psychoanalyst with a private practice at 7 East 94th Street. He was white, Jewish, and considered a "pioneer," who'd written several articles on the social and cultural aspects of psychoanalysis.[16] She went into therapy at twenty-four as an act of self-scrutiny, frustrated by the emotional barriers she'd erected and depended on, by an attendant loneliness she seemed unable to escape.

Nor was she able to escape a tortured sleep, "bound in that most terrible of nightmares—not being able to wake or move,"[17] or the confusion of dreams in which the faces of women competed, were contorted, and erotic desire both affirmed and haunted her. Nor could she escape the sense of unfinished business with her family and father, that "great and inescapable pain."[18]

Lorde later claimed that Clement Staff's marriage was on the brink of divorce: the two of them were romantically involved and intended to marry once his divorce was finalized.[19] Whether that claim was true or not, it was a significant indication of her evolving attraction to white men, even though she thought of herself as lesbian now. Moreover, it signified a sexual personality that was lesbian *and* bisexual, and would permit her to enter into marriage in a foreseeable future, as did many women then who married men but were or became sexual with other women.

On March 25, 1958, Staff died in Mt. Sinai Hospital, of an unexplained "long illness." His death was a shock to Lorde and came two days short of the eighth anniversary of Genevieve Johnson's death. Staff was the second person in her life to die relatively young. Lorde struggled to reckon with her shock and grief. "When I have learned to foreaccept the certainties of life," she wrote, "all of whose names is [*sic*] dead, I shall have learned my living." A month later, she wrote in her journal,

> And there will pass with your passing
> Little of beauty not your own:—
> Only the light from common water—
> Only the grace from simple stone.[20]

The death of Clement Staff left Lorde on her own to fathom the intricacies of her recurring nightmares, loneliness, and emotional struggles. She became terribly depressed. Several untitled poems in her journal were anchored to images of death and ravaged sleep, such as this one:

> I dreamt of betrayal one icy night
> And before the grey dawn shed its light

> I hung my shackled arms & wept
> What had been done me while I slept

and this one:

> Now has come to me almost all I can know of
> death and to my love, the foolish path to light.
> What it was she sought I do not know, and
> seeks again & shall not find . . .
> Before the death is all of me I must
> go now, before the memory of light is
> eaten into darkness also, and I become
> some witless ravening anger slinking
> thro the street I learned to cherish . . .[21]

Lorde sought out the assistance of another therapist, a Dr. Rosenbloom. Rosenbloom had an office on West End Avenue. She saw him weekly, and he treated her free of charge because she was a student. Described by her as a "very liberal, very responsive white male," Rosenbloom nursed her through what Lorde characterized as a year of "an almost suicidal depression,"[22] though she hadn't actually attempted suicide.

Lorde was adept at keeping separate the different social worlds she inhabited, and at Hunter College no one knew of her battles with depression. She became actively involved with *Echo*, a student literary publication which she edited and contributed a few poems to. *Echo's* office was next door to the office of the Student Council, in the back of which was housed the Student Government Office. Both offices had a steady stream of students going in and out to work, meet, and gather. In that whirl of activity, Lorde met Blanche Wiesen, who'd entered Hunter in the fall of 1958.

The oldest of two daughters of Jewish parents, Blanche was straight out of high school—where she'd distinguished herself as an athlete—and seven years younger than Audre. Her mother, Sadonia Ecker Wiesen, was an educational and legal secretary. A food importer in 1958, her father, David Theodore Wiesen, later became a bus driver active in

New York City's Transport Workers Union.[23] At Hunter, Blanche was active in student government, eventually becoming president of the Student Council and then vice president of Student Affairs for the National Student Association (NSA) for the northeast region. Dissatisfaction with the NSA's stance on racial issues subsequently led her to a founding role in Students for a Democratic Society (SDS).[24]

Audre and Blanche became friends immediately, socializing together at gay bars. Blanche found Audre "dazzling" and "flirtatious." Audre became her first female lover. The relationship between them went on for some time, non-binding and periodic, as Audre ("who never had just one person at a time")[25] and Blanche each maintained other lovers. Their friendship was to be lifelong, their paths separating and intertwining.

The decade that had seen feverish anti-Communist sentiment and an emerging civil rights movement was coming to a close. The 1950s had also seen the birth of the age of television, which helped to popularize a family-centered ideology aimed at rigidly defined roles for women and men within families.[26] Television shows such as *Leave It to Beaver* and *The Adventures of Ozzie & Harriet* echoed social expectations of these roles, glorifying them in the "ideal" American family, which was white, uncritically patriotic, and heterosexual. Racism and segregation defined black people as culturally deviant and black families as pathological. Contesting these perceptions while articulating the deviance of racism, black writers such as James Baldwin and Lorraine Hansberry[27] directed white America's gaze toward its own pathologies. Internationally, the Cold War reconfigured global relations; and having triumphed over communism during the Korean War (1950–53), America was poised against its former ally, Russia, as "the voice of the free world." Fidel Castro's guerrilla campaign against the reactionary Batista dictatorship in Cuba would be successful, ushering in the Cuban Revolution by the end of the decade. Polarizations abounded: capitalist versus Communist; white versus black; rich versus poor; normal versus abnormal.

In 1959, Lorde graduated from Hunter College and entered Columbia University's graduate program in library science. Bordered by Harlem, Columbia became yet another stage upon which she juggled carefully inhabited, intersecting worlds. She worked during the daytime, took classes at night, and was still involved with the "gay-girls" scene in the East and West Village. But her life at home was disintegrating. Marion had become increasingly dissatisfied with her inability to land a steady job in New York City and to create her own niche there. She decided to move back to Stamford. The breakup depressed Audre, yet the experience of living with Marion had assuaged, if temporarily, an untenable loneliness. It shaped a significant model for Lorde's desire to be linked with other women erotically, and to have a meaningful life, neither of which she was willing to choose between.

FIVE

"A s a Black lesbian mother in an interracial marriage," Lorde later reflected on her life in the 1960s, "there was usually some part of me guaranteed to offend everybody's comfortable prejudices of who I should be."[1] But Lorde was publicly silent, for the most part, about the details of her seven-year marriage to Edwin Ashley Rollins. In the film of her life, *A Litany for Survival: The Life and Work of Audre Lorde*, her only comment about Ed Rollins was that he "was the only man I ever considered marrying."[2] The reasons for this uncharacteristic silence were framed by the dissociation often accompanying less than amicable divorces and by Audre Lorde's public, near-mythic persona as lesbian. For his part, Ed never spoke publicly about his ex-wife, maintaining a silence of more than two decades and breaking it only after she was dead.

When they met, she was twenty-seven. He was thirty, a graduate of Columbia University's law school and working for the city doing title work—a job requiring him to check the titles of properties owned or soon-to-be owned by the city, before the city sold them.

The son of a Protestant family, Ed had been raised in Scotia, New York, near Schenectady. His father's mother was Native American; the family's mixed blood was visibly apparent in his father's darker skin. Ed had a younger sister. A beautiful, sensitive boy more interested in books than roughhousing, his mother dressed him in velvet. On Saturday afternoons she took him to musical events to instill in him a sense of culture.[3] He grew up loving opera and was particularly fascinated with Maria Callas, whom he adored. He was temperamentally closest to his mother, Edith. His father, Neil, a real estate agent and a "man's man," liked to hunt and was ever tough on and disappointed with an only son who had none of his more manly inclinations.[4] By the time Ed was twelve or thirteen, he knew he would not live or make a career in the sheltered, upstate New York world of his parents. His values were different from theirs. When asked during a casual family discussion once if he'd consider marrying a black person, the teenaged Ed said yes.

Ed Rollins kept secret from his family's certain disapproval an early attraction to boys and men. Although he was never exclusively homosexual,[5] these early patterns of secrecy would follow him into adulthood and become a troubling aspect of marriage. At seventeen, only weeks after his mother suffered a nervous breakdown and was institutionalized in a mental hospital, Ed wanted out of his family. Too young to enlist on his own, he asked his father to sign the papers giving him permission to join the U.S. Navy.[6] Wanting to join the navy was an overtly "manly" act; it was the first time his father was ever truly proud of him.[7] With his father's permission, Ed ran away from a family in which he had become an outsider.

By the time Audre met Ed, he'd been discharged from a naval unit attached to the Marines in Korea and was sharing an apartment near Columbia on 114th Street with John Gloster, a former service buddy who was now his best friend. John was Irish American, originally from Springfield, Massachusetts, and gay. Ed himself had "been at that point gay for fifteen years for all practical purposes." Although he'd dated women from time to time, he had had very little sexual contact with them. Ed had been engaged to a woman whose material aspirations conflicted with his disinterest in a corporate career. He led Audre to believe his ex-fiancé might have realized he was gay.[8] But at thirty, Ed's biological clock was ticking. He wanted kids and was looking for a wife who suited him.

Long before they actually met, Audre and Ed heard of each other through Margie Gumpert, a white woman and mutual friend. Margie attended Hunter High School for a time but did not graduate from there. Exactly when she and Lorde met is not clear, but they were introduced by a former Hunter High School associate. She'd divorced her first husband with whom she'd had two daughters, and was then married to Lou Murdoch, a technical writer who wrote manuals for machinery. She had one son with him. Margie exercerised a counterculture persona[9] and filled her Riverside Drive apartment with art and antiques.[10] A liberal, she was involved then with organizing support at the local Democratic level for John F. Kennedy's presidential bid. Playing matchmaker, Margie orchestrated a small afternoon gathering at her apartment on 160th Street, to which she invited Audre and Ed. It was the spring of 1961.[11]

At the gathering, the conversation was laced with pro-Kennedy politics. Margie's circle included, amongst others, Don and Paula Copelman; her husband, Lou; Roland Turner, a black musician, and his white wife Diana; Neal and Martha Einson, whom Audre had first known as Martha Klempner when they became friends at Hunter High School in the early fifties. Martha's keen intelligence, cynical wit, assertive personality, and almost masculine but delicate features[12] were attractive to Audre.

Born and raised in New York City to a Jewish father from New Jersey and a mother who was a Russian Jew, Martha's family was working class and liberal. She grew up influenced by her maternal grandmother, Dora Bogen, whom she described as "very left wing." Bogen felt the Communist Revolution was a good thing in Russia and should happen in the United States as well.[13] After graduating from Hunter High School, Martha earned a degree in social work from Adelphi University. In 1953, while working as a proofreader for Prentice-Hall Publishers, she met Neal Einson. They married the following year and eventually raised a daughter and a son. Audre and Martha had gone their separate ways but never lost touch.

Audre was not involved in the Kennedy campaign and had only

attended the gathering at Margie's insistence. Audre and Ed paid little attention to each other that afternoon; later, each complained privately to Margie of their disappointment after having finally met.

Margie Gumpert's afternoon party was one of many held that spring into summer. From late July to September, there were relatively small gatherings of fifteen to sixteen people at the Copelmans' Bronx apartment, at Neal and Martha's home in Springfield Gardens, Queens, back at Margie's. Most of those who attended were married couples. But in this group, marriage did not necessarily prove heterosexuality or monogamy; independently, both Audre and Ed were having an affair with Margie.[14]

At first, Ed only pursued friendship with Audre. Audre kept her distance, playing up an arrogant, self-centered persona which made getting to know her, except on social terms she controlled, difficult. She reinvented herself in this crowd as someone who didn't like parties, making it known she preferred one-to-one social situations.

In time, Audre became the focus of Ed's attention. Ed misread her unaccompanied presence in the group to mean she was unattached. But in a lesbian context, Audre saw herself as far from unattached, engaged as she was in a series of concomitant affairs. She maintained an intimate relationship with Blanche Wiesen; occasionally dated a frustrated dancer, Elaine Paul; and became involved with Yolanda Rios, a young Puerto Rican woman. For the moment, Ed was not the focus of her attention.

Audre and Yolanda met sometime between 1959 and 1960, at a party in Brooklyn given by one of Audre's cousins, Gerry Martin. Something of a playboy, Gerry had a number of girlfriends, of whom Yolanda was one. Audre thought he was trying to get rid of her, as he'd become more interested in his newest girlfriend. At the party, he asked Audre to take Yolanda off his hands. Partly as a favor to her cousin but more because of an immediate sexual attraction, Audre befriended Yolanda, who was eighteen years old then, and was at least seven years Audre's junior.[15]

Although Lorde was only sexually attracted to Yolanda initially,[16] in time she came to care for her sincerely. Lorde empathized with Yolanda's experiences as a girl who'd also grown up feeling unloved by her mother.

She convinced Yolanda to go to school to earn a general education diploma. In turn, Yolanda adored Lorde, looking up to her as mentor and role model. Lorde rewarded that adoration with friendship and understanding, even as some of Lorde's more "highbrow" friends were privately critical of her involvement with Yolanda.[17]

Relationships such as theirs—in which loving merged the physical, erotic, and mental planes, and was defined by Lorde's internal aesthetics rather than obvious physical beauty—were characteristic of Lorde; she often loved people who hadn't had a sense of being truly loved before they met her.[18]

By now, Lorde had finished at Columbia with a master's degree in library science and was working as a young adult librarian at the Mount Vernon Public Library. She also had a bright, sunny two-bedroom apartment at 5 Monroe Street, within a six-block walk of the library, and situated in a comfortable integrated neighborhood. The move from the East Village to Mount Vernon was a significant one, signaling an autonomy Lorde had not experienced previously.

She was financially self-sufficient for the first time since leaving her parents' home. She did not have to worry now whether she had enough money to buy food, shoes, or clothes. She was employed as a professional, with the chance to work with books, with young people, and to put into practice what she believed about the power of books and language. The library had few books by or about black people available to the young black teenagers who hung out in its reading rooms and were watched with great suspicion by the head librarian, Mrs. Larch, who thought they were not serious readers. But Lorde liked them, thought it important they were in the library taking out books and subversively provided them with stories about black adventurers she hid in her desk.

Bouts of depression still drove her to Dr. Rosenbloom's West End Avenue office, even as her sense of autonomy grew. Yet her education, professional status, and apartment in the integrated Mount Vernon neighborhood, were symbolic of her parents' dream to rise from poverty to self-sufficiency. Lorde had fulfilled their dream—and surpassed it.

Just as the sixties inspired a new generation of civil rights activists, the decade also gave rise to the "sexual revolution." For some, this revolution opened the doors between race and sex and desire. Audre Lorde was no stranger to pushing at these boundaries, and she became part of a smaller, "very intimate group of friends,"[19] which included the Einsons, Ed Rollins, Margie and Lou Gumpert.

Primarily in their later twenties and early thirties, they came from working-class backgrounds, were extremely intellectual, witty liberals, and considered themselves outcasts.[20] They shared a dream of the country's political possibilities and experimented with visions of a new social order—one beyond racial and sexual boundaries. They became an extended family. Within the group, the lines between heterosexuality, homosexuality, bisexuality, love, and friendship blurred. Irrespective of gender, sex between the friends was no secret. For her part, Audre had "a long and very very intense love, sexual relationship" with Martha; was having "a really long and intensive sexual relationship" with Margie; and had a "very intense, but not very long" sexual affair with Neal Einson.[21]

Lorde was the only black female in the group, the only avowed lesbian, a poet, and single. She exploited the control that being single and desired afforded, managing a flow of friends who were lovers to her Mount Vernon apartment. But she limited their access to it and to her, seeing them one at a time and only when she wanted to. After work sometimes, she'd consent to an intimate evening spent with Martha or Neal or Margie Gumpert; and then, sleep-deprived, would consume amphetamines or cups of coffee in order to be alert at work the next day.

As the only black professional working in the library then, Lorde's self-sufficiency was tested at two critical moments. The first involved an incident orchestrated by black women who worked for the Westchester County Library, with which the Mount Vernon Public Library shared a building. Most of the library clerks were black women who lived in either Yonkers or Mount Vernon, where the tendency then was to conservatism. Unlike them, Lorde "dressed strangely" and wore her hair in an afro. Lorde felt outside their "really rigid, tight sisterhood"[22] and kept to herself; she remained aloof and socially reserved.

The Mount Vernon staff, black and white, regularly took a tea break in a room in which there were also lockers. One day, at teatime, as Lorde opened her locker, a straightening comb and iron fell out of it. These objects were an obvious hint from the black female library clerks: do something with yourself and with that nappy hair. When the comb and iron fell out "in front of all these white people," Lorde felt deeply betrayed and even more isolated.[23]

The incident cut into a ragged, old wound. Love, hurt, anger, separation, and self-hate formed the emotional clay that characterized Lorde's relationships with other black women. She remained distrustful of them. Her intimate relationships with black women were much more casual than those she had with white women, who became longer-term lovers and friends. Except for Joan Alexander Sandler, whom she'd known for years, she didn't have close black women friends and was more of a voyeur of black lesbian life in the bars and at house parties given by them. Lorde moved in social circles in which she was often the only black female, insulated from criticism by other black women. Though she was deeply hurt by the incident, she responded stoically with the mark of self-sufficiency defined by that stiff upper-lipped attitude drilled into her by her mother.

As in many other places around the country, talk of air-raid trials and practice drills heightened in Mount Vernon. The Cold War era was an unstable one. The language of peaceful co-existence was ever endangered by saber-rattling and nuclear proliferation. Mount Vernon's municipal leaders led the town's drive to be ready in the event of a nuclear emergency. Its mayor decreed that all public institutions and civil servants were to participate in an upcoming civil defense drill, including the staff of the public library.

As a student at Columbia, Lorde had become a member of the local chapter of the National Committee for a Sane Nuclear Policy, often known simply as SANE. She did not believe in air-raid drills, and informed her supervisor she would not participate, though she agonized over the decision. Dr. Rosenbloom disagreed with her. He expressed the strong opinion that her decision was self-destructive, threatening the security of a good job. Her job was, he advised, more important than her principles.[24]

On the appointed day, Lorde abstained from participation in the civil defense drill. She was verbally reprimanded for doing so, but she did not lose her job. Rather than seeing her decision as self-destructive, Lorde saw it as self-confident. In her mind, abstaining from the drill was the first political act to give her a sense of self-determination.

Lorde was disturbed by Rosenbloom's advice. Expert or not, he was wrong; her principles did matter, to her if not to him. As well, Rosenbloom was charging for her sessions now, since she had a job and could afford to pay. But she was paying for bad advice, she thought. Soon after the air-raid-drill protest, she wrote him a letter terminating him as her therapist.

The price of autonomy was high, for sure; but the break with Rosenbloom had its financial rewards, too. Not having to pay for therapy sessions left her with more money to spend, and Lorde, calculating it could be spent on clothes and traveling, "felt this tremendous sense of freedom."[25] She took advantage of a month-long vacation from the library due her and went to California that May to visit with Elaine Paul. She'd met Elaine when they were both students at Hunter College. Elaine was deeply political, and, thereafter, she had a profound effect on Lorde's sense of politics.

Elaine Paul had grown up in San Francisco and then moved to New York to become a dancer, only to find the New York dance world hyperconscious of body size, discouraging to dancers who were too "heavy" or had the "wrong" body type. When her father died, she moved back to California at her mother's insistence but longed to return to New York. She'd written to Audre often begging her to come out and visit. Elaine's mother didn't want her to go back east, and certainly not alone. Elaine hoped her mother might have a change of heart if she and Audre went back to New York together.

Around the same time, the South was experiencing a wave of "Freedom Riders," mostly young black and white northerners organized by the Congress of Racial Equality (CORE), whose mission was to travel south together on buses and challenge the segregated rule of interstate travel. The much-publicized, bloody attack on Freedom Riders en route to Jackson, Mississippi, by a white mob in Montgomery, Alabama, was all over the news in 1961.[26] Audre was captivated by the idea of the Freedom Rides. As her visit neared, she and Elaine planned to come back across the country together, go to Jackson, Mississippi, and take part in them.

In San Francisco, Lorde got her first driver's license and she and Elaine took off in Elaine's mother's car. They drove south to Santa Rosa, and then on to Yosemite National Park, where they camped out. Their plan was to follow El Camino Royale down to Mexico, but the road had only recently opened and much of it was just dirt. Going as far as they could, they stopped off in Hermosillo, Mexico, for a week before driving back to San Francisco. They were near broke but still intent on the trip to Mississippi.

The thought of the two young women taking off now for Mississippi terrified Elaine's mother, who got down on her knees and begged them not to go. Racial violence in the South's hotbeds was not to be taken lightly. While Lorde empathized with the civil rights protests, she hadn't fully considered she might endanger her life. Mrs. Paul's appeal was a reality check, and the two young women were dissuaded from going to Mississippi. With only enough money for bus fare, they took a five-day Greyhound bus trip back to New York.

But the trip to California tweaked Lorde's sense of adventure. When she returned to Mount Vernon, to her apartment and job at the library, she had a deepened sense of stability. Survival itself, she knew now, had been a precarious adventure fraught with the possibility of not making it, with bouts of depression severe enough to question sanity. But she'd done more than survive. In opposing the Mount Vernon air-raid drill and Dr. Rosenbloom's advice, she'd acted on what she believed. It was, after all, 1961; and America was being transformed by individuals, communities, and organized movements of citizens openly acting on what they believed. Though she had not yet fully embraced the civil rights movement decisively, she was beginning to be convinced of a self-authorized power to engage the social problems of the world around her.

By summer's end, Lorde began to tire of having lovers she slept with and then sent home to someone else. As the seasons changed and fall approached, she felt lonely and wanted a primary lover of her own. During this time, Ed Rollins became more of a presence in her life. He began to call on her and visit.

At first, she hardly desired friendship with him, even as she found him sexually attractive and had heard from Margie Gumpert he was good in bed. Over time, though, she allowed the friendship between them to develop; she found him interesting, if at times peculiar, and became more emotionally involved with his life, political work, and ideas. She liked him: he was conversational, gentle, and affectionate.

Too, she recognized Ed was an iconoclast like herself, an outsider with whom she shared an affinity. But Ed was intent on getting married; and whenever he'd raise the subject in conversations with her, Audre made it clear she was not the marrying kind.

That November, Ed invited her to take a trip with him up to Scotia. He'd told Audre quite a bit about his mother and family, and she was curious about his people. Chiefly to satisfy that curiosity, she agreed to go. She'd always wanted children and, unbeknownst to Ed, she'd been thinking about having children with him. Audre met Ed's mother, father, sister, and brother-in-law during what turned out to be a fairly pleasant experience, despite the feeling of being on display. Ed's family thought she was nice but wanted assurance there was nothing serious between them. While not revealing his own feelings, Ed assured his family Audre was not interested in marriage.

The fall of 1961 waned into winter, as Audre focused on turning the friendship into a sexual affair. Ed wasn't interested in another affair. He wanted something more now, a commitment. Audre wanted nothing to do with commitment. Yet the longer Ed held out sexually, the more she wanted him.[27] As the Christmas season neared, Audre saw her opportunity.

The library was throwing a Christmas party and Ed wanted to go with her. Audre was reluctant to invite him along at first. In spite of her individualism, she'd promoted an image of herself at the library as righteously black and was unsure how she would be received in the company of a white man, especially one as uninhibited as Ed could be. In addition to his professional image as a lawyer, dressed in suits and his eyeglasses, Ed had a flamboyant, campy style he came to be known for. Considered very handsome, even beautiful, Ed danced the lines between "masculine" and "feminine" fashion. Like a character out of a play,[28] he wore flowing capes, spoke in a florid prose, and was dramatically Oscar Wilde-ish.[29] To Neal and Martha Einson, he was a strange, very peculiar fellow who hung around Margie Gumpert's friends but had no friends of his own, and was "ostentatiously gay"[30] in a circle where subtlety ruled. Shortly before the party, Audre seduced Ed, satisfied that the sex between them was fair exchange for his presence at the party. But Ed was appropriately social and understated as her guest. Afterward, relieved that nothing untoward had taken place, Audre felt a closeness with Ed that united them against the thinking of a more provincial world.

Now that they were intimate, Ed raised the subject of marriage again. While she found him likable, sexually compatible, and his ideas on children in sync with her own, Audre was interested in neither a husband nor marriage, just yet. At heart she was a lesbian; her relationships with Yolanda Rios and several other women continued.

From the start, Audre and Ed made known to each other their same-sex desires. As their courtship evolved, they also came to understand that neither was interested in a conventional marriage, though both believed in the conventions of marriage and that they could raise children in a new kind of family.[31] They were idealists, rebelling against mainstream norms; young professionals, even as Ed had failed the bar exam and prepared to take it again.

Much of their intimate time was spent at Lorde's apartment, fixing the relationship on Lorde's territory and encircling it with her insistence on one-to-one, private relationships. Lorde needed and cultivated a sense of control, covering her paranoia about privacy and compartmentalized emotions. She had a prudish self-image she protected and projected. She did not like to be talked about by other people, except in terms that she set. Shortly after their first dinner and formal date, Ed made the mistake of informing her of a casual discussion he'd had with Margie Gumpert about it. Even though she'd often discussed the intimate details of Margie's sexual affair with Ed, Audre roundly insisted that Ed was not to discuss with others what was private between them again.[32]

Spending as much time with Audre as she allowed, Ed commuted back and forth between Mount Vernon and Manhattan. Audre embraced Ed with measured reserve. He was a satisfying lover, with whom she got along well. He deferred to her, became dear to her,[33] but she questioned his motives. Was he trying to score points, using her to prove how liberal he was? Cultivating friendships with "Negroes" was a popular form of white liberalism; many white liberals were famous for announcing at cocktail parties that some of their best friends were "Negroes."[34] But Audre was not Ed's first black lover.[35]

In a letter to her dated November 10, 1961, Ed questioned his own motives, admitting to confusion and confessing to a penchant for thinking in ways that mixed up his thoughts and motives. He listed his motives in nine points intermingled with the reasons for his attraction: she was a soft-spoken black woman with nimble hands, whose face he liked, and whose presence added something to the group he was now a part of. Ed questioned if what he felt was more than lonely. Wondering whether he'd been self-serving, he asked himself if she was his private answer to the race problem.[36] Ed struggled with what his initial motives may have been, and with the intense vulnerability accompanying this openness; he ended his letter with a declaration of his feelings that was both hopeful and genuine.

Christmas 1961, Ed went up to Scotia to spend the holidays with his family. While there, he informed his parents he'd been seeing a black woman he now wanted to marry, not mentioning that it was Audre. His parents welcomed the news he was at last interested in marriage; but his mother, particularly, found objectionable the idea of marriage to a black woman, causing Ed to cut short his visit and return to New York City even more determined. He immediately went to see Audre.

That Christmas night, Ed proposed to her. Audre skirted an immediate response, saying they would talk about his marriage proposal in the morning. The next day, she grilled him on his sincerity, his intentions, testing his answers for signs of how deeply he'd thought; testing his resolve even further at one point by suggesting Ed didn't know what he was getting into.[37] Although they loved each other and she felt she could handle Ed, she was not in love with him. Lorde needed time to think through the contours of such a marriage. What would it mean to marry a white man in the heat of the civil rights movement and the black revolution? What would it mean about her own blackness? What would it really mean to have interracial children? Her own biological clock was ticking, and though she wanted children now, she wasn't sure she was strong enough or stable enough to have them on her own. Ed did not want children outside marriage. He was deeply concerned others might think he did not want to marry her because of her race; he worried that any children they begot outside a marriage might suffer.[38]

She ruminated over Ed's proposal, testing the idea with her closest friends. Neither Margie Gumpert nor Martha Einson thought marrying Ed would be a good idea. Audre was particularly disappointed with

Margie's response, because Margie knew Ed intimately. Marion Masone took a trip from Stamford to Lorde's Mount Vernon apartment just to beg Audre not to marry Ed; she offered to resume their own affair as an alternative. But from Audre's perspective, any consideration of marriage was not antithetical to loving women. And there were other disappointing responses initially; her mother was not convinced a white man would ever want anything more than sex from a black woman.[39]

The opposition upset Lorde, and pushed her and Ed closer together. As they discussed the reactions of friends, it became clear that the racial and sexual agendas of those around them were self-serving at best. Though they were of dichotomous worlds as black and white, and subaltern cultures as lesbian and gay, America was in the throes of social transformation; they had at their fingertips the possibility of creating a new kind of marriage. A week after Ed proposed, Audre agreed to marry him, with the stipulations that they loved each other but were not in love, and that they could make the marriage work despite what others thought.[40] Days later, Ed bought Audre an engagement ring he insisted she wear.

Toward the middle of January 1962, Audre took Ed to her sister Phyllis's house. It was Ed's first meeting with her mother. Mrs. Lorde politely interrogated Ed until she was satisfied as to his intentions. Ed took pains to let her know they were honorable. Audre and Phyllis were in the kitchen eavesdropping and were amused at how well the two understood each other and got along.

Audre married Ed on March 31, 1962, at St. Mary's Church on 126th Street between Amsterdam Avenue and (Old) Broadway; a week later, Ed took the bar exam once again. Outfitted in a yellow and white Chinese *chiong som*, a sheathlike sliver of a dress, Audre looked shapely and elegant, her body now evidencing the thinning side effects of continued amphetamine use. Her mother and sisters attended. Phyllis was maid-of-honor; Ed's friend and roommate, John Gloster, was best man; and the officiating minister was a friend of Ed's.

No one from Ed's family came to the ceremony. Mrs. Rollins was distraught her son was actually marrying a black woman. Before the wedding, Mr. Rollins had written to Ed, warning that this marriage would kill his mother.[41] Though less concerned about race than his wife was, Ed's father had issues of his own: Ed was too flighty, not ready for marriage, hadn't been able to hold down a decent job for more than a year, and what if they had children? He doubted that the marriage would last or whether Ed could support a family; he himself was too old now to support any children if Ed could not.[42]

There was a sizable crowd in attendance, but the wedding was a disappointment to some of Lorde's lesbian friends, including Marion Masone, who refused to attend. At the Eleanor Roosevelt House at Hunter and the reception afterwards, Ed "thought it was hysterical and Audre thought it was kind of funny too"[43] that several of her women friends were sitting in a corner together, the sour on their faces apparent. Martha Einson asked Audre if she'd invited all the women she'd ever slept with to the wedding. To which Audre replied, "it looks like it."[44]

The honeymoon was hardly lavish, but a romantic "get acquainted week"[45] spent with the phone off the hook at Lorde's apartment and trips in a rented car to beaches around the city. An odd pairing by any account—a black woman who was lesbian and a white man who was gay—they'd married within less than a year of meeting each other and had reinvented themselves into a young interracial couple.

Shortly after the wedding, Ed moved out of his apartment and into Audre's; which, aside from its convenient proximity to Audre's job, established her home as their first. Audre kept her position at the library, and two months after they were married, Ed passed the bar exam. He invited his parents to join him, Audre, and Mrs. Lorde at a formal induction ceremony to be held at the Appellate Division Courthouse, in Manhattan, that June. Mr. and Mrs. Rollins came down to New York to attend, meeting Audre's mother for the first time. Though Mr. Rollins would become more accepting of Audre in time, Mrs. Rollins remained stoically opposed to the marriage.

At the start, domestic life together was pleasant, though there were disagreements, differences in personalities, and the newness of marriage. Audre and Ed socialized with other couples and regularly visited with Phyllis and her family at their home in the Bronx. Eventually, most of Audre's women friends got used to the idea that she and Ed were married.

While life now included marriage to Ed, there was still her poetry.

Lorde began to write more. Much of what she had written up to this point was unpublished. The year she got married, however, two of her poems, "Father Son and Holy Ghost" and "Coal," appeared in the anthology *Beyond the Blues*, published by a small press in England.[46] "Father Son and Holy Ghost" aired Lorde's repressed feelings about her father's death, nine years afterwards. The title entangled religious patriarchy with textual memories of his ghostlike silence and physical dominance:

> I have not seen my fathers grave.
>
> Not that his judgment eyes have been forgotten
> Nor his great hands print
> On our evening doorknobs . . .[47]

Years later, when the poem was republished in *Coal*, she made changes to its line structure, the placement of commas, and changed the line "Misty from the worlds [sic] business" to "drabbled with the world's business,"[48] a revision that replaced the image of her father as vague with a more accepting one of him as a man dragged down by life. The later spacing between the first line and first stanza was a particularly notable revision, which recast the "silence" between that line and the subsequent stanza as visually loud.

At its most obvious, the union between Audre and Ed was a social experiment. Beneath the skin, the marriage broiled with slow-cooking problems that seeped out and surfaced. Audre knew as little about living with a man as Ed knew about living with a woman. She was dominant and authoritative. He was submissive enough, but he had an orthodox sense of his role as provider, "an image of what he thought the perfect husband was and he tried to be it." He doted on her—anything Audre wanted she could have. But Audre demanded that Ed be emotionally responsive.[49] She was prone to fits of heightened irritability (another side effect of amphetamine use) and explosive anger, becoming verbally abusive and violent over seemingly petty things.

Once, at a Thanksgiving dinner at their apartment, Martha and Neal Einson watched in disbelief as "she crawled all over him"[50] for eating the tail of the turkey, her favorite part. At other times, she'd throw a plate, shoe, or pot at him for aggravating her, or physically beat on him when she felt he wasn't responding emotionally. Ed was rarely in contact with his family; except for John Gloster and Margie Gumpert, he had no former friends of his own that he and Audre associated with. He was prone to secrecy—particularly when it came to financial matters and his homosexual liaisons. Whereas Audre brought lovers home who were known to Ed, Ed did not, acting out, over time, a closeted homosexuality with strangers that infuriated Audre.

By July 1962, Audre was pregnant with her first child. As an expectant mother, she stopped taking amphetamines, ate a balanced diet, gained weight, and blossomed into pregnancy. Even before the child was born, and without benefit of sonography back then, she'd argued fiercely with Ed that the baby was a girl. Being pregnant engaged Audre in a romance with her body's production symbolic of an eternal state of fertility, as she embraced its corporeal and poetic states.

NOW THAT I AM FOREVER WITH CHILD

. . .

The swelling changed planes of my body—
And how you first fluttered, then jumped
And I thought it was my heart.[51]

In August, Lorde's fertility as poet was amplified. Eight of her poems,[52] dating between 1952 and 1962, appeared in volume 2 of the Heritage anthology, Sixes and Sevens, edited by Paul Breman and published by his London-based small press. Having spent his college years in Europe living under the cultural isolation imposed by German occupation forces during the war, Breman's later discovery of the blues inspired his search for the poetry of black Americans and devotion to its publication as he sought to illuminate the particular relationship between creativity, race, and social condition.[53] In response to Breman's query, each contributor to the anthology was asked to introduce their work with a comment addressing that relationship. Lorde wrote:

I am a Negro woman and a poet—all three stand outside the realm of choice. . . . All who I love are of my people. It is not sim-

ple. . . . But what is in my blood . . . comes the roundabout journey from Africa. . . . This is the knowledge and richness I shall
give my children proudly. . . .[54]

In October 1962, American reconnaissance planes discovered Soviet
missile bases in Cuba. As President Kennedy ordered a blockade of
Cuba, demanding the removal of missiles, Lorde fretted that the Cuban
missile crisis and the possibility of an ensuing nuclear war threatened an
already fragile world, not to mention the security of her unborn child.
Five months pregnant by December, she quit her job at the Mount Vernon Public Library.

At the time, Lorde's ideas about having and raising children were
unconventional. She insisted Ed accompany her to birthing classes; that
he be allowed in the delivery room when the moment came; that their
baby would stay with her rather than in a nursery with other newborn
infants. She wanted to breast-feed and joined La Leche League, which
provided educational assistance to women interested in breastfeeding.

Lorde reestablished contact with Marion Masone, whom she missed
dearly, asking Marion to be the baby's godmother. Masone agreed. On
March 16, 1963, Audre gave birth to a daughter, Elizabeth ("Beth") Marion Lorde-Rollins, at New York Hospital in Manhattan.

Word of the impending March on Washington dominated the news.
Both Audre and Ed wanted to go. Audre prepared for their attendance at
the march in August by weaning Beth. Leaving their daughter in the care
of her sister Phyllis, Audre and Ed drove from New York to Baltimore,
with Elaine Paul and Yolanda Rios accompanying them. They stayed
overnight there in Blanche Wiesen's apartment.

Blanche, now living in Baltimore, was enrolled as a graduate student
in history at Johns Hopkins University, where she was working on a master's degree and ultimately earned a PhD. She remained politically
active, protesting against the war in Vietnam and on behalf of the civil
rights struggle. In the years to come, she would be briefly married to
Sam Cook, a librarian. While married, she met Clare Coss at a Vietnam
protest meeting of the Women's International League of Peace and Freedom.[55] Clare was also married at the time. A playwright and psychotherapist, she was a New Yorker by way of New Jersey and New Orleans; and

was, up until then, a little sheltered. Falling in love with Blanche Cook and later meeting Audre and Ed was her introduction to gay life.[56] Blanche and Clare eventually divorced their respective husbands, and as a lesbian couple would become two of Lorde's closest, lifelong friends. The morning of the historic march, Blanche joined the group for the drive into Washington, D.C.

The August 28 March on Washington was Lorde's first decisive embrace of the civil rights movement. She was in awe of the more than 250,000 people who attended: the massive, integrated people's protest overwhelmed her. The possibility that racism in America could be ended in her lifetime seemed a real enough dream that day. She was never to forget the shimmering pool between the Lincoln Memorial and Washington Monument where heat-exhausted marchers cooled their feet, or working in a tent alongside Lena Horne as they helped make coffee. As morning turned to afternoon, there was speech after speech from the speaker's podium, but Audre and her party left before witnessing first-hand Martin Luther King, Jr.'s, now immortalized seven-minute speech; they listened to it on the radio in the car on the drive back to Baltimore before heading home.

Lorde's life was now defined by a "poetic excitement,"[57] in which motherhood, marriage, and the political climate were utmost concerns. Preoccupied with child care and married life, she wrote few poems, substituting reading poetry for writing it. Or she'd stockpile scraps of paper in her pocketbook, the baby's bag, wherever, on which she'd jot down images and phrases to make of poems later. Other times, she'd pull out and read old poems she'd written, reworking them.

Yet the idea that she had settled down was hardly true. While happy being a mother, new motherhood proved stressful. A bright baby, Beth was colicky initially, woke her up at night, cried all day, and had to be breast-fed on schedule. Stressful too was Lorde's conversion from prima donna in a social world in which her needs and desires were primary to the demanding realities of motherhood, which made those secondary. Lorde's identities as lesbian and mother were not synonymous, creating a dialectic in which those identities were both unified and in conflict.[58] At times, needing to feel the freedom she'd formerly exercised, Audre expelled milk for Beth and left her in Ed's care; she took off for hours then, and once for a couple of days on a fishing trip with some lesbian friends. She justified these spontaneous absences to Ed by doggedly pointing out he was a parent, too. She felt like she had two children instead of one, resenting the additional burden of Ed's expectations and dependency on her.

Audre was becoming disappointed with Ed. To her, he had a great sense of history but seemed removed from their own roles as interracial parents within the defining context of the sixties. The racial import of the moment to black people was something he wasn't living and breathing every day—or so she felt. The notion that she was "forever with child" wove through the few poems she found time to write. In some, her poet's gaze was personal; in others, political. The bombing of the Sixteenth Street Baptist Church in Birmingham, Alabama, on September 15, 1963, killed four little black girls, whose lives were brutally stilled at the hands of white segregationists. Birmingham was a symbol of hard-core segregation and a focal point of the civil rights struggle. If Ed, father of a little black girl himself, could not put himself in their black parents' shoes, Lorde certainly could, penning a poem to memorialize them.

> SUFFER THE CHILDREN
> Birmingham, 1963
>
> . . .
>
> But who shall dis-inter these girls
> To love the women they were to become
> Or read the legends written beneath their skin?
>
> Those who loved them remember their child's laughter.[59]

Credited to "Audre G. Lorde," the poem appeared in the January 1964 issue of *Negro Digest*. It was framed above by snapshots of the faces of the four little girls: Denise McNair, Addie Mae Collins, Carole Robertson, and Cynthia Wesley. Below, a slice of a photograph depicted the church's bombed-out windows.

In September 1963, Ed was fired from a job with a conservative firm and began doing freelance title work. He was still involved with his political work, and, as a ward leader to whom others turned because of his astute leadership, was considering going into New York City politics himself. To Ed's credit, but unrealistically, he didn't figure his black wife or his homosexuality as obstacles to that path. At the same time, he seemed withdrawn and depressed to Audre. When John F. Kennedy was assassinated in Dallas that November, Ed became even more depressed, since he had idolized Kennedy and saw his presidency as a hopeful symbol for Democrats across the country. By December, Ed was still without a salaried job.

As Beth's first Christmas rolled around, Audre was determined to make it festive, despite Ed's depression. She cooked and invited friends over. The next day, she and Ed and the baby went to visit Mrs. Lorde, who'd returned from a trip to Grenada with her sisters. When they got back home, their apartment had been ravaged by fire. Ed had a habit of leaving cigarettes burning, and though they'd both smoked and promised not to do so in the baby's room, he'd left a lit end dangling off the edge of the dresser. It fell into an open drawer, smoldering there for hours until the fire caught, consuming the apartment in smoke. The place was no longer fit to live in. Audre and Ed salvaged what they could of their books, furniture, and Audre's smoke-damaged clothes. They moved in with Phyllis and Henry and their kids. By January 1964, Audre was pregnant with her second child.

It soon became evident that living with her sister's family was a bad idea. A relatively conservative couple, Phyllis and Henry objected to Audre and Ed's shows of affection (even though it was only handholding) in front of their children, something they did not believe in and did not do themselves. They offered to rent a hotel room as an alternative. Shortly thereafter, Audre, Ed, and Beth moved into a studio with kitchenette in a hotel on 73rd Street and Broadway; they looked for a more permanent place to live, toughing out the winter in a state of flux.

Ed freelanced as much work as he could hustle up, driven to recoup the financial standing he'd had at the beginning of their marriage. When he wasn't involved in politics, he worked day and night, and was often not at home. With another baby on the way, and their financial situation rocky, Audre turned to Phyllis and her mother for emotional support.

In time, they moved to a tiny, three-room apartment on Broadway and 149th Street, only blocks from where Lorde's family had once been the first black family to move into a building on 152nd Street.

LANGSTON HUGHES was the first poet to extend himself to Lorde professionally. Between 1949 and 1950, he was briefly associated with the Harlem Writers Guild, then housed in the Harlem branch of the YMCA. He'd met Lorde and remained interested in her work. The most prolific writer to emerge from the Harlem Renaissance, Hughes's name was synonymous with the voice of black writing in America and abroad for more than four decades; and he'd become the preeminent black literary figure, aging, during the sixties, into his reputation as the "Dean of Negro Writers."[60] Hughes's record with respect to black writers, and black women writers such as Gwendolyn Brooks and Lorraine Hansberry, was generous. He deliberately sought out Audre Lorde.

Hughes was editing a poetry anthology. He wrote to Lorde, inquiring if she'd like to submit some poems for consideration.[61] In a letter to Joan Sandler,[62] Audre recounted a bodacious tête-à-tête with Hughes in which she challenged what had, in her mind, generally passed as "Negro poetry," with its themes of victimization and lynching, arguing that was not the kind of poetry she wrote, and implicitly challenging Hughes's work as well. Though she'd rashly prejudged the anthology, she submitted some poems anyway.

When Ruth Baharas returned to New York from Poland, she went to visit Audre. Though she was not surprised Audre was pregnant, she was surprised to find her married, even though she thought Ed a bright man. Ruth was also surprised by Audre's general deportment, the decisiveness of it in sharp contrast to the younger, indecisive Audre she'd known. Audre assured Ruth she was still a lesbian, an assurance Ruth felt was unnecessary since she understood, without need for language, that Audre's feelings for women were "something very deep in her."[63]

The year 1964 culminated in the birth of Audre and Ed's son, Jonathan Frederick Ashley Rollins,[64] on August 31; and in the publication of two of Lorde's poems in the anthology *New Negro Poets, USA*, which Hughes edited.

Gwendolyn Brooks's foreword defined the period as one in which

"Negro poets" had to write and remember they were Negroes at the same time; unable, unlike white writers, to embrace the genre without infusing metaphors, sonnets, and stanzas with a racial reality. Even those poets whose work seemed to renounce a deliberate racial stance, Brooks noted, spoke in a racial voice, testifying to an inescapable consciousness.[65] The anthology was divided into five sections. Brooks's comments brought into the fold of "Negro poetry" poems that were a range of lyrical, protest, personal, descriptive, and reflective statements.

Lorde's poem, "And Fall Shall Sit in Judgment,"[66] appeared in the first section of lyrical poems. An ode to fleeting and misnamed love, resonant with earlier influences of the Romantic poets she admired, its sixteen lines boasted a melodic rhyme scheme each second and fourth line of a stanza. Her other poem, "Pirouette," appeared in the last section of reflective poems.

> . . .
>
> Your hands reading over my lips for
> Some road through uncertain night
> For your feet to examine home . . .[67]

Written in 1957, during the period of Lorde's first claims to lesbian identity, the poem's understated message was typical of lesbian work of the period.[68] The version published in Hughes's anthology differed significantly from a later version in which the last line, "I cannot return," was revised in subsequent publications to read, "I am come home."[69] Lorde altered the final line to reflect the politicized lesbian community of which she had become a definitive and outspoken member.

On a day early in June 1965, Audre was driving in Manhattan and stopped at a street corner, waiting for a red light to change. Someone who'd stolen an army truck rammed into the black Rambler she and Ed now owned, dramatically demolishing the rear end and involving Audre in a terrible accident. Jonathan, ten months old, was in the car with her and suffered minor injuries. Audre suffered whiplash injury to her neck and back, which severely hampered her ability to pick anything up—especially the children, who had to be lifted onto her lap by Ed for months afterwards. Unable to write also, her spirits sank.

SIX

NEW HOUSING complex of high-rise buildings opened on Harlem's Upper West Side; some of its spacious apartments overlooked the Hudson River and the New Jersey shoreline. In the wave of original tenants, Audre, Ed, and the two children moved into 626 Riverside Drive, Apartment 20B, in 1966. Their three-bedroom apartment had a view of the Palisades. Beth and Jonathan were still young enough to share a bedroom and their parents shared another, leaving the third for Ed's use as an office. Ed quickly became involved with the building's affairs, going to community meetings and sitting on its board of directors. The new apartment lifted Lorde's spirits, but she had a nagging feeling of wanting more sustained engagement with her work.

Shortly after Audre and Ed had married, Yolanda Rios married Bill Butts. Eventually, they moved into an apartment on the thirteenth floor of 626 Riverside Drive. When Yolanda gave birth to a daughter, Stephanie, three years younger than Beth, she and Audre shared a bond as new mothers, raising and baby-sitting each other's children.

As Beth and Jonathan grew, Lorde's approach to raising them was progressive. She made her own whole-grain bread, and way before any-one else was discussing it, she questioned the causal effects of sugar and dyes on hyperactivity in children. Lorde was aware of all manner of health and science issues, answering the children's questions about sex and the body in an age-appropriate manner. As kids, Beth and Jonathan were dressed in the same kind of clothes, and encouraged to be physi-cally affectionate with each other. They were never talked down to or left out of conversations about the civil rights movement or the war in Viet-nam. Although they were not allowed to watch television indiscrimi-nately, they could watch the evening news. Walter Cronkite's televised face became integral to their young lives. When they could read, she read *The New York Times* with them. Her children were taught to see themselves as part of a larger extended family whose members, unlike the outside world, were united by racial and sexual differences rather than terrified of them.

From early on, Lorde insisted the children understand the global consequences of living in a society of plenty. One Thanksgiving, she bullheadedly announced they were all going to fast the whole day, as a way of remembering the world's starving children. When Beth went to the refrigerator, filled a bag with food, and suggested her mother send some to the starving children so they could have their own dinner, Audre laughed, but did not waver; she instructed the children that everyone had to learn to live with less, so everyone could have more,[1] even though when Christmas rolled around each year, she and Ed indulged the chil-dren, spending money on gifts and decorations.

Even so, Audre was not totally divorced from her own upbringing. Like her mother, she was formidable and intense, her authority unques-tionable. Though she differed from Mrs. Lorde in that she was more openly affectionate, she was also a strict disciplinarian. Her anger seem-ingly came from out of nowhere sometimes, the force of it chaotic and illogical to the children, but Audre rarely, if ever, struck them; the act of spanking was left to Ed.[2] The memory of her own mother as a parent who was physically abusive, who—as she wrote—"used me for her own dissatisfactions,"[3] loomed in Audre's consciousness. And Audre under-stood herself as a woman harboring tremendous anger. She was so frightened of her own capacities, she vented rage on inanimate objects.

Rather than hit Beth for doing something wrong once, she emptied a drawerful of Beth's clothes onto the floor in an enraged fit, and then demanded Beth clean up the chaotic mess.[4]

Lorde warned her children not to act out in front of white people, especially in public. And she adopted with them the same bloodcurdling look to keep them in line that her mother had used on her. Although they were allowed out to play, Lorde espoused a fear of the outside world borne of her mother's, but was more sophisticated. She cautioned Beth and Jonathan against running in the street, lest they be shot by a policeman assuming their involvement in something bad. As she'd learned from her parents, personal matters between her and Ed were never discussed in front of their children. While she listened to the music of singers like Joan Baez and Edith Piaf, the children were not exposed to black popular music at home and learned nothing about popular black dances from her. Lorde's attitude echoed her parents' practice of disallowing certain cultural practices associated with "common" black life in their home.

Ed's career as a lawyer was floundering, and by now he was hiding from Audre the truth of their financial situation; the pressures on him as sole provider overburdened his sense of responsibility. When Lorde found out Ed was having money problems, she was infuriated he couldn't admit to not being able to pay the bills and that he'd placed in jeopardy the well-being of their children. Ed's situation may have brought a definitive halt to the conventional role-playing—making him the breadwinner and her the homemaker—that had seeped into their marriage. This also ended an uncharacteristic period of financial dependence for Lorde. Audre took a job in the library of the St. Clair School of Nursing on 66th Street, working the 4:00 P.M. to midnight shift.

In retrospect, Lorde thought Ed was better than most men. But the kind of man he was played into her sense of survival and need to control. She admitted as much to herself in a later journal: "I have learned that control seemed a key to survival . . . that I married Ed to control him."[5] Lorde's perception of Ed's malleability made it possible for her to recover a sense of dominance and authority as she reinvented their marriage. She gave him no choice but to be primary caretaker of the children, to feed, bathe, and put them to bed when she went to work; this action permitted her to "call the shots" again, and much more aggressively. To Ed's way of thinking, and what he'd seen of his parents' marriage, men didn't need to communicate with their wives: women talked; men didn't. Audre's intensified insistence that Ed communicate his innermost feelings was contradictory to his more traditional notions of masculinity, causing him to resist the feminization of his intimate self. Growing angrier, Audre's response to Ed's increasing silence was to berate and even physically attack him.

According to Lorde, Ed became more secretive than ever about his outside sexual life. That their own sexual life was sporadic and he was sexually engaged with men was not the issue to Lorde. The issue was dishonesty and denial. Ed would be gone for hours on one pretext or another, and she instinctively felt he was out picking up men. When he came back, she'd ask him what he'd been doing. Ed would refuse to talk, avoiding her interrogations as to why he didn't bring his lovers home, as she did, and be up front about whom he was with. Ed defended his actions by insisting it was different for him. Audre, who admittedly knew little about male sexuality, let alone male homosexuality, judged him by her standards, finding it unfathomable he would be sexual with people whose faces were those of strangers rather than friends. At times, Ed would confess to disliking the part of himself that was homosexual. Pressing him to be more honest and self-accepting, and reasoning that it was bad "for the children to have a father who didn't accept all the people he was," Audre suggested Ed go into therapy.[6]

Lorde was now "running the world"[7]: ruling over the children, Ed, their household, and working to keep them financially afloat. Intermittently, she was also assisting Mrs. Lorde. She went to her father's old office to help out as her mother, getting along in years, attempted to maintain a semblance of the real estate business Mr. Lorde had bequeathed her. Audre juggled a hectic schedule, sleeping only three or four hours a night. She returned to relying on amphetamines to stay alert. Her reliance on speed again resulted in an incremental weight loss because of the drug's ability to suppress the appetite. This dependence on stimulants was periodic and did not develop into lifelong drug abuse.

She also was "running" relationships with several women. Of these, the relationship with Yolanda Rios came to have the most needy aspect to it. As their lives intertwined with children, husbands, intimacy, Yolanda demonstrated an intense love for Audre.[8] Ed liked Yolanda for the most part, perceiving her as a good-hearted person. But he also thought she wasn't her own best friend and was a user of others,[9] in unhealthy ways. Audre was more tolerant of Yolanda's emotional dependency, but she tired, in time, of the confusion Yolanda's needs caused her.[10]

The "world" that Lorde saw herself in charge of was turned on its head early in 1967, when a Reverend Sofeld contacted her asking for an interview. Sofeld was taking a course on black writers and was assigned a paper on a writer of his choice. He'd chosen Audre Lorde as his focus, following the path of her work from the anthologies edited by Pool, Breman, and Hughes. Lorde's ego was stroked by his interest, and she agreed to the interview. Sofeld came to her home and took her out to lunch. He was suave, friendly, and pleasant, and Lorde made available all of her old poems for his review.

By spring, the paper was finished and Sofeld gone. He mailed her a copy of his work in April. When Lorde read his seven-page analysis of her work, she was devastated. What had become—Sofeld asked—of the early promise of this bright, talented poet? Look at her now, married, with children, and no new poems in the last two years. What a shame. His words felled Lorde and, reading them, she broke down in tears. Was she really a has-been at only thirty-three years old? Was her promise as a poet gone? Sofeld's paper inflamed Lorde, redefining her intensity as a writer.

Unlike Ed, who was using the third bedroom as an office, she had no designated workplace of her own in the apartment. So she moved a desk given to her by her high school friend, Diane di Prima, into their bedroom, announcing that this space was now her poetry corner. She also demanded Ed take care of the children three hours every Sunday afternoon—her poetry time. The desk, the corner, and the hours alone allowed Lorde to structure herself as poet for the first time since she'd married.

Revising drafts of poems primarily, she threw herself into intense activity, her efforts disappointingly rewarded by rejection slips from white editors of mainstream publications who found her unsolicited poems of no interest. But the decision-making power of white editors and publications over the aspirations of black poets was being challenged by an emerging black cultural movement from which Audre Lorde was to benefit.

An outgrowth of the civil rights and Black Power movements, the Black Arts movement was in full swing by the late 1960s. Discarding any persona as "Negroes" begging for integration, black artists situated themselves as the cultural arm of the social and political changes surfacing in black communities nationwide. Because of this new cultural movement, a plethora of writers became household names in black communities; they included, amongst others, LeRoi Jones (Amiri Baraka), Sonia Sanchez, Nikki Giovanni, Don L. Lee (Haki Madhubuti), Ed Bullins, Larry Neal, and Gwendolyn Brooks. Ideologically, the Black Arts movement paralleled the Black Power movement's nationalist concerns for black self-determination. As an aesthetic and spiritual sister of the political movement, it promoted a radical reordering of Western cultural aesthetics, the traditional role of the artist, and the social function of art. The main thrust of artists aligned with it was to speak to the spiritual and cultural needs of black people vis-à-vis their racial oppression. The Black Arts movement condemned "protest literature" for its implicit appeal to white morality, as black writers turned their gaze away from a fickle, paternalistic white readership and toward the black community. Credited as the first to articulate the contemporary notion of black arts, the poet and dramatist LeRoi Jones (Baraka) was its leading practitioner and spokesman.[11]

As its thrust was self-determination, the Black Arts movement gave rise to a number of magazines, publications, and alternative presses. Following Hoyt Fuller's model at the more established *Negro Digest, The Journal of Black Poetry, Soul Book, Black Dialogue, Liberator,* and *Black Expression* were some of the better-known independent publishing outlets for black poets. Alternative presses such as Broadside Press (Chicago), Jihad Press (Newark, New Jersey), Third World Press (Chicago), Black Dialogue Press (New York and California), and Drum and Spear Press (Washington, D.C.)[12] aimed to support black literature and define a new black literary aesthetic shaped by militancy, black nationalism, and liberation politics. They called for a new literary aesthetic of blackness, in opposition to white cultural aesthetics.[13] Several perspectives coalesced around those culturalisms intrinsic to black Americans: language forms, style, "soul food," community values, music, and viewpoints as an oppressed people.

The leading voices of the Black Arts movement were black male writers and those black women—like Sonia Sanchez and Nikki Giovanni—whose early writings reflected an "acceptable" kinship with black men and suppressed gendered perspectives inconsistent with a monolithic, "authentic" blackness. In contrast, Lorde's more lyric, understated poetry was out of sync with these raced designs. Her later poetry, however, would more explicitly reflect a politicized, self-inflected black consciousness.

Much older than these writers and more renowned, Gwendolyn Brooks's literary career had long been distinguished by mainstream literary prizes and publications. Harper published her first book, *A Street in Bronzeville*, in 1945. In 1946, she was the recipient of two prestigious awards for poetry, a Guggenheim fellowship, and a grant from the American Academy of Arts and Letters. Four years later, she won the Pulitzer Prize for poetry. Between 1945 and 1963, Harper published five of Brooks's works. The voice of Brooks's early work was that of a poet whose lyric, imaginative turns of language transcended race.[14]

In what is now a well-known turning point in her career, Brooks attended the Second Black Writers' Conference at Fisk University in Nashville, Tennessee, in 1967. There, she was electrified by a contagious energy emanating from a new generation of black writers, including LeRoi Jones and the poet Ron Milner, whom she heard read at the conference. Brooks credited the younger writers and the conference atmosphere as the moment she entered into a new consciousness.[15]

A mother figure to younger, radical black poets and writers of the later sixties, many of whom participated in a writers' workshop she held at her home in Chicago, Brooks's engagement with them was the source of her conversion to a more militant voice, unseen in her work of the 1950s. Harper published *In the Mecca* in 1968, but Brooks now shifted away from publishing only with a mainstream house. Between 1966 and

1975, she published eight books with Broadside Press, founded by Dudley Randall in 1965. Brooks's shift to Broadside legitimated Randall's efforts and positioned her to affect the careers of scores of others, including Audre Lorde, ultimately.

FALL 1967 FOUND Audre overtaken by a debilitating case of the Asian flu that made juggling a chaotic schedule more difficult. Both Beth and Jonathan, now four and three years old, respectively, were enrolled in nursery school at the New Lincoln School—a private, progressive institution where the students were mostly white. The New Lincoln School was then located on 85th Street, between Fifth and Madison Avenues. At the nursery, Beth and Jonathan were among a handful of black children. Audre cultivated in both a sense of themselves as black rather than interracial; as they got older and could read the black-oriented comic books she procured for them, she took care to instill a knowledge of black history and privileged blackness as their essential identity. In contrast, Ed brought home white-oriented fairy-tale books and did not discuss the European traditions informing them.[16] Although Lorde departed from the child-rearing practices of her own parents, who had avoided family discussions of racism, she duplicated for her children the private school experience her parents had provided for her, as well as their belief in the value of a private education as intrinsic to the children's status as different.

Lorde was now working three days a week as head librarian at the Town School, a private school on East 76th Street attended by children from upper-class white families. Managing the children's schedules and her own gave her little time to attend to her flu symptoms. She was thankful when Elizabeth Maybank, a neighbor of theirs who lived in the same building, returned home. A black woman originally from the South, Mrs. Maybank had gone back for the summer after her husband died. She'd acted as a baby-sitter on past occasions. Audre welcomed her return as Mrs. Maybank nursed her through the flu and helped out around the house. A telephone call from Diane di Prima brought Audre back from a certain feeling that the flu—and life in general—was killing her. That call changed her life.

At the time, Diane headed The Poets Press, an independent press devoted to publishing poetry. She had founded it in 1964 and, assisted by grants from the National Endowment for the Arts, was publishing her own work as well as that of other poets. It was time, she urged, for Audre to get a book out.[17]

Born in New York City the same year as Lorde, Diane grew up under the influence of her grandfather's anarchistic philosophy. Like Audre's, Diane's life was shaped by an early knowledge of herself as poet. After Hunter High School, she attended Swarthmore College from 1951 to 1953. College life was too conventional for Diane and she left Swarthmore to explore the bohemian scene in Greenwich Village; there she became part of the jazz-centered, coffeehouse culture of the "Beat Generation." Her immersion into bohemian life was the backdrop of her friendships with Allen Ginsberg and Jack Kerouac, and her association with a number of other Beat poets, including William Burroughs, Frank O'Hara, and Michael McClure.[18]

Di Prima's early poems fixated on love and were often sexually explicit. Influenced by the jazz she heard in coffeehouses and clubs, her work rejected traditional formal restraints as she sought to marry avant-garde approaches to design, meter, and rhyme.[19] In 1958, her first collection, *This Kind of Bird Flies Backward*, was published by Totem Press in New York; the press specialized in literary broadsides and was started by LeRoi Jones,[20] with whom she had a relationship. The book established her reputation, a small press audience, and her sense of countercultural engagement. By 1966, she had had four more books published by various presses.

Sick, but encouraged, Lorde shaped a manuscript together: most of it repolished versions of poems written in high school.[21] Titling it *The First Cities*, her manuscript was in the mail to Diane by Thanksgiving. At Christmastime, she expended the last of her energy in preparation but was still too sick to enjoy the excitement of the children and the family's traditional holiday dinner with friends. By New Year's, she was bedridden again.

The second week in January 1968, she received another life-changing call. Audre was recuperating on the couch when the phone rang, so Ed answered it. The caller was Galen Williams. The National Endowment for the Arts was providing a grant to support a poet-in-residence at Tougaloo College, a historically black college in Jackson, Mississippi. Audre had been recommended as its recipient. Her initial response was hardly positive: she was sick, there was the kids, she couldn't do it. There were her fears. One, she would be taken seriously as a poet, in a public way, and the idea of that frightened her. Two, she was terrified of going south.[22] Six years had passed since she and Elaine Paul flirted with the idea of joining the Freedom Riders in Jackson, Mississippi; segregationist backlash against the civil rights movement was now legendary. But Ed insisted she accept, promising to care for the children in her absence. Just weeks later, taking a leave from the Town School, Lorde left Manhattan for Jackson, Mississippi.

SHE ARRIVED EARLY in February. Once she'd settled in on campus, Clare Lovelace, who headed the English Department, formally introduced her to the Tougaloo community at an assembly. She was expected to use the residency to work on her own poetry, give public readings, and perhaps sit in on a class or two. As Lorde moved about encouraging students to attend a reading, the idea occurred to her to do more than was expected. A small group of eight to ten aspiring poets responded to her suggestion they meet with her in a workshop setting.

When the poetry workshop convened, Lorde was terrified. She knew nothing about teaching poetry, and had little or no formal knowledge of poetic theory. Nor had she ever been in this kind of relationship with black people before. Except for one white female, all the students were black, militant, and wore afros. She was the first adult they'd seen on campus wearing an afro. They saw their own blackness reflected in hers. Lorde had no idea how to proceed. For her, this was going to be a trial by fire.

She began by asking her students why they wanted to write, talking to them about poetry, and searching through the bank of connections between feelings and writing. She felt they needed access to literary models beyond those offered in their English courses, mimeographing and distributing to them poems by other black poets.

The workshop's racial and sexual dynamics quickly intensified, as the more militant students aired their feelings about whites. Lorde dreaded the vulnerability of any exposure she did not initiate, and revealed to them, "the father of my children is white."[23] Laying aside the problems surfacing between herself and Ed, she defended not the marriage, but the right to determine one's own relationships irrespective of racial or social dictates. Initially, her openness engendered the students' hostility and disillusionment, but blackness, she'd reasoned, "was not an easy question to be resolved."[24]

Lorde felt she owed it to these young people, and herself, to be honest. After all, these were students who, like her, had to deal with the sound of bullets shot from guns at night by members of the White Citizens' Council, whose intimidation tactics included using the periphery of Tougaloo for target practice. The White Citizens' Council attracted middle- and upper-class whites opposed to desegregation. Unlike the cruder tactics employed by the Ku Klux Klan, its members generally resorted to more sophisticated strategies of economic harassment, political pressure, and propaganda in order to preserve white supremacy and segregation between the races.[25] Under these circumstances, Lorde felt that keeping Ed's race a secret would have been to live a lie.

Lorde's revelation opened the students to engage a more complex black reality, one in which they could be pro-black, discuss racism, and still relate to her as a black woman married to a white man. They could examine their own firsthand notions of blackness, not just the rhetoric of blackness. Together, she and her students came to see the emancipatory potential of their identities when articulated as both self-constructed and historic; embracing the boundaries of identity while at the same time not being limited by them. At Tougaloo, the seeds of what would become Audre Lorde's theory of difference first sprouted into language.

Around mid-February, Yolanda Rios came down to Tougaloo to celebrate Audre's birthday with her and to bring Audre the unbound proofs of *The First Cities*. Holding them in her hands, Audre realized the book's publication would thrust her into public scrutiny.

Frances Clayton had also come to Tougaloo, as an exchange professor in psychology from Rhode Island's Brown University, Tougaloo's sister college. Blond, blue-eyed, and the youngest of nine children, she was born in Illinois on September 10, 1926. She grew up in a poor white farming family. Working the land and responsibility for chores defined an early childhood framed by the depression. Frances's father was a minister and the family's poverty followed them as he moved from town to town, ministering. Despite material lack and a flock of children, the Clayton household was one in which order prevailed. An intelligent but shy girl, constantly uprooted, Frances made few friends.[26]

Education proved to be her salvation. In 1949, Frances graduated from Indiana University where she'd trained under Burrhus Frederic (B. F.) Skinner,[27] a leading proponent of behaviorism—the school of psychology explaining behavior in terms of observable responses to environmental stimuli and rewards. Two years later, she graduated from Brown University with a master's degree in science. Few women in the 1950s chose, or were encouraged to choose, behavioral psychology as an academic arena in which to make their mark. Fewer still achieved prominence or stature in the highly competitive, male-dominated field. But after earning a PhD in psychology from the University of Minnesota in 1954, Clayton began her academic career as a behavioral psychologist; she taught first as an instructor of psychology at Minnesota in 1954–55, and then as an assistant professor at Brown, 1955–56. "A wunderkind"[28] at only age thirty, her research on animal behavior marked her as a rising star. With just one year under her belt as an assistant, Clayton was promoted to associate professor of psychology at Brown in 1956, becoming the first woman to be tenured in psychology there.

Though a wonder in academia, the few available details on Frances Clayton's adult life sketch a woman who was lonely and had ambiguous personal relationships with men. By the time she met Audre, Frances had refused two or three marriage proposals.[29] In the twelve years between 1956 and 1968, she lived alone in Rhode Island, devoting her time to teaching, laboratory work, and research. She was forty-one and Audre thirty-four when they met.

As Frances drove off campus for a trip back to Rhode Island the weekend of Yolanda's visit, Audre introduced the two women to each other. Yolanda became jealously suspicious of an as yet unstated, albeit evolving, relationship between them.[30]

The Tougaloo residency initiated a new identity for Lorde as poet-teacher. She'd never worked as a poet before, and in this informal setting, nurturing students, she learned to teach by doing it, formulating a theory of practice that would become a signature mark of her teaching style in ensuing years.

Under her direction, the workshop's members churned out a remarkable flood of poems. Lorde herself wrote furiously, beginning, for the first time in a long while, a notebook with poems, fragments of poems, and drafts; most of these would form the poems of her second collection, *Cables to rage*.[31]

Inspired by her students, Lorde put in a call to Galen Williams, who now headed up Poets and Writers, a fledgling organization devoted to promoting and funding literary activity. She pleaded with Galen for additional monies to print a magazine of poems by the young writers at Tougaloo. Galen came through with a small amount, and Lorde edited *Pound*, a magazine devoted to their work.

The six weeks Lorde spent in Jackson bound together her experiences at Tougaloo and her relationship with Frances Clayton as the two women fell in love. In a conversation with her daughter years later, Audre confided to Beth the dynamics of a partnership that permitted both her and Ed to have loving friends, though, at the time, her first commitment was to Ed and their marriage. If Ed had been willing to work on their marriage, Audre speculated, she might never have had to choose between Frances and him.[32] However that explanation suited Audre, falling in love with Frances was an *emotional* commitment she'd not made either to Ed or to any of her other "loving friends." The implications of that commitment weighed on her as the residency drew to a close:

> We are not twins
> And I shall make my judgement
> Upon you
> Heavy as my hand on your thighs
> Heavy as my heart beating on your stomach
> Heavy as difference between us.[33]

Lorde returned to New York in mid-March. After teaching at Tougaloo, she was no longer satisfied being a librarian and working in the Town

School's lily-white atmosphere, even as she returned to it. She was in love with Frances Clayton. She still loved Ed, but their marriage was in certain trouble. Ed was even less communicative now, his depression more pronounced. He behaved like "an ostrich with his head in the sand"[34] and Audre thought him an "emotional zombie."[35] She insisted they should enter into couples therapy, but Ed refused to go. His reaction to Audre's announcement that she and Frances had become lovers was one of passive acceptance. He told her he was happy for her. But happy for her was not enough; if the marriage was going to continue, she demanded, he'd have to participate in working on it. Either the relationship was going to change or it was going to end. She'd never been one for ending relationships, preferring their rebirth into friendships; but Frances Clayton was going to be a permanent part of her life, she knew, and what her students had taught her had changed her.[36]

The First Cities was published in April 1968. Dudley Randall reviewed Lorde's first collection in the Negro Digest. In addition to book reviews from time to time, he wrote articles for the Digest.[37] At Broadside Press, Randall's reputation as publisher of some of the most important works by black writers defined a significant contribution to twentieth-century American literature.[38] His generous reviews drew attention to the works of emerging writers.

A native of Washington, D.C., Randall showed an early interest in poetry. At age thirteen, he won first prize for a sonnet he submitted to the poets' pages of the Detroit Free Press. Having earned a master's degree in library science from the University of Michigan in 1951, Randall worked as a librarian during the fifties. Amongst the earliest books published by Broadside were two of his own, Poem Counterpoem (1966), co-authored with the poet Margaret Danner, and Cities Burning (1968).

Broadside was the American distributor for Paul Breman's Heritage anthology series and Randall was familiar with the steady development of Audre Lorde's publishing record. Though his review made clear he did not think Lorde a "nature poet," he remarked upon her references to nature as metaphors charting the changing seasons of love and relationships in her poetry—her use of natural images untypical of the more urban images raging through the poetry of her peers. Randall drew attention to the fresh quality of her language, noting an absence of stridency, unlike the more rhetorical and confrontational poetry of her contemporaries. He defined the collection as a "quiet, introspective book."[39] As word of the publication of *The First Cities* spread, Lorde's excitement was palpable.

There was a symbolic opportunity to revisit Tougaloo on April 4. Many of her beloved students, members of the Tougaloo Choir, came to New York to do a fund-raising concert for Tougaloo, with Duke Ellington, at Carnegie Hall. As a freelance assignment for the *Clarion Ledger*, a Jackson-based newspaper, Lorde was to cover the concert and write an article about it. She was seated up front listening to the choir singing "What the World Needs Now Is Love" when the concert was interrupted by the announcement that Martin Luther King, Jr., had been shot and killed in Memphis, Tennessee. The entire house broke into tears, as did Ellington and the choir. Albert Honeywell, head of the Tougaloo Choir, urged the young people to finish the song in tribute to King.

The murder of Martin Luther King, Jr., was a bitter irony. In cities across the nation, black people erupted—looting, rioting, unsure of the enduring relevance of non-violent protest in a society wholly implicit in King's death. When civil order was finally imposed, a collective black rage had exacted $45 million in damages as payback.

Lorde was also unsure what would become of a world ever on the brink of peril. She'd developed a lingering fear of world destruction fueled by living through the Cold War. Black rage, and white America's historic indifference to that rage, seemed now to have set the stage for race war. Whether it happened or not, the possibility was real to her.

That year—1968—also saw growing public opposition at home to America's involvement in the conflict between North and South Vietnam. Audre adamantly opposed the war, marched in protest against it, and vehemently disagreed with Ed, whose hawkish views at the time seemed to her the uncritical, macho ranting of an ex-serviceman. It was another sign their lives were going in different directions and, for Audre, Ed's initial belief that America belonged in Vietnam was intolerable. In time, she came to view Ed's early perspectives on the war as the subtext of an unspoken resentment toward her; she admitted to years of her own conceited, often violent efforts to change him which made his resentment justifiable.[40]

The response to the publication of her first book of poems was largely positive and Lorde now fielded requests to do public readings. It was at one such reading in Harlem that she got a phone call from Neal Einson, in May. Martha was in the hospital, clinging to life. Audre left the reading and went to Martha's side immediately.

Neal and Martha had been in their Volkwagen bus that evening, on the Bruckner Expressway in the South Bronx. He was driving, she was in the passenger seat. The expressway was under construction then and stretches of it were dimly lit. The driver of a Chrysler plowed into the back of the Einsons' bus, claiming never to have seen it. Martha's head went straight through the windshield.

At Jacobi Hospital, the doctors on staff determined there was no damage to Martha's skull. Soon after she was admitted, however, her brain began to swell and she lapsed into a coma. In order to save Martha from brain damage and certain death within forty-eight hours, her doctors administered ice therapy, wrapping her in an icy blanket which lowered her body temperature. She remained in a coma for almost two months. Audre visited daily; she stayed by Martha's side hours at a time, calling Martha's name and entreating her to come back. Though Martha was not responsive, Audre believed she would regain consciousness. Whether or not Martha was going to be a vegetable remained to be seen.

As Martha fought her way back to life, Audre wrestled with the course of her own. Her demands on Ed persisted and their emotional life together was unraveling. Frances Clayton was living back in Rhode Island, 165 miles away, and part of Audre's heart was with her. The other part was wanting to teach.

Yolanda Rios was unhappy about Audre's relationship with Frances. Now enrolled as a student in the SEEK Program at City College,[41] she'd shown a copy of *The First Cities* to Mina Shaughnessy, director of the SEEK Writing Program there. She urged Shaughnessy to read it and to hire Audre. Prevailing on Shaughnessy put Audre in Yolanda's debt.

That summer, Audre, Ed, Yolanda, and Bill rented a house off Lake Hopatcong, in New Jersey. Ed and Bill could only come out on the weekends because they were working, so Audre, Yolanda, and the kids spent the bulk of the time there. Audre kept up her visits to Martha, chronicling the stages of Martha's miraculous but difficult recovery in an epic, double-voiced poem:

> On the first day of July you warned me again
> *the threads are broken*
> you darkened into explosive angers and
> refused to open your eyes . . .[42]

Frances accepted Audre's invitation to spend some time at the rented house, temporarily ending their separation. It was her first meeting with Ed and her first introduction to Beth and Jonathan, and to members of the Lorde-Rollins extended family who visited at different times. Frances's shyness made her appear unfriendly and uptight in Audre's circle.[43] Figuring the relationship between Audre and Frances would run its course, as others had, Ed made no demands during Frances's stay—miscalculating, as he did so, the perceptible shift in Audre's emotional and erotic life.

Apparently, Yolanda did not like Frances. Audre was both sister figure, and lover to her; Frances's presence threatened those bonds. Yolanda did her best to remain important to Audre and central to the lives of their children. But over time, she became jealous of Frances's centrality in Audre's life and singled out Frances's race as an issue of contention.[44]

Mina Shaughnessy followed up on Yolanda Rios's suggestion. In September 1968, Lorde began teaching at City College, on 138th Street and Convent Avenue, in the SEEK Program. The expectations accompanying the program's mission were high and emotionally charged. Those hired to teach had a single semester, at best, to raise the academic skills of the mostly black students who would not have gotten into college by passing entrance exams first. SEEK students registered for remedial courses in the liberal arts. The idea was that, upon successful completion of those classes, they would then be better positioned to compete with the general pool of applicants to City College and other City University of New York (CUNY) campuses. At SEEK, Lorde joined a stellar constellation of young, gifted, poet-writer-teachers also hired by Shaughnessy; they included Toni Cade Bambara, Addison Gayle,

David Henderson, Barbara Christian, Adrienne Rich, and June Jordan. The moment could not have been more alive, or more dramatic.[45]

Although the Tougaloo experience had been successful, this was to be a more formal classroom setting. Responsible for teaching grammar and composition, Lorde entered the classroom fearfully each day, but she relied on her instincts; she admitted her trepidations to her students and taught herself the rudiments of grammar as she taught them to her class. She came to see these rudiments as arbitrary, liberating as well as restrictive. Tenses were, she learned, simply a way of ordering time. While teaching her students the purposes of grammar, she taught herself to write prose.[46]

Aside from the high-pressure atmosphere at City, there was Ed to deal with at home; the differing needs of a young daughter and son; reading poetry to them before they went to bed; keeping up with Martha's eventual but slow recuperation; being supportive of Neal; and finding money for the children's scholarships. Then there was longing for Frances; their letters back and forth; and above all writing, after the children were asleep, at the kitchen table, late into the night.

Her new poems explored themes familiar (love, relationships) and new (the postmortem accompanying a first book). When several of them appeared in *Cables to rage*, discerning readers leaped upon the obvious lesbianism in the lengthy poem, "Martha":

> . . . and yes Martha
> we have loved each other . . .
> no Martha I do not know if we shall ever
> sleep in each other's arms again.

Less attended to, though no less important, was another poem:

ON A NIGHT OF THE FULL MOON

> . . .
>
> your lips quick as young birds
> between your thighs the sweet
> sharp taste of limes.[47]

The images of this poem fleshed out a rich, layered, female language of love. Read alongside "Martha," the two poems signified incremental, public disclosures of Lorde's lesbianism.

While at City College, Adrienne Rich formally introduced herself to Lorde one day on campus, having seen her in a number of program meetings. Adrienne was born and raised in Baltimore. Her father, Arnold Rich, was a professor in the medical school at the university. He was Jewish, though her mother, Helen Jones Rich, was not. He had a sense of himself as an outsider, did not want to be labeled as a Jew, and disdained any association with the Jewish social world of Baltimore; a perspective which led to his family's isolation from others.[48] A graduate of Radcliffe College, Adrienne Rich had already published several acclaimed collections, including her first, *A Change of World* (1951), selected by W. H. Auden for the coveted Yale Series of Younger Poets Prize. Auden's Introduction to the book praised her mastery of form, delicacy, and emotional restraint.[49]

As a young writer, Rich was under the influence of male poets she admired in college—Dylan Thomas, Wallace Stevens, Robert Frost, and Auden himself. Learning from them the art of craft, her early style followed the prevailing academic poetic ideal: the poet's voice, neither male nor female, yet filtered through male personas, was that of a generic masculine speaker.[50]

In 1953, she married Alfred H. Conrad, an economist teaching at Harvard University, with whom she had three sons: David, Paul, and Jacob, born in 1955, 1957, and 1959. The family moved from Cambridge, Massachusetts, to New York City in 1966, when Conrad began teaching at City College of New York. By then, Rich had published three more collections: *The Diamond Cutters and Other Poems* (1955); *Snapshots of a Daughter-in-Law: Poems, 1954–1962* (1963); and *Necessities of Life: Poems, 1962–1965* (1966).

In *Snapshots of a Daughter-in-Law*, she began her transition to a more self-conscious examination of the social position of women, their relationships to others and to cultural institutions, repositioning herself as subject within a process of feminist consciousness-raising. With *Necessities of Life*, the shift in her work became even more overt. In that collection, Rich undertook the process of reinterpreting women's lives and

acknowledging foremothers, such as Emily Dickinson, which characterized much of her subsequent writing.[51]

She'd bought a copy of *The First Cities* in the CCNY bookstore, read
it, and was greatly impressed with Lorde's poetry. They talked and met
for lunch a few times afterwards. When Lorde left City College to teach
at Lehman College, another CUNY campus, Rich stayed on at City,
weathering the storm of her husband's death in 1970.[52] The two poets
saw little of each other during that period, and Adrienne Rich moved on
to Boston to teach at Brandeis University.

THE WATERSHED YEAR of 1968 for Audre closed on her role as midwife
at the home birthing of Diane di Prima's daughter, Tara.[53] The night
before Christmas Eve, Diane readied a loaf of bread to bake and placed
it in the oven. When her waters broke, she called Audre. Audre hopped
into her car and sped onto the West Side Highway, encountering a traffic jam of last-minute Christmas shoppers which made the trip from her
Riverside Drive apartment to the Village, and the Hotel Albert where
Diane was living, a longer ride than usual. Throwing off her coat and
pulling on a pair of sterile gloves she'd bought and kept ready for this
purpose, Audre arrived just in time to catch Diane's baby as it came out.
Afterwards, Alan Marlowe, Diane's husband at the time and father of
the baby, emerged from a nearby room along with several other male
friends of theirs. And the bread, now ready, was consumed with some tea
by all who'd gathered.

IN THE SPRING semester of 1969, the dramatic atmosphere at City College blew up with revolutionary fervor. Black and Puerto Rican members
of the student body, demanding "open admissions," called for a strike.
The demand for open admissions was principled upon the idea of more
democratic access to higher education, particularly within the City University of New York; a "public" system, which purported to service the
city's college-bound hopefuls, the university still largely remained closed
to the vast majority of students of color. In spite of the liberal-minded
philosophy behind a program like SEEK, its students bore the stigma of

their separation from the general student body in much-publicized remedial classes. The realization of separate and unequal access to education resonated with earlier demands for the desegregation of public schools and institutions of higher learning in the South. On the City College campus, it sparked "the revolution in the north."[54]

Business as usual ceased at City. The students set up barricades, occupied buildings, and forced an end to all classes. Symbolic of the Black Power movement, the red, black, and green liberation flag replaced the American flag on campus. With empathetic faculty and community supporters backing their demands, bringing them food, blankets, and other necessities, the students' strike lasted some six or seven weeks and received national media coverage.[55]

Audre Lorde and Yolanda Rios also supplied the students with soup and blankets, and were uncritical supporters of the student movement until their firsthand discovery that some of the female students in those occupied buildings were naively submitting to sex with the brothers in the name of the revolution.

In the meantime, some faculty, unable now to teach, disappeared from sight. Others, who felt politically committed to the students, sought an alternative site at which to hold classes. Classroom space at Intermediate School (I.S.) 201 in Harlem was made available. For the duration of the strike, the classes taught at I.S. 201 became known as "Harlem University." Lorde was among those who taught her classes there. She was at I.S. 201 every day, handing out assignments.[56]

By now, the emotional and sexual focus of Lorde's life was Frances Clayton. She still insisted that Ed go into therapy, that she knew what was best for him, that he was not living up to his potential as a human being; the monotony of her nagging covered up the guilt she was beginning to feel as she entertained thoughts of ending the marriage. But the vow to "love and cherish 'til death do you part" chained Audre to her Catholic upbringing and a family history in which no one got divorced. She and Ed were barely speaking: emotionally turned off, she'd asked him to sleep on the couch.

That summer, Audre took the children with her to Rhode Island for a visit with Frances. Although modest in its decor, Frances's home smacked of an obsessive neatness. Everything had and stayed in its place; in the kitchen utensils were hung up in order and spices racked alphabetically.[57] Its museumlike order had none of the chaos of the Lorde-Rollins home, where the presence of children and the clutter of daily preoccupations were self-evident. In time, Audre would come to depend happily on Frances's need for order.

During the two-week visit, Audre assured Frances their relationship would continue, but she was going to leave neither her family nor her children, and when the two weeks were over, she was going back to Ed. When Frances began to suggest marriage may not have been what Audre wanted any more, Audre denied that, suspecting Frances of ulterior motives and sidestepping the issue of her own indecision.

Ed now saw the relationship between Audre and Frances for what it was. He accused Audre of abandoning him; of emotional demands for communication that were insatiable; a need for love that was too much for him.[58] When Audre told him she thought they should have a trial separation, Ed was jolted by the possibility that their marriage might end. He did not want a separation, fearing they'd never get back together. And in an effort to save the marriage, he offered Audre an olive branch: joint therapeutic sessions. Audre agreed to marriage counseling, knowing it was but a Band-Aid to a hemorrhaging wound. She no longer wanted Ed or the marriage.

PART THREE

"Uses of the Erotic . . ."
(1970–77)

SEVEN

W HAT LORDE WANTED now was to reinvent herself: she wanted a life wholly grounded in lesbian identity. She wanted to fuse that identity to power, as a woman and a poet. She would come to identify its potency as "the erotic . . . a resource within . . . that lies in a deeply female and spiritual plane, firmly rooted in the power of . . . unexpressed or unrecognized feeling."[1] Lorde felt that expressing and recognizing her deepest feelings could position her to take responsibility for them. She also felt that taking responsibility, as a woman, could lead to making use of "the erotic" to resist oppression and as energy for social change.[2] As she wrote in her journal: "I am lustful now for my own name."[3] That name would be defined by her relationship with Frances Clayton, her children, her poetry, and the feminist movement. She would find that name by embracing an African, female-centered spirituality.

In the meantime, Lorde began teaching at Herbert H. Lehman College in the Bronx in the fall of 1969, and was in her second term there in 1970. The Education Department of Lehman instituted a program to aid new teachers working in New York City's schools. Since most of the students in the public schools were black, the program aimed to broaden traditional theoretic approaches to teaching them. Lorde's course, "Race and Education," proposed an examination of the effects of racism upon black Americans. The majority of the young teachers who registered for her course were white women; one or two of the mostly female class were black.

Assuming the now familiar approach that had proved tried and true in past classes, Lorde encouraged her students to make a connection between personal experience and learning. They were required to consider the effects of racism upon themselves, and to alter their own race-based assumptions and those of the world around them.[4] She also required that they discuss what they were prepared to do to end racism, countering their notions of education as racially unbiased. Her white students resisted examinations of racism. Her black students were unable to recognize their own internalized racism; they rarely finished her course out, perceiving it as having no intrinsic value to them.[5]

Left with a majority of white students, Lorde insisted they examine white perceptions of black Americans through discussions of commonly held stereotypes. Her students were neither used to nor prepared for such self-scrutiny and they responded with guilt, anger, and silence. After one class, Lorde wrote in her journal, "some hostile" and "no one stayed after." More than once, her students fled the room immediately after class.[6]

She was not popular with the students at Lehman. They were intimidated by her[7] and showed little of the adoration she'd felt from students at Tougaloo or City College. Teaching at Lehman was emotionally costly, the inability to connect with the too few black students frustrating; and the onus on her to teach white people about their racism was draining. By the end of her second term, she began to feel this was a job for someone who was white.[8]

Lorde kept up the marriage-counseling sessions with Ed and their therapist, Jack Theta. On one hand, she still insisted the onus was on Ed to change and make the marriage work. On the other, she insisted on a trial separation. Ed argued against separating, his sense of abandonment increasing. Theta tried to help the couple over their differences, but he came to see a trial separation as a useful solution. As the months went by, Lorde vacillated between wanting out of the marriage and her own feeling she was indeed abandoning Ed. But if one thing was clear, it was that she no longer wanted to live with him.

Despite the physical distance, Lorde's developing relationship with Frances Clayton was emotionally satisfying. Clayton was seven years older, stable, clearheaded, intelligent. Clayton was loving, and unlike Ed, responsive. She wasn't one of the "gay-girls" of Lorde's sexual coming-of-age, and had no history tied to Lorde's other lovers and friends. Clayton was adventure on new terrain. Lorde was passionately in love with her. But Clayton wanted more than Lorde's accustomed brand of "friendship." She wanted a live-in relationship ultimately. She pressed Lorde to be more definitive about the possibilities of their future.

In March 1970, Lorde and Rollins drew up a trial separation agreement. That summer, she took the children with her to Rhode Island to be with Frances. From there, she called Rollins, told him she was returning at the end of August, and that he had to move out. She knew then this was going to be more than a trial.

Beth and Jonathan knew nothing of their parents' breakup. The full weight of it struck them the day they saw their father packing. Assuring the crying children he would see them often, Rollins moved out of their 626 Riverside apartment into first a studio, then a two-bedroom, in the Broadmore Hotel at 103rd Street and Broadway. Rollins later blamed himself, in part, for the separation because he was preoccupied with a struggling career, constantly absent from home, passive, and satisfied with the marriage as it was. His children and family meant everything to him; being separated from them would deepen his depression over the next five years.[9]

Rollins's departure left Lorde with a mixture of feelings. For the first time in a long while, she felt free from the tensions of marriage. She now had another opportunity to construct a life for herself, and for her children. Yet her relief was accompanied by a sense of failure: she had not been able to uphold her commitment to Rollins. Lorde was afraid now of her ability to sustain a committed relationship; afraid of what would happen to Frances Clayton, for example, in the future, if she could not. As much as she'd insisted on the separation, she was depressed by its actuality. Though Frances came to New York some weekends to be with her,

Audre wanted to be alone, to come to terms with her sense of failure. Were it not for Elizabeth Maybank, who assumed some responsibility for housekeeping and taking care of the kids during this period, Lorde could not have balanced single parenthood, working, and writing.

The threads of her life were snaking together in a self-propelled design of their own that year. Five years before the publication of *The First Cities*, Paul Breman had offered to publish a collection by Lorde, but she hadn't taken his offer seriously. During a brief meeting between the two of them in 1969, Breman reminded Lorde of his standing offer.[10] Prompted by the reminder, and testing him, Lorde gave Breman a book-length manuscript. True to his word, Breman published Lorde's next book, *Cables to rage*, in 1970.

The jacket of *Cables to rage* sported an imposing head shot of the poet, with gray tints that bragged of a natural, intellectual femininity. Scarred by a childhood of feeling "fat, black and ugly," Lorde decidedly made no attempt to conceal her lack of conventional beauty with artificial applications. Neither exceptionally attractive nor ugly—in her own words, "plain"—Audre was privately insecure about her looks; she compensated in public by being charming, dramatic, and vain. She wished she'd had high cheekbones and a longer neck, and consciously imitated the stylized pose she believed to be that of movie stars: chin tilted up, head back and showing her best side. But poor eyesight sometimes betrayed her vanity: she would fall or stumble clumsily.[11] Except for periods when the use of amphetamines caused her weight to drop considerably, Audre remained conscious of herself as a large-framed woman, adopting into her wardrobe as she grew older the looser-fitting African outfits that would become her signature look and turn the image of her body into a political statement.

Cables to rage, consisting of eighteen poems, codified a transitional stage in which the writer contemplated who she was to become.

> . . .
> the shedding of my past in patched conceits
> . . . a book of leavings
> now
> I can do anything I wish[12]

The only review on record appeared two years after publication, in the March 1972 issue of *Poetry*. Mike Doyle, a poet, reviewed a hefty twenty-five books published by Canadian poets, mostly with small presses. Prompted by celebrations of Canada's centennial, his review sought to articulate the specific contours of Canadian poetry, responding to a strong nationalist impulse in Canada's cultural life that was not surprising given that country's resistance to absorption by the United States.[13]

Why *Cables to rage* was included among the works Doyle was assigned to review remains a mystery, except if placed alongside the comments of Douglas Lochhead and Raymond Souster, editors of *Made in Canada: New Poems of the Seventies*, an anthology Doyle also reviewed. Doyle quoted the editors' assertion that the variety, excitement, and technical excellence of contemporary Canadian poetry was unmatched by any save for poetry produced in the United States.[14] Enter Audre Lorde; a yardstick by which to measure Canadian poetry.

Doyle was undecided as to whether or not Lorde and Robin Skelton, an Irish poet, were "two ducks among the swans, or vice versa, or whatever." His assessment of *Cables to rage* was brief and dismissive: "Lorde writes free verse (whatever that is, anymore), of no particular note."[15]

But Lorde's exposure within black literary circles was steadily gaining ground. The *Journal of Black Poetry*, a San Francisco–based quarterly, published one of her poems, "Rooming houses are old women" in its first Pan-African Issue. The next (Winter–Spring 1970) issue embodied an ideological break with Western cultural aesthetics, and a reclamation of black images and history definitive of several revolutionary journals of the time. The year before, the *Journal* had published "Conversation in crisis," a poem Lorde wrote in 1962 as a response to an argument between herself and Rollins. In the *Journal*, it was accompanied by a black-and-white photograph of a young black couple embracing and smiling—the woman's smile more defined, less pained, than her male counterpart's.

The photograph was typical of the *Journal's* politics, which were punctuated by a bias inscribing black male oppression as more severe than that suffered by black women. Often, it made use of visuals in which black women appeared friendly, communicative, and non-threatening, juxtaposing them against images of imposing, hostile-looking black men.

Neither of the poems selected for the radical journal was hyper-"black" in tone, but their successive publication built upon editorial statements in the annual poetry issue of the *Negro Digest*, in 1968. The editors of the *Digest* identified the moment as one in which the "new Black Renaissance" was evidenced by a growing number of poets "confronting their experiences and giving vent to their imaginations without apology." Significant to this proliferation of poets was the unique opportunity the black community now had in determining its best poets and when those poets spoke to and for black people.[16] Inclusion in the annual poetry issue was certainly a mark of distinction, and Lorde's poem, "Naturally," placed her work alongside that of Dudley Randall, Sonia Sanchez, LeRoi Jones, Don L. Lee, and Gwendolyn Brooks, all of whom were prominently identified at the radical center of the new literary renaissance.

On the surface, the language, imagery, and racial appeal of "Naturally" made it an obvious choice for inclusion. Yet the poem was a tongue-in-cheek dig at the rhetoric of newly found black pride. An oversimplified reading might assume Lorde's uncritical embrace of a nationalist agenda tied to black economic power. But as was proven time and again, nothing about Audre Lorde was simple, and the poem's final statement served her critique of black pride rhetoric as lacking in sustenance:

> . . .
> But I've bought my can of
> Natural Hair Spray . . .
> Still thinking more
> Proud Beautiful Black Women
> Could better make and use
> Black bread.[17]

The original draft of "Naturally" appears in Lorde's journal after poems written in August 1968 and before an untitled one written while she was at Tougaloo, dated "2/22," which recorded observations on housekeeping. This chronological confusion was consistent with Lorde's habit of inconsistently dating drafts, leaving out dates totally, and recycling journals that were only partially used to write in them again later. Contrary to the assumptions of friends and intimates—and even to what she said about her own journals—Lorde did not always make use of her journals as diaries in which she wrote daily, detailed every event in her life, or recorded those events fully.

THE LEHMAN EXPERIENCE left Lorde hungry for engagement with black students. Because of public demands for open admissions within the CUNY system, the John Jay College of Criminal Justice in Manhattan now admitted a more representative population pursuing a liberal arts education. For the first time, black and Puerto Rican students enrolled in classes with the city's uniformed personnel. Lorde seized the moment. She revised the course she'd taught at Lehman and talked the dean of John Jay into a course on "Race and the Urban Situation."

Lorde began at John Jay as a lecturer in the English Department, becoming the first black member of its faculty. She taught her course and a second one geared to remedial writing instruction, which she handled by using creative writing techniques. From the start, Lorde's course was heavily attended, its potentially explosive mix of black and white police and black and white working-class students heightened by the ready revolvers the police wore visibly.[18] Over the next two years Lorde revised and perfected a series of lectures on racial stereotyping, institutionalized racism, and the stages and mechanics of oppression, wedding them to discussions on race, class, gender, black history, and literature. Her journal notes made several references to the participation of black people in their own oppression; in particular, she cited the black middle-class identification with white material culture, and romanticized notions of black pride, as detrimental to black progress.[19] Oddly, she documented nothing as substantial about the remedial writing course.

Lorde threw herself into teaching at John Jay, covering up a deepening depression. As the months wore on and Frances Clayton came and went, she found their separations increasingly unbearable. After one such separation in November, Lorde drafted two brief pages dated "11/26/70" that were neither written in a journal nor clearly a letter actually sent to Clayton. Nevertheless, she "conversed" with Frances, writing of the four days since her departure as being "like a year of emptiness" and expressing her feeling that Frances was "isolated in the middle of that vast forest on the island inside of me—unreachable."[20] But torn between wanting Frances with her and wanting to be alone, Lorde eventually insisted on time to herself, and Clayton's trips to New York ceased.

Lorde now felt she'd driven away the two people she claimed to love. She wrote of Frances's pain at having to leave her, comparing it with the "figmentary and symbolic pain—also strong but so different"[21] she herself felt after Rollins left. Admitting to missing Rollins at times since, Lorde sought to assure herself of the difference between what she felt then and now:

> but I have never felt this rending loss—
> this aching <u>hole</u> in me that I know as
> the lack of you.[22]

Three days later, her tone was more sober. Inscribing two more pages dated "11/29 70," she carried on her conversation with Clayton, explaining her feeling they were living in a dream, albeit painful, but that she and Clayton would awaken out of that pain and toward each other "to face new and different terrors."[23] Praying she was not wrong about the dream state as test period, Lorde spelled out what she saw as "problems" for them as a couple:

> 1) In our very existence I see us as part of the revolutionary vanguard—how is less clear. But what that means in terms of our relationship to other revolutionaries cannot be determined only on personal attitude convenience or whim. By committing ourselves to each other we also commit ourselves to a larger dream— a re-organization so to speak—and have common cause—if not common ideology to other revolutions.[24]

Lorde tied their connection to other revolutions to a "what-if" example of a male SDS fugitive appearing at their door; and to knowing on what grounds they were separate from him and united with him in common opposition to the patriarchy. She insisted on their individuality, but linked their relationship to engaged struggle, noting: "Since our existence rocks the boat we must be prepared for other rougher waters."[25]

The other "problem" she outlined spoke directly to differences in their personalities. Basically shy, Clayton was prone to be less conspicuous and more comfortable in the background. Lorde was comfortable with confrontation, and even sought it out. She asked:

> 2) Do you need as much withdrawal as you say you do? Or is that the only way you see now so far to protect what the we will make less needful of protection? Is there potential real pleasure for you in rubbing up against others, that you have not yet discovered— less than I sometimes think but more than you find possible at this time?[26]

In four pages dated "12/14 70," Lorde extended the conversation with Clayton to one directed more at herself. She wrote of a dream she'd had two nights in a row. The dream was revelatory, reminding her of important things she'd forgotten, having more to do with herself than with Clayton. She recalled only the vaguest details: "something about your present, & wanting to breathe—and a lesson I wanted to teach. . . ."[27] Lorde interpreted this dream as clarifying a distinction between physical desire and emotional well-being. Before her recurring dream, she'd associated her pain with an absence of Frances's body. But the dream spoke to Audre of three things she wanted: to have Frances present; to feel alive; and to learn from the past. It forced her to realize the pain she felt would not be lessened simply by having Frances's body, but by having Frances with her wholly.[28]

Lorde admitted to a fear that Clayton would not want her, or that the price of wanting her was too high for her lover to pay; inferring in a cryptic explanation, "because of who/what I be," that Clayton (like Rollins) might become overwhelmed by Lorde's demands, need for love, and need for freedom beyond love's boundaries. And there was another fear:

> You will contradict other needs I want
> to fulfill like my children my
> committments [sic] to living black and
> subversive my comfort my image (erroneous)[29]

The fear that Clayton would contradict the fulfillment of "other needs" signaled more complex differences between them. Frances Clayton had no children. She did not express an articulated political identity as white, whereas Lorde did so as black. Clayton worked within institutions but did not overtly work to change them, trying to fit into them rather than not. Lorde saw living "subversive" as an immutable aspect of her being.

The fear that Clayton would contaminate her comfort level and image spoke also to Lorde's fear of vulnerability. It was the same fear she'd faced down at Tougaloo. Now the case was not exposure of an interracial "heterosexual" relationship with a white man, but of an interracial lesbian relationship with a white woman; the latter more problematic than the former, given her increasing literary engagement with an even more radicalized black community. Rumors about her lesbianism had long circulated in black artistic and intellectual quarters, but Lorde kept her lesbian world nestled within her mostly white, liberal social circles. She was not out publicly, and she was courting a fragile acceptance within the black community, the home she longed for within it as hazardous as the specter of certain disapproval and rejection. Just as she needed Ed Rollins to reinvent herself as fertile, she needed Frances Clayton to redefine herself as lesbian.

At the end of this triplet of writings, Lorde concluded that her only option was to be alone while she resolved the relationship with Rollins: "I am equal to whatever I must do with Ed as long as F & I are not together."[30] Only then could she be sure she'd acted out of her own strengths and not Clayton's.

By now, a debate began over whether or not a Black Studies department would be established at John Jay. There, as elsewhere, the push to establish such a department called for a radical restructuring of the institution in terms of hiring more black faculty and staff, and institutionalizing a black intellectual presence.[31] Lorde inserted herself into that debate, going to meetings and contributing to strategic discussions; she blunted the absence of Clayton by an immersion into the politics there.

Rollins kept his promise to Beth and Jonathan, seeing them on a regular basis—far more now than before he'd moved out.[32] He visited twice a week, stayed for dinner, brought Audre flowers, wined and dined her in an attempt to repair their lives. But his desperate efforts were all for naught. Lorde did not want a reconciliation. Angered, Rollins accused her of getting him out of the house under false pretenses and of not giving their marriage a chance. Lorde felt she'd given the marriage a lot of chances, and now it was over.

Rollins threatened to take Lorde to court, charge her as an unfit mother, and take full custody of their children, though he did not follow through with those threats in the end. In 1971, Lorde and Rollins finalized a separation agreement. Rollins built in a clause preventing her from moving out of state with the children,[33] a clearly retaliatory move which anticipated the possibility that once rid of him, Lorde would take the children to Rhode Island and live there with Clayton.

Lorde once recounted a rare retaliatory move of her own the day she signed the agreement. She'd picked up "this girl" at Snookie's, a gay bar on 14th Street, took her back to the woman's hotel room on Eighth Street, and "almost" beat her up. She was unable to recall "this girl's" name and rationalized the moment as "not my shining hour."[34] But why had she, on the day that began her legal freedom from Ed Rollins, exhibited such violent anger toward a girl one can presume was white? Was she acting out some warped sense of power, powerlessness, or freedom? How did this behavior fit, in her mind, with the dominance associated with picking someone up and the submission to sex—presumably—with a stranger ? How did it fit with loving Frances Clayton, whose whiteness she passionately respected as "difference"? And how did it fit with her official engagement of the feminist movement when, in the fall of 1971, one of her poems appeared in *Woman: A Journal of Liberation?*

Written the year before, "Who Said It Was Simple" foretold Lorde's complicated embrace of feminism, her locations as black and feminist within the movement, and her competing feelings of love and hate for white women as individuals and allies in struggle.

. . .

Sitting in Nedicks
the women rally before they march
discussing the problematic girls
they hire to make them free . . .[35]

Lorde's embrace of the women's liberation movement intersected with the political ferment of the movement as it unfolded in New York City particularly. At the time, the cultural arm of the movement gave birth to a proliferation of magazines, newspapers, and grassroots publications devoted to women. Coffeehouses and bookstores opened as public spaces catering to a female clientele; and popular demand rose for readings by women poets and writers.[36] Ideologically, the movement's activism on behalf of an end to women's oppression based on gender coordinated with Lorde's longstanding feelings about the "place" of women in the private and public spheres. On a more personal level, Lorde came through the door of the movement in need of a politicized home.

She had not been at home as a young activist in the progressive circles of the early fifties, in which black people were welcomed but homosexuals frowned upon. She had not been at home in the "gay-girl" bar scene in the later fifties because she was black. She was not at home in the current black liberation struggle because she was her own kind of "black," and suspect as a lesbian. These communities had allowed her to express separate aspects of her identity. But Lorde understood her multiple identities as representing "the very house of difference."[37] Without a community that welcomed all of her identities at once, she had been unable to construct an integrated, political self—one that would emerge "blackened and whole."[38] At the outset, the feminist movement presented itself as a longed-for home. As she became more publicly involved with white feminists, though, Lorde's stance as a radical black lesbian would challenge their perspectives on sexuality, the meaning of feminist sisterhood, and race.[39]

BY 1971, Lorde and Clayton had decided to live together. As Lorde and the children were legally restricted to residing in New York State, Clayton agreed to give up an established life in Rhode Island and relocate to the city. The search for a suitable house to purchase took more than a year and coincided with Lorde's efforts, beginning in February 1972, to divorce Ed Rollins.

Though it had a basement, backyard, and an attic as the kids requested, 207 St. Paul's Avenue on Staten Island was a diamond in the rough. With no gate or fence around it, the property was unkempt and exposed. There was no cement walkway, dirt everywhere, the lawn hadn't been mowed in months, and the backyard teemed with weeds and discarded junk. The three-storied house was covered on the outside with a fake brick, burgundy-colored asphalt paper. Inside, the kitchen drawers had melted crayons everywhere, the mustard-colored carpet was filthy, and the basement unfinished. It looked like a money-guzzler to Clayton, but Lorde, seeing its possibilities, fell in love with it.[40]

Moving there meant relocating to the city's most conservative borough politically. Yet the promise of living in a house of their own, just a ferry's ride from Manhattan, was a reasonable compromise; and it was suitable for Frances, who was basically a rural person and insisted upon being surrounded by trees and space. Audre and Frances closed on the house by June, and that summer, with the help of Beth and Jonathan, they set about making it livable and establishing life as a family.

Once into their new home, the couple established clear boundaries between themselves and the children physically. The second floor housed their individual studies, a guestroom, and their bedroom, which Beth and Jonathan were not allowed to enter. In effect, the second floor was private. Beth and Jonathan lived on the third floor; and the two floors functioned, emotionally, as separate households. Beyond the physical arrangements, establishing life as a family meant a series of difficult adjustments.

At nine and eight, respectively, Beth and Jonathan were accustomed to living in a predominantly black neighborhood and going to private school with children who were mostly white. They now found themselves living in proximity to white kids with very different social attitudes from the ones they'd known, who thought them nerds and did not like them because they were black. The black kids who lived around the corner on Clinton Street disliked them because they were racially mixed, spoke differently, and appeared to be stuck up.

Beth and Jonathan also had to adjust to public school, where the atmosphere was assuredly less privileged and the general population more streetwise. Until then, they'd lived a fairly sheltered life in a world primarily informed by their mother's politics and social circles. They found the other children tough and threatening. On more than one occasion, they were beaten up and chased home from school.

At first, Lorde thought the kids were having problems because she and Clayton were lesbians, a fact unknown to their neighbors initially. She soon discovered Beth and Jonathan were simply not fighting back and defending themselves. One day, as the three of them were in the car, they passed by some of the neighborhood toughs. Seeing that these kids were no bigger than her own, Lorde was livid with Beth and Jonathan for acting cowardly. The children's interpretation of their mother's oft-stated political belief in non-violence, however, was at the core of their confusion as to the difference between self-defense and wanton violence. In direct contradiction to how she'd raised them, Lorde now demanded that Beth and Jonathan assert themselves; she insisted there was a time and place to fight back, to be violent. Eventually, Jonathan and Beth fought back and the tougher kids left them alone. Fighting back, standing up for oneself, was an essential component of Lorde's worldview. Transmission of that worldview to Beth and Jonathan became critical to raising them not only as intelligent, socially conscious people, but as "warriors."

In the ensuing years, living on Staten Island had other drawbacks. Lorde and Clayton did not hide the fact that they were lesbians, nor could they hide the obvious fact that their relationship was biracial. The entire family was often the target of hate and prejudice. On one occasion, a bag of human feces was dumped on their porch overnight. At times, Lorde imagined hordes of white people marching up St. Paul's Avenue to get them; she believed a race war, in which she would be a primary target, was imminent. Lorde and Clayton kept a stash of food in the house in the event of such a race war or a tornado, the latter possibility setting Clayton's teeth on edge because she'd grown up in a part of the country in which tornados were a frightening reality. Lorde had a tendency to be paranoid, but her fears were more than paranoid responses. She did not delude herself about the physically idyllic culture of Staten Island or how unsafe their lives could be at any moment.

Beth and Jonathan also had to make adjustments in their relationships with their father. Before the move to Staten Island, they saw their father on Mondays and Wednesdays. Now they only saw him on weekends, when he'd pick them up on Friday and return them on Sunday, refusing ever to enter the house Lorde and Clayton shared. Lorde and Rollins had little personal contact beyond that to do with making arrangements for him to spend time with his children. As Rollins became more and more delinquent with child-support payments, Lorde took him to court, winning a judgment against him. Rollins's anger toward Lorde bled over to the children, and he stopped calling them. Between 1976 and 1978, as Beth and Jonathan entered their early teens, he had little contact with his children. Beth eventually wrote her father, telling him he needed to do something about not communicating with them. Rollins did finally make contact with them, but Jonathan was angry with his father and refused to see him for another year.[41]

For Clayton, the decision to relocate meant the difficulty of finding employment. She had glowing recommendations, but her applications for employment were met with suspicion. Clayton's desire for a horizontal move within academia seemed inexplicable, especially since she was at the top of her research career at Brown University and had been engaged in several significant projects there.[42]

Inexplicable, too, was a career in which her scholarship seemed arrested. An entry in *American Men and Women of Science* listed no publications—an odd comment on the professional expectations of a "wunderkind" in her field. Clayton may have encountered conditions familiar to women in the academy: opportunities to publish, especially in highly competitive fields dominated by men, are fewer; women may provide research for male colleagues or contribute substantial work to articles "authored" by men for which they are not credited. Clayton's name disappeared from subsequent editions of the directory. Whatever the reasons for her disappearance from the "official record,"[43] she'd abandoned a promising career at Brown. She eventually accepted a position at Queens College, teaching psychology, later becoming licensed as a psychotherapist with a private practice.

Between 1972 and 1973, she suffered terrible asthma. At times, she could hardly breathe and an oxygen tank had to be installed in their home to assist her. Formerly an avid skier, she became less active in New York City, put on a lot of weight, and smoked a lot more.

Clayton also had to accept Lorde's friendship with Blanche Cook, several years her junior, who had known Lorde's children much longer and had a more playful side to her personality. With a past, and intimate, history between them, Lorde and Cook shared a language of memories that excluded Clayton, and made her jealous from time to time. But Clayton was living in Lorde's world now, which included an extended family of Lorde's intimate friends.

Clayton was not used to raising children. But for falling in love with Audre, she would not have chosen to have children in her life. Still, she co-mothered Beth and Jonathan, and brought to the household an obsession with order. She did all the food shopping, cooked twice a week, and took care of the wash for herself and Audre; seeing to it, as part of their chores, that the children did their own wash and cooked family meals twice a week themselves.[44] Clayton's insistence on order belied an intolerance for unstructured living; when she became a part of the family, there were "family meetings" every Sunday, at which issues—principally chores, a list placed on the refrigerator during the week before—would be hashed out and discussed.

Lorde was happy to have an ordered household. With Clayton in charge, it was easier to devote herself to her writing and public life. It pleased her that her second-floor study had "a force field around it"[45] which kept everyone out. Lorde often took Beth and Jonathan to her readings, but when she read out of town, Clayton was at home with them. As Lorde conceded the bulk of domestic responsibility to Clayton, she came to think of and need Clayton as her wife.

Clayton married Lorde's life: she gave up the emotional solitude of her own in return for friends who became hers, children who became hers, and fame and success that became hers vicariously. Save for her blood family, and the patients she eventually retained, Clayton lived in Lorde's circle. In time, she grew insecure and dependent—an aspect of her persona that Lorde appeared to cater to, out of need, love, and because of the shifting power dynamic between them.[46]

In certain respects, Clayton fulfilled Lorde's hunger for mother love. Lorde's affairs with women were not generally ones with peers, but with younger women who idolized her. On a deeper emotional level, those affairs left her wanting. As an older woman, Frances certainly fit the bill as a symbolic maternal presence, taking care of Lorde's most basic needs. But there was an aspect of the relationship between them that duplicated Lorde's experiences with her true mother: Clayton was often jealous, threatened by Lorde's desires for a public life, and chastised Lorde for being a crazy artist.[47] Clayton could not, however, satisfy Lorde's primal need for black mother love. In November 1972, Lorde noted in her journal:

> I have looked and looked for the black woman who would really be my mother—who could tell me how the lies we swallowed in the tenderest winters could be toughened and explored and thrown away, who would name me hers and sanction my suffering not by removing it which she could not because it echoed hers, not by reducing it because within lay the key to all our future powers, but by a recognition that would heal the gaps within my strength. Who would recognize me as both proud and loving.[48]

In the early to mid-1970s, there was no feminist, and certainly no public, discourse on lesbian parenting, let alone on interracial lesbian couples as parents.[49] Making the road as she walked it, Audre counted on Blanche Cook and Clare Coss—the core of their extended family— to help her and Frances raise the children. After Bernice Goodman came into their lives, they turned to her for guidance also.

Bernice Goodman was a psychotherapist whose ad Lorde read one day in *The New York Times*. Shortly afterwards, she arranged an appointment at Goodman's Third Street apartment in the East Village. She knew little about Bernice initially, except that she was a lesbian and a feminist.

Goodman, like Clayton, was seven years older than Lorde. A Jewish southerner originally from Hot Springs, Arkansas, she'd gone to college at the University of Wisconsin in the late forties, making her way to New York and graduate school at Columbia University in the early fifties. She began private practice in 1969 and worked as a consultant for the Department of Health, Education and Welfare from 1971 to 1972. In 1972, she co-founded the Institute for Human Identity in Manhattan, with which she was affiliated until 1976.

Goodman's was a maverick personality, and her practice of therapy blurred the lines between friendship and professional engagement. Not only did she become Lorde's therapist, she became Clayton's therapist, and Cook's and Coss's as well. Goodman exercised few, if any, boundaries, befriending them all and becoming part of their extended family. She ate dinner at Audre and Frances's house, accompanied them on short trips with their friends, and insinuated herself into their lives. As their therapist, she became part of their family meetings, participating on a fairly regular basis as their guide.

While relying on their extended family, Audre and Frances built into their parenting specified time without the children; they saved one month out of the summer for themselves, when Beth and Jonathan went to camp or to visit cousins in Washington, where Audre's sister Phyllis and her family now lived. Within the bounds of this structured freedom, Lorde continued to shape independent identities as lesbian and mother despite her public pairing of these personae.

By 1972, Adrienne Rich was back in Manhattan, living on the Upper West Side. After her return, she and Lorde began to see a lot of each other; they shared, in those early days, an eager support of the feminist movement and an association that was to develop into a significant, life-long friendship. Rich's work was now firmly engaged in the dynamic between social vision and personal, individual experience.[50] On those occasions when Lorde took a day's leave from her domestic life in Staten Island to come into the city and "visit the ladies,"[51] they'd meet for lunch—often at O'Neal's Balloon, a well-known midtown watering hole for the artistic crowd, across the street from Lincoln Center. "The ladies" also included Cook, Coss, and Yolanda Rios—with whom Lorde maintained an ongoing affair she deliberately kept secret from Clayton.[52]

In the past, Lorde had been open about her affairs, but Clayton was possessive. She was not as sexually experienced as Lorde, and did not subcribe to the idea of sex-with-friends that Lorde acted upon. Lorde led Clayton to believe their relationship was monogamous, but Clayton would find out over time that she'd been misled.

Although Rios would have preferred to be first in Lorde's life, her position as the "other woman" fed a mutual need. Lorde's trysts with Rios gave Rios false hope, gave her something over Clayton to dissipate her jealousy. Lorde needed to feel loved, constantly. She needed to feel respected, recognized, and desired. She equated sex with love—and with intimacy. Lorde believed she didn't really know a person unless she slept with them; she bedded, or attempted to bed, women she knew or was attracted to "as part of the challenge of friendship."[53] Her sexual aggressiveness was part of a need to control every aspect of her connection to other women.

DUDLEY RANDALL WAS well acquainted with the two books Lorde had already published. Gauging the greater impact of Broadside Press upon the careers of black American poets, Paul Breman asked Randall to publish her third, but initially Randall hesitated. Lorde and Randall's accounts as to why he hesitated differ significantly, yet the discrepancy between the two is defined by contradictions within the larger black social reality and not necessarily by variances in the truth, or by the personal dynamics between them.

In Randall's version of the moment, he feared publishing Lorde's manuscript would overextend Broadside Press's capabilities; and he was reluctant to do so until Gwendolyn Brooks intervened, convincing him otherwise. Brooks was Broadside's most distinguished poet and Randall was indebted to her for the unmitigated support she gave to his press. He had great respect for her, and her assessments of the work and merit of younger black poets influenced his own judgment.

Alternative presses, such as Breman's and Broadside, had nowhere near the publishing and marketing budgets available to mainstream houses. Still, Randall's fear was inconsistent with Broadside's impressive productivity. Between 1966 and 1972 alone, Broadside Press brought forth numerous books of poetry by Don L. Lee (Haki Madhubuti), Sonia Sanchez, Gwendolyn Brooks, Nikki Giovanni, Margaret Walker, Etheridge Knight, and Margaret Danner. As the most successful of the black independent presses, Broadside helped to shape the literary careers of Marvin X, Askia Muhammad Toure, Keorapetse Kgositsile, James Emanuel, and scores of lesser known poets. Commonly known as "the Broadside Press poets," the poets Randall promoted wrote within a prescribed blackness, which was nationalist and heterosexual. To publish a poet whose work already showed signs of lesbian engagement was risky, and would have "overextended" what the black community was "capable" of handling from its presses and chosen poets.

On a broader level, the black community was in the throes of the struggle for black liberation. Prominent, often self-appointed, spokespersons for the community publicly expressed an intolerance of homosexuality, perceiving it and other indices of difference—the women's liberation and gay liberation movements, for example—as divisive and furthering the community's vulnerability.[54]

Yet knowledge of homosexuals and homosexuality was not at all foreign to black people—many of whom personally knew an "aunt," "uncle," a "single" man or woman who was gay or lesbian. In the churches of many black working-class urban neighborhoods, black gay men, especially, had long been known to number among choir members, even as an embedded Christian ethic disavowed homosexuality. While "faggots" and "bulldaggers" were tolerated presences, their sexuality was not. They were not to articulate a public position as gay or lesbian and bring "attention" to themselves. It was privately known among black civil rights leaders that Bayard Rustin, one of Martin Luther King, Jr.'s lieutenants and an architect of the 1963 March on Washington, was gay, although he was not out.[55] Black entertainers whose careers openly pushed at the boundaries between gender and sexuality paid a price for doing so when they attempted to find employment outside their more liberal artistic circles.[56]

In Lorde's version of why Randall hesitated to publish her, Randall wanted to publish the collection but claimed not to understand one of the poems. The second stanza of "Love Poem" was explicitly lesbian and threatening to Randall's comfort level:

> And I knew when I entered her I was
> high wind in her forests hollow
> fingers whispering sound . . .[57]

After receiving her manuscript, Randall called her on the telephone, questioning her about the gender of the speaker in "Love Poem." She understood his question as homophobic. When she responded that she was expressing love for a woman, Randall asked her to delete this poem from the work.[58] Ultimately, Lorde acquiesced, sacrificing "Love Poem" for the prospect of another published book. Privately, she believed that acquiescence left her vulnerable, that she'd let Randall use her lesbianism against her; she felt betrayed by her own need for the black community's embrace. Even so, the personal dynamics between Lorde and Randall remained amicable.

Lorde's third collection, *From a Land Where Other People Live*, was published by Broadside Press in 1973. Once again, Lorde's poetry catalogued her preoccupations with birth, children, love, familial relationships, women. Yet her poetic voice had evolved. There was a maturity, flexibility, and meticulousness to it. With *From a Land Where Other People Live*, Lorde's voice shifted away from the seasons and earth as its general metaphors toward a more specific urban context. At the thematic matrix of that shift was Lorde's identity as black and woman, her anger at social injustice, and a recognition of the personal as global; all of which were essential to the book's—and Lorde's—power, becoming dominant subjects and metaphors she threaded through succeeding works.[59]

As a result of their mutual connection to Broadside Press, Lorde and Sonia Sanchez became friends. By 1973, Sanchez had published five books with Broadside, including *We a baddDDD people* (1970), a work that epitomized her early experiments with disrupting white English grammatical patterns and privileging black speech patterns. Sanchez was born in Birmingham, Alabama, the same year as Lorde. Her mother died when she was a year old, leaving Sonia and her sister to be raised by extended family members. She grew up stuttering and shy. As a child, Sanchez wrote poetry in her head, hiding whatever she did write down from a sister who derided it as "stupid stuff." When Sanchez was nine years old, her father moved them to Harlem. Like Lorde, Sanchez attended Hunter College, graduating with a degree in political science in 1955.[60]

During the 1960s, she emerged as one of the most militant black female poet-activists of the period. She exercised an innovative, razor-sharp poetic style that employed the use of chants simulating West African languages, which she felt recovered an oral tradition muted by the historic experience of black enslavement. Offering ear-splitting experiments with words and rhythm, Sanchez's early sound poems were anti–white America, and were forged by the influences of Malcolm X, black popular culture, and the Black Arts movement. Although recognized for her pro-black, revolutionary politics, Sanchez was criticized by both black and white people for being too strident.[61] In the late sixties, her political activism led to an association with the poet Etheridge Knight, who was in prison at the time. They were married and later divorced.

In the early 1970s, Sanchez joined the Nation of Islam, an organization well known for its inflammatory, anti-white rhetoric. Membership in the Nation brought Sanchez more criticism. The perception of Sanchez as a black woman who was beginning to operate outside of a prescribed blackness took hold after a 1972 production of her most popular play, *Sister Son/ji*, at the New York Shakespeare Festival Public Theatre. Essentially a monologue, the play exposed contradictions and weaknesses within the black revolutionary movement because of its anti–black woman ideology and practice. When Sanchez elaborated upon that theme in a subsequent play, *Uh Huh; But How Do It Free Us?* (1975), she voiced sentiments that were unpopular with black men in the movement and made her politically unpopular in certain quarters.

A prominent figure in New York's black literary circles before she moved to Massachusetts to teach at Amherst College, Sanchez was long aware of the rumors, if not the fact, of Lorde's lesbianism. Initially, her views on homosexuality reflected the homophobic climate of black "revolutionary" politics. Years later, Sanchez admitted she questioned then the significance of an articulated sexual politics to the liberation of black people.[62] But Sanchez's brother was gay—a fact she'd long known, yet never discussed. In time, Sanchez's alienation within the Black Arts movement framed her relationship with Lorde. As their association developed, it was defined by a common though dissimilar location as black women who were outsiders.

Lorde did not share Sanchez's spiritual and political perspectives, and she made that fact clear to Sanchez. Still, she welcomed the relationship between them, often offering generous, critical comments on Sanchez's work.[63] Lorde nurtured the evolving friendship in part because she respected Sanchez as a sister poet and freethinker but also because Lorde herself wanted to be recognized by heterosexual black women—a recognition that would both assuage her own alienation from the black community and serve the goal of solidarity she believed crucial to black women's liberation overall.

From a Land Where Other People Live was nominated for the 1974 National Book Award for poetry, a nomination shared by Adrienne Rich, Alice Walker, and Allen Ginsberg. The nomination gave Lorde and Broadside Press a certain literary currency. It was an influential factor in a second printing of the book by Broadside, which boasted the nomination on the jacket.

At the time, Alice Walker was also living in New York City and the three female recipients knew each other. After receiving news of their individual nominations, they spoke to each other by telephone. Seizing the moment as an opportunity to act jointly on their feminist politics, they made a pact and drafted a statement, promising each other should one of them be chosen, she would read the statement on behalf of the other two. When the award for poetry was announced, it went to Rich and Ginsberg, who, as co-winners, shared the 1974 prize. Walker did not attend the April 18 ceremony held in New York City, but Lorde did, joining Rich on stage. In keeping with the pact, Rich read their statement.

In content, it was a feminist manifesto proclaiming women's struggles for self-determination, and denouncing the historic silence imposed upon multiple communities of women. Rich accepted the award, noting the token recognition of women in American society:

> . . . We symbolically join together in refusing the terms of patriarchal competition and declaring that we will share this prize among us, to be used as best we can for women. We appreciated the good faith of the judges for this award, but none of us could accept this money for herself, nor could she let go unquestioned the terms on which poets are given or denied honor and livelihood in this world, especially when they are women. . . .[64]

Dudley Randall was also at the ceremonies. Lorde was gracious and introduced him to Rich. Afterwards, she and Randall were driven to a

celebration cocktail party at the Biltmore Hotel, in a limousine chauf-
feured by a representative of Rich's publisher.[65]

TOWARD THE LATTER part of April 1973, Lorde took a trip to Barbados,
where she "ran away to rest to be alone." As Barbados was the island of
her father's birth, the trip signaled a symbolic quest to get to know him
and his real home. She took with her a copy of Adrienne Rich's *Diving
into the Wreck*. Lorde's papers do not make clear whether she actually
sent the following letter to Rich, which was written that summer and
after the Barbados trip, but she recorded her feelings about Rich's latest
collection in her journal. "Dear Adrienne," she wrote in part, "I was so
lucky to have plucked it from my mailbox on the way to my plane—I
heard you sing. Out of the heart of me to my heart."[66]

Lorde's "letter" alluded to her attraction to Rich, whose "soft/sharp
beauty" she loved, and whose face flashed on and off for her between
Rich's "tough, welcome & tender" words. Measuring "the shrinking distance" between them as their developing friendship, Lorde was generous
with her feelings for Rich as poet, citing the hope, reassurance, and
vitality Rich's poetry ignited in her. "I am reminded that I am more whole
that circumstances and echos whould have me believe I am," she concluded, unmindful of her grammar or spelling, "and being reminded of
that I am become more whole still and more strong, more myself."[67]

Lorde arrived in Barbados on April 19, checking into a beach complex
off Hastings Road in Bridgetown. Although she could hear the water
right beyond the road, she was immediately disappointed that the rented
apartment had neither a view of the water nor was it right on the beach.
Even so, Lorde found Barbados "gorgeous." She was struck by the smell
of the island; by the sight of Barbadian school girls uniformed in brown
and gold minidresses, matching derby hats, and ties; and by the match-
box houses in endless variation and scale. On her first day, Lorde noted,
"the telephone calling is endless";[68] an indication that she was annoyed
by constant interruptions from Staten Island.

The following morning, Lorde rose early, intent upon greeting the day
with a swim. The beach was "empty and delicious"[69] and she was fascinated by the coral. While at the beach, she spotted a young boy with a

speargun and knife. She asked if he had been fishing. The boy told her he'd caught a baby octopus but would not go back into the water again that day, as island lore deemed it chancy to go into the water on Good Friday. Though she spent the morning on the beach, she took the boy's words to heart and did not go back in for another swim.

Touring the island by taxi, she saw cane growing everywhere; she noted the bend of the trees in one direction due to the constant persuasion of trade winds, and that away from the coast, the inland area was extremely hilly. Seeing this triggered a memory of language she'd no doubt heard her mother use: "up some hill & down some gully behind gods back." Observing the hilly terrain through her own eyes confirmed that what her mother saw "is for true."

The drive around the island took Lorde through the parish of St. James, where houses of varying shapes and sizes looked like dollhouses to her. The perception of them as dollhouses in "stages of repair and dis-repair" resonated with the symbolic aspect of her journey, which she obviously hoped would reconstruct her father's past, her own, and the psychic disrepair she felt still between them. While passing through, she had "the strangest feeling" that St. James was a part of her history and that "somewhere here my bones were being promised."[70] She could not help but wonder in which one of those "doll houses" the part of her that was her father began. Recording her intuitions later, Lorde placed quotation marks around them, as if her feelings had been told to her, literally. As on more than one occasion in Barbados, Lorde's intuitions about her father's past had the effect of apparitions: they came to her as both real and surreal.

Over the weekend, she acquainted herself with island life in Bridgetown proper, exploring its streets, tourist attractions, and shops on the Saturday. Finding the streets crowded, the morning heat too much and even the best shops unappealing, she thought the whole scene exemplified Frances's worst nightmares about New York. She reckoned the reason so many Barbadians had migrated elsewhere was because Barbados was overcrowded. She'd planned to go to Grenada while in the Caribbean, but discovered the Air Calypso office was closed on Saturday and would be closed on Monday as well, in observance of the Easter holiday. At the Pan American office, she learned the airline charged an additional U.S. $71 for first class. Although she'd been determined to fly first class to her mother's homeland no matter what, she couldn't bring herself to actually pay extra for the luxury.

Lorde was not necessarily frugal when it came to money, but she never had much beyond what was essential, was conscious of spending it and of her propensity for shopping. She "reported" her restraint to Clayton: "I have finally conquered—or been conquered—whichever, but no shopping this trip."[71] In the next breath, however, she confessed to having bought one pawpaw at the market and some trinkets at a Women's Self-Help Shop near the harbor. The shop sold flowers and embroidered handiwork by young and older women. Lorde rationalized her purchases as stemming from an inability to resist women, rather than a lack of self-restraint.

She spent the bulk of that Sunday lazing on the beach. Her excursion around Bridgetown the day before had left a bitter taste and she wanted to be away from its overcrowded hustle and bustle.

Several days later, on her last day, she made a pithy entry in her journal: "I can't go to Grenada after all."[72] She'd hoped to go to Grenada on Tuesday, April 24. Over the weekend, news of an airport strike and rioting there circulated around Barbados, as did rumors of minor gunfire and incidents involving thrown glass. When the airport closed down on Monday, passage between the two islands by boat became the only means of traveling; and by then, there was no more available space on the boats. The unlucky were stranded in Grenada until Tuesday. With the airport strike still unsettled, Lorde's chances of getting to Grenada before returning to the States became negligible, as did any hope of weaving up the holes in the quilts of her parents' lives.

Her time in Barbados coming to a close, Lorde began to feel sorry she would soon leave, but she missed Frances terribly. She was conflicted over whether or not to call home. On the one hand, she wanted to be called. On the other, she was paranoid about the telephone operator, convinced the operator was listening in on her calls. In the end, she decided not to make the call since talking by telephone was an insufficient replacement for having Frances there with her.

The morning before Lorde left Barbados, she made a visit to the registry in Bridgetown. She got there at 9:00 A.M. but was told to come back after noon. Killing time, she wandered about, noting there were fewer people out, less traffic, and the general atmosphere more casual than it had been the previous Saturday. She returned to the registry office promptly at noon.

There, after two and a half hours putting to the test her research skills as a librarian, she found no official record of her father's birth. The fruitless search raised several suspicious possibilities in Lorde's mind: his birth had not been registered (which she thought highly unlikely); someone made a mistake; her father was older than she thought he was, or younger; or someone had lied. Given the scant information she had and her understanding that he was twenty-six when her parents migrated to New York, Frederick Byron Lorde was probably born sometime around 1898. Lorde's journal notes abruptly end without clarifying whether or not she searched the registry's records of earlier years for proof of her father's birth. Nor do her notes indicate whether she in fact found proof of birth of others born around the same time, which would add credence to her suspicions. Lorde concluded that Frederick Byron Lorde was younger than her mother; and that Linda Lorde lied about her own age because she was older than Byron but couldn't admit to being so.

Although unable to close the gaps in her father's past, the week alone in Barbados had a restorative effect. In the absence of an official record, she'd discovered much she could associate with him: he'd come from this sun, this beach, this water. He'd come from this island, which had no quartz, but was rimmed with coral all around. He'd seen these cane fields, houses; these sheep who looked like goats and had no wool but whose coats were warm brown. He'd seen these coco palm trees. He'd surely heard that a coconut falling from a mature tree could kill you if it hit you on the head. He'd known of the mongoose imported to eradicate the rats which were a problem themselves now because they preyed upon domestic animals as well. Surely it was here that Byron Lorde learned the song, "Sly Mongoose—Dog Know Your Name," which Audre now remembered hearing him sing. And more than likely, it was here that her father's love of local politics, of political talk among men, was rooted in the saying, "Scratch a Bajan, find a politician."

He'd seen what was left of the plantations, where cane harvested by slaves was pressed by windmills; and may have known of the place that was once a separate island where smallpox victims were housed in the eighteenth and nineteenth centuries, but was now joined to the mainland as a touristy conglomerate of craftshops and houses called Pelican Village.

As the trip ended, she had to admit she loved having the week alone. Although Barbados was not her ideal island retreat when all things balanced out, Lorde still speculated, "I could even live here (thats the way I measure places)."[73] She'd heard Barbados was considered the most successful multiracial society amongst all the islands, with a population that was 92 percent black, 5 percent white, and 3 percent classified as "oriental" and mixed. But she wondered how Barbadians actually classified themselves, remarking upon seeing some whose skin tones were the color of her mother's and whose hair ranged from straight to kinky. She doubted just how "multiracial" Barbados really was. From what she'd seen, its racial stratification reflected its class structure. Hotel owners, shopkeepers, and others of the merchant class were almost always white and that unclassifiable mix of "light." Politicians were more frequently darker and all shades in between; but becoming a politician, she observed, seemed to be a road open to anyone clever enough—irrespective of skin color. In the parish of St. Johns, there were enclaves of very poor white people, most of whom were cane workers, living side by side with black people. They were descendants of the second wave of a conscripted class of whites who came to Barbados after indentured white labor was no longer profitable, when slave labor and sugar cane production were the basis of the island's economic structure in the mid-eighteenth century.

Lorde ended her notes with a final comment on avoiding writing about the previous evening. She'd smoked some marijuana after a telephone conversation with Clayton. The conversation had been unsatisfactory and she felt a drag or two would be a helpful farewell ritual as she packed. She'd spent the balance of the evening experiencing a stream of hallucinogenic fantasies, none of which she could trust to detail by writing them down.

BACK AT HOME, Lorde's reputation as poet was solidifying. In spite of the fact that her work was insufficiently known relative to her talent, she now published a string of poems in black periodicals, small literary magazines, and several anthologies. The emergence of feminist publications such as *Aphra, 13th Moon,* and *Amazon Quarterly* in the early seventies extended her readership in feminist and lesbian circles, and she responded to more requests to do readings for audiences of women. It was during one such reading in 1973, at a woman-owned combination bookstore-coffeehouse on West 72nd Street, that Lorde publicly came out as a lesbian.[74]

The bookstore-coffeehouse was packed with women, among them Adrienne Rich. Since giving in to Dudley Randall's editorial pressure, Lorde decided not to worry any more about who knew she was a lesbian.[75] She initially addressed this topic within the context of a feminist, rather than black community. For Rich, who was also in the process of coming out, it was "a staggering moment"[76] as Lorde dramatically delivered "Love Poem"—the poem Randall had objected to—in its entirety.

The reading gave dimension to Lorde's reputation as lesbian poet. As she and Rich individually shaped their public identities as lesbians over time and their friendship became a matter of public record, they were often asked to read together, to appear on the same bill at benefits, speak-outs, and conferences, linked as feminists, cultural icons, and poets whose publishing careers had been long and consistent by then.[77] One black, the other Jewish, they conveniently fit a desire within the movement to be seen as integrated.

Lorde's public claim to a lesbian identity was a process of intertwining moments. "Love Poem" appeared in the February 1974 issue of *Ms.* magazine, which brought her lesbianism to the attention of a wider feminist audience. After its publication, she tore the poem from the magazine and tacked it up in the English Department at John Jay. Her motivation for doing so was self-protective. By then, the debate over black studies there had been complicated by a separate demand for Puerto Rican studies, which led to discussions on creating two new academic divisions instead of one. She'd opposed initiatives to wed the two at an administrative level. Lorde's uncompromising stance had put her at odds with more moderate colleagues, leaving her with few allies, especially in the English Department, where she now perceived her colleagues as enemies. She believed they were attempting to discredit her among the black students, amongst whom her militant racial stance made her quite popular. She'd posted her poem to defuse efforts to use her lesbianism against her;[78] and also to have the upper hand that honesty afforded.

Her fear of being rejected by the black students fueled the images of "Blackstudies," a poem she began drafting in 1973:

> In a room on the 17th floor my spirit is choosing
> I am afraid of speaking
> the truth . . .

The foundation for the poem had been built at Tougaloo, her experience there a constant referent as Lorde recognized its recurring impact. Facing down the certain isolation and rejection that admitting open lesbianism to any constituency of the black community would engender, she grappled with the cost of honesty:

> I do not want to lie. I have loved other
> tall young women deep into their colour . . .
>
> I am afraid
> that the mouths I feed will turn against me . . .

The architecture of the finished poem permitted Lorde a flight into honesty, and into herself as black woman–mother–teacher:

> . . .
> My students wait outside my door . . .
> for what I am sworn to tell them . . .
>
> Stepping into my self
> I open the door . . .[79]

Although not one of the poems she became best known for, "Blackstudies" marked a significant turning point in Lorde's relationship to the black community. As with "Love Poem," it fused the erotic as a source of power to other themes in her work.

After *From a Land Where Other People Live* garnered the National Book Award for poetry nomination, Dudley Randall was anxious to publish Lorde's next book; he coaxed her to let him see another manuscript, which she did. Thematically, *New York Head Shop and Museum* was sufficiently "black" to make Randall comfortable with Lorde's ever complex and textured blackness. But Lorde was more confident now and insisted her next book would have to include "Love Poem." This time, Randall acquiesced.

When *New York Head Shop and Museum* was published by Broadside in 1974, it signaled Lorde's mounting self-confidence as a poet. The voice elaborated upon the maturer voice in *From a Land Where Other People Live*. The urban landscape upon which Lorde gazed was an hallucinogenic nightmare: in "A Sewerplant Grows in Harlem," New York City's children succumb to drugs, the invisible make themselves visible in scrawls of graffiti, and the environment defecates upon all human hope:

> . . .
>
> Have you ever risen in the night
> bursting with knowledge and the world
> dissolves toward any listening ear . . .[80]

With this publication, Lorde altered her personality as poet, emerging as a more authoritative, powerful speaker, one for whom the power of self-determination became a focus. Several of the poems remarked upon this added dimension to Lorde's voice, but none more clearly than "Blackstudies," with which the book concluded. An intricate, five-part narrative, abounding with images of demons, fallen gods, outgrown myths, and references to a blackness she would not swallow uncritically ("Visions of chitterlings I never ate/strangle me in a nightmare of leaders/at crowded meetings to study our problems"),[81] it prophesied Lorde's rebirth as poet, woman, and maker of her own myths. As she put it in another poem, "New York City 1970":

> For how else can the self become whole
> save by making self into its own new religion?[82]

New York Head Shop and Museum marked an end to Lorde's relationship with Broadside Press, though she was recognized by the press in
1975 with its Broadside Poets Award. The reasons were not specified by
either Lorde or Randall, but Lorde's deepening involvement with the
feminist movement certainly lay at the heart of her shift away from the
heterosexist reputation of the press and the poets it generally published.

LORDE HAD ALWAYS wanted to go to Africa. The time was never more
right than now: the house was in good shape; her life with Clayton and the
children was established; both she and Clayton were financially stable
enough to afford to bring the entire family on the trip. She'd turned forty
that year and her fourth book was out. As the semester at John Jay drew to
a close, she canvassed friends for names to contact while in Africa, taking
into account suggestions that she carry copies of her books with her.

Having taught herself African history, Lorde felt her ancestors originated on the continent's west coast,[83] the focal point of the Atlantic slave
traffic. She had no specific genealogical evidence for her intuitions,
which were part of a broader search for a place she could belong to spiritually. She had not yet been to Grenada, but before leaving for Africa,
Lorde tried to find out from her family's older members what, if any, stories had survived and might affirm her belief that Grenadians had
retained some West African culturalisms.

Lorde and her brood left New York City on July 13, 1974, on an Air
Afrique flight, bound for a five-week tour of Africa, including Togo,
Ghana, and Dahomey (renamed the People's Republic of Benin in 1975).
Lorde saw herself "living through a moment that was unreal"—the
dream-reality sensation amplified by having set herself free from a sense
of being "anchored." The trip marked an opportunity to actualize her
"longest dream," but this dream's reality was embedded in a region of
Africa in the throes of postcolonialism.

When their plane landed in Dakar, Senegal, to refuel, its passengers
were deplaned. Lorde's first impressions of Africa were idyllic images of
the bustling airport at dawn, full of beautifully attired Senegalese and
fashionable young women sporting intricate, braided hairstyles. The
sight of so many slender bodies immediately made her conscious of her

own size. She was also conscious of the fact that it had been "a long time since I've been surrounded by a language I could not speak."[84] Although armed with a few phrases essential to the tourist, her unfamiliarity with French reminded her of being in Mexico, where she'd had only the rudiments of Spanish to rely on. The language barrier was disconcerting; but a day later, when they were in Lome, the capital of Togo, she felt "impatient and peaceful both at the same time."[85]

Once they were settled into their rooms at the Hotel Le Benin, Audre sent a telegram home. The handwritten version was addressed to Mrs. Linda Lorde, but then Audre thought twice about sending it to her mother, scratching out her mother's name and replacing it with her sister Helen's name and address. The telegraphed message was brief:

> Arrived safely at beautiful Lome.
> Love
> Audre[86]

In Lome, she was impatient to experience the city, its smells and people, and the sense of peacefulness she had was one of being "near a home part of me."[87] Although the quick descent of nightfall there reminded her of Barbados, Lorde did not like Lome in fact. A sea of French-speaking people crowded its streets, and little boys fascinated with Beth made her leery of male attention to Beth for the first time: "I am finding it very very disconcerting & threatening the way men & boys hit—however gently & gallantly—on Beth."[88]

To her, the Hotel Le Benin was an expensive tourist trap, with dull food. At the hotel and on the street, the Togolese she encountered were less interested in her than in her tourist dollars. Save for a museum and cathedral they visited on their second day, there was little to see and little evidence of craft culture. She concluded Lome had a Coney Island-esque quality ("This is really Far Rockaway"),[89] and before leaving, she noted, "I really very much feel Lome lives on others' leavings."[90] Still, Lorde carried away from Lome what was for her a recurring image in its variations: a woman busy with fetching water, accompanied by a younger woman or older one, washing her pots or baby in the street at dawn before going to the market.

Lorde and her family arrived in Accra, Ghana, on July 18, after three hours aboard a crowded bus that was stopped frequently and during which their passports were constantly checked since the road between Togo and Ghana was the focus of a border war. Lorde immediately felt looser and freer, and she was happy to be in an English-speaking, much friendlier country. After one night's stay at the University of Ghana in Akuafo Hall, however, the hard single cots and bugs in the room reminded her of Mexico City and she felt too old to be so uncomfortable now. The next morning, they all agreed better accommodations were in order. They lucked out with a comfortable, two-bedroom chalet that became available only after she produced the children; their presence convinced the hotel receptionist that she and Clayton were not just a couple of strange street prostitutes.

Ghana was closer to that "home part" of Africa Lorde was searching for. Being there affected her sensually. She was fascinated by the natural landscape. She inhaled the constant aroma of corn and plantain baking; the corn growing everywhere had a heady smell that was dry and rich. The smell of Accra, its food, the proud, erect bearing of women carrying their wares on their heads, all reminded her of Barbados. Once, while dining in Kumasi, the rock cake dessert drew her back to the memory of Newton's—a West Indian bakery in Harlem where her mother bought rock buns sweetened with the taste of Grenada.

She came to learn that the sandstone she saw was called laterite, a deep red rock. As they traveled along the roads, the red dust that clung to their hands and hair was from the laterite; though they washed away the earth red color daily, it was the color that permeated the creative consciousness of West Africa and so much of the African art she saw.

Ghana offered Lorde cultural knowledge Togo had not; it was there that she felt, "I've inherited a wealth of treasures and new ways."[91] Ghana introduced Lorde to the culture of its Akan peoples; to their brassmaking arts and aesthetics; to the *akua'ba*, the fertility dolls carried by pregnant women to ensure the birth of beautiful children. Each craft village she visited had its own specialty. In the villages of Darboa, Pankrono, Awhia, and Bonwire, she witnessed how beads, pots, stools, and kente cloth were made. Lorde was particularly fascinated with the adinkra cloths of the Asante: the elaborate, traditionally hand-stenciled symbolic designs were individually named, and were proverbs encoding historical, allegorical, or magical information.[92] Many of the stamped messages were variations of phrases she remembered hearing from her mother and other Grenadian kin.[93]

Visits to historic landmarks and museums were high on her agenda. Every city they went to, they visited at least one as Lorde searched for the spirit of Africa she had traveled more than seven thousand miles to find. At the Shrine of Kumfuo Anokye, they were let in to see the OBosom Dan, the fetish room. There they were told the ways of the spells by a very old man who spoke no English, but through a translator told them also of the tortoises sacred to the Asante and the Tree of God, the four branches of which were the points on a compass. Outside the white walls of Castle Osu, old Christiansborg, Lorde and her family looked upon the grave of W. E. B. Du Bois. Standing at Du Bois's gravesite just fifty yards away from the Atlantic Ocean, Lorde began to visualize, for the first time, what had taken place on Africa's west coast three hundred years before.[94]

The emotional realities of the African slave trade, and the participation of Africans in it, hit hard again during a Cape Coast tour to Saõ Jorge d'El Mina Castle, the infamous holding pen built by the Portuguese. Situated on the beach only yards from the dark, furious waters of a foreboding Atlantic Ocean, *El Mina* ("the Mine") had been originally intended to house a wealth of gold the Portuguese expected to plunder from Africa's "Gold Coast." By the sixteenth century, the "gold" it stored was black flesh.[95] Led by their Ghanian guide, Felice Rockson, Audre, Frances, Beth, and Jonathan descended down into levels of a bat-infested dungeon, reliving, as Rockson conjured it, the horrific history palpable in its smell and walls.

For Lorde, there remained "old old dreams in the stone of Elmina."[96] At the deepest level, the bats were populous; and there they saw an altar lit by a single candle, erected as a monument to those Africans who disappeared in the slave trade. Jonathan found the experience upsetting[97] and Beth believed she could see the docked sailboats of European slavers, the exodus of the confused and captured, and could feel the spirits of the African prisoners.[98] *El Mina* felt sacred to Lorde and she could write neither about it or Cape Coast in her journal. "The pen in anything but poetry," she summarized her feelings, "would dwarf if [sic]."⁹⁹

In Ghana, as in Lome, Lorde was fascinated with fleeting, almost mythic, visions of African women who appeared in stark juxtaposition to contemporary scenes. One morning in Accra, on their way to visit the library and the British Arts Council, they passed a young woman Lorde described as "black & nubile & naked except for a string."¹⁰⁰ She was in front of Parliament House, a modern-looking edifice of white stone located on the busy 28th February Road. The woman was washing herself in the street, with water from a small bowl. Near her was a small pile of cloths. An hour later, on their way back, she was still there, mirage-like, squatting in the gutter as she pounded and mixed a concoction of leaves and herbs upon a flat stone. All the while, the heavy morning traffic slowed and detoured around her, neither she nor it disrupted by the other's presence. Such moments were obvious comments upon a clash between the traditional and modern worlds of postcolonial Africa, and Lorde's need for the mythic competed with reality.

Indeed, at the market in Accra, Lorde encountered Ghanaian women who were shrewd businesswomen despite their traditional assignment in the market arena. During her first attempt at bargaining, Lorde got such a tongue-lashing from one cloth dealer, she decided then and there never to attempt bargaining again, partly because she was embarrassed and partly because the woman was a much more formidable force than she had imagined encountering.

The realities of Ghanaian women's lives were both confined by tradition and hidden beneath it. After seeing a play one night, Beth kept asking where all "the women warriors" were, acknowledging what she'd been told but had not yet seen. Several days later, Lorde wondered where they were, too, remaining hopeful she would find them: "I am looking forward to finding some woman legends."¹⁰¹

If the presence of "women warriors" and even everyday women was hard to ascertain, this was in direct correlation to the near invisibility of Ghanaian women writers and their literature. By 1974, Ama Ata Aidoo, perhaps Africa's best known woman writer and a native of Ghana, had published two plays, *The Dilemma of a Ghost* (1965) and *Anowa* (1969), and a collection of short stories, *No Sweetness Here* (1970), all initially published in Europe by the London publisher, Longman. In short, until the second half of the 1960s, African literature was defined and dominated by male writers. As a group, their greater access to the tools of literacy and education (particularly abroad), as well as their location as men arising out of deeply gendered societies in which women were expected to assume traditional roles as wives and mothers, provided the basis for a sustained literary productivity. That sociocultural history shaped an image of the African writer as male, and established male characters as the traditional and central subjects of African literature. The appearance of Flora Nwapa's novel *Efuru* on the Nigerian literary scene in 1966 coincided with the publications of Aidoo, and work by the two women pioneered the emergence of complex female African characters who were central to their own narratives, defying the traditional expectations both as Africans and as contemporary women. Still, at the time of Lorde's visit to Ghana, African women writers were little known and a social anomaly. When Lorde appeared, unannounced, at the Arts Council to leave copies of her book, she was disheartened: "I'm tired of offering my books to places & hands that don't know me or really want them."[102] Although she rationalized her disappointment by noting she had not expected to be greeted with open arms, Lorde's ego was bruised at the perceived lack of interest in her work.

As she traveled through West Africa, her search for an ancestral female self, for "some woman legends," became the basis for a deeper realization of the unity of the male and female energies in African thought, if not practice. That unity was the erotic core of an African ancestral self. One afternoon at the Cultural Center in Kumasi, during a performance of traditional dance and song, Lorde observed that many of the dancers were older women and men. What struck her about their dancing was the fluidity of sexual energy between them, the complementary understanding between their hands, bodies, and feet that simultaneously eroticized the feminine and masculine and eternally linked them. Much of what she experienced in Ghana would make its way into her poetry, though Lorde did not write any poems while in Africa, storing away these images and experiences until her return to the States.

Nearly a month had passed by the time Lorde and her troupe were touring Dahomey. By then, the wear and tear of the trip had become an issue. Lorde expected Beth and Jonathan to handle being in Africa, but culture shock, the fact of their young ages (Beth eleven, Jonathan ten), and the length and exhaustive nature of the trip itself sometimes conspired against their best efforts. Being in Africa was certainly no vacation for them. They rose early in the mornings and went to bed late. They had to adjust to hotel and travel conditions, could not drink the water, and the local food, which delighted Lorde's palate, was often too spicy for them. At times, they were irritable, mischievous, or quarreled with each other.

Jonathan's journal gave a day-by-day account of their activities, since Lorde required them to write in their journals daily or draw a picture of what the day had been like. Though he took to much of the sightseeing, he was sick more than anyone else and at varying times was affected by the heat, the food, or simply bored—especially on days when they spent considerable hours in their hotel rooms or traveling between countries. In Lome, he found the fact that his and Beth's room was connected to Lorde and Clayton's constricting because they couldn't make noise and be themselves. In general, he was happier whenever the living arrangements gave him and Beth some freedom from the physical proximity of the grown-ups.

Jonathan's account of the market scene in Accra between Lorde and the cloth dealer pointed to the strain between his mother and Clayton he sometimes witnessed: when Lorde stopped to buy and bargain after she herself had said there was to be no buying, Clayton became angry and the two of them got into a heated argument; then Clayton left Lorde and the children at the market and returned to their chalet.[103] As the trip wore on, moments of tension between Lorde and Clayton affected him as they alternately, or leniently, exercised authority. He and Frances, especially, got on each other's nerves. Early in the trip, during one of their family meetings, he'd been told he was selfish, which he found disturbing, and he wrestled with that perception for the balance of their stay in Africa.

His journal also recorded how much he and Beth relied on each other, since they often were separated from the grown-ups at bedtime, between meals, and between activities. Once in Kumasi, the leg on Beth's bed broke as she rolled over. The two of them tried, unsuccessfully, to fix it. When their mother came in and discovered the broken bed, she was so angry she accused Beth of being a liar. Jonathan immediately came to his sister's defense, protecting Beth's integrity and testifying to the truth of her story. In Abomey, Dahomey, as Lorde and Clayton lingered at a craftshop, Beth was surrounded on the street by a group of African children who begged for chewing gum. Beth gave away all she had, but when there was no more, they began to hit her. Again Jonathan came to her defense, distracting the children by handing over his own supply of gum. As well as being protective of his sister, he was generally appalled by what he saw of African street children, perceiving them as greedy and irritating. Like his mother, he was conscious of the attention Beth got from boys, but what he saw was that Beth liked it. By the time they were in Dahomey, he was tired of being nice and vacillated between liking Africa and wanting to be home.

In general, Lorde was much less protective of her son than her daughter in Africa. Beth was hardly ever out of her mother's sight. During a taxi ride back to their chalet one evening in Accra, Jonathan sat up front with two young men. When one of them put his arm around Jonathan, Lorde viewed the gesture as gentle rather than disconcerting or threatening, and symbolic of people's friendliness, particularly when one of the young men told Jonathan he thought the boy had an African face. But even at home, and as he grew older, being a boy in a lesbian household meant that Jonathan often had to fend for himself.

Though Lorde raised both her children to view themselves as black, in West Africa Beth was particularly aware just how American they were. She became conscious of the conditions under which Africans lived; of having more money, especially for candy and chewing gum, than African children had. A servant class of Africans waited on them in hotels. At one point in Ghana, Beth and Jonathan were severely chastised by Lorde for eating some chocolate in the hotel lobby and being unmindful of the African children close by, staring at them. When Lorde came down to the lobby, she was furious and near tears as she whisked them away to their room. She was ashamed that they had not offered the other children any chocolate; punishing them for acting like ugly Americans, she banished both to their room for the balance of that day. At other times, she understood that Frances was constantly nagging the children about their manners and behavior, that they were not enjoying Africa as much as she was but were trying to. Africa notwithstanding, it was hard for them to make friends generally. When they behaved according to her expectations, she felt warmly toward them.

Lorde did not believe Frances was at all happy being in Africa, but she didn't know what to do about that because it seemed to her that Frances wasn't really expressing her feelings. Also, Frances seemed most at ease when they stayed indoors, especially at the chalet where they all played card games. When Lorde observed Clayton reading a book or magazine from home, she assumed Clayton was just biding her time. Lorde thought Clayton wanted time alone, together, away from the kids, but they were in a foreign country and she didn't want to do that. She felt they were struggling to work out their communication problems, despite periods of not speaking to one another. Lorde's perception of Clayton's moods, or of how Clayton experienced being in Africa, made her impatient with Clayton when she wrote about their interactions in her journal.

Differences in how they were treated based on race were a problem, too. In Ghana, particularly, where she'd presumed racial kinship between herself and the black population, Audre was deeply offended when waiters and hotel personnel served Frances first or looked to Frances to make decisions or pay the bill, ignoring her. The assumption that theirs was an employer-servant relationship in which the power dynamic favored Clayton was humiliating to her. At times, both attempted to disrupt that assumption by playing up moments in which Frances acted out the part of a white woman serving a black one, making a point of leaning over and grandly lighting Audre's cigarette in full view of any African watching.

Nevertheless, in Dahomey, Lorde found keys to the Africa she was looking for. While staying at the Hotel Du Port in Cotonou, Dahomey's largest city and chief port, she and her brood took in some of their last sights of Africa. They toured Cotonou, Porto-Novo (the capital), and Ouidah, a former "Slave Coast" city-state where Africans captured inland were brought, examined by ship surgeons, and then branded on the breast with the identifying marks of the French, English, or Dutch companies so each nation could distinguish its property from that of the others.[104] Lorde felt Ouidah was the spiritual center of Dahomey, and more than any other place in Africa, she felt that Dahomey was home. There, in the synthesis of Yoruba and Dahomean deities, she found what she believed was the religion of her foremothers and her spiritual connection to them. She found Seboulisa, the goddess of Abomey (once the inland capital of ancient Dahomey), who was worshipped as "the mother goddess of all." She found Oshumare, the Yoruba rainbow-snake deity, who signified unity between aggression and compassion. Oshumare was also known as *Da Ayido Hwedo* to the Fon people of Dahomey, for whom the deity signified the union of female and male energies and was sometimes represented as a pair of twins. She learned of Oboto, the sea-goddess, *Yemoja-Oboto* to the Yoruba. She found Mawu-Lisa, the highest deity of the Fon, whose combination of female (*Mawu*) and male (*Lisa*) aspects represented the union of the Moon and the Sun as a Fon ideal.[105]

For Lorde, the spiritual knowledge of Dahomey revealed the connections binding the deities of Dahomey to the Yoruba pantheon, which had traveled with and been transformed by the spiritual practices of African captives throughout the African diaspora. Constructing her own version of "Africa reblended"[106] once she got back home, Lorde transformed the name of the Ewe-Fon sea-goddess, Avrekete,[107] into the phonetic "Afrekete"; thereafter she signed much of her correspondence: "In the hands of Afrekete."

The day before they were to leave Dahomey, she had her hair styled in the tight narrow braids wrapped with thread known to Dahomean women as *akai*. Leaving Dahomey, and Africa, saddened her, and she wasn't ready to go. But Lorde took from Africa what she needed: a spiritual location; the knowledge of original ancestors; a corporeal reality that was unique, timeless, and complex; and a lust to operate upon the world's stage. When her time in Africa was over, Africa in Lorde had just begun.

EIGHT

T HE AFRICA LORDE brought back became the stage upon which
her public persona emerged in the late 1970s: she increasingly
appeared at readings and in public wearing a dashiki shirt and a
gele, the signature head wrap of African women. She was adorned in
beads and jewelry. She became living proof of African foremothers and
of their spiritual fusion within her. Lorde became her "own new religion."[1] As a reader and speaker, she was masterful—her delivery elo-
quent, her intonation musical. She embodied "the erotic," and this
vision proved critically necessary for other lesbians and feminists.
Lorde's embrace of the erotic as a source of resistance was consistent
with her identity as outsider. But embracing that identity meant negotiating contradictions related to her family and work, which in turn
shaped more complex meanings of the term "outsider."

In the months after her return, though, Lorde wrestled with a bout of
depression and despair. She dreaded being back at John Jay. She was
unsure if her depression was related to Jonathan and his emotional well-
being growing up in a household of females[2] with lesbian parents.

Jonathan was now ten years old, and seeing his father only intermittently. She understood that the balance of power at home favored Beth,
a scenario she increasingly felt needed to be corrected for Jonathan.
She'd introduced Jonathan to Robert Turner as a friend of hers, telling
her son that she thought Bob would be a good person for him to hang
out with. Exactly when and how Robert Turner became a "friend" of
Lorde's is unclear, but it is reasonable to speculate that Lorde, a
resourceful person, had sought him out, met him in advance, and
trusted him enough to entrust her son to him; hoping that by befriending
Jonathan, Turner would prove to be someone masculine Jonathan could
look up to and confide in.

A tall, friendly, rather muscular black man, with a mustache,
Turner—who was living with a white woman—was in fact a perfect big
brother surrogate. On Saturday mornings, Lorde took Jonathan to the
Staten Island ferry, where he rode alone across to Manhattan carrying
with him an envelope for Turner. Turner would meet Jonathan at the
ferry, then spend several hours taking him to the zoo, to the park, or to
his house in Manhattan; at his home he encouraged Jonathan to talk as
they built models of airplanes, ships, and artillery guns.[3]

Lorde also suspected that another source of her depression was
Frances Clayton. The tensions between them during the trip to Africa
were fresh in her mind. She loved Frances, but resented her lack of self-
direction.

Lorde wanted to put some distance between herself and her therapist Bernice Goodman, telling Goodman she would not see her for a
while. Part of the ambiguity she felt toward Goodman was complicated by her sexual fantasies about Goodman. As Goodman continued
to act non-traditionally, she clouded rather than clarified issues; this
left Lorde with mixed feelings about an entangling, all-encompassing
relationship.

Moreover, she felt slighted by *Black World* (formerly *Negro Digest*)
recently. When she searched the September 1974 issue, she found no
mention of *New York Head Shop and Museum*. She wanted, once again,
to stop caring about being recognized by the black community, to be
someday freed of that need.

Lorde encouraged Beth and Jonathan to be thinking people rather than children for whom someone else did all their thinking. She explained the world to them as she thought it should be; and exploded into a rage, not only at their tormentors but often at them, when they suffered any indignation, any pain, she could not immediately remedy. It infuriated her to be reminded of their pain as outsiders. The reality of their alienation was surely on her mind as she fine-tuned "Now Am I Stranger Within"[4] in her journal (a play, perhaps, on the title of her earlier poem, "Now that I Am Forever with Child"), later changing the title to "School Note":

> . . .
>
> My children play with skulls
> at school
> they have already learned
> to dream of dying . . .[5]

As the year ended, Lorde recorded fragments of several poems, distilling into them her experiences in Africa, the children's lives, herself. Significantly, the most complete were drafts of the poem about her children and one invoking Seboulisa, the Dahomean goddess. Lorde was convinced that a maternal, spiritual bloodline had been revealed to her in Dahomey—one which had been subconscious, but which was now a useful conscious reality. As "mother goddess of all," Seboulisa embodied an archetypal African foremother. She was also legendary for having one breast, the other having been eaten away by worms of sorrow. Lorde adopted Seboulisa as her spiritual mother. With the winter upon her and her depression aggravated, she called on Seboulisa for comfort:

> . . . Give me the woman strength
> Of tongue in this cold season . . .[6]

On March 21, 1975, Lorde's divorce from Rollins was finalized on grounds of irreconcilable differences. Lorde appeared at the County Courthouse in Manhattan, with her attorney, Harold M. Weiner. Neither Rollins nor his attorney, Ernest Neidorff, appeared. Rollins had not been present on January 30, and had not answered a court summons.

The presiding judge, Seymour Bieber, awarded Lorde custody of the children, $365 in child support due (which Rollins had not paid while they were in Africa), and $750 for legal fees.[7] Lorde insisted the divorce papers decree she could resume the use of her maiden name, which she'd used inconsistently. Thereafter, both the title and copyright pages of her books bore only the name Audre Lorde.[8] She celebrated her freedom with Clayton, Cook, and Coss. Cook and Coss brought a huge cake, decorated with a tongue-in-cheek inscription: "To Audre, the gay divorcee."

Several months after deciding to put some distance between herself and Bernice Goodman, Lorde vacillated about remaining in therapy. She believed she no longer needed Goodman as mentor, that she'd learned all she could from her. Lorde felt that Goodman focused less and less on her real pains: the enduring sense of rejection she experienced from her mother; the sense that though she'd divorced him, Rollins had replaced her in her mother's life; that his whiteness and maleness made him the third child her mother always wanted, rather than her; as well as the terrible, generalized isolation she endured. And Goodman left a lot to be desired as a therapist. She confused Clayton and Lorde, calling Lorde "Clayton" during therapeutic sessions. Nor did Lorde want to be reduced to the sum of her longings and her pains, which was Goodman's focus, but which she thought "noble in context, and only in context do they have meaning to the others who will come to read and seek illuminations after I am dead, and they are in their time of growth." Over the course of their sessions, Lorde had come to understand that the pain and isolation she felt would neither destroy nor immobilize her. Nor were they consistent or forever. She was strongly attracted to Goodman; and she could see beyond her "endless fantasies" of Goodman, a woman who was alternately beautiful and ugly, wise and foolish.[9] But Lorde was torn between realizing Goodman's limitations and remaining in therapy—for her own sake and for Clayton's. She finally decided to continue as Goodman's patient.

By 1975, Lorde was becoming better known, a fact that fueled her ambitions as a poet. She felt she had prominence and stature now, but the appearance of her poems only in periodicals and small magazines confined her work to a limited audience. She believed she had a bigger audience and could reach it. She also believed her books, all published by small presses, were hampered by poor distribution. Lorde's poetic accomplishment was not in question, but she was caught in the paradox between wanting to be seen as a genuine artist and known as a celebrity. Driven in part by ego and in part by talent, Lorde believed she now deserved better. Affiliating herself with a mainstream publishing house required getting a literary agent. Her friends—including Bernice Goodman and her gynecologist, Marcia Storch—suggested she contact Charlotte Sheedy, a feminist.

Sheedy had been employed in publishing for some years, starting out as a secretary and working her way up to editor. As an editor, she handled what were called "women's interest books"—books on fashion, gardening, cooking, and decorating. During the sixties, she became a radical activist, whose involvement with the antiwar movement led to draft counseling and jail. After the 1968 assassinations of Martin Luther King, Jr., and Robert Kennedy, Sheedy began to see the publishing work she was doing as insignificant. In addition, she had three small children and was leaving her husband. Sheedy wanted to teach history at that point, and she decided to return to school. In 1970, she began at Columbia University as a graduate student intent on teaching history at the college level.[10]

While at Columbia, she supported herself and her children by becoming a literary scout for a number of publishers. One of them, Dial Press, had first-refusal rights on any manuscripts she brought in, but she could sell the manuscripts that Dial turned down to other publishers. After nearly four years of going to school during the day and working at night proofreading, copyediting, and reading manuscripts, Sheedy began to believe she'd made a terrible mistake. It could take ten more years to get a PhD and she would be fifty by then. She was hideously in debt and had three children to raise. One night at dinner with Joyce Johnson, an editor at Dial to whom she'd sold a number of books, Sheedy confessed her dilemma: she was about to be forty, she couldn't continue in school, she believed her radical past made getting a conventional job impossible, and her children were in school and she needed to be home with them.

Johnson suggested Sheedy work from home as a literary agent, and that she canvass the authors whose books she'd placed to see if they would let her represent them. Although she had been in publishing thirteen years by then, Sheedy felt she knew nothing about being an agent, but when she began making calls to authors the very next day, the responses were all positive. After that, she charged some stationery to a credit card and started representing authors. She rose at 6:00 A.M. so no one would see her delivering manuscripts on her bicycle because she didn't have money for postage. In 1974, she opened her own agency. When she met Lorde in 1975, the agency was somewhat established and her clients were primarily feminist academics.

Sheedy had read Audre Lorde's work and knew of her nomination for the National Book Award. Even before meeting Lorde, Sheedy thought her a gifted poet, with real possibilities for becoming a politically important, well-known writer. She was flattered when Lorde came to see her. From the first day that Lorde walked into Sheedy's West 86th Street office, Sheedy agreed to represent her, becoming Lorde's only literary agent in life and remaining so after her client's death.

Lorde was the first poet Sheedy represented. Few agents represented poets in those days since poetry offered prestige but not profit. But Sheedy's feminist politics and her belief in the quality of Lorde's poetry drove the working relationship, and friendship, between them.[11]

Sheedy began sending Lorde's manuscript, "Coal," to major publishers. At the time, white publishers and white agents paid little attention to poets generally, and less to black poets. Despite the outpouring of black writing in the sixties, few white publishers considered black poetry a viable market. Lorde's work was rejected by a number of them.

In part, Lorde viewed Sheedy as someone who could ease her way in the publishing world and act as a buffer, but she was in no sense a typical client. She made her own decisions, never relinquished authority over her work, and often gave it away or signed contracts without Sheedy's knowledge.[12] During her early days with Sheedy, Lorde gave several poems to Diane di Prima to publish. Di Prima was living in California by then. Though her Poets Press had disbanded in 1969, she resumed publishing activities in 1974, establishing Eidolon Editions, another alternative press. Di Prima had a grant from the National Endowment for the Arts, wanted to publish Lorde, and asked her to submit something. At work on many of the poems later to comprise *The*

Black Unicorn, Lorde sent di Prima a manuscript containing just seven poems. It was a curious, if not mercurial, decision, considering that Lorde now believed the small press route meant being published in a small way. She didn't tell Sheedy about this manuscript until much later, when it was about to be published as *Between Our Selves*. Then Lorde shrugged off not informing Sheedy first, dismissing it as just a few poems she gave di Prima for her little press, and not important.

Unlike the first time she had published with di Prima, Lorde did not leave the jacket design to di Prima's discretion but sent her own drawing, depicting two crocodiles whose trunks intersected. This was an Asante adinkra symbol she'd discovered in Ghana. The proverb translated into "they share one stomach yet they fight over food." Lorde also chose an Asante symbol for a linguist's staff for the frontispiece: a bird looking backward, meaning "mistakes can be corrected." The proverbs were the subtext that wove the collection together, and reflected the process of Lorde's spiritual transformation in Africa. She dedicated *Between Our Selves* "for Frances," borrowing from "School Note" a vision of the difficult life they faced:

> *for the embattled*
> *there is no place*
> *that cannot be*
> *home*
> *nor is.*[13]

As the collection's "last word," Lorde included an appealing head shot of herself, like a neo-adinkra symbol, wearing African attire.

Widely ignored by critics of Lorde's work, *Between Our Selves* was a significant, concise collection, which introduced an African-based spiritualism that was infusing and transforming Lorde's poetry. In "Solstice," for example, references to the ritualized use of drinking pots and straw baskets, and to guardian "spirits / who are angered by our reluctance / to feed them," signaled Lorde's desire to reflect traditional beliefs of the connection between the living and ancestral worlds.[14]

The seven poems in *Between Our Selves* shaped some of the questions and paradoxes Goodman's therapy had not succeeded in untangling for her. In one—"Outside"—she wove through feelings of being a child hurt by her own blackness. Lorde constantly debated what it meant to be black, refusing to accept an "easy" blackness. This was both a source of her sense of isolation and gave her the distance from which to critically speak of difference: In her journal notes for 1975–76, she wrote that

> I have a right to be black. I have a right to be different and I have a right to survive. I have a right to join with other different human beings who are also black, Blackness doesn't mean we are one lump of chocolate poured on the face of eternity. Until each of us can love herself & himself fully, in all our contradictions, we will never survive as a people in this land because we will never survive as individuals.[15]

In the title poem, "Between Ourselves," Lorde signaled a willingness to forego the black community's elusive embrace, though not the black liberation struggle, for a more complex accounting of its history and her own:

> . . .
> Under the sun on the shores of Elmina
> a black man sold the woman who carried
> my grandmother in her belly . . .[16]

In several of the poems, she addressed the destructive forces operating against black children—her own and the community's. "Power" epitomized the rage she felt upon learning a white New York City police officer had been acquitted of murder charges after killing a ten-year-old black boy. The boy, Clifford Glover, had been shot from behind by Officer Thomas Shea at 5:00 A.M. in the South Jamaica section of Queens, on April 28, 1973. Lorde returned from her trip to Barbados two days before the incident.[17] She was driving home when she heard the news of the policeman's acquittal on her car radio. Sickened with fury, blinded by rage, Lorde pulled over, stopped the car, and started to write the poem; she wondered if the police officer had been a student at John Jay, if she had seen him in the halls.[18]

Along with most of black New York, she followed months of media coverage. Of the twelve jurors hearing the case, eleven were white men. Mrs. Ederica Campbell, a supervisor of probation investigations for the State Supreme Court in Manhattan, was the only woman on the jury, and the only black person. After acquitting Officer Shea of the murder charges on June 12, 1974, some of the jurors were interviewed by the press. One juror, Angelo Sicurella, inadvertently identified the gender of the juror who'd held out the longest against a verdict of acquittal as "she," then recognizing his slipup, said that "she or he" had given in and voted with the majority. Mrs. Campbell herself stated, "They almost killed me, and I almost killed them."[19]

Lorde identified both with the pain the slain boy's mother now bore and with Mrs. Campbell, who had been forced, by fear of a white male majority, to side with them in the end. In "Power," she connected her rage at the killing of Clifford Glover to the racism which caused black people to self-destruct:

> until she let go the first real power she ever had
> and lined her own womb with cement
> to make a graveyard for our children.[20]

INITIALLY, W. W. Norton rejected the manuscript of "Coal." Published herself by Norton, Adrienne Rich's claim of having nothing to do with Norton's subsequent acquisition of it was a modest one. Her quiet input was no doubt instrumental to a change of heart on the part of John Benedict, her editor. A distinguished poet, whose work was highly regarded in the mainstream, Rich's status lent weight to her assessments, and was certainly the nudge Benedict needed. Sometime in 1975, Benedict called Charlotte Sheedy, encouraging her to resubmit Lorde's collection. Sheedy did so, and he called again, offering a contract and modest advance. At Benedict's request, Rich sent a letter in support of Lorde's work.

Lorde was absolutely delighted that Norton wanted to publish her. Yet she resented the means to the end. Rich was influential in opening the door for her there and she was certainly grateful.[21] She knew Gwendolyn Brooks had intervened on her behalf when Dudley Randall initially hesitated to publish her. She'd enjoyed the support of Langston Hughes, early on. But she felt belittled that a better known poet, someone white, someone black, anybody, had to intervene in order for her to get published.

Lorde traveled for much of 1975, giving readings at colleges, universities, public libraries, and community spaces. This spurt took her through Louisiana, Pennsylvania, South Carolina, New York, New Jersey, and Detroit. Lorde fancied being in demand and having an audience. At the same time, she was conscientious about doing readings and felt it her mission to pursue colleges and universities where there were black student organizations. She answered mounting requests, turning down none of them, including gigs she didn't get paid for. When answering the requests became unmanageable, Lorde asked Sheedy to take over handling her speaking engagements and to get her more money, which Sheedy did, negotiating increasingly better fees. Money was an issue because there was never enough. Despite her salary from John Jay, Lorde was often broke: she had Beth and Jonathan to support, the house and a mortgage, a car in constant need of repair, therapy to pay for. Though they had an established, middle-class life, Audre and Frances lived modestly, didn't indulge in expensive evenings out generally, and socialized among a private circle of friends. Lorde depended on the earnings from her poetry readings to help support her family.[22]

As her public life intensified, she wrestled with several paradoxes. She began the new year, 1976, frustrated by "this curse of writing," imploring herself to be disciplined and to have "The courage to Create. To turn myself into a living wire stretched between heaven & hell at war." It was odd to her that she would speak of "loathing" writing, her "life's blood"; a thought as paradoxical as that she loathed Frances, or the children. But she considered she might "have to encompass even those frightful thoughts."[23] She did not imagine her life or work without Beth and Jonathan but saw self-preservation as an imperative. "The children must be themselves, but not out of my blood & bone," Lorde wrote. "I will help them but I cannot sacrifice myself to them."[24] She was thinking of Jonathan, in particular: orchestrating a relationship between her son and Robert Turner had ultimately proved painful for Jonathan.

The relationship lasted for several months, and the two did become friends. One Saturday, while on the ferry, Jonathan held the envelope his mother had given him up to the light, his curiosity getting the best of him. Through the thin paper he could see a check inside, for $50, made out to Robert Turner. It didn't take long for Jonathan to figure out Turner was getting paid to spend time with him. Jonathan was devastated, feeling furious, and betrayed. When he confronted his mother, she confessed Turner was not only getting paid but that he was a psychiatric social worker as well. Jonathan refused to see Robert Turner again.[25]

Lorde was lonely and terribly unhappy, recording, over several months, sketchy details of how Clayton often hurt her; musing about how to accomplish Clayton's freedom and her own; at once loving and hating her partner. Over the course of their long relationship, Lorde publicly extolled the racial differences between them as creatively useful. Privately, those differences were a source of deep-rooted tension.

When the first edition of *Coal* was published in 1976, a list of Adrienne Rich's publications appeared at the back. At the time, the works of one poet were often listed in the works of another, if they seemed to have an affinity. It was—and still is—industry practice for a publisher to advertise other books in paperbacks. The practice itself was not unknown to Lorde. Broadside Press also advertised a roster of poets and their publications in other books it published. However, seeing Rich's books advertised in hers made Lorde furious in spite of herself.[26] She admired Rich as a poet, but she felt deeply competitive against her because Rich was better known, more celebrated—and white.

Lorde went to see Charlotte Sheedy about the matter, insisting that Norton not advertise Rich's books in hers. Sheedy hadn't given the matter a second thought before Lorde brought it to her attention. She credited Lorde with a change in her own business practice, as from that day forth the Sheedy agency put a standard clause in its contracts that no books of authors represented by Sheedy's agency could contain advertisements for the works of other authors without the agency's express approval.[27]

Nevertheless, becoming a Norton author marked a significant turning point in Lorde's publishing career, not least because of the addition of her name to its elite roster of contemporary American poets. With

Norton's stamp of approval, Audre Lorde became the first out black lesbian to crash the gates of the literary mainstream. And yet, while Norton's publication of *Coal* and subsequent collections certainly positioned her vis-à-vis the mainstream, Lorde would remain an outsider, validated by periodic access to its attention. Despite publishing five of her fourteen books under the Norton imprint, Lorde's work was—and still is—generally ignored by male-dominated literary criticism; and it has yet to transcend the homophobia that keeps marginal her identity as lesbian.

BYRON LORDE ONCE told his youngest daughter the two moles on her feet were signs she'd travel a lot. That September, Lorde went to Russia, at the invitation of organizers of the African-Asian Writers Conference. Were it not for Clayton, Lorde would have been unable to travel as much as she did. It was Frances who made Audre's absence from home and Beth and Jonathan possible. Without the assurance of Clayton's salary, the family could not have maintained the middle-class lifestyle they were accustomed to. Lorde's gross salary at John Jay barely crested $30,000 a year even though, as faculty, she was a "big draw." Yet it was precisely because she was published, increasingly sought after as a poet and public intellectual, that she could negotiate time away from John Jay as frequently as she did. Lorde was thrilled with the invitation to be the American observer to the conference, which was being convened by the Union of Soviet Writers. The memory of her trip to Ghana still vivid for her, she was especially anxious to meet and be in the company of the African writers.

Lorde dated her arrival in Russia as September 10, 1976,[28] but a new passport she'd applied for was not issued until September 20. According to her journal, she was in Moscow three days before she made note of the date, September 28.

From all indications, Lorde arrived in Russia on Saturday afternoon, September 25, stepping off the plane into a bone-biting wintry Moscow which was raw yet seemed familiar. She was met at the airport by a woman named Helen, her guide and interpreter. It was a thirty-mile ride from the airport into Moscow proper, and along the way the landscape reminded her of northern Westchester, New York, in late winter.

Lorde stayed at the Hotel Younnost, originally a youth hostel and now one of Moscow's international hotels. She did not speak Russian and initially found the task of ordering dinner at the hotel daunting: "Then I remembered my phrase book & would be damned if I'd let an unspeakable, unreadable language do me out of a russian meal." Later that evening, the view from her room window, the lights on the skyline, the outline of a railroad bridge, and the intermittent flash of tail lights from automobiles all reminded her of "100 nights along Riverside Drive."[29] The more she saw of Moscow, the more she thought its crowded hustle and bustle was much like New York.

Despite the rainy, gray weather, Lorde and Helen went sightseeing most of that Sunday. She saw the university, several historic plaques, and the home of the Bolshoi Ballet. Although she never got to, she wanted to visit Poetry Hall and the Aleksandr Pushkin Museum. Her interest in Pushkin was piqued by his reputation as the "father of Russian literature," founder of modern Russian poetry, and his African ancestry.[30] Touring Moscow with Helen, she got a glimpse of life in Russia from her interpreter's perspective: the constant fight against the cold; the fact that almost everyone had lost a family member in World War II, the "Great Patriotic War"; and that Russian women mourned the lack of men.

By Sunday evening, Lorde began to wonder what other women would be attending the conference. Then she met Ama Ata Aidoo, the Ghanian writer, who was also staying at her hotel. She'd wanted to meet Aidoo since being in Ghana, and her first impressions were of a soft, beautiful, iron-willed woman. Later, however, she remarked upon Aidoo with some disappointment after witnessing an argumentative discussion on revolutionary politics between Aidoo and Helen. While disappointed in both women, she was particularly disenchanted with Aidoo, of whom she'd expected more, faulting Aidoo for the very same iron-willed quality she'd noticed at first.

As the actual conference site was in Uzbekistan, five hours south of Moscow, the entire delegation, including members of the press, was flown there the next day. By the time they landed in the capital city, Tashkent, it was nightfall. They were greeted at the airport by a welcoming crowd, television cameras, and children dressed in indigenous costumes who presented each member of the delegation with flowers. The weather in Tashkent was tropical and on the drive from the airport to the hotel, the scenery reminded Lorde of Ghana.

Much of Tashkent had been rebuilt after an earthquake in 1966. Seeing it by next day's light—especially Old Tashkent, which survived the earthquake—Lorde felt even more that it looked like Ghana or Dahomey, with its market stalls, corrugated tin roofs, adobelike houses, its mix of old and new. Even the flowers and trees reminded her of West Africa. In contrast to people in Moscow, the people of Tashkent struck her as warm-blooded and expressive.[31] She also noted they were Asians who considered themselves Russian. Lorde did not think race or racism were non-issues amongst individual citizens of the USSR, but she did think that because there was an articulated state position against nationalism, there was a unity among its diverse peoples.[32]

The historic realities of non-Western oppressed peoples were a given at the conference, which brought to the Soviet Union delegates from several African, Asian, and Middle Eastern nations. The aim was to facilitate their introduction to one another, and to foster solidarity between them. Lorde recorded sketchy observations on the content of the conference itself, noting snippets of statements made by delegates and speeches during which she heard no mention of the struggles of black Americans.[33] Why she'd been invited as an observer rather than an active participant now confounded her. It seemed to be a contradiction that she was there at all. She tried to raise the question of her presence with several members of the Union of Soviet Writers. Each time, however, she felt their answers were polite but circumspect.

Had she been granted a recognized platform as were others, Lorde would have certainly given voice to the struggles of black Americans in an international forum where solidarity between oppressed peoples was a constant refrain. But Lorde's presence as an American observer, while recognizing black struggles for freedom, decentered them within the context of struggles against colonialism and imperialism in the Third World, where resistance to American and European foreign policies shaped such struggles. The African-Asian Writers' Conference provided Lorde with firsthand consideration of the notion of solidarity between oppressed peoples, adding even deeper meaning to her notion of being an outsider.

NINE

S HE WAS FORTY-TWO now and life was going well. She was increasingly in demand as a poet, which created more opportunities for her to travel. It also created a sense of being powerful, which sometimes brought out an arrogance in her. Moreover, Lorde had a solid reputation as a feminist lesbian literary figure. She had a vision of her own and other women's poetry as important to transmitting notions of women's culture. She'd overcome her personal fears in pursuit of a self-defined life. Where her work and reputation were concerned, she had nothing to fear.

Early in November 1976, Lorde went to the West Coast, to do a brief reading tour in Los Angeles and San Francisco. The two days in California gave her an opportunity to see Pat Parker, to whom she'd been introduced by Wendy Cadden—a graphic artist and typesetter—in 1969. Cadden was a close friend of Parker's and her lover was the lesbian feminist poet, Judy Grahn.[1]

Originally from Houston, Texas, Parker was the youngest of four daughters of a mother who was a domestic worker and a father who retreaded tires for a living. Racism, Jim Crow segregation, and poverty

defined her childhood. In 1962, Parker moved to California after graduating from high school, eventually earning an undergraduate degree from
Los Angeles City College and a graduate degree from San Francisco
State College. The same year she moved to California, she married the
playwright Ed Bullins; she divorced him in 1966 and then married
Robert F. Parker, whom she also divorced.[2] Like Lorde, Parker began
writing early in life. As her publishing career evolved, her work was also
distinctive for breaking silence on the question of free speech, and of
domestic abuse—an issue Parker was particularly haunted by. One of
her sisters was murdered by an ex-husband with a history of abusing his
wife. In *WomanSlaughter*, Parker's third collection of poems,[3] she confronted society's entrenched unwillingness to protect women from
domestic abuse and legal structures which refused to prosecute their
abusers to the fullest extent.[4]

Parker was out when she and Lorde first met in 1969, but Lorde was
not. Cadden facilitated the meeting between them at Parker's apartment, where the two poets spent the night up reading and sharing each
other's poetry.[5] Before the night was out, Lorde offered Parker two auda-
cious pieces of advice: she urged Parker to pay more consistent attention
to her craft; and to leave her lover. Before she died of breast cancer in
June 1989, Parker intended to include several new poems in a reissue of
her fourth collection, *Movement in Black*. In an expanded edition of that
work, the poem "For Audre" began with Parker's quintessential rawness,
and was a humorous account of their meeting and Parker's response to
Lorde's advice:

> Who is this bitch?
> I mean really . . .[6]

As their long friendship developed, they saw each other whenever
Lorde was out west or when Parker came east, time and schedules
allowing. Parker visited with Lorde in Staten Island, where she met
Frances, Beth, and Jonathan; and Lorde was fond of the fact that Parker
had a daughter, Anastasia Jean. Although money was a constant issue for
her, Lorde extended herself to Parker on more than one occasion. She
knew Pat made a lot less than she did, and sent her money for postage

and other necessities. When Parker organized a writers' workshop for women in prison in the mid-seventies, Lorde offered several hundred dollars to support it.[7] After an October 1983 reading together at the University of Oregon, Lorde sent Parker a letter: "The enclosed check is part of what I feel belongs to you as a sister Poet from what I was paid in Eugene, given that you did one reading & I did two."[8] While Lorde thought no one person was to blame, she felt that the financial arrangements were badly handled, wanted to be sure things between herself and Parker were clear, and was concerned the money matter might be used to pit them against each other in some petty way.

Lorde did not generally regard women who were greatly younger than her as peers, particularly when they were writers too. For all she admired and adored Parker, who was ten years her junior, this new woman was no exception. Lorde's letters to Parker between 1974 and 1989[9] suggest a bullheaded delight in playing the big sister role. Whether Parker solicited advice or not, Lorde schooled Parker on the business of writing: prompting her to compile a list of women's groups and bookstores she could read at on the East Coast; sending lists of people and places to contact for readings, making absolutely clear which ones she endorsed and which not; suggesting times of the year when it was best to come east for readings. When Parker was about to take a job with the Poetry in the Schools Program in San Francisco, Lorde wrote to say she was sending a newsletter from the Teachers and Writers Collaborative (TWC) in New York. Lorde claimed in that letter to have worked with TWC several years earlier, but she had not. Poets and writers who worked with the TWC taught in the public schools, which Lorde had never done. Nevertheless, she offered Parker the following advice:

> The thing about these Poetry in Schools gigs is this: get in there, give the kids what you can (and from you that's a lot) make a lot of bread, which is possible if you play it right, but don't stay around too long. AND DON'T TRUST ANYONE IN IT. Play it cool, keep your mouth shut when you're not poeting, and don't get *too* buddy-bud with the poets you work with. Protect yourself <u>at all times</u>, and the kids, if you can.[10]

In one letter, she chastised Parker severely for not having contacted Galen Williams, the director of New York City's Poets and Writers, when she'd told her to. Lorde understood Parker needed money as much as she needed exposure, and she was irritated with her for not following through:

> you have not yet written to Galen Williams, which is a mistake. Get it together, lady. Of course it's not REALLY important on the cosmic scale of things; we both know it, but like every other kind of grease, it helps to keep the kinks at least manageable and I know you know what I mean.[11]

On a more personal level, throughout their relationship, she chided Parker for not sealing envelopes containing letters, for not writing back in a timely fashion or not returning her telephone calls promptly. She continued to read and comment upon Parker's poetry, but Parker grew to resent Lorde's perception that she was not working hard enough at her craft nor as disciplined as Lorde insisted she must be.[12]

Parker wore her working-class lesbian sensibilities on her sleeve, neither denying nor blunting them for public consumption. In person, she was unapologetic, forthright, and had long articulated her own racial and class locations as outsider. Seeing Parker again that November in 1976, Lorde could not help but feel that "Pat Parker illustrates to me again how much of a sucker harpie blowhard creampuff I really am."[13]

Though she appreciated a chance to glimpse the West Coast women's scene, Lorde felt less challenged by the experience than she'd expected. She was as much hungry for dialogue as she was for a captivated audience at her readings, but she found the L.A. women especially low key in comparison to those in New York, despite their commitment to feminist community. Many of the lesbian women she met in California made their living doing blue-collar work as truck drivers, cooks, lineswomen, and circuit checkers for Pacific Gas & Electric; but Lorde felt there was much more to class consciousness than they articulated—or seemed willing to do in her presence. The absence of dialogue around this topic, and class privilege, was dreary and frightening. Frightening, too, were familiar patterns of unexamined racism, and she wondered if it were really possible to alter the outcomes of those learned patterns. Lorde was beginning to see now the necessity for linking analyses of racial, class, and sexual oppressions. If the trip to California offered no other challenges, it gave her an opportunity to reflect critically on what was needed to alter those patterns.

When she was in San Francisco, Lorde stayed at two communes. Observing the communes to be models of the differences between patriarchal and female society, she felt that the women residing in them led interesting, separatist lives. Yet her general impression of lesbians in Berkeley was that they were into fewer stereotypes as butch and femme, fat and thin. Their racism less obvious, they were into pseudo-poverty, did not interrogate assumptions based on privilege, and had raggedy politics as feminists because of their indifference. By the time she was on her way back to New York, Lorde had learned enough of the "internecine warfare" between bisexuals and gays, bisexuals and heterosexuals, gays and heterosexuals, lesbians and feminists and lesbian feminists, between black and white and working class and middle class, between San Francisco and Berkeley gays, to conclude that what was most divisive about the feminist movement—in California as elsewhere—was the politics of exclusion within it.

LORDE'S TRIP TO Russia in September 1976 was hardly a memory when, four months later, she was in Nigeria as a member of the first American contingent to the Second World Black and African Festival of Arts and Culture (FESTAC '77), which was held from January 15 to February 12, 1977, in Lagos. Its predecessor, the First World Festival of Negro Arts, had been held in Dakar, Senegal, in 1966. At the end of that festival, Nigeria accepted an invitation to host the second one in 1970. In 1967, longstanding ethnic tensions between the Ibo and the Hausa peoples came to a climax when the Ibo proclaimed the independent republic of Biafra. The resulting civil war between secessionist Ibo and Nigerian forces, during which more than 1 million Biafran civilians died of starvation, lasted until Biafra's surrender in 1970. Nigeria's unstable political climate made holding the festival there impossible. It was rescheduled for 1975, then postponed again when Nigeria could not commit the necessary resources.

By 1977, Nigeria was recognizably the richest black-ruled nation on the continent. The source of its newly found wealth was oil. Appropriating control over realizing the festival, the military-led Nigerian government took it out of civilian hands, and committed itself to FESTAC's success. In preparation, the government spent an estimated $40–$60 million to construct the National Theater—a maze of public and performance spaces where many of the cultural events were showcased. It also ordered reconstruction of the 60,000-seat National Stadium, another site for the festivities. New expressways were built to relieve the traffic jams Lagos was legendary for. The Nigerian government spent nearly $80 million more to underwrite the building and operational costs of a sprawling housing complex six miles outside Lagos where the festival's participants were housed and fed at its expense. The 15,000-unit complex, FESTAC Village, was slated to be used after the festival to alleviate a housing shortage.

After years of planning by international organizing committees, a global call went out to the black cultural world inviting representative delegations to Nigeria. In the United States, word of FESTAC spread slowly, then more rapidly as rumors of a "free trip to Africa" circulated. Black Americans from every walk of life scrambled feverishly for the chance to be among those to go. Many did not even have passports; some had no money. Confusion over when or if FESTAC was to become an actuality, as well as the earlier postponements, made it difficult for many of those who were formally invited to reshuffle personal and professional schedules at the last minute. Andrew Young, then U.S. Ambassador to the United Nations; members of the Congressional Black Caucus; and Democratic Representatives Yvonne B. Burke and Charles C. Diggs had already persuaded the State Department to charter a plane for the 192-member American contingent. Later, they convinced it to charter another, to rush a second contingent of 252 black Americans that was to come two weeks later.[14] In all, the 444-member American contingent was the largest in attendance at FESTAC '77, and the largest single group of black Americans to return to Africa at one time.

The flight from JFK International Airport to Lagos was long, and the plane packed. There was a virtual "Who's Who" of black artists, grassroots organizers, academics, and other representatives of the black American cultural world on board. Lorde knew some by name if not by sight, but kept largely to herself. The plane stopped to refuel in Madrid before continuing on to Africa, passing over the Sahara Desert. The largest desert in the world, stretching east to west across North Africa, the Sahara seemed infinite to Lorde. The sight of desert unfolding into desert was scary, even as she was captivated by moving over its persistent reddishness, its shifting terrains and textures. The desert felt to her "truly male and frightening," but high above, metaphorically straddling it, Lorde began seeding the poem "Sahara":

> Plateaus of sand.
> Dendrites of sand.
> Continents & islands and waddys
> Of sand . . .

The first American contingent arrived in Lagos the afternoon of January 13, two days before FESTAC's official opening. During her first hours in Nigeria, Lorde was intent on taking off alone. She found the teeming coastal capital much like New York City and terribly noisy. Nigerians honked their car horns incessantly, there were no traffic lights or policemen at key intersections, and the traffic jams reminded her of those on the Long Island Expressway in summer.[15]

As anticipated, FESTAC '77 was the most significant international gathering of the black cultural world to be held in post-independence Africa to that time. It was a mecca for more than seventeen thousand black artists, who came from the Caribbean, Australia, South America, Canada, Europe, the United States, as well as throughout Africa, and attracted to Lagos almost half a million spectators. Representative of those who'd survived slavery, colonialism, genocide, discrimination, and apartheid, black people came from every nook and cranny of the globe. Never before had so many had an opportunity to reforge links to Africa, to see the world through a common vision of black eyes, and to witness the unbroken thread of their common African heritage as inspired, timeless, and enduring. At times, some of the African American participants were so overcome emotionally, they cried hysterically, their tears a visceral reaction to the haunting, historic fact of their separation from the home of their ancestors.[16]

The aims of FESTAC's organizers were grand: to ensure the resurgence and propagation of the cultures, cultural values, and civilizations of the African diaspora; to promote black and African visual artists, performers, and writers, facilitating for them a global audience and greater access to worldwide outlets; to encourage, through cultural production, a return to origins in Africa by those uprooted to other continents; and to promote international and interracial understanding.[17] The subtext of these aims was that the cultures of the African diaspora had been exploited by those of Europe and the West for far too long. FESTAC also had a political component: its spirit addressed the need for a united front against all forms of human oppression, and solidarity with liberation movements, such as that in South Africa, of the time. Despite their differing historic oppressions and exploitations, many saw and expressed such realities as the potential basis for organizing politically against a common enemy.[18]

The atmosphere at FESTAC '77 and in Lagos was intoxicating. New delegations arrived daily. There was a constant buzz of activity, day and night. The hum of black people speaking a host of different languages, and understanding each other nonetheless, created a soundtrack that was its own music. Inside FESTAC Village, there were multiple "villages"—compounds representing different nationalities within walking distance of each other; this made it possible to "travel" the black world, partaking of its sights, colors, and foods.[19] The sounds of rehearsals permeated the villages nightly, and every evening after dusk, the drumming would start. "The music would swell," Lorde wrote, "and my blood would start to run fire."[20] There were non-stop presentations by traditional dancers, plays, films, exhibitions, readings, concerts, ceremonies, special events, and endless discussions on solidarity, revolution, and history.

Lorde kept a polite distance between herself and other members of the American delegation, anticipating and heading off hostility toward her as a lesbian. At home, Lorde knew her embrace of feminism and gay liberation set her apart from those more involved or identified with the black liberation struggle as a racial construct only, and she was unwilling to make herself a target of further isolation in Nigeria. Reading the subtext of FESTAC as heterosexual, she felt it was safer to appear straight, and she'd forgotten how easy it was to be straight in public, particularly around black people.[21]

She also stayed out of the fray and intrigue within the American delegation, watching as Ron Karenga—a cultural nationalist, self-styled radical, and professor of Afro-American Studies at San Diego State University—positioned himself to be its leader. By the fifth day, the absence of some key name people—including Ossie Davis, Haki Madhubuti, Addison Gayle, Jeff Donaldson (a Howard University professor of art and chairman of the U.S. delegation), and others—became the subject of gossip and speculation. Dissent and division snaked through the contingent. Some felt that those who were staying in hotels, especially, had better accommodations than they did, and complained about an absence of comfort they were used to as Americans. Living conditions at the artists' compound became increasingly camplike and its facilities overtaxed. Many of the black American artists began to move out, scrambling for any hotel room they could find, their sense of solidarity giving way to more personal needs for comfort. As Karenga jockeyed for power, there was an uneasy shifting of groups and cliques.[22] Standing apart, Lorde felt that the delegation lacked cohesiveness and common cause, and that Karenga was a source of the dissent and division within it. She was determined not to get caught up in the delegation's internal struggles. She had her own agenda: "I came here to spread my word, to seek words of others, and to share whatever sustenance our different visions offer."[23]

Those particular dynamics aside, Lorde constantly wrestled with a need to please and to be approved by other black women at the same time she was mistrustful of them. Leery of trusting or assuming sisterhood with straight black women, few of whom were proponents of feminism or gay liberation at the time, she was superficially friendly with other black women in the delegation yet remained paranoid that they were being secretive, harboring information, around her.[24]

Lorde did allow herself to open up to one black American woman, however. A native of Florida and an artist-in-residence in Tampa at the time, Mildred Thompson had studied art at Howard University in the 1950s, where she'd been deeply influenced by her mentor, James Porter. A professor of art history, Porter was an eminent painter with an illustri-

Audre, in her first communion dress, on the steps of St. Mark the Evangelist, 65 West 138th Street, Harlem, circa May 1944. (*Courtesy of the Lesbian Herstory Educational Foundation/The Lesbian Herstory Archives*)

Audre (left) at age 22, and a friend, Felicia, Woolworth's Department Store, 1956. (*Courtesy of Gloria Joseph*)

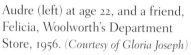

Audre Lorde

Cables to rage

Cover, *Cables to rage*
(*Courtesy of Charlotte Sheedy*)

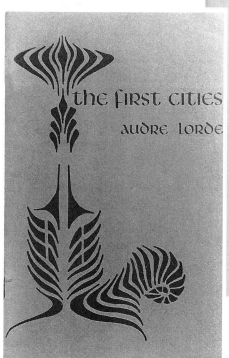

To Mephi — who walked thro the streets of some of these cities with me.

the first cities

"And nobody sleeps in the August house when the bells of Corn are ringing"

Autographed to her friend, Mephi
(*Courtesy of Charlotte Sheedy*)

Cover, *The First Cities*, 1968
(*Courtesy of Charlotte Sheedy*)

Promoting Kitchen Table: Women of Color Press, at the Second Women in Print Conference, Washington, D.C., 1981 (from left to right): Barbara Smith, Audre Lorde, Cherríe Moraga, and Hattie Gosset. © 2004 JEB (Joan E. Biren)

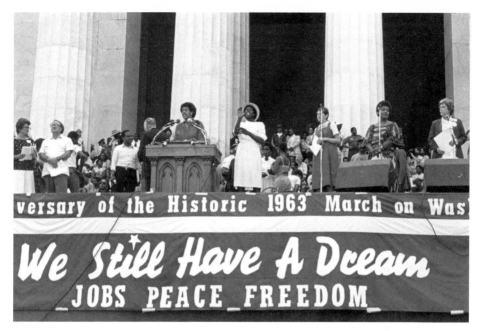

Audre Lorde (second from right), waiting for her turn to speak, at the 1983 March on Washington for Jobs, Peace and Freedom. © 2004 JEB (Joan E. Biren)

With a delegation of black women writers in Cuba, January 1985: *Front row* (left to right): Mari Evans, Alexis De Veaux, Rosa Guy, Cuban poet Nicolas Guillen, Jayne Cortez, Toni Cade Bambara, Audre Lorde, Mildred Pitts Walker. *Back row* (left to right): Gloria Joseph (partially obscured), Cuban poet Nancy Morejon, Verta Mae Grosvenor, sculptor Mel Edward. (*Courtesy of Spellman College Archives*)

At the dedication of The Audre Lorde Women's Poetry Center, Hunter College, December 1985 (from left to right): Clare Coss, Frances Clayton, Audre Lorde, and Audre's sister Helen Lorde. (*By permission of SISA, the Sisterhood in Support of Sisters in South Africa*)

Three of the Founding Mothers of the Sisterhood in Support of Sisters in South Africa (SISA), at the dedication of The Audre Lorde Women's Poetry Center, Hunter College, December 1985 (from left to right): Audre Lorde, Gloria Joseph, and Johnnetta Cole. (*By permission of SISA*)

On the beach in Carriacou, her mother's birthplace, a year after the 1983 U.S.-led invasion of Grenada. (*By permission of Gloria Joseph*)

Audre Lorde and Gloria Joseph, in full beekeeping regalia, at their home in St. Croix, circa 1988. (*By permission of Howard Francis*)

Gloria Joseph (left) and Audre Lorde, front yard of a rented house, Christmas, 1989, Virgin Gorda, after being detained for several hours when customs officials in Tortola refused them entry because of Lorde's dreadlocked hair. (*By permission of Blanche Cook*)

At a book fair in Canada (circa 1982), from left to right: South African writer-activist Ellen Kuzwayo, Gloria Joseph, and Audre Lorde. (*By permission of Dagmar Schultz*)

During one of the last years Audre taught at Hunter College, circa 1985.

Audre and Gloria in Hawaii, July 1991, during the solar eclipse, standing on lava near the Pelé crater. (*By permission of Blanche Cook*)

Audre, on the balcony of her friend Dagmar Schultz's house, Berlin, Germany, either 1991 or 1992. (*By permission of Dagmar Schultz*)

A poetry reading at the Studio Museum in Harlem, circa 1977, from left to right, poets: Jodi Braxton, Patricia Spears Jones, Rikki Lights, and Audre Lorde.

ous career dating back to the Harlem Renaissance.[25] After graduating from Howard in 1957, Thompson spent a year at the Brooklyn Museum School in New York. Between 1959 and 1961, she studied at the Hamburg Hochschule für Bildende Kunst, in Germany. On Porter's recommendation, she left the United States to return to West Germany in 1964, living there and teaching art for nearly ten years.

Thompson's departure from the United States during the heyday of the civil rights and Black Arts movements served as a "universal" narrative in her work, which was absent politicized discourse on black art. In the 1960s and 1970s, her work indicated a brief flirtation with expressive social realism. Her early etchings were reminiscent of Henri Matisse and had a distinct figurative quality to them. But early in the seventies, Thompson moved away from the human figure as a mainstay of her work, developing into an abstract painter, printmaker, and sculptor.[26]

Thompson thought of herself as an expatriate and did not separate her identity as black from her identity as American, eventually disavowing any claim to being American. She'd traveled between art worlds in the United States, Europe, and Africa; and her work was better known abroad than it was in the States.

Mildred Thompson struck Lorde as "a beautiful, powerful sister."[27] She fondly retold the story of watching Thompson, who went out early in the mornings to collect wood, hammering the pieces together for a canvas stretcher in an alley of the compound. Lorde dramatized the story of how she became smitten with Thompson, embellishing it with unmitigated romantic intrigue: she'd met and had an affair with Thompson, while she was in Africa with Clayton and the children, two years before. Lorde did have an affair with Thompson, but it crystallized after they met in Nigeria and during the brief period Thompson lived in Washington, D.C., in the mid-eighties, where Lorde saw her at every opportunity. As she got to know Mildred Thompson better, Lorde became disenchanted that the artist lacked identities as black or woman, which she believed created an essential dishonesty in Thompson's work. But that belief limited Thompson to Lorde's own definitions of "black" and "woman."

Thompson shared one essential quality with Lorde: she refused to be bound by expectations of race and gender. Unlike Lorde, she was an

American who wasn't defined by living in America—a perspective on American "blackness" that was new to Lorde. Nevertheless, over the course of their affair, Lorde gave Thompson four of her poems, for which Thompson created a series of abstract pen-and-ink drawings in a sketch-book, entitling the series "Journey Stones: love poems,"[28] after Lorde's poem, "Journeystones: I–XI."

Thompson was adept at self-promotion, making good use of available opportunities, or creating them. Once, when other visual artists didn't show up in the right place at the right time for a scheduled interview with a television crew from the Nigerian Broadcasting Company, she saw no reason not to go on with the interview alone, inviting Lorde to seize the moment with her. Lorde saw Thompson as a wheeler and dealer, and believed that she was chiefly responsible for a taped reading Lorde was asked to do at the Nigerian television studio some days later.

On January 20, Lorde read at the National Theater, having given her material in advance to be translated as was protocol. Despite the immense crowds that generally attended FESTAC events, and having the spotlight for a moment, curiously, Lorde recorded no notes on her own reading or subsequent reactions to it. Nor did she ever publish the details of her experiences in Nigeria. But Lorde was not alone in her silence. Only a handful of the black Americans who went to FESTAC '77 wrote about what it was like to be there, and most of those were affiliated with the black press. Much of the white American press ignored FESTAC. None of the black American writers published a major piece on the events in Nigeria, despite the fact that FESTAC was life-altering and shaped lasting personal and artistic bonds between artists who participated in it. Its magnitude became nearly impossible to delineate beyond themselves.[29] Even so, the impact of the moment was undeniable: after being in Nigeria and reading at FESTAC '77, Lorde saw herself upon an international stage,[30] and—unlike in Russia—she was heard.

By the second week, the State Department began to exert pressure on the American contingent to return home, as the second contingent was on its way. News of the arrival of a second contingent had floated around for several days, but there was some confusion as to whether its arrival meant the first group had to go. Having been welcomed during the opening ceremonies to thunderous applause, black Americans were a powerful presence at FESTAC; they played a pivotal role in the cultural and scholarly components of the festival. As word surfaced they were actually leaving, the Nigerians were also confused as to why. Lorde believed the reason was because the U.S. government wanted to control the number of American blacks attending FESTAC '77 at one time, and that it was fearful of the impact of a clearly successful FESTAC.[31] The night before their departure, Lorde and Thompson spent the evening together. Lorde left Nigeria on February 1, bound for home.

IN FEBRUARY 1977, *Chrysalis* was launched. Dedicated to a feminist articulation of women's culture, the quarterly was published in Los Angeles. From the start, *Chrysalis* gave voice to some of the more enduring, critical ideas of the feminist movement's radical edge. Some readers objected to the magazine's lesbian content, others criticized deficiencies in analyses of lesbian experiences; but the editors defended their policy of inviting reflections upon the sexual diversity of women within the feminist movement and the larger society where such reflections were more generally denied, silenced, or distorted. In time, *Chrysalis* became an important feminist quarterly, providing a platform for an emerging body of feminist cultural theory as espoused by Lucy Lippard, Michelle Cliff, Joanna Russ, Mary Daly, Blanche Weisen Cook, Adrienne Rich, June Jordan, Susan Griffith, Marge Piercy, Marilyn Hacker, and Audre Lorde, among others. Several months before the magazine's debut, its publisher, Kirsten Grimstad, and one of its editors, Susan Rennie, invited Lorde to act as poetry editor. Since Lorde was in New York, poetry submissions were to be sent directly to her by mail.

Lorde intended to send Grimstad and Rennie a letter making clear what would be her editorial approach, but she did not begin crafting it until December 5, 1976. In the letter, she identified women poets as warriors—an identity appropriated from the legendary Amazon women of Dahomey she was so fascinated with. "I do believe," she began, "the poets are our modern amazons—riders defenders explorers of the loneliest outposts of our kingdoms." Lorde's knowledge of African history and culture was often motivated by her own needs to use it, and was figurative rather than necessarily literal; on occasion, she took poetic license with it. But the statement defined a significant poetic aesthetic that was appealing to her personally and to her vision of other women poets. Alluding to erogenous zones of her own body which guided her intuitions, Lorde also wanted the editors to know how she would make decisions on submissions. She was known to make off-color statements she well knew were shocking, and she took delight in playing the "bad girl." However, now she was also thinking out loud what was to become a more realized theory of the "uses of the erotic": "I must tell you," she forewarned them, "very little of true power, few of my decisions come from above my chin—only the force of explanation and persuasion." Lastly, Lorde wanted to make clear,

> Poetry of Crysalis [*sic*] must mirror sing warm scream the highest of our journeys the bloodiest of our failures the most bizarre and precious of our dreams the most difficult of our future uncharted arrivals and the agonizing elations of reconstructing the route & journeys so we may come again.[32]

As poetry editor for *Chrysalis* over the next two years, she read thousands of submissions, literally, culling from them selections for twelve issues of the quarterly. It was a herculean task, but Lorde was an efficient, sagacious poetry editor and used her position with the magazine to publish emerging poets, including Patricia (Spears) Jones, Jodi Braxton, Sandra Maria Esteves, Sara Miles, Lois Elaine Griffith, and Honor Moore.

She also used it as an opportunity to repay debts to some friends. Lorde owed a great deal to Diane di Prima and Adrienne Rich, both of whom helped to define critical moments in her literary career. In part, publishing them was a way of showing her gratitude. Publishing Pat Parker's work also gave Lorde an opportunity to acknowledge her debt to Parker as the first out black lesbian she'd known. Although Lorde did not feel she owed a debt to June Jordan, they were peers, she wanted Jordan's respect as a black woman, and admired her as a poet, having met Jordan when the two were teaching in the SEEK Program at City College during the sixties. While their public personas differed sharply, there were similarities in their early backgrounds.

Like Lorde, June Jordan's early childhood was framed by a sense that her father would have preferred to have had a son; and she too was conscious of being a child who was not only the wrong sex but the wrong color.[33] Raised in Brooklyn, she shared with Lorde the experience of growing up in a strict, working-class Caribbean (Jamaican) household which bred in her a sense of fear and insecurity at having a disapproving, physically abusive parent—in her case, her father. Jordan's poetic sensibilities were evident early, shaped in part by delighting in the speech and storytelling of an uncle who lived upstairs in their Hancock Street home, and also by parents who introduced her to poetic passages in the Bible and to the poetry of Paul Laurence Dunbar. Even so, Jordan's parents wanted her to pursue a conventional life. Her father wanted her to be a doctor and her mother wanted her to marry one. Neither could envision her as a poet.[34]

By the time Lorde and Jordan met at City College, Jordan was active in Harlem's grassroots politics, divorced, the mother of a son, Christopher, and establishing her life as a writer. A prolific poet by the 1980s, Jordan also emerged as a political essayist whose progressive politics offered up searing commentary on national and international issues.

As Jordan's activist and literary reputation took hold, she achieved acceptance for characteristics Lorde lacked. Fiercely outspoken on the present and future of black America, Jordan's racial solidarity and personal relationships with black men, public and private, earned her respect from other black activists and artists. She was published by mainstream houses from the start—a recognition that Lorde, who'd been publishing longer, waited years for. Jordan's reputation vis-à-vis the national black community afforded her the embrace, the heterosexual approval, continuously denied Lorde. Though not wholly acceptable among hard-core black activists of any stripe at the time, Jordan's bisexuality made her less a target of scorn, relatively speaking, than did Lorde's well-known lesbianism. Whereas Lorde began to open her readings with the pronouncement that she was a "black, lesbian, feminist, mother, poet warrior," Jordan did not see the need for Lorde to articulate an identity as lesbian especially; and she felt distanced from Lorde's complex definitions of herself as more than black.[35]

Lorde and Jordan crossed paths over the years. They attended each other's readings on occasion, and saw one another at literary events around the city. Lorde had a fleeting attraction to Jordan which she would have loved to be mutual. They never really became friends, perhaps because as personalities they were too similar—both were fiery and politically brilliant. Their tough exteriors belied the fact that they were sensitive to slights, real or imagined.

When Lorde learned that friends had referred Jordan to Charlotte Sheedy, she became jealous that Jordan might receive Sheedy's nurturance, and appealed to Sheedy not to take Jordan on as a client.[36] But her jealousy was misplaced, and selfishly driven by a sense of herself as *the* celebrated black feminist. Lorde had indeed shaped black feminism significantly, and led the charge long before others entered the fray. Her popularity and visibility within white feminist and feminist lesbian circles granted her an enviable cachet, even star status. Still, in terms of other black women writers who were her peers—Alice Walker, Toni Morrison, Sonia Sanchez, among them—Lorde was one of a substantial group defining black women's literary traditions and shaping black women's perspectives on white and black feminism.

Nevertheless, Lorde longed to be recognized by Jordan. In a letter dated March 23, 1977, Lorde recalled a reading that month at the Donnell Library in midtown Manhattan, where she was introduced by June Jordan. She was fraught with anxiety beforehand because Jordan was introducing her and she could not really hear what she said. After the reading, Beth took away Jordan's introduction to read and later gave it to her mother. Lorde was moved to discover Jordan's recognition of her as a poet. "I had not realized before," she wrote, "that you knew—recognized what I've been trying to do, and I have wanted you to recognize me for a long time because I respect the way your head works, your fire and your pain, and have come to value your opinion more than I can say, which is different from loving you, which I do also." The longed-for recognition and approval from Jordan that she now felt she had permitted Lorde to risk vulnerability: "I have always wanted an emotional openness between us, and what is so interesting & valuable to me is that I must now re-read my own messages, since obviously I mis-read yours."[37] But Jordan was cautious about befriending her, and separated respect for Lorde's work from personal engagement.[38] For her part, Lorde understood Jordan as an important black poet; she saw to it that two of Jordan's poems appeared in the third issue of *Chrysalis* in 1977.[39]

In the late seventies, Lorde began her seminal relationships with Michelle Cliff and Barbara Smith. Cliff was born in Kingston, Jamaica, into a middle-class, light-skinned family. British colonialism in Jamaica had created a caste system of privilege based on skin color in which "white" or light-skinned Jamaicans were viewed as—and were—better off and socially separate from darker-skinned Jamaicans. Considered among the lightest, Cliff learned early the social distinctions between light and dark, and the social status based on color. When she was still a young child, she and her immediate family moved to New York, where she lived from age three to ten. As middle-class, light-skinned Jamaicans who neither sounded like nor looked like more "typical" Caribbean immigrants, they assimilated into the world of Manhattan, and were perceived by others as white.[40]

Cliff spent the balance of her youth back in Jamaica, educated at private girls' schools run by white English women and creole Jamaicans. A pervasive British colonial presence informed her life back home. Because of her "white" looks, she was taught to identify with British culture and deny her African heritage. She would come to terms with her identity as a "white black woman"[41] later in life. In an essay published in 1983, Cliff explored the complexities of disengaging from the silence and repression scored by a colonial past, at the same time she sought to construct a new identity as Caribbean subject, lesbian, and woman of color.[42]

When she was of college age, Cliff left Jamaica and returned to New York. After graduating from Wagner College on Staten Island in 1969, she landed a job in 1970 at W. W. Norton, where she worked for a year before going to London to attend graduate school. Having finished at the Warburg Institute there three years later, Cliff returned to New York in 1974 and to Norton, as a copy editor. She'd worked on Lorde's first collection with Norton, *Coal*, and was a manuscript editor at the time of Norton's publication of *The Black Unicorn*.[43] In 1976, she began a lifelong association with Adrienne Rich. It was Rich who introduced Cliff to Lorde.

Cliff and Rich became part of a group of several women who gathered regularly to talk about their writing and writing-related issues. Originally the group consisted of Audre Lorde, Frances Clayton, Blanche Cook, and Clare Coss. They met once a month at Bernice Goodman's East Village apartment, which doubled as her office and was where she also saw them all as clients. Goodman had published several articles in her field, and was writing a book, *The Lesbian: A Celebration of Difference*, at the time.[44] Cliff and Rich joined the group in 1977 and, later, so did Joan Larkin and her lover. Goodman's lover, Deanna Fleischer, an artist, also participated. Though the group started out with good intentions, it proved a mistake to hold their meetings at Goodman's home. Goodman could not separate her roles as therapist and sister writer. The incestuous nature of her primacy as a shared therapist ultimately undermined the group's dynamics. While Goodman maintained her relationship as therapist to all of them, the group, as such, fizzled out a year later.

Lorde tried to turn her attraction to Rich and Cliff into opportunities to bed them, separately. She once told Rich she could not, in principle, trust a white woman she had not slept with. Neither Rich nor Cliff was interested in Lorde sexually and both resisted her persistent attempts at seduction.[45]

Michelle Cliff was twelve years younger than Lorde and Lorde treated her accordingly, much to Cliff's dismay, especially in light of Lorde's relationship with Rich, whom Lorde both viewed as an equal and wanted to be considered equal to artistically. At the same time, Lorde's longing for a Caribbean connection underlined her interactions with Cliff. As Cliff embarked upon work on *Claiming an Identity They Taught Me to Despise*, the first of several books to explore the psychic fragmentation and longing for wholeness endured by light-skinned black women, and centered in the Caribbean, Lorde wrote to Cliff offering generous encouragement: "I'm very excited by the direction you're taking with On Reclaiming An Identity They Taught Me to Dispise [*sic*]. The pieces that wipe me out are the pieces directly out of the you, they are incredibley [*sic*] strong. And I want more of them, you are the life and substance and depth of this struggle. . . ."[46]

By then, reading and commenting upon each other's work was an integral aspect of the friendships between Cliff, Lorde, and Rich. As Lorde's letter also indicated, she'd sent Cliff and Rich the draft of a new

poem and was anxious to know how they felt about it, believing it unfinished and unsure that what she'd intended was, in fact, on paper. Before
mailing the letter off to Cliff, Lorde realized she'd gotten the manuscript's title wrong but nudged Cliff to consider:

> . . . I was feeling Reclaiming, not claiming,
> because it was yours to begin with and you knew
> it, which is why color was so charged, so shameful.
>
> reclaim, to rescue from an undesirable state, to
> demand or obtain the return of.
> claim, to ask for as a right.
>
> So as a black woman, you're in the process of
> expanding that definition, but it's been yours
> all along. . . .[47]

After the publication of *Claiming an Identity* in 1980, Cliff endured a
rash of criticism from white and black women threatened by the book's
complex formulations of race and racial identity. Black women readers
were angered by Cliff's claim to blackness, and white women were star-
tled by how it exposed false notions of racial (white) purity. Throughout
all the hue and cry, Lorde remained a staunch supporter.

Cliff was grateful for the generous attention Lorde gave to her writing. But there came a point when she felt Lorde stepped over the line
between being helpful and controlling. They were having dinner at a
restaurant one Sunday evening, two years into their friendship. As Cliff,
Rich, and Lorde sat talking, Cliff announced plans to work on an essay
about Virginia Woolf. Cliff and Lorde got into a heated discussion over
the merits of writing about Woolf. Lorde argued that writing about Woolf
was a betrayal of black people. Cliff planned an approach that would
examine Woolf's life, as a writer, in the context of her racism. Neither
gave an inch of ground to the other, and the conversation escalated out
of proportion to its subject. When it was over, Lorde was furious, and
Cliff felt Lorde had tried to exercise control over who she was as a
writer, and as a woman of color.[48]

Afterwards, Lorde reflected upon the incident in her journal. She felt that the volatility between them was about much more than Virginia Woolf, "that what was being fought did not need fighting over," and that they were each trapped in their own stubbornness. Cliff was important to her in many ways, and she did not want the friendship between them to sour, or be lost. Yet their differences were a matter of what Lorde saw as

> a basic difference between us as black women—certainly under-
> standable in terms of our individual histories. We each of us are a
> bridge between the different selves within us, black and white. I
> was raised black, with a knowledge secret though it was of white-
> ness inside as well as out. She [Cliff] was brought up white with
> a knowledge of blackness outside but not in.

That "basic difference" framed, Lorde believed, differing attitudes con-
cerning racism. She was convinced there was nothing to be learned from
Woolf, whom she'd read long ago and thought too narrow in perspective.
Woolf was long dead, "frozen in changelessness."[49] The potential for
white women to develop and act out of a consciousness of their own
racism was the hope Lorde held onto in her public and private engagement with them.

Nor did she share in the admiration for Virginia Woolf in the feminist
community which now made of Woolf an icon. She wanted to get past
the friction between herself and Cliff, and hoped they might. In the end,
the blow-up between them proved to be a temporary impasse, as much
an indication of the bitterness Lorde felt at always having to battle
against white women's racism as of the nuances and contours of her lasting friendship with Cliff.

BARBARA SMITH became important in Lorde's life because of her instrumental role in Lorde's relationship with an organized, black feminist
community. Also several years Lorde's junior, Smith was born in a poor
urban area of Cleveland, Ohio, into a working-class family headed by
strong-minded women. One of twins, she and her sister, Beverly, were
raised by their mother, Hilda, a grandmother, and a maternal great-aunt,

Phoebe. Like thousands of black southerners during the Great Migration, Smith's great-aunt moved north from rural Georgia in the late 1920s, becoming the first of several sisters to do so.[50] Barbara seldom saw her because Phoebe worked as a live-in cook for a wealthy white family. Her mother, Hilda, worked full time, leaving the house each morning before anyone else had risen.

When she was six years old, Barbara, Beverly, and their mother moved into the house owned by another aunt, LaRue, and her husband—who eventually left LaRue because she was "too involved" with her family. Barbara's father was not a part of her life, and with LaRue's husband gone, her early years were shaped by black female kin who worked hard, valued notions of home, loved each other, and did "women's work" and "men's work." By the example of their own lives, they taught Barbara and her sister to be decent, respectful, to work, and to rebel.[51] As she was to write much later in life, these women formed early prototypical models of black feminists.[52] In 1955, when Barbara was just nine years old, her life was forever altered when her mother died.

During the early 1960s, Barbara was in high school when she attended her first demonstration protesting the death of a white minister who had laid down in front of construction equipment about to break ground for a new segregated elementary school. That demonstration began her life as an activist. In college, she participated in black student organizing and actively opposed the war in Vietnam. After graduating from Mount Holyoke College in Massachusetts in 1969, she earned a master's degree from the University of Massachusetts.

Wedding activism to critical thought in the 1970s, Smith emerged as one of the foremost black feminist theorists. In 1978, she shocked an audience attending the panel on black women writers and feminism at Howard University's National Black Writers' Conference when she presented a path-breaking essay entitled "Toward a Black Feminist Literary Criticism."[53] Smith's essay was the first to insist publicly upon the experiences of black lesbian writers, their critical relationship to the larger community of black women writers, and the homophobia aimed at silencing their very existence. It argued the necessity for reading the politics of race, gender, class, and sexuality as crucial determinants of the lack of recognition suffered by black women writers, particularly those who were lesbians.[54] In the 1980s, she became a champion of the movement to establish black women's studies, co-editing with Gloria T. Hull and Patricia Bell-Scott *All the Women Are White, All the Blacks Are Men, But Some of Us Are Brave* (1982). An anthology of writings by black women, this was the first work to identify and legitimate black women's studies as a viable field of scholarship.

Smith lived in Boston from 1972 until 1981, when she moved to New York City. She knew of Lorde before they'd actually met, having used several books published by Broadside Press in black literature courses she taught at a number of colleges in the early seventies. During her own process of coming out as a lesbian in the mid-seventies, and in search of literature on lesbian and gay life, Smith happened upon an issue of *Amazon Quarterly* in a Boston bookstore. To her surprise, Lorde was listed as poetry editor, and Smith wondered if Lorde was lesbian.[55] Taking Lorde's association with the quarterly as a clue, she asked people she thought might know if Lorde was in fact lesbian.[56]

The actual face-to-face meeting between the two of them came during a 1976 convening of the Modern Language Association (MLA), in New York. At the time, Smith was on the faculty of the English Department of Emerson College in Boston, and the first person of color to serve on the MLA's Commission on the Status of Women in the Profession. The commission was critical to the development of women's studies nationally. Appointed in 1974, Smith began her tenure in 1975, serving through 1978 and eventually becoming a co-chair. Smith spearheaded the commission's efforts to compile a listing of black and Third World women scholars, especially those in the field of literature. Although scholars in other fields and those without academic affiliation were not excluded, the purpose of the listing was to form the basis of a directory that would aid in promoting a communications network among black and Third World women teaching in college, and to encourage scholarship in black and Third World women's studies. Smith attended the December 1976 MLA meeting partly because the commission was responsible for substantive programming, which was part of the MLA's annual conventions. In addition, the MLA had a gay caucus and sponsored a number of programs featuring women and lesbian writers. Lorde was in the audience of one of the plenary sessions when Smith rose to speak.

"Is it possible," Smith posed the question, "to be a black lesbian writer and live to tell about it?" Only partially rhetorical, Smith was grappling with whether or not she could expect to have a career as a lesbian writer. She put the question hoping for a response from someone much further along as a writer than herself.[57] Lorde took Smith's comments as reason to believe she had not been telling her own stories loud enough.[58] Though her poetry readings in New York particularly were often attended by a smattering of black and Latina lesbians, the majority of lesbians who came were white. Lorde was so impressed by Barbara Smith's comments, she began to consider the idea of writing prose. After introducing themselves, Lorde and Smith began to correspond by mail. Smith joined an inner circle of women with whom Lorde kept in constant touch.

Lorde's communications with her closest friends served as a lifeline. She habitually called Blanche Cook, Clare Coss, or Charlotte Sheedy as early as 6:00 A.M. To Sheedy, Lorde would often complain about how she was being treated as a writer, disgorging details of the latest slight against her, furious over a racial incident or someone's racist behavior toward her. The letters and conversations with Adrienne Rich, particularly on the subject of race, were important to Rich's work.

Lorde pushed Rich to examine race as both a historic and a contemporary construct, forcing Rich to articulate positions of her own in a new way. The fact that they had a loving, trusting friendship, and respected each other intellectually, made it more possible, as time went by, for them to talk about and confront race. Rich was in no way naive about the subject of race or racism; nor did they always agree when they talked. But just as they critiqued each other's poetry, Rich wanted and invited the exchange between them as friends and like-minded activists. In that way, Lorde was an indispensable figure to Rich. Rich understood she was getting from Lorde something she was not getting anywhere else—and with love. As Rich began work on an essay entitled "Disloyal to Civilization," she showed a draft of it to Lorde. Lorde responded that Rich was glossing over the history of black and white women's relationships, and sentimentalizing them. Though terribly upset and hurt by Lorde's comments, Rich took them into consideration.

Back in Boston, Barbara Smith was acting on an idea she'd hit upon while at the MLA Convention. By then, she'd been traveling a lot, speaking on college campuses, as one of the earliest proponents of what was to become black women's studies. She'd met a number of other black feminists and lesbians on the East Coast and noted their growing critical mass. At the same time, they were isolated from each other and frequently ostracized within black communities. At Smith's urging, the Combahee River Collective, a Boston-based grassroots organization (of which Smith, Demita Frazier, and Smith's twin sister Beverly were founding members), initiated a series of retreats for black feminists and lesbians.[59]

The first retreat took place over the weekend of July 8–10, 1977, at a private home in South Hadley, Massachusetts. Seven more were held between 1977 and 1980 at sites on the East Coast.[60] The weekend-long gatherings produced intense political discussions among highly educated social activists engaged in varying social movements, and permitted a radical, politicized black female space to develop—one in which intellectual debate fertilized political strategies. These gatherings were opportunities to share creative work and exchange copies of hard-to-find materials about black women by black women. By virtue of their intimate nature, the retreats were also opportunities for some to explore more private liaisons.[61] Among the more consistent retreat attendees who were not founding members of the Collective were Cheryl Clarke, Lorraine Bethel, Sharon Page-Ritchie, Cassie Alfonso, and (Akasha) Gloria Hull. Lorde joined the first retreat and continued to participate in coming years.

ON ARMISTICE DAY, November 11, 1977, Lorde finally reached her gynecologist, Marcia Storch, on the telephone. Storch confirmed half the fear sparked by her own self-examination. There was something wrong in her right breast and exploratory surgery was definitely necessary. The prospect of surgery horrified her, and she reeled from the "what-ifs" she now had to think about. If the prognosis was bad, which was the other half of her fear, there would be so many more things to consider because "bad" meant the possibility of metastasized breast cancer that could certainly shorten her life. She was only forty-three and felt there was still so much to do and say. "Bad" also meant money worries, pain, what to tell her children, when. She wanted to be honest but didn't want to frighten Beth and Jonathan, who were now just budding teenagers. Nor did she want to lean too heavily on them. She could lean on Frances, and did, throughout that day and in the days ahead. Though she felt strong, she was shaken, and wondered how long she could maintain her strength. "I don't want this to be true. Any of it,"[62] Lorde determined in those early hours, weighing whether or not to have surgery.

The next day, she wrote:

> It feels like I've been in training for this for years—for the final testing of the manner in which I say I choose to live my live.[*] The refinement of pleasure I wished to examine and have begun to— the power which I release into work and the satisfaction thereof. These things will work now if at all.[63]

The worst-case scenario was that she would die soon and painfully. The least of what could happen, she felt, would be some pain and disfigurement. Lorde tried to focus on other things. It was a sunny, promising day. From her office window, she could see the sails of boats in Staten Island Bay just beyond her house. But no matter how she tried to distract herself, she had a feeling whatever lay ahead was going to be dire.

As the days went by, Lorde bounced between emotional states. She was angry. She cried. She felt empowered, almost relieved, when she agreed to have a biopsy. Two physicians affiliated with Beth Israel Medical Center in Manhattan confirmed there was a tumor in her right breast and concurred that she had a high risk of breast cancer.

Lorde had always "listened" to her body. She felt there was cancer in her. She did not know why this was happening to her, nor what she could have done differently to prevent it. She slept less and less, tortured by fury. She had fantasies of chopping her right breast off, like a she-wolf chewing off a paw caught in a trap. She had to think about letting go of

---

[*]Lorde may have meant to write "life" here instead of repeating "live." The sentence is reproduced as she recorded it in her journal.

something that was precious to her but no longer needed. Maybe that was what she was supposed to learn, if she survived learning it.

"I wish to survive and that has always meant war,"[64] Lorde reminded herself. She began to think of her right breast as no longer a part of her. It had betrayed her, harbored an evil that could now destroy her. She'd lived up until now with a fear of being vulnerable and alone. She told friends about the tumor and impending surgery. Adrienne Rich assured her she was part of a community of women who would face this crisis together. That assurance meant more to Lorde than she could tell Rich at the moment. It also helped her to focus on her love of women and her work.

Lorde prepared to leave for a reading in Worcester, New York. She thought facing an audience chancy, and was unsure if she could pull the moment off. She wanted to see if she could handle being away from Clayton, her mainstay. If she stopped working now, she might never start again. She'd begun to write some prose about her childhood, her father, and her son, and she wanted to finish those projects. There was the manuscript of "The Black Unicorn," which she still needed to shape up before sending it back to John Benedict, her editor at Norton. Then there were the poetry submissions to *Chrysalis*, and a piece by Clare Coss she wanted to follow up on.[65] Staying focused on her work had a calming, curative effect. But spiritually, Lorde felt she was being overtaken by, and becoming, the goddess Seboulisa: "I never thought Seboulisa would overtake me in this fashion—that I would become her so completely that even the symbol of her breast eaten away by worms of sorrow should become mine."[66] Her affinity for Seboulisa now seemed the fulfillment of a mutual destiny.

At the same time, Lorde's fury over what was happening to her personally was inflamed by fury at other events. She was incensed by news of the killing of Randy Evans, a fifteen-year-old black youth shot by Robert Torsney, a New York City police officer who claimed he'd discharged his weapon while succumbing to an epileptic attack. The killings of children in apartheid-ruled South Africa, shot down on the streets of Soweto as they sang freedom songs, were a vile reminder of America's hypocrisy, its pretense of concern for human rights in other countries. The blatantly racist murders of black children in the United

States and South Africa infuriated her; and she felt deeply the connections between liberation struggles at home and over there. The struggle to survive made martyrs of black people, and casualties easily mistaken as the enemy. While Lorde felt her own self "a casualty in a cosmic ecologic war,"[67] she did not want to relinquish her power by envisioning herself as a martyr. She was determined to survive, and to teach.

Shortly before the Thanksgiving break, Lorde painfully told her students at John Jay she was going into the hospital for surgery. She felt as if she were becoming a statistic and she was more afraid than she'd ever been. During the Thanksgiving holiday, she and Frances went to Atlantic City for two days. While there, they took endless steambaths and rode along the boardwalk in a rolling chair. Doing so reminded her of a photograph she'd once seen of Gertrude Stein and Alice B. Toklas, also riding in a rolling chair along that very boardwalk. The similarity between moments lifted her spirits. Lorde thought Atlantic City was the kitsch capital of the earth, but she thoroughly enjoyed being there with Clayton.

On November 29, she went into Beth Israel Medical Center wondering if she would survive, wondering how she might have enjoyed what may have been the last weeks of her short life a bit more. For nearly three weeks, she'd thought of little save her body, its mortality. How was she going to put into action the notion of living fully, should she survive?

Two days after the biopsy, December 1, Lorde was told that the tumor was benign. What she'd learned living "in the fire of anxiety"[68] she didn't want to forget, yet the extreme relief she felt was tinged with anger. She was angry with herself for not knowing all along it was benign, and at her doctors for frightening her so.

Several months before, Lorde had been invited to speak on a panel at the upcoming December meeting of the MLA in Chicago. Sponsored by the Commission on the Status of Women in the Profession and the Gay Caucus of the MLA, the panel was entitled "The Transformation of Silence into Language and Action" and had been conceived by Julia P. Stanley, who was also to be its moderator. The other invited speakers were Adrienne Rich, Mary Daly, and Judith McDaniel. Lorde planned to address the theme of lesbian invisibility in contemporary literature; she'd decided she owed it to herself to amplify her voice, to make sure it was loud enough to be heard by those she was not yet reaching—in particular, younger black lesbians who might be in attendance as Barbara Smith had been the year before. After the cancer scare and biopsy, however, she felt she couldn't do it; it was no longer important and there was no way she was going to go.

Lorde spoke to Rich about her decision not to attend the MLA panel. Rich planned to present an essay entitled "Disloyal to Civilization: Feminism, Racism, Gynephobia."[69] Despite the painful push and pull between herself and Lorde over it, she'd valued Lorde's insights, as well as Cliff's and those of other feminists with whom she shared drafts of her work. It was Rich who suggested Lorde talk about what she'd just been through. At first, Lorde could not see the relevance of her experience to the panel. But as they talked, she began to sense connections between her own self-imposed silence and the panel's theme.[70] The conversation with Rich bolstered Lorde's resolve: she began setting down on paper connections between being a black lesbian poet, life and death, fear and silence.

Assuming the panel's title, Lorde delivered her speech, "The Transformation of Silence into Language and Action,"[71] on December 28. Beyond coming out, it was her most revelatory statement to date. Lorde admitted to those listening the acute fear she felt during her ordeal, and the fear she felt now while speaking. She spoke of her reliance on other women who saw her through it, helping her to become a warrior in the struggle to survive. She implored women in the audience to examine what silences they too lived with, acquiesced to, were becoming casualties of. She'd come face to face with the reality of death, the final silence, she told them; and now she knew there were no silences worth keeping.

Linking race, sexuality, and difference, Lorde seized the moment to air another difficult truth: racism within the women's movement perpetuated black women's invisibility, and had links to the failure to bridge differences between women in spite of notions of "sisterhood." Few white women in the movement then, whether lesbian or heterosexual, were willing to scrutinize the power dynamic inherent in racial disparity or the ways in which they benefited from their own unexamined racism. The issue of white women's racism was left to feminist women of color to articulate, generally at the risk of suffering white women's guilt, tears, and anger. Lorde found their racism unbearable and tiring, and she remained vigilant and outspoken about it; yet she refused, at the same time, to be tokenized by her own popularity amongst white feminists. As much as she desired their adoration, Lorde repeatedly risked her popularity by publicizing issues others could not—or refused to—see.

The transcript of the full panel's remarks was published in *Sinister Wisdom*, a feminist journal, the following year; but in later years its title—"The Transformation of Silence into Language and Action"—became a truism credited to and most associated with Audre Lorde. The essay offered a legacy of quotable "Lorde-isms." "Your silence will not protect you" became popular amongst a younger generation of lesbian and gay activists of color, white feminists, and aficionados of her work worldwide.

While Lorde's speech garnered the compassion of many who heard it, it was no doubt unexpected and unsettling. Afterwards, despite the emotional toll the speech took on her, she was glad she'd gone to the MLA. But fear of the possibility of cancer, of susceptibility to it, never left her. This fear of a life-threatening disease was greater than any fear she'd ever contended with. Thereafter, the magnitude of that fear split Lorde's life in two. Though she continued to evolve as a writer, activist, and woman, fear of cancer seeded Lorde's second life.

the second life

PART ONE

"The Black Unicorn"
(1978–83)

TEN

ORDE DID NOT succumb to her fear of cancer. For nearly a year, she staved off thoughts of the possibility of a life threatened, becoming engrossed in living out an energetic creativity. "A new year of fruit. I am glad to be alive and real—on the journey and most equal to it,"[1] she wrote in her journal as 1978 began. Barbara Smith was glad, too. After hearing Lorde's presentation at the 1977 MLA Convention, she felt the moment "represented a kind of milestone" and was even more convinced now of a black lesbian feminist cultural awakening connecting with political consciousness. In a letter to Lorde dated January 10, 1978, Smith wrote, "Can I say again how alive your being alive makes me feel?!"[2]

As well as putting finishing touches on poems comprising *The Black Unicorn*, Lorde's seventh collection, she turned her attention to tackling prose. She'd become convinced prose was the vehicle to a larger audience[3] and had several projects in mind. She'd crafted a bony outline of them in her journal at the end of 1977, wanting to be sure to write down her intentions since she seemed "to be loosing or losing every scheme of this prose thing."[4]

The intuitive, schematic reach of the outline gives little indication of what Lorde had in mind exactly, except that she planned five pieces which she titled "Standing on a Street Corner," "My Father," "Washington," "Staten Island Midnight," and "My Mother's Mortar." Early in January, it occurred to her why one of the pieces, "My Mother's Mortar," was not as forthcoming as she'd wanted it to be.

> Now I know. The ending of My Mothers Mortar hasnt [sic] come because I am reluctant to plunge into the conqueror, the urge to destroy and to beleaguer as the distorted concomitant bred by social abnormalities which accompany or dilute the unborn movement which is black and female and creative and fullsome.[5]

Lorde's reluctance to "plunge into the conqueror" mapped the dynamics of articulating an eroticism attached to her mother, whose body was to her simultaneously "erotic and dangerous."[6] That eroticism was both explored and exploited later in *Zami*, as she integrated "My Mother's Mortar" into the larger coming-of-age-as-black-and-lesbian narrative driving the work.

In evolving versions of "My Mother's Mortar" drafted in her journal, Lorde recalled the summer she was fifteen, her naïveté at the onstart of menstruation, and the sensuality associated with the pleasure of grinding spices using her mother's mortar and pestle. As she deleted and then reinstated an early statement about a sexual fantasy focused on her mother, Lorde's drafts show some indecision as to whether or not to include the following passage: "And for years afterward whenever I thought about the way I smelled that day . . . I would have a secret fantasy of my mother, her hands wiped dry from washing and her apron untied & laid away, looking down upon me lying on the couch and then slowly thoroughly making silent love to me."[7] Ultimately, she resolved the issue by revising her fantasy in *Zami* into a mutually erotic lesbianesque scenario of herself and her mother "touching and caressing each other's most secret places."[8] The publication of "My Mother's Mortar" in the summer of 1978 was a transformative step, as it signaled Lorde's foray into fiction.[9]

The beginning of a new year's "fruit" found Lorde also tussling with drafts for two strategic essays, "Man Child: A Black Lesbian Feminist's Response" and "Scratching the Surface: Some Notes on Barriers to Women and Loving." Though she resisted the notion that she wrote theory,[10] both essays would prove to be significant contributions to contemporary black lesbian thought.

She'd been invited by Robert Chrisman, editor of *The Black Scholar*, to contribute to a forthcoming 1978 issue called "Blacks and the Sexual Revolution." By the late 1970s, black discourse on the impact of the larger sexual revolution on sexual politics in black communities had reached feverish, if not hysterical, proportions—particularly amongst nationalists and traditionalists who viewed the feminist, lesbian, and gay liberation movements as antithetical to the black liberation struggle.

Lorde filled several pages of notes in her journal, exploring "some ideas—feeling, pulses." She wanted to address "the Black Scholar man," to introduce herself to him as black lesbian poet-mother, and to reach a larger black audience: "And if our struggle was one dimensional Sex Color Class we would have only one quest, one conquest, but our own lives have shown that this is not so." Given the theme, it was an opportunity to confront black homophobia and paralyzing notions of blackness: "There can be no separation because of our differences, which we must recognize and cherish and protect as fiercely as we do our common struggle. . . ."[11]

Lorde's notes made fundamental her black feminist "pulses," as she recorded a flurry of fragmented thought on black women: as African warrior women and as a mythic "we," who once fiercely defended the name of royal husbands and now needed to defend themselves, to ask "what excess of bravery and endurance and triumph can we milk from ourselves in the name of our faces and our sisters and our daughters." At one point, thinking about "a black female aesthetic" made her "hot in the pants" and she teased out sentences about how "the black woman moves her beauty into a cosmic force"; a black aesthetic different from that associated with the Black Arts movement. Lorde rhapsodized over beauty as force, as "a fundamentally female concept"; about the earth as "stroking to bring forth seed," cresting on an analogy of the earth to black women: "it is also intrinsically black meaning deep and maternal. And it moves beyond color. . . . I know that each piece," Lorde noted, "must speak to someone else some woman black or white somewhere needing affirmation she is not alone."

Lorde flirted with several styles throughout the essay—the poetic, the polemic ("My Sisters, In Blackness, I come to you as from another country. . . ."), and tropes of Dahomean female ancestors and black women's mythic struggles—feeling her way through an anthology of ideas, historic and contemporary. Even so, her ideas were not coalescing and, as she did more frequently, with increasing conviction, Lorde appealed to Seboulisa: "Oh goddess help me this feels all so important—that I understand all that moves me—important for myself—my survival which is tied to the other larger importance—for someone else some-where to know we existed before and went through enough to leave word behind saying—Struggle sister."

By the end of her first set of notes, Lorde had worn out these approaches, but not before collapsing into a sexualized reference to black women which she addressed to Clayton: "Frances I find something in their bodies that is particular and needed." Her ideas finally exhausted, Lorde concluded these notes convinced that "Somewhere in all this must be buried the theme for the BS piece on the Sexual Revo-lution"—but somewhat overwhelmed: "this feels so."[12]

That she grappled with essay writing had as much to do with the importance and nature of the pieces as with the demands of the genre. The other piece she was working on was a focus on being lesbian and raising a son. She'd been asked to contribute an essay on the subject to *Conditions*, an alternative women's magazine founded in 1976 by a col-lective of writers—Elly Bulkin, Jan Clausen, Irena Klepfisz, and Rima Shore—that emphasized work by lesbians. In a letter to Adrienne Rich written some time between late July and the first days of August, she expressed frustration with the writing process: ". . . I've taken <u>2 months</u> count it, friend, two months to write this paper about Jonathan for Con-ditions and Adrienne honey tell me there's got to be an easier way!! I may have as you say an enormous well but I'm very short on patience or per-spective." Having sent Rich a draft, she was anxious to hear her com-ments although willing to wait until they could speak in person when she and Frances joined Adrienne and Michelle Cliff in Vermont later in August.[13]

Frustration aside, Lorde was underestimating how much perspective she had as she applied herself to drafting the essay, even as she felt impatient with the drip-by-drip aspect of writing it. In her "first notes for a paper on Sons,"[14] Lorde took a position on male children radically different from that adopted by proponents of feminist separatism, who touted visions of a world without men, denying a more complex, holistic understanding of femaleness and maleness. For Lorde, feminist separatist ideology was, as any ideology of "easy blackness," patently simplistic, creating "those easy identities that we pull over ourselves, like water blankets, that usually wind up smothering us." She was critical of those who chose to be politically fashionable, and maintained:"To be what is fashionable, what is easiest to be, is always dangerous."[15] She consistently resisted taking any stance that meant forfeiting one identity for another, a position congruent with her sense of "learning to live in harmony with your contradictions."[16]

In a subsequent set of notes, Lorde wrote that she wanted "to write a simple how to, knowing there is no way to tell another" lesbian how to raise a son. And in the next sentence, realizing she could only speak of how it was between herself and Jonathan, any theory of lesbian mothering of sons, she decided, was best left to someone else.[17] "Our sons are a piece of ourselves—or reflect a piece of ourselves as women that we are reluctant to acknowledge."

Lorde's perspective on raising a son who would feel for himself, who would not rely on a woman to do so, was rooted in what she believed to have been part of the difficulty during her marriage to Ed Rollins: "The most important message I have for my son to keep him from committing his father's fatal errors is 'I do not exist to do your feeling for you.' "[18] She well understood the ways Beth had a gender advantage over Jonathan: "Sons—boys have no role models—Our girls have us as positive role models—the boys have nothing—they are trail blazers—they are making their own definitions of self as men."[19] Lorde consulted with Jonathan while writing about him, incorporating his voice and youthful perspectives in her essay.[20]

At the time she was writing "Man Child: A Black Lesbian Feminist's Response," Jonathan was fourteen years old. In her later notes, Lorde congratulated herself that Jonathan had had the "advantage of sampling

a non-sexist relationship" free from "those natural assumptions" generally driving power dynamics in heterosexual couples. She and Frances
had made attempts to question, evaluate, and measure their feelings
toward power and its expression. Yet however much Lorde and Clayton
interrogated notions of power, Lorde's critique of "those natural assumptions" inherent to heterosexuality and patriarchy was defined by the fact
that she and Clayton were an interracial lesbian couple. Lorde noted, "J
has had a model—not of a relationship certainly, but of relating."[21] She
admitted that Jonathan lived in a household in which "power was clearly
female."[22] This assertion resisted masculinist notions of power, and contradicted the idea that power was something women should be ambivalent about or suspicious of. Lorde also accepted that she had no easy
answers for her son's survival as a black man,[23] defined, as it was, not just
by his lesbian parents but by the historic oppression of black men in a
racist culture.

As an adult, Jonathan's assessment of his progression from child to
man was a comment upon the singular position he held within their
family and household, Lorde's stance as lesbian feminist mother, and a
level of emotional independence he was forced to assume:

> Manhood in the household in which I grew up was something
> that was left entirely to me to define. My mother provided a list of
> things that were repugnant in other men. Society provided a list
> of things that were required in every quote man end quote. And I
> was left to find for myself the definitions that would provide the
> operating structure within which my personality would grow and
> exist.

Unable to "live by negatives, which is what my mother was giving," and
refusing to be defined by a society for which he had little respect and
whose definitions of manhood were "completely anathema" to his
beloved mother, Jonathan was left to his own devices to define what
being a man and manhood meant.[24]

Drafting "Man Child: A Black Lesbian Feminist's Response" positioned Lorde to consider the impact of raising a son within an "honest"[25]
interracial lesbian household, as practice. Equally important was the

opportunity it afforded to address oversimplified solutions to oppression of any kind. This point was at the nexus of Lorde's "theory of difference." It distinguished her from white feminist writers of the time whose critiques of women's oppression lacked the complexity of racialized analyses. In short, as an out black lesbian mother, Lorde put forward a more complex discussion of lesbian mothering; going against the grain of—and widening—the vision of feminist discourse on male children and, by extension, the potential of men as allies[26] rather than simply as generalized "oppressors."

When she returned to drafting notes for *The Black Scholar* piece, which she later titled "Scratching the Surface: Some Notes on Barriers to Women and Loving,"[27] Lorde was more focused, outlining four points she fleshed out as essential arguments. For one, she thought it critical to make the point that racism, sexism, and homophobia stem from the same root: an inability to tolerate difference, or to recognize the potential of difference as a beneficial force. Second, she wanted to make a point about black women bonding, as an aspect of black women's traditional relationships with men, and by citing mythic, historic, and actual contemporary examples of the Amazons of Dahomey and West African women's market guilds. Her third point was "the double face of racism/sexism"—defining sexual politics in the black community.

In making her fourth point about "self-propelled, self-motivated & self-defined" black women, Lorde explored several pages of thought noting aspects of black women's sociosexual history; linking black men as sexual prize, the threat of black male disapproval, black women's spiritual memory, black fear of black lesbians, the intransigent, unaddressed racism of white women, and racial hostility (both from within and without) as errant, prevalent behavior amongst oppressed peoples.[28] She also included here information she'd discovered in the published narrative of an Efik-Ibibio woman of Nigeria who'd had a lifelong relationship with another African woman.[29] In sum, "Scratching the Surface" outlined the transcending themes of Lorde's essays and speeches, from that point on, vis-à-vis black women's lives within a black community.

"This is the year I pass into the fish—," Lorde noted on the day of her forty-fourth birthday; "the sun now goes into Pisces at 7:21pm and I was born around 9pm on 2/18/34 and it was in Aquarius then. It does all seem to fit the pattern of my living—I feel myself moving into a Piscean head the last couple of years."[30] Ever since her days as a member of "The Branded," Lorde had turned to occult practices such as astrology and the *I Ching*—an ancient Chinese divination system also known as *The Oracle of Change*—as ways of interpreting intuitions, dreams, circumstances, time, and destiny. The "Piscean head" she felt herself moving into reflected a deeper translation of the private self as public self. She now defined overcoming the isolation engendered by keeping "the private" private as an essential, revolutionary act of her own and other women's survival.

That deeper interrogation of the private was embedded in one of Lorde's most celebrated poems, "A Litany for Survival,"[31] of which she'd drafted pivotal segments as early as April 1977. Beginning then with the lines, "you have been imprinted with fear/like a line in the center of your forehead," Lorde shifted to a more intimate voice, replacing the pronouns "you" and "your" with "we" and "our" as she wrote the following stanzas:

> . . .
> When the sun rises we are afraid
> it might not remain
> When the sun sets we are afraid
> it might not rise again
> When our stomachs are full we are afraid
> of indigestion
> When our stomachs are empty we are afraid
> we may never eat again.
>
> When we are loved we are afraid
> that love will vanish
> When we are alone we are afraid
> love will never return
> When we speak we are afraid
> our words will not be welcome
> but when we are silent
> we are still afraid.[32]

The poem's "we" at once made particular and universalized the private, speaking to the fear associated with the private, and to the importance of articulating the private as an act of survival. Lorde's frugal use of the refrain, "we were never meant to survive,"[33] endeared the line and the poem to her audiences and readers. As one of her most memorable poems of the late 1970s and into the 1980s, "A Litany for Survival" helped to frame the intensity of her emotional impact upon lesbians, gay men, feminists, and those with other radicalized identities.

Lorde's sense of herself as passing out of the influence of the sun in Aquarius—one life—now and into a second life influenced by the sun in Pisces ("a Piscean head") resonated with a transformation in her literary reputation as poet solely. She had an ambitious creativity: in addition to "My Mother's Mortar," she was at work on fragments of other autobiographical fictions she completed and published as self-contained pieces, ultimately framed by their inclusion in *Zami*. One recounted a childhood longing for "a friend, a little sister" and fantasies about how to "acquire this little person."[34] Another recounted a family summer vacation during which one night, because the entire family slept in one large room, she shared a bed with her older sisters—relishing an atypical chance to listen to the stories they entertained each other with, inserting herself into the activity, much to Helen's disgruntlement. As a self-contained segment of a projected book-length manuscript-in-progress she now called "Prosepiece," Lorde interwove the two fragments, titling the narrative "Of Sisters and Secrets" for its publication in *The Lesbian Path* (1980).[35]

A week after she turned forty-four, Lorde accompanied her mother to New York Infirmary Hospital, where Mrs. Lorde was admitted late in February. The diagnosis was that Mrs. Lorde was suffering either from a myocardial infection or from a potassium-sodium imbalance, and Lorde worried her mother might be fatally ill.[36] She still had in mind a return trip to the Caribbean, to see Grenada. She'd planned to take Frances with her and to leave on January 20, but a severe snowstorm forced them to cancel their plans that day. Their new departure date was set for March 17. As it drew near, Mrs. Lorde's health improved, and Lorde recorded a brief comment in her journal that her mother looked and felt better.

Beneath the comment about her mother, Lorde inscribed the following passage:

waters in the
The locks and dams of my living
are coming together—the parts are
disolving [sic] between the water dikes.
Once the sluices are open, energy
can flow like water back & forth
from & to all the different parts
of my existance [sic], reinforcing & taking
sustenance from wherever necessary.
That is the meaning of #29, the abysmal.[37]

She'd consulted the *I Ching* by proposing a question and had received this passage as her "answer," the twenty-ninth hexagram, K'AN, both trigrams of which denote "water, dangerous." Exactly what question she asked the *I Ching* is unclear, but her interpretation of the meaning of the twenty-ninth hexagram as "the abysmal" captures both the sense of a "perilous chasm" ahead and the ability of water to flow ever onward, maintaining its true nature even while running through a dangerous abyss.[38]

LORDE AND CLAYTON arrived in Port of Spain, Trinidad, on Friday, March 17, leaving for Grenada early the following morning. Lorde made no notes on the stopover in her journal, except to assert a pithy comparison once in Grenada: "The Grenadians & the Barbadians walk like an african people. The Trinidadians do not."[39]

The cab they took from the airport in Grenada to their hotel on Grand Anse Beach was driven by Claudius Thomas, a gentleman from Grenville—the same parish in which her mother had lived—who responded to Lorde's queries about the parish and informed her he "knew the old lady." At first glance, Lorde's notes do not clearly indicate who "the old lady" was, but ensuing references suggest she was speaking of her mother's older sister, her aunt, Sister Lou. After checking into their room, she and Frances sunned on the beach, which Lorde noted "was alive with sea eggs." Having arrived on the island on Saturday, market day, they then made their way up Grand Anse Beach and north a short distance to Market Square in St. George's, where they bought some spices and fruit.⁴⁰

Lorde's first observations of Grenada confirmed her maternal connections to it: "Grenada. I am here. This is in truth a lush & beautifully verdant haphazard island," and, "This is the country of my forebearing mothers, the women who defined themselves by what they did." Though in awe of their beauty, Lorde was also struck by a sense of the paradox defining the island-homes of her parents: "Grenada and Barbados will always be poor enough to stay healthy though many children die." Even today, agriculture and tourism still drive Grenada's economy, providing skilled and unskilled jobs for a laboring class. Middle-class enclaves dot urban sections of the island. For the average Grenadian, poverty and purchasing power are shifting realities on an island where the land provides an abundant source of edibles, the surrounding waters provide a rich source of seafoods, and most consumable goods are expensive, imported items.

In those first hours in Grenada, Lorde recalled racial aspects of her mother's influence upon her. She noted that her own racial ambivalence, what she called "my schizophrenia," had come "highly recommended" by a mother who taught her never to trust white people or anyone darker than herself. She could see more clearly the historic deference to white values and white, or near-white, standards of beauty in the culture her mother grew up in, and she experienced a sense of compassion for Mrs. Lorde, commenting, "my mother had a hard row to tow" and "what a crazy mixed up set of schemata or values she grew up in."

Lorde could now begin to consider deeper meanings of her mother's stories about Grenada: how Mrs. Lorde's knowledge of the healing uses of herbs had no context in New York; how strange it was for her mother to observe that "Pumpkin was a decoration to them [American women], and they treated their husbands better than they cared for their children"; how Mrs. Lorde's cultural dislocation, the psychic rupture conditioned by migration to America, resulted in an aggregate unfamiliarity with this new world: "There was so little that she knew in the strange one's country. How the electric worked, where the free milk for babies fund handouts occured [sic] and at what time." The memory of a mother who pinched her daughters' arms to make them behave while wandering through the galleries of the Museum of Natural History brought an understanding of a woman who "was over-anxious tense and afraid."[41] In these sympathetic journal entries, Lorde recorded central themes of what was to become *Zami*.

That Sunday, she and Frances spent the early hours of the day sunning and walking on the beach. Escaping the sun in the afternoon, they retired to their room; there they devoured the fruits they'd bought at the market, and sat on their veranda drinking rum punch, reading, and writing postcards. Their one complaint centered on fussing with the hotel's staff about not having enough water to drink. The next day, they decided to go to St. George's where the island registry was located.[42]

Just as on her trip to Barbados Lorde had attempted to discover her father's premigration history, so now she researched as much as she could about her mother's life in Grenada. Birth and death records were kept at the Health Department in St. George's. When she and Frances arrived there around eleven-thirty that morning, it had already closed. They returned at 1:00 P.M and filed requests for information on Linda Belmar and Lorde's maternal grandmother, Elizabeth Noel (Ma-Liz).[43] According to her notes, Lorde learned that Ma-Liz had been born in 1868 and died sometime between 1931 and 1932, and that Mrs. Lorde was born between 1897 and 1898.

Tuesday, March 21, was the vernal equinox and Lorde thought it "a good day to go to Grenville."[44] Claudius Thomas had agreed to be their driver. In addition to visiting Sister Lou, she wanted to see some of the places immortalized in her mother's stories: Noel's Hill, Taylor's Anglican School, McNeilly's Store, the Catholic church on Grand Bras Hill, the place where her mother walked down the hill to the sea. "Excited and anxious at the same time,"[45] she wondered if Sister Lou would be able to talk, what she looked like, and whether she remembered Linda.

Lorde did not record specific answers to those questions, although she noted Sister Lou's telephone number in her journal at the conclusion of some fragmented references to rum, Telescope Beach, big palm leaves, Mount St. Catherine (the highest point on the island), coco fermentation, red french cashew, calabash tree, and flamboyans. More than likely, this enigmatic list represented snatches of conversation with Claudius Thomas and what she learned of the landscape during the long, hilly drive from Grand Anse northeast to Grenville. In the midst of these notes, Lorde jotted down an unexplained sentence, "Mr. Hutchinson knew my mother well,"[46] and wrote in overly large letters the surnames NOEL and McNEILLY—each followed by question marks.

The following day, Lorde noted: "This has been a rich trip, although yesterday was a strange day. I feel a ghost has been laid to rest, but I dreamed confusing dreams last night full of light-skinned people I did not know, but was involved with in some way." She'd read in the newspaper that someone named Innocent Belmar had been killed in Grenville and marked that item in the paper.[47] Though she'd made no notes addressing Sister Lou in detail, Lorde did record that "The mystery of the Noel, McNeilly, Belmar Lorde clan/groups grows & grows. I never know what the shore hides, nor what the women refuse to tell."[48] And though she felt "a ghost has been laid to rest," their meeting raised several unanswered questions. How was she related to the McNeillys, if she was? Who was Gordon Hutchinson exactly? Why did her mother speak of working in McNeilly's store and Sister Lou of working in Alfred Noel's store (her maternal great-grandfather)? Why didn't anyone want to speak of Mignon Noel, her great-grandmother? Was Mignon white or black? Why had Ma-Liz's brother, Matthew, been so cruel to Linda and her sisters? Why did that Mr. Hutchinson want to know where she was born?[49]

Lorde and Clayton remained in Grenada for the balance of the week; they left on Saturday, March 25, on a flight for Trinidad en route back to New York. In her journal, she made no mention of whether or not she went to Carriacou, the tiny sister island a ferry ride away where her mother was actually born.

Two weeks after her return to New York, Lorde sent a business-related letter to Kirsten Grimstad. While always encouraging *Chrysalis* to embrace a diversity of women writers—the growing list now included Barbara Smith, Lorraine Bethel, (Akasha) Gloria Hull, and others involved with the black feminist retreats—Lorde noted that she was deeply concerned about the magazine's treatment of poetry. She praised the editors for having done "an incredible job of keeping Chrysalis afloat in the face, I know, of personal and economic adversity" and reiterated her belief in *Chrysalis*'s "great potential" to be "a vigorous and effective journal of women's culture." But she hardly took the editorial board to task for giving minimal space to poetry and for an absence of aesthetic primacy where poetry was concerned:

> . . . At some point, the Board must make up its collective mind about the function of poetry in Chrysalis. You may decide to exclude poetry from the magazine, although I think that would be a very unwise decision. But in a Journal of Women's Culture, to include poetry as less functional than breaks between articles, partakes of the same western european mind-fuck that masquerades as serious scholarship in the patriarchal academic media. . . .[50]

Poetry was not the magazine's focus, but Lorde felt a deep responsibility to the poets whose work she championed. She was impatient with the way the magazine presented their poems, and that it delayed publication and allowed typographical errors by the printer.[51] In short, she criticized the editors' "shocking insensitivity to the needs of the poem as a work of art."[52] Also, the editors' plans to do a poetry issue remained unfulfilled. Since the magazine had already announced those plans, Lorde aired her concern about the volume of poetry she'd been holding onto in light of their stated intentions.[53]

Kirsten Grimstad—at this point managing editor—responded to Lorde's letters during this period. Grimstad cited financial stress, the editors' efforts at fund-raising, and other reasons why varying issues were delayed—including defective paper. In one letter, Grimstad also noted that the interpersonal tensions between the editors had been a burden, but that those tensions were finally subsiding. There was a renewed spirit of cooperation between them, and a commitment to work together in spite of their differences.[54] Lorde had an appreciation for the financial and emotional stresses associated with feminist efforts at publishing, and was openly sympathetic to the Chrysalis editors, but she did not waver from her sense that the magazine disrespected, if not sacrificed, poetry and poets within its pages.

WHEN "SCRATCHING the Surface: Some Notes on Barriers to Women and Loving" appeared in the April 1978 issue of The Black Scholar, it did so alongside articles by scholars and activists such as Angela Davis, John-netta Cole, Elizabeth Hood, Assata Shakur (JoAnne Chesimard), Nathan Hare, and Robert Staples, all of whom put forward varying perspectives on race, gender, and sexuality. Lorde's essay was distinguished from the pack by virtue of being the first by an out black lesbian to be published in a journal whose targeted audience was black intelligentsia. The article heralded Lorde's desire to engage black public discourse on her own terms: "The black lesbian has come under increasing attack from both black men and heterosexual black women . . . the black lesbian is an emotional threat only to those black women who are unsure of, or unable to express their feelings . . . for other black women, in any meaningful way. . . ."[55]

As far as promoting more complex notions of blackness and black women's sexuality, the essay's publication represented a watershed moment in African American letters: a major achievement both for Audre Lorde and for an emerging generation of black lesbian writers.[56] However, Lorde was not completely satisfied with it. In an interview with Adrienne Rich published in 1981, she noted that "The piece was useful, but limitedly so because I didn't ask some essential question . . . I had not asked myself the question: Why is women loving women so threatening to black men, unless they want to assume the white male position?"[57] As hindsight, her assessment suggests why she thought she was only "scratching the surface."

By mid-1978, Lorde was engaged in expanding her literary contacts and her definitions of herself as poet. In addition to producing essays, she drafted segments of "Street Corner," a narrative that recounted "how being young and black and gay and lonely felt"[58] while living on the Lower East Side and going to the mostly white lesbian bars of the 1950s. At the invitation of Ginny Vida, the editor of the 1978 anthology, *Our Right to Love: A Lesbian Resource Book*, she'd lifted the piece nearly intact from her journal; it was submitted under the title "I've Been Standing on This Street Corner a Hell of a Long Time!" Significantly, Lorde's narrative was the first to follow an introduction to the anthology's segment on "The Spectrum of Lesbian Experience," which acknowledged the persistent racist and class-conscious attitudes that women of color and working-class white women encountered within a white, middle-class-dominated feminist movement.[59] But if there was one work in 1978 that illuminated her literary transformation, it was *The Black Unicorn*.

Most of the sixty-seven poems comprising *The Black Unicorn* were written between 1975 and 1977. In Lorde's judgment, the poems included were indicative of intensely "productive years."[60] It was slated for late fall publication,[61] but a letter to Adrienne Rich suggested she had copies sometime between mid-July and early August. In that letter, Lorde remarked, "The Black Unicorn did come out—which I've been doubting for the last 6 weeks—and its 'real purty' as a speckled pup." Consoled by the fact the book was a reality now, she followed up with a parenthetical aside: "The print is execrable; the red is a little off; the quotes are not what I've [sic] have chosen; the back looks naked; the photo is sappy, but the poems make me wake up in the middle of the night wondering when I'll ever write something like that again."[62]

The Africa that Lorde saw, felt, dreamed of, and discovered in legends while visiting its west coast in 1974 and 1977 became the overarching metaphor in *The Black Unicorn*. Fully embracing both experiential and acquired knowledge, Lorde sculpted *The Black Unicorn* into a bold state-ment on the meaning of connection to Africa to her; at the back she even included a glossary of terms upon which many of the poems depended. During an interview shortly after publication, Lorde stated she'd orga-nized the collection of poems "because they seemed to spark a particular dialectic in that order. It wasn't chronological."[63] Beginning with the nine poems in Part I, *The Black Unicorn* situated Lorde's embrace of Africa in the bonds between women as sisters, mothers, and daughters, and in the legendary goddess-mother figures of Seboulisa and Yemanjá (the Yoruba goddess of the oceans, mother of other goddesses and gods, who is sym-pathetic to women). As R. B. Stepto's review suggested, in "From the House of Yemanjá" for example, she established a personal connection which offered up "new renderings of the legends that surround them":[64]

> My mother had two faces and a frying pot
> where she cooked up her daughters
> into girls
> before she fixed our dinner.[65]

In the title poem, "The Black Unicorn," Lorde also located the meaning of Africa at "the boundary between unnaming and renaming,"[66] asserting the existence of an oppressed, corporeal black unicorn, in contradistinction to Western mythic stories of the unicorn as benign, virginal, and white (free):

> The black unicorn is restless
> the black unicorn is unrelenting
> the black unicorn is not
> free.[67]

This title poem resonated with the image on the book's jacket: a photographic rendering of a headdress worn by the Bambara people of Mali (West Africa) known as the Chi-Wara. The best known version featured a highly stylized carving of an antelope head, its flowing mane resting upon a majestic, arched neck. Used in rites re-enacting myths centered on the birth of agriculture[68] and traditionally worn by dancers performing in pairs in the fields, the Chi-Wara ensured fecundity and communal power and was believed by the Bambara to have been sent by the Creator to instruct them in the cultivation of corn. Interestingly, the curvature of the long-horned image used for Lorde's book is associated with a mythical combative antelope who is a male buck; the female doe is characterized as having straight horns, no mane, and carries on her back her short-legged offspring.[69]

Reconfiguring "the boundary between unnaming and renaming," the poems in Part I defined Lorde by what she was not—not of the West, spiritually, and not white—and redefined, in the poem "A Woman Speaks," what it meant to be woman:

> . . .
> I have been woman
> for a long time
> beware my smile
> I am treacherous with old magic . . .[70]

In touch with her "own ancient, noneuropean consciousness of living as a situation to be experienced and interacted with,"[71] Lorde's reclamation of African epistemology conflated an Africa in the West, an adaptation and transformation of European culturalisms, and black survival as it had been historically shaped by the New World.[72]

Having established "African history and mythology as a basis for her imagery about women,"[73] the poems in the remaining three sections of *The Black Unicorn* took more contemporary positions on Lorde's bonds with women as intersections of the political, personal, and erotic. In "For Assata" (Part II), Lorde responded to the imprisonment of Black Panther Assata Shakur (née JoAnne Chesimard). One of the most vocal black female revolutionaries in the 1970s, Shakur had been a target of J. Edgar Hoover's campaign to disrupt and defame the impact of radical black nationalist organizations. During a shoot-out between state police troopers and three Black Panthers—including Shakur—on the New Jersey Turnpike in May 1973, Shakur was wounded, then captured after a brief chase. One of the state troopers, Werner Foerster, was killed in the shoot-out. Four years later, on April 16, 1977, Shakur was convicted of his murder and sentenced to life imprisonment.[74] While noting briefly the perils of sisterhood, the poem illustrates Lorde's sense of connection to a history that bound black and white women warriors:

> . . . Assata my sister warrior
> Joan of Arc and Yaa Asantewa
> embrace
> at the back of your cell.[75]

Several poems in Parts III and IV—including "Therapy," "Recreation," "Ghost," "Bazaar," and "Solstice"—share a thematic concern with women's bodies as locations for the tension between home (the familiar) and a new world (what must be made anew). In "Fog Report," Lorde converses with a lover, interrogating that tension, and concluding on images necessary to remaking the bonds between them:

> I am tempted
> to take you apart
> and reconstruct your orifices
> your tongue your truths your fleshy altars . . .[76]

Reviews of *The Black Unicorn* would be decidedly mixed. *Booklist* observed, "Thick with need, knowledge, and blackness, *Black Unicorn* is a not-too-gentle collection of poems." Citing a "quality of quickness" to the work's rhythm, the reviewer also noted that *The Black Unicorn* bantered about a number of subjects, including black motherhood.[77] Rochelle Ratner, poetry columnist for the *SoHo Weekly News*, reviewed the book for *Library Journal*. Ratner called attention to Lorde's consistent concern with her identity as woman in poems that were "hard-edged, compelling, and vital"; she elaborated on Lorde's ability to slip "gracefully into her various personae" in historical and contemporary relationships with other women.[78] *Kirkus Reviews* was unequivocally insistent that "The poems offer little in the way of an emotional center but rely, rather, on references to obscure African rituals, places and objects."[79]

On the other hand, the review in *Choice* commended Lorde and *The Black Unicorn* for the same things *Kirkus Reviews* found wanting. Acknowledging that Lorde had been a "strong lyrical figure in Afro-American Life," and her multiple identities as woman, mother, teacher, lover, the reviewer went on to note, "Now she has added another self— the spirit that has gone to Africa and become imbued with the symbols, rituals, the intensities of life there."[80] The poet and critic Hayden Carruth, in a review in *The Nation* in which he commented on a number of books of poetry released that year, admitted that *The Black Unicorn* was a book he felt divided about. On the one hand, he didn't care much for Lorde's writing, which he thought teetered too close to the commonplace and led him to wonder why contemporary black poets hadn't achieved, in his estimation, the eloquence of their Francophone Caribbean and African counterparts. His obvious bias toward black writers writing within European linguistic traditions aside, Carruth also said that her "best poems move me deeply."[81]

Andrea Benton Rushing and R. B. Stepto both praised Lorde's fresh approach to an African past as a vehicle for reimagining the feminine. Writing for *Ms.* magazine, Rushing proclaimed that Lorde's approach to that past was "a sane corrective for those excesses of 1960s cultural nationalism which urged black women into polygamous and deferential relationships with men."[82] Stepto's review in *Parnassus: Poetry in Review* echoed Rushing's. Beginning with the pronouncement that *The Black Unicorn* was "a personal triumph for Lorde in terms of the development of her canon" and "an event in contemporary letters," Stepto cited Audre Lorde and Jay Wright as the only two North American poets who had the talent to write poetry that went beyond oversimplified references to African gods and traditions. Noting an essential difference between the two as Lorde's embodiment of the feminine and Wright's embodiment of the masculine in West African cosmologies, Stepto asserted that both poets shared "abilities to create a fresh, New World Art out of ancient Old World lore," making use of a communal, historic, prophetic, and personal voice generally associated with the African griot. He went on to claim that the goal of *The Black Unicorn* was to present an invigorating, powerful, magnificently feminine voice modulated by feminist timbres, which shaped and made accessible "Lorde's particular envisioning of a black transatlantic tradition."[83]

LATE IN JULY 1978, Lorde attended the Fourth Black Feminist retreat (she had not attended since the first retreat a year earlier). During the retreat she concluded in her journal, "I don't fit into this group." There were several reasons why she did not "fit." The women were a generation younger than she was. Though certainly a model for them as an older lesbian, Lorde's persona as mother figure, as authority, intensified the generational differences. Since the black feminist retreats were a project of the Combahee River Collective, there was a fluidity between the two groups in terms of key personalities, participation, and membership. Lorde was not at the center of either, although she was a significant, albeit centrifugal, presence at retreats she did attend. Nor were they a group over which she had control; as activists in their own right, they had articulated, political agendas. Furthermore, they promoted an identity politics as black women and, unlike the groups of white women Lorde primarily interacted with, she had no racialized upper hand, in that regard, in their company.

Lorde also made note of two particular "assumptions" she felt at odds with during their discussions: that it was inappropriate to have a male lover, and inappropriate for women in the group to be lovers except within the context of a serious relationship. In contrast to their purism, and as she had lived her life, both of these "assumptions" were foreign to her; both precluded exercising the sexual fluidity she had practiced in the past and the sexual spontaneity with women she desired and cultivated presently, at and away from home. While Lorde accepted that the group would provide black feminists a base of emotional support, she saw these women as "a literate/political group that does not value physical activity."[84] However, "physical activity," the erotic component of their political work, did become a subtext of their gatherings, ultimately creating a tense, disruptive dynamic when some relationships went awry.[85] Lorde no doubt saw in these younger women opportunities to turn their admiration of her into affairs of the moment and was disappointed by their insistence that "we are here for courageous political action" even when individual behavior contradicted that claim.

Lorde distilled from their discussions "that we mustn't discuss white women in terms of love & affection."[86] Within this group, such discussions were tricky, particularly since their goal to institutionalize black feminism meant an ideological separation from white feminism and white women. At the same time, desire—in the context of difference— shaped and unleashed notions of sexual freedom between black and white lesbian women, and common cause often necessitated recognizing white women as allies. Further, some women at the retreats, including Lorde and Barbara Smith, were involved with white women intimately.[87] The issue of relating to white women, as lovers and allies, would surface during the fifth retreat a year later.[88]

When Lorde got back to Staten Island, she and Frances followed through with their summer plans, as was family custom now, once Beth and Jonathan went off to camp on July 28. Some days after the children were gone, Lorde wrote to Adrienne Rich.

In her letter, Lorde thanked Adrienne for directions to the place Rich and Cliff kept in Vermont, and informed her waiting friends that she and Frances planned to spend Friday and Saturday at Tupper Lake in upstate New York, before taking the ferry across to Burlington to join them. She looked forward to their company and to talking with them "in the cool of the evening green." Lorde also briefly mentioned a prose piece, "Tar Beach," which she'd found herself drafting (". . . and this swam up like a silky mermaid begging to be written")[89] while working on notes for a paper she was to give at the Fourth Berkshire Conference on the History of Women, at Mount Holyoke College, toward the end of August.

The tale of a brief affair with an intriguing black woman named "Afrekete" (Kitty), "Tar Beach" framed frank descriptions of lesbian love within the storied context of the couple's introduction at a black lesbian house party in Queens, during the 1950s; there, in sharp contrast to the plot of "I've Been Standing on This Street Corner a Hell of a Long Time!," racial sameness supplanted racial difference in providing a spiritual, much-needed home for Lorde that was at once physical, erotic, and emotional. Significantly, "Afrekete" lived in a reimagined Harlem. And, as Lorde scripted it, the end of the relationship provided a telling metaphor of her relationship to her birthplace:

> We had come together like the elements erupting into an electric storm, exchanging energy, sharing charge, brief and drenching. Then we parted, passed, reformed, reshaping ourselves the better for the exchange. . . .[90]

Once in Vermont, Lorde felt closer to her work as poet, writing in her journal of "the work expressed in my tongue however stumbling." She also felt at peace in the natural environment there, and reveled in the solitude of having no one around for miles except her friends.[91] It was a welcome respite before heading off to the Fourth Berkshire Conference.

Organized by women historians, the Berkshire Women's History conferences were a response to their historic isolation within the male-dominated American Historical Association, and to the developing significance of women's studies in academe.[92] For some lesbians who planned to attend, the fourth conference was framed by protest as word spread there would be no papers on lesbian history presented.[93] At a time when gender studies also was emerging as a discipline, the exclusion of papers on lesbian history was seen as an affront to many. In the weeks prior to the conference, Barbara Smith took the lead in coordinating the presence of members of the black feminist retreats. She sent out copies of the formalized program, information on the protests, and travel and registration instructions, urging their attendance.[94] By the time the conference began, the protests had produced separate meetings, including a general meeting open to anyone interested in the history of sexuality,[95] which began the first night.

Though not a traditional paper on lesbian history, Lorde's paper, "Uses of the Erotic: The Erotic as Power," presented on August 25, historicized the suppression of the erotic. It pioneered the notion that women needed to reclaim their erotic energy, which had been suppressed within them.[96] As Lorde claimed, "when we begin to live from within outward . . . we begin to give up, of necessity, being satisfied with suffering and self-negation. . . ."[97] Although "Uses of the Erotic" did not overtly address what a later generation of black feminist theorists would define as the burden of a historical legacy overshadowing black women's bodies and, therefore, the particular difficulty of reclaiming an erotic black female body, it was a first "in linking the erotic to power and resistance."[98]

After the Berkshire Conference, Lorde returned home, where she typed a letter to Barbara Smith. As well as promising to send a revised copy of "Tar Beach" and touching "on all the loose ends I mean to talk with you about and always forget," she praised Smith's presentation at the conference and the impact of Smith's work upon her own:

> First, I want to tell you again what a good job you did at the Berks. I really envy you your ability to stand flatfooted and correct, and assemble a coherent and elegant presentation from your wealth of work, and to do it so eloquently. . . . I'm sending you a copy of my Berks paper because I want you to have it. In some way that I myself am not clear about, there are pieces of it that belong to you, or that would not have been expressed without that place which is you in my heart, and I am thankful to you for that.[99]

With activities drawing to a close, Lorde reflected on that summer, in her journal, as one during which she'd felt safe and secure. Though she wrote some, she hadn't pushed herself to write, and was pleased with how much and what she'd completed. She felt she'd worked hard, under pressure, and had produced: for other women, certainly, and, more accurately, for herself. The essays, the new book, the prose pieces she'd written and published, her appearance at the Berkshire Conference, were all work she'd accomplished in solitude. In Vermont, she'd worked encircled by a world of loving women friends and felt, as she wrote in early September, "Those 4 glorious days on the hill—I had never allowed myself to experience that particular kind of closeness & space both at the same time before with any one other than Frances."

Lorde interpreted the experience of "that sweetness of womanspace" as a sense of being able to work or play in communion with other women. Within that kind of space, she believed, connection to the erotic was allowed to flow, energizing women—and their connection to each other—at a visceral, creative core. It was a feeling she did not want to let go of, and she was momentarily "depressed at coming back to the world—it is as if the sun has gone out in more ways than one."[100]

On Labor Day, during her regular self-exam, Lorde discovered "the huge lump"[101] in her right breast. She'd lived in fear for almost a year now of the possibility of cancer. It was a possibility that filled her with terror and dread. Lorde's decision to be hospitalized and undergo a second biopsy was shaped by an overarching "rage to live that became an absolute determination to do whatever was necessary to accomplish that living."[102] How to do so was a decision that only she could make.

Unlike the first scare, but because of it, this time Lorde was much more prepared. In the days before entering Memorial Sloan-Kettering Cancer Center, with assistance from friends, she researched information on alternative therapies to cancer treatment; considered the impact of diet and nutrition on cancer prevention; and studied the efficacy of such conventional medical practices as radiation, chemotherapy, and surgery (mastectomy). Throughout, she relied on an emotional network of close women friends who mobilized around her, among whom were Blanche Cook, Clare Coss, Michelle Cliff, Adrienne Rich, her sister Helen, Bernice Goodman, and Frances Clayton, first and foremost.

Lorde underwent her second biopsy on September 19. The following day, she summed up the enormity of the results:

> . . . I was operated upon and it was malignant. The work I did last year was not in vain, but it all seems so monstrously unfair. My sabbatical, the book that may never get written, but I insist I will—I must.[103]

Lorde's journal also records a list of questions she had for her oncologist, Dr. Peter Pressman. She was interested in discussing other alternatives to radiation, mastectomy, and chemotherapy—such as nutrition therapy. She wanted to know if her decision was to have a mastectomy, would it be better to have it at Lenox Hill Hospital or at Sloan-Kettering. She wanted to know if the lump she felt was the malignancy or the cancer that was part of it. Lorde also wondered about the implications of the lesion being close to the nipple. Was that significant and, if so, how significant? How long had it been developing—was there any connection to the last lesion, in terms of its course, effect, or otherwise? This last question appears to be the only one Lorde got an answer to, noting after it a single underlined word: "<u>years</u>."[104]

In addition, she needed to know how long she would be hospitalized after a mastectomy, and questioned the impact of surgery on the use of her arm and chest muscles. As several of her questions suggested, Lorde was leaning toward mastectomy—radical surgical removal of the breast—and already had determined she would have surgery if the biopsy proved the tumor malignant.

The day before her mastectomy, which was scheduled for September 22 at Sloan-Kettering, Lorde wrote:

> I'm glad I had this extra year, and that my right breast was so precious to me. The anger I felt last year faded, and I'm glad because my breasts have always been dear to me and it would have been a shame not to have enjoyed the last year of one of them. I feel very dear towards it, and yet now I'm prepared to lose it in a way I wasn't quite ready to last November.

Over the course of the previous ten months, she'd wrestled with an intuitive feeling that "this would be the final outcome." Despite the first diagnosis that the tumor was benign, she'd had a sense that

> It never seemed like a finished business for me, why exactly I don't know. But this year inbetween was like a hiatus, an interregnum, in which I came to accept, without thinking consciously of it, the emotional fact/truths of what I had come to in those hor-

rendous 3 weeks last November. . . . I think my body sense was that a malignancy was there somewhere, and would someday have to be dealt with. Well, I'm dealing. Wish I didn't have to, but glad I had all this time to learn to love me. In a different way.

Having researched alternative options to surgery, she'd found them unsatisfactory. Nor did she believe in radiation or chemotherapy: "I think they are destructive. But I have not seen any evidence that surgery is bad, at worse it may be unnecessary. But it is my life I am gambling with, and I can't take that chance!" That night, the gamble came sharply into focus: "7:30PM. If I cried for a hundred years I couldn't express the sorrow I feel right now, and the loss."[105]

The following morning, September 22, Lorde noted: "Today is the day in the grimy morning, and all I can do is cry."[106] She also noted a reference to Eudora Garrett, the woman she'd fallen in love with in Mexico in 1954, who'd been the first she'd known to have had a mastectomy. Much later, when writing about that morning in "Breast Cancer: A Black Lesbian Feminist Experience," she would elaborate, remarking: "Eudora came to me in my sleep that night before surgery in that tiny cold hospital room so different from her bright hot dishevelled bedroom in Cuernavaca, with her lanky snapdragon self and her gap-toothed lopsided smile, and we held hands for a while."[107]

ELEVEN

L ORDE UNDERWENT A transfiguration after her mastectomy—she was physically transformed, and her postsurgery personality exalted the change. Reprioritizing her life, determining what were to be legitimate uses of her energy[1] and her work, became her central mission now. In her son's words, "After she got cancer in 1978, her life took on a kind of immediacy that most people's lives never develop. The setting of priorities and the carrying out of the highest prioritized tasks assumed a much greater importance. . . ."[2] During the initial days of her hospitalization and recovery, Lorde considered: "There's a kind of protection the bleak unfeeling walls of a hospital give that allows me to look into the face of death and still dare to be joyful. I want to move toward death if I must with the certain knowledge that I leave some thing rich and part of the Great Going Forward behind me."[3]

She contemplated resigning as poetry editor for *Chrysalis*, informing Adrienne Rich what she was thinking before telling the *Chrysalis* editors. Rich's history with the magazine and its editors was independent of Lorde's, but her loyalty to Lorde crisscrossed with loyalty to her other relationships within their intersecting circles. Writing to Lorde in mid-October, Kirsten Grimstad acknowledged that they were shocked to hear about her surgery and concerned for her well-being. She remarked on the possibility of Lorde's departure from the magazine as outlined by a letter from Rich; noting that Rich had mentioned Lorde was retiring as poetry editor, assumed the *Chrysalis* editors knew that, and wanted to suggest a replacement. Grimstad expressed a mixture of surprise and sadness at the possibility Lorde might no longer be actively engaged with the magazine. At the same time, she hoped Lorde would stay on as a contributing editor. In closing, she acknowledged that she knew it'd been hard for Lorde to work with editors who were living on a different coast. But she hoped Lorde felt positively about her relationship with *Chrysalis*, as the editors felt positive about her.[4]

The strain of working with the West Coast women—artistically, racially, and geographically—had been long brewing. But Lorde had also weathered a personal insult more sharply felt than any other. On September 1, before her surgery, she'd sent a letter to Grimstad informing her of the publication of *The Black Unicorn*. Lorde also mentioned that *Chrysalis* was to receive a review copy, and spoke of her discussion with Robert Chrisman, at *The Black Scholar*, about the possibility of running "an exchange ad" for her book in each magazine. She ended: "Let me know what you decide and what happens."[5] Characteristic of *Chrysalis's* editorial and organizational problems, neither Grimstad nor any of the other editors responded to Lorde's letter with any immediacy. This fueled her sense that not only did the editors ignore the needs of poets, they ignored *her*.

Proof of that now was to be found in Grimstad's October letter. Though sympathetic to Lorde's surgery, Grimstad made no reference to *The Black Unicorn*, mentioning instead that the editors had heard about Lorde's essay on the erotic from Adrienne Rich and Blanche Cook, and that they were very interested in having a look at it.[6] Lorde was certainly interested in having "Uses of the Erotic" published, but she was just as interested in promoting *The Black Unicorn*, a work of major importance to her. She sent Grimstad a second letter:

> . . I urge you to have it reviewed for Chrysalis. It is an important
> book, and speaking as it does out of the consciousness and con-

nections of an African-American lesbian feminist poet, of course it has already come under advance attack from the straight white press. I feel it is really important that the feminist media not ignore The Black Unicorn the way, for the most part, it ignored my last book, Between Ourselves.

If you need any help finding a reviewer, just let me know.[7]

As part of reprioritizing her life, Lorde sought to make significant changes in her diet. Still convalescing in the early part of November 1978, she traveled to Houston and San Francisco to do poetry readings. The trips were soon after her operation, but in the immediate moment Lorde saw them as a chance to gain some perspective: "I really needed the space—the distance of a continent from the site of it all—this or that—a perspective."[8] In retrospect, she felt that the passion and energy to return to work came from having written "The Uses of the Erotic." "The existence of that paper enabled me to pick up and go to Houston and California, it enabled me to start working again. I don't know when I'd have been able to write again, if I hadn't had those words."[9] While reconnecting with old friends like Diane di Prima, Lorde visited with Dr. Alice Francis, a chiropractor.

Dr. Francis encouraged Lorde to eat less red meat, chicken, and fish, and more vegetables and grains. She also urged her to consider decreasing her intake of vitamin E as the vitamin overstimulated the hormones. As Lorde understood Dr. Francis's explanation of the cancer phenomenon, the cancer-producing factor was still in her body and was a product of a hormonal imbalance that would normalize in four to five years, once her hormones settled. In addition, Dr. Francis told Lorde her pancreas was underfunctioning and needed to be encouraged by enzymes, and she gave Lorde some whole pancreatic matter and trace minerals to take.[10]

Changing her diet meant changing lifelong eating habits, but Lorde was determined to get healthy so that the cancer would not return. In the years she was "cancer-free," Lorde frequently discussed her various diets and eating regimes as part of her six-o'clock calls to Charlotte Sheedy; and she also shared with Sheedy a sense that she needed to control her rage, to deal with and release her anger, as she began to think it was her rage that produced the cancer.[11]

One instance of unnecessary frustration centered on Helen Jaffer, a feminist Lorde had become acquainted with on a previous trip to the West Coast. Jaffer's response to the poem "A Litany for Survival" at a reading in San Francisco caused Lorde's temper to flare up. "I must remember that when Helen Jaffer said that she recognized Litany as a cancer victim's poem I did feel like hitting her. Is that something I can't look at? Does that give it more credence? And I looked at it & it still doesn't feel right inside me. Is that defensiveness?"[12] Though she'd written that poem long before her diagnosis, she'd thought of it and other work—particularly "The Transformation of Silence into Language and Action"—as indicative of her body's sense of cancer as a fact in her life.[13] The prescient nature of her work was unsettling, even to her.

In December 1978, Lorde considered starting another project: "I want to start a new book today. I want to lay this heavy one to rest, beginning with the fear of that time before my first biopsy, and ending really with the coming back of the light after the amputation of my right breast for cancer."[14] Lorde viewed this "coming back of the light" in the context of "an altered sense of mortality."[15] She wrote in her journal: "I am also coming back into the light of my work my life what I want most to do, undaunted by the false sense of security an apparently unthreatened life seems to offer."[16]

The decision to write about her cancer experience was both an act of resistance and an extension of her ideas about translating—and politicizing—the private. Many women before her had had their lives altered by facing, or surviving, breast cancer. But a cult of silence and erasure kept women's experiences with breast cancer a secret, and Lorde felt that "terrible wrongs are being done to women by others & themselves."[17]

One of the first horrors of a mastectomy—beyond the physical pain which is a great and carefully held secret, and the fear of a life-threatening cancer, is the conspiracy of the cancer-cartel to insist to every woman that she is not really different—that with a little skillful patience & a few ounces of foam or silicone gel she can pretend to herself & the world that nothing has happened.[18]

Lorde's discussions with her surgeon, Dr. Peter Pressman, and her study of research on postmastectomy options raised serious doubts about breast reconstruction. For one, though silicone gel implants had been used in non-malignant breast augmentation, there was no conclusive evidence the substance itself was not carcinogenic. Nor had there been large-scale studies of women having postmastectomy reconstruction which provided sufficient statistics to demonstrate whether breast reconstruction did or did not have an effect on cancer recurrence. An even more dramatic reality was the possibility that the additional surgery necessary to insert a prosthesis under the skin might stir up otherwise dormant cancer cells, and an implant might mask any recurrence of them, making a diagnosis difficult.[19] Although "free" of breast cancer now, Lorde well understood the possibility of recurrence. But she was determined to survive as a warrior, not a victim.

Defining the loss of her right breast then as "an honorable wound," Lorde adamantly resisted wearing a prosthesis; not only was it, in her mind, a signifier of pretense (". . . that the fake is just as good as the real since it looks almost the same. . . ."),[20] but it also meant succumbing to market-driven standards of the feminine and female beauty. Lorde did not just translate the private; she embodied an exaltation of it, giving it a specificity, particularly as her writing came to encourage public gaze upon "the political as framed by the significance of the everyday."[21] Or, more succinctly, upon her own body: black, eroticized, transformed.

In general, women who have survived breast cancer by mastectomy have to battle shame, fear, loss of beauty or sexual appeal, feelings of social and familial isolation, disfigurement, stigmatization, and the difficult road to recovery in a culture that equates "real" womanhood with physical "perfection." Lorde herself was not immune to an array of feelings:

> What does it mean to lose a limb. A woman to lose a breast? Me to part with a treasured part of me? . . . Coming to terms with loss. What does that mean, making it my own? It is my own or it wouldn't be my loss. The unspeakable. (1) Will she cherish my body now I am damaged? (2) Did I do this to myself? 3. What can I learn & how shall I teach it? 4. How do I give up that huge place of feeling forever?[22]

The loss of her right breast was traumatic, and profoundly painful. Mediating that trauma and pain as she healed physically went well beyond politicizing the loss as an "honorable" reminder of a war uniquely female: "During the following hospitalization, mastectomy & its aftermath, I passed thro many stages of pain, despair, sadness & growth. As I moved thro them, sometimes with no choice, I began to feel that I had lost a breast only to become a more whole person."[23] The notion of herself as "a more whole person" underscored Lorde's transfiguration. As a breast cancer survivor now, she integrated within her multiple identities yet one more identity. Lorde's bravery in the face of amputation can be explained by her irrepressible personality: she'd invented a compelling persona as "outsider" from which she derived strength, status, and a public platform. She had a self-actualized notion of beauty and what was beautiful. And she willingly risked self-exposure—turning the lessons of her life into opportunities to teach others what she'd learned. Lorde genuinely believed that her survival was a political issue.

The desire to write about her cancer experience was one process. Actually doing so was another, in part because writing prose remained a challenge and Lorde was less comfortable with "the kinds of linear thinking" it required.[24] Early in 1979, she struggled with the two processes.

For three months, she'd wanted to write a piece on cancer as it affected her life and consciousness as a woman, a black lesbian. She'd wanted to address the implications of breast cancer, "the threats to self-revelation that are aligned against a woman who seeks to truly explore those questions, those answers," but discovered she "could not even write about the outside threats to vision and action because the inside pieces were frightening." Reasoning through why she'd delayed the process, Lorde admitted to herself a reluctance to begin writing. "Yet what I want to talk about & say," she further admitted, "comes distilled from my own experiences so the reluctance is a reluctance to deal with my own experiences and the conclusions drawn from them. It is also, of course, a reluctance to living or re living—giving new life to—the pain." She likened the physical and psychic pain of separating from her breast as "at least as sharp as the pain of separating from the mother as in seeing her from an equidistant point. But I did make it once so I can make it again." As her journals of 1979 and 1980 reveal, Lorde saw writing about her experience as a crucial process of "focusing from the periphery to the center."[25]

The journals Lorde kept between 1979 and 1980 also record an urgency to recall and order the stories of her life, from childhood to consciousness of herself as lesbian. Lorde did not view the individual prose pieces she was writing and publishing as part of a concerted work of fiction until after her mastectomy; then, the need to tell her stories became infused with reflection upon the sources of her survival. Those sources were embodied in women who'd loved her—not necessarily in easy relationships—and began with her mother.[26] As the notion of a book took shape in her mind, and its working title, "I've Been Standing on This Street Corner a Hell of a Long Time!" emerged, Lorde wove together material threaded from her readings on the strengths and weaknesses of child-rearing practices of Caribbean and African American women, and her own childhood and life as a young black lesbian in New York in the 1940s and 1950s.[27]

She set out to write "a particular kind of fiction" that was "made up of work that is autobiographical as well as material that is historical in the respects of the public domain, and also mythic material." By her own account, consciously constructing the work this way was an attempt to avoid questions about its authenticity,[28] given her understanding that authenticity existed not only within but beyond the singular life in the context of history and mythic narrative. "Writing prose," Lorde reflected on the process, "has taught me a new way of viewing the world & my passage through it—a more linear and expansive—also wider and more apperceptable [sic]—way of community with myself and about myself to others and about others."[29]

Not four months after Lorde's mastectomy, Frances Clayton's mother died. Lorde traveled with Frances and two of her sisters to the funeral in Fairfield, Ohio. In the company of Clayton's family, Lorde felt she "must walk lightly here; there are so many interrelationships between these people that I'm not privy to, that I can't really interfere." She thought Frances's family treated Frances "shamefully," especially her sister Ann. Lorde felt that Clayton either denied or avoided recognizing how she was being treated. Lorde also noted she'd tried to remind Clayton of her real life but thought that Clayton resisted that reminder, giving Lorde a sense she was interfering indeed.[30]

As the *Chrysalis* editors were pursuing a reviewer for *The Black Unicorn*,[31] Lorde made up her mind to sever her relationship to the magazine. She wrote to say so to Kristen Grimstad on January 15, 1979, noting that she'd also informed poets who were inquiring about their work. Lorde outlined what was to be done with several packages of unread manuscripts she was sending to *Chrysalis*, and added that she expected the editors would now deal with any further poetry inquiries, but that she would continue to respond to poets who contacted her directly until March. However, she'd already selected the poetry for several future issues and was still invested in her responsibility to those poets. She also suggested the names and gave addresses for several poets who might be asked to serve as guest poetry editors—including Joan Larkin, Honor Moore, Patricia (Spears) Jones, June Jordan, Pat Parker, and Judy Grahn.[32]

By now, Lorde was determined to publish her writing on breast cancer sooner rather than later. With "The Transformation of Silence into Language and Action" already circulating,[33] she sought a venue for another essay that was specific to why she'd refused to wear a prosthesis. She completed "Breast Cancer: Power Vs. Prosthesis" in March 1979 and submitted it first to *SAVVY*, a newly established magazine targeted to women professionals. "Breast Cancer: Power Vs. Prosthesis"[34] was Lorde's condemnation of the social pressures generally visited upon women's perceptions of their bodies and upon women facing life after a mastectomy: "Women have been programed to view our bodies only in terms of how they look and feel to others, rather than how they feel to ourselves, and how we wish to use them. . . ."[35] When *SAVVY* published Lorde's essay, it proved a mixed blessing. She promptly wrote to the editor, Sue Edmiston, itemizing her concerns.

The biographic note accompanying the piece in *SAVVY* had said she was a poet but excluded any mention of race—a fact Lorde saw as inseparable from her identity as poet. She told Edmiston that if it was an editorial decision to exclude that information, doing so was an error *SAVVY* could ill afford, particularly if it did not want to incur a reputation for ignoring black women professionals. Equally egregious to Lorde was the photograph that accompanied her work. She was "quite disturbed" by the decision to pair the essay with a picture of "a thin, young, white woman hiding her breasts, whose body language screams defeat, and the very opposite of everything the article is saying," and she added, "If there was ever a picture of woman as victim and vulnerable, that was it."[36] The tone of Lorde's letter was gracious throughout, even as she took SAVVY's editorial staff to task for an insensitivity to racial issues and for replicating patriarchal notions of women's bodies.

Lorde's constant challenges to white women to analyze unexamined racism intensified now as she considered the body of work she'd produced and what were its legitimate uses. On May 3, she began a letter to Mary Daly. Daly had sent Lorde a copy of her latest book, *Gyn/Ecology: The Metaethics of Radical Feminism* (1978).[37] A highly original, dense meditation, synthesizing philosophy, literary criticism, history, poetry, and feminist rhetoric, *Gyn/Ecology* sought to incite "a linguistic revolution" as a path to women's empowerment, and was ultimately hailed as "a landmark in woman-centered analysis."[38]

Daly was born in Schenectady, New York, in 1928. She'd attended co-educational Catholic schools from elementary through high school, completing undergraduate studies at a small Catholic women's college and then earning a master's degree in English from Catholic University. An Irish Catholic from a working-class family,[39] Daly's childhood had been shaped by the depression and World War II. She had a rebellious personality, and her career-long confrontations with religious patriarchal institutions began in the 1950s when American universities discouraged admission of women into graduate programs in theology. Undaunted, Daly moved to Switzerland, where she studied philosophy and theology. When she returned to the States, America was being transformed by the civil rights, antiwar, and feminist movements, all of which were to affect her evolution as a radical.

In 1966, Daly joined the faculty of Boston College's Theology Department, publishing her first major work, *The Church and the Second Sex*, in 1968. The book took on the Roman Catholic Church, accusing it of sexism within Christianity and an open hostility toward women.[40] The publication and subsequent publicity caused her to be fired, but Boston College reluctantly rehired Daly after 2,500 students protested her dismissal.[41] Her second book, *Beyond God the Father: Toward a Philosophy of Women's Liberation* (1973), shaped her evolution from radical Catholic to post-Christian feminist, marking her as a leader in a spiritual movement urging women to move beyond Christianity and Judaism as traditional religious constructs.[42]

In the 1970s, Daly, a self-styled radical lesbian feminist, emerged as an icon of the separatist discourse in feminism which argued against the "reformism and co-optation" of the mainstream movement; it put forward, instead, a philosophy of the "woman-identified-woman" and women's culture separate from any association with patriarchy.[43] Furthermore, Daly became convinced of the ways in which language shaped and limited consciousness, and her work exposed intersections between cultural institutions, ideologies, and atrocities perpetrated upon women. More generally, it had a decided influence upon lesbian and gay spiritualities. As a feminist theologian, Daly's analyses of Christianity and Catholicism were highly regarded by feminist scholars, particularly those who had read her two previous books.[44]

Daly and Lorde had not crossed paths after their appearance on the panel at the 1977 MLA Convention. In the interim, Lorde had sent Daly a copy of *The Black Unicorn*. She was a reader of Daly's work, especially *Beyond God the Father*, where she found Daly's critique of Catholicism especially helpful in coming to terms with and demystifying her own Catholic indoctrination.

Lorde began the draft of her letter by thanking Daly: "I want to thank you for having Gyn/Ecology sent to me. So much of it is full of import for me, useful and generating, and reaffirming." She noted that the silence between them since the MLA panel was self-imposed and self-protective: she'd decided shortly before the MLA Convention she would never again speak to white women about racism because doing so was a waste of energy since their guilt and defensiveness made being heard so difficult, and white women were better positioned to speak to each other. Lorde no doubt felt that way, but it is doubtful such a decision was one she could have stuck to. Her private and public relations with white women continued to define her willingness to engage racial differences. From that location, she could write of her belief in Daly's "good faith toward women," in Daly's "vision of a future within which we can all flourish," and in Daly's "commitment to the hard sometimes painful work necessary to effect change."[45] She also wrote of her excitement as she began reading *Gyn/Ecology*, especially the opening chapter on the ability of the patriarchy to perpetuate itself through myth.[46]

But the body of the draft letter was a critique of *Gyn/Ecology* as circumscribed and myopic. While acknowledging Daly's copious research, Lorde wondered why the author had confined her discussion to white, Western European, Judeo-Christian goddess images, and had not included examples of African goddess mythology. Allowing Daly this "narrow"[47] scope, she noted two other aspects of the book by which she was even more troubled. For one, there was Daly's chapter, "African Genital Mutilation: The Unspeakable Atrocities." As Daly described it, the ritualized excision and infibulation of African female genitalia was one of five ancient and modern atrocities that were perpetrated upon women globally, and patterned what she defined as the "Sado-Ritual Syndrome": a patriarchal, state-sanctioned murder and dismemberment of the goddess, of the self-affirming essence of women.[48]

Daly began her chapter with the point that some incarnations of the "Sado-Ritual Syndrome," such as the genital mutilation of African women, were unspeakable on two accounts—their nature as linguistically "inexpressibly horrible" acts, and the entrenched taboos against writing, speaking about, or naming them. She anticipated criticism by noting that Western critiques of such atrocities, including her own indictment, were neither racist nor imperialist, and served the larger cause of women's emancipation vis-à-vis a "planetary patriarchy." It was in black women's interests, Daly contended, for feminists of all races to speak out against African genital mutilation and to see her discussion of the practice within the pattern of other "barbaric rituals/atrocities"[49] she named.[50]

Lorde did not see it that way. In her view, Daly focused the book's only discussion of African women "as preyers upon each other—as instruments of each others destruction"; this was, in her mind, a self-serving distortion of black women's history.[51] The distortion and erasure of black women's history were historic and cultural agendas driving Lorde's critique of Daly's work at a time when even the most "radical" white feminist intellectuals had little, if any, knowledge of black women's history or were concerned with the complexities of that history.

In that regard, Lorde's critique of Daly's work was an aggressive attack on white feminist scholarship in general.

Moreover, Lorde was troubled by Daly's use of her own work to introduce that chapter. As she had throughout *Gyn/Ecology*, Daly integrated excerpts from a number of poems and other writings by women to frame her chapters. With permission from Broadside Press, she'd taken an excerpt from one of Lorde's poems in *New York Head Shop and Museum*, "A Sewerplant Grows In Harlem Or I'm A Stranger Here Myself When Does The Next Swan Leave."[52] Lorde accused Daly of having misused her work, illegitimately extracting from it what might make her own work legitimate in the eyes of black women particularly, and not making use of black women's words to illustrate other aspects of her thinking that were non-racial in context. In fact, Daly had used an excerpt from a poem by Pat Parker in a later chapter in just such a context, but Lorde did not address that example.[53]

In sum, the draft fluctuated between patience and anger as Lorde remarked upon their mutuality as outsiders ("We need each other, outsiders do, for consciousness, support, connection all the necessities of living on the border"). At one point, Lorde's anger overtook her and she made the following insertion: ". . . but I feel since you have not recognized me, I have been in error, & no longer recognize you." She closed the draft by making a point about their inherently different positions as black woman and white woman vis-à-vis patriarchy. Finally, she asked Daly to respond to her perceptions and thanked her for what she'd gained from Daly's work, calling this letter her repayment for what she'd learned.[54]

On May 6, Lorde posted Mary Daly an extended, three-page version of that draft. She also sent copies to Adrienne Rich and Michelle Cliff, with the following typed note:

Dear Loves,

Since this is a very grim and disturbing letter enclosed herewith I thought I'd include something else to delight you, maybe.

3/21/79
she said

it's not enough being
different
you have to cherish it, too.
If I was to wait
until I was
right and proper
before I spoke my mind
I'd be sending holographic messages
on a ouija board
little cryptic complaints
from the other side.[55]

Any careful reader of *Gyn/Ecology* could ascertain Daly's indebtedness to Cliff and Rich, among others, as influences upon her work. She had acknowledged Cliff as "a witty sharer of ideas as well as an excellent copy editor." And she had acknowledged that Rich had been "ineffably encouraging and enspiriting," helpful to the book's process, and an inspiration through "her own work and sharing of criticism."[56] Lorde knew of their professional and personal association with Daly, a highly touted icon of the feminist movement. Thus, on a deeper level, sending Rich and Cliff a copy of her letter to Daly signaled a break with white feminist ideology and an articulation of her own intellectual space as black feminist, within a synchronous space articulated by commas: black, lesbian, feminist, mother, poet warrior. As its most visible proponent within the white feminist community, Lorde established a discursive space for contemporary black feminism; defining, in the process, the limitations of white feminists' fixation "on the primacy of gender as an oppression"[57] and the limitations of white feminist theory as applications of radical thought.

Lorde's belief that Daly's work mirrored that of other white feminists whose scholarship compounded black women's oppression justified raising questions about it with Adrienne Rich, whom she loved and felt close to. But the social-political terrain between them was murky. Rich was friends with Mary Daly. Although Rich did not encourage it, Lorde felt there was a "charged sexuality" between herself and Rich. That it was unexplored prevented her from both exercising total control over

Rich or trusting Rich completely, and she came to distrust that part of Rich she believed consorted with her enemies.[58]

Rich's principled differences with Lorde highlighted bifurcated allegiances. She was deeply loyal to Lorde, but resisted jumping on Lorde's band wagon when Lorde publicly differed with white feminists they knew in common. As time went on, she also resisted acting as a surrogate voice for Lorde; and she resisted, too, a complete allegiance that would require her to sever her own bonds with white feminists and write them off simply because Lorde was angry with them. Rich's stature as a cultural icon within the feminist community was itself complicated. She was one of few celebrated white feminists to acknowledge racism within the movement; this position put her in disfavor with some who saw discussions of race, as well as class, as a distraction or divisive and threatening to the movement's gender focus and cohesiveness. Rich's stature provided needed currency with which to engage less race-conscious feminists in a more progressive discourse. She recognized her own development toward that discourse as one that was in process, and sought to engage other white women in ways that were constructive,[59] if not less confrontational. But just as she refused complete allegiance to Lorde, she also refused complete allegiance to Daly.[60]

Her differences with Daly aside, Lorde's mind was bent on the possibility of publishing a compilation of journal excerpts written prior to and in the aftermath of her mastectomy. Edited into one piece and entitled "Breast Cancer: A Black Lesbian Feminist Experience," she sent the work, with a cover letter, to Kirsten Grimstad at *Chrysalis* on May 20. Seeing this now as "the second part of a longer work, <u>A Cancer Journal</u>," Lorde insisted on knowing whether or not *Chrysalis* was interested. She saw feminists and feminist publications as her first audience. "I would like this to appear first in a feminist publication," Lorde directed Grimstad, "since I feel this subject of breast cancer as a personal experience for feminists is one that has met with enormous silence. . . ."[61] On May 31, she wrote to Deborah Marrow, now managing editor at *Chrysalis*, acknowledging the editors' intent to publish "Uses of the Erotic," but urging them to publish the excerpt from *The Cancer Journal* instead.

Arguing that "Uses of the Erotic" was in its second printing as a pamphlet and was to be included in published proceedings of the Berkshire

Conference on Women in History, and thus was already available to the feminist community, Lorde urged Marrow toward her way of thinking: "I think the Cancer Journal excerpt is a silence-breaker that is desperately needed in the lesbian/feminist community." She also begged Marrow to publish a formal announcement in the next issue that Lorde was no longer poetry editor or to just remove her name and address from the masthead, as she was getting flak from poets whose work she was no longer responsible for.[62]

With no definitive answer from *Chrysalis*, her sense of urgency pro-voked by a short-fused temper, Lorde submitted the journal excerpt to *Sinister Wisdom*. *Sinister Wisdom* published "Breast Cancer: A Black Lesbian Feminist Experience" in its Summer 1979 issue. When Issue #9 of *Chrysalis* was published in the fall of 1979, "Uses of the Erotic" appeared in it, but there was no review of *The Black Unicorn* as had been promised.

BY NOW, THE Combahee River Collective was active in several commu-nity efforts. Though neither widely known nor widely accepted in Boston's black community because its members were out lesbians and feminists,[63] the group's support for multiple issues affecting the lives of black women helped it develop a track record within some sectors of the black community as an informed contributor to the community's bread-and-butter issues.[64] As such, members had supported Kenneth Edelin, a black doctor at Boston Hospital arrested for manslaughter after he'd per-formed an abortion. They also supported the defense in the case of Ella Ellison, a black woman accused of murder after having been seen in an area where a homicide had been committed. They'd picketed along with the Third World Workers Coalition in support of the hiring of black labor-ers for the construction of a new high school in the black community.[65]

These activities formed the basis for organized interactions with other progressive community activists, including those opposed to the death penalty in the state and to violence against women.[66] The Collec-tive's consciousness-raising efforts among black women who were not feminists, particularly groups of black church women, broadened their base as community activists; this facilitated opportunities to define how a black feminist politics was necessary to understanding and resisting black women's oppressions, and proved significant to articulating the issue of violence against black women.[67] In the 1970s, violence against women became an issue of increasing importance to feminists who viewed sexual violence, such as rape, as a particular form of oppression threatening women's liberation.[68] But at the time, it fell to black feminists to particularize sexual violence suffered by black women—namely, rape, sexual harassment, pornography, physical abuse, and fatal harm.

Between late January and the end of May 1979, thirteen women were murdered within a two-mile radius in Boston. Twelve were black and one was white. Except for one, all of the murdered women's bodies were found in Roxbury, Dorchester, and the South End—predominantly black neighborhoods in the city. Several had been strangled, some were stabbed to death. Two were dismembered, two were buried after they'd been killed, and several of the dead women had been sexually assaulted. After the sixth black woman was found dead early in April, a memorial protest march and rally was held in Boston's South End.[69] Most of the speakers were black men, who viewed the murders as racially motivated and urged black women to protect themselves by staying indoors or by finding a man to accompany them whenever outside. That the murders were perceived as racial, solely, did not sit well with many feminist lesbians at the rally.[70]

A resident of Roxbury, Barbara Smith kept Lorde informed of the murders, sending her Xerox copies of buried articles which appeared in the city's white newspaper, the *Boston Globe*, and the more extensive coverage in a black weekly, the *Bay State Banner*.[71] The murders cut a deep emotional gash in Smith and other black feminists based in Boston. Lorde encouraged Smith to keep her abreast of the Boston events as they unfolded; she made paying attention to them a priority.

Smith's correspondence with Lorde chronicled the Combahee River Collective's activism in response to the murders. In one letter dated late in May, she informed Lorde of "a hectic week" of meetings and of a particular street action they'd participated in which involved painting stenciled messages about the murders at or near the sites where the women's bodies had been found.[72] Angered and frustrated by the view that the crimes were simply racial, Smith drafted a political statement on behalf of the Combahee River Collective, analyzing the murders as conditioned by the politics of racism and sexism that devalued black women's lives and made possible such unchecked violence.[73] The statement was quickly approved by several other members of the Collective. Ultimately, it cited statistics on abused women, offered black women suggestions for self-defense strategies, and included a list of Boston-based organizations working on the issue of violence against women.

The Combahee River Collective had ten thousand copies of its statement printed and distributed as a pamphlet, changing the title, *Six Black Women: Why Did They Die?*, each time another murder was reported. Community response was overwhelmingly positive, and the pamphlet established the Collective as indispensable to black and feminist groups organizing to resist violence against women.[74] Smith's letter linked the Collective's activism to plans for the fifth black feminist retreat in July; she suggested that a proposed black women's benefit poetry reading, at which Lorde had agreed to read, be held concurrent with the retreat.

Yet in the year-long hiatus between the fourth and fifth retreats, Lorde harbored conflicting emotions about the younger women and her need for them. She wanted to see them, but she did not want to stay with them.[75] Sharing living space during the retreats was an expected convenience and part of the intimacy between the women. Lorde's ability to compartmentalize her feelings and social worlds was an effective, self-serving tool. But that ability now masked a problematic reality as she sought allegiances with a more politicized generation of black lesbians. She loved black women intrinsically and wanted to be loved by them. Yet in the company of other black lesbians, Lorde's ego conflated their adoration for her, power over them, and seduction. Early in her friendship with Barbara Smith, for example, she'd told Smith she was coming to Boston to do a reading and wanted to stay at Smith's house instead of a hotel. Smith agreed to the arrangement, realizing only later Lorde meant to use the opportunity as an occasion to seduce her.

Although she admired Audre, Smith was neither attracted to her nor interested in what would be, in essence, an extramarital affair with Lorde, who'd boldly asserted she generally related to women "in one of two ways, either as lover or as mother." Smith's refusal to accept either of the two options proposed by Lorde ultimately meant they "hammered out a friendship"[76] over time that was based on shared politics and respect for each other's work, and established a boundary between herself and Lorde's desires. Just as loving white women represented the "creative uses of difference" for Lorde, loving black women raised issues about racial sameness. Lorde's belief that there was no "easy blackness" did not just define her position as black lesbian in relation to the black community at large, but redounded to her relationships with black lesbians—especially those to whom she was attracted but who were not attracted to her.

The Fifth Black Feminist Retreat was held at the Cambridge Women's Center in Boston the weekend of July 6–8. In addition to Barbara, Barbara's twin sister Beverly, Audre Lorde, Demita Frazier, and Sharon Page-Ritchie, the participants included Cheryl Clarke, Phyllis Bethel, Gloria Joseph, and Yvonne Flowers. Joseph recorded notes on the weekend's sessions, which were later expanded by Barbara Smith and posted afterwards to all who had and had not attended. The notes described the group's interest in taking advantage of opportunities to publish in several feminist magazines; an offer on the table from Beacon Press to do a book on black feminism which the Smith sisters were negotiating; and the upcoming national March on Washington for gay rights in October, at which there would be a Third World Gay Conference.[77] Most significantly, the retreat notes included a page listing nearly two dozen items indicating the growth and development of the black feminist movement within the past year. Among them were a rise in black feminist grassroots organizations; an increase in black feminist and lesbian networks nationally; artistic collaborations, which were defining an emerging black lesbian and feminist culture; nascent organizing efforts amongst black academic women; and the perception that black lesbians were less engaged with providing racism consciousness-raising for white women and becoming more identified with black women.[78]

If proximity to younger black women was the issue for Lorde, supporting and promoting their political activism was not. The Fifth Black Feminist Retreat sponsored two poetry readings as benefits for organizations working in response to the twelve murdered black women.[79] The readings were held that Friday and Saturday nights. On Friday night, at the Solomon Carter Fuller Mental Health Center in Boston, Lorde shared the stage with a number of local poets, including Kate Rushin, Diana Christmas, and Fahamisha Shariat Brown. At the Sanders Theatre at Harvard University in Cambridge on Saturday night, she and Adrienne Rich read before an even bigger crowd. A black journalist who'd come to the reading wanted to interview Lorde for an article she planned to submit to a Boston alternative paper. Lorde declined the interview, encouraging the reporter to interview local women writers instead. The reporter did so, but the newspaper was not interested in running a story about the lesser known black poets.[80] Lorde was not publicity-shy, but there were times she preferred to support the efforts of other women, highlighting a generosity toward them as writers and activists that would become legendary.

"Need: A Choral of Black Women's Voices" had its debut that weekend. Lorde wrote the piece as a poetic response to the Boston murders. Dedicated to Patricia Cowan[81] and to Bobbie Jean Graham, the last of the twelve black women to be murdered, "Need" reconstructed the brutality of their deaths.[82] It was also Lorde's way of paying tribute to the senseless sacrifice of countless other black women whose deaths were the nightmares informing her words. In composition, "Need" departed from Lorde's usual poetic style and suggested a chorus of black women's voices in performance. Within the three sections, the poem harmonized four voices: "I," "P.C. [Patricia Cowan]," "B.J.G. [Bobbie Jean Graham]," and a chorus, "ALL." Beginning with her own voice, "I," in the first section, Lorde invited listeners into the unrecorded acts surrounding the killings of black women:

> I: This woman is Black
> so her blood is shed into silence . . .

This section then allowed the voices of "I", "P.C.," and "B.J.G." to alternate in three-part harmony, fusing them as "ALL" at its end:

> ALL: And how many other deaths
> do we live through daily
> pretending
> we are alive?

Narrating the gruesome specifics of Cowan and Graham's murders, Lorde's "I" was absent in the second section as she questioned, through the other women's voices and the chorus, the need black men have for black women, and the price of that need:

> B.J.G.: And what do you need me for, brother,
> to move for you, feel for you, die for you? . . .

Throughout the poem, Lorde lashed out at the futility of an unexamined racial solidarity with black men who wore the faces of black women's abusers and killers; exposing, as violently fake, the nationalist rhetoric of black manhood:

> ALL: . . . calling me black goddess black hope . . .
> black mother
> you touch me
> and I die in the alleys of Boston . . .

In the final section of "Need," two voices prevail as Lorde first speaks for herself:

> I am wary of need
> that tastes like destruction . . .[83]

The poem ends with the chorus repeating, "We cannot live without our lives"—a line attributed to the lesbian feminist writer and activist Barbara Deming, which Lorde had seen used on a banner made by the Combahee River Collective linking Third World women and the issue of violence against women.[84] As a critique of the racism and sexism operating against black women, "Need" became one of the first poetic statements to question the paradox of racial solidarity, "in defense of an elusive Black unity,"[85] for black women.

TWELVE

ORDE'S CONTINUING association with *Chrysalis* grew worse. As she saw it in a July 20 letter addressed to the editors, they were unable to treat with her as a peer; were deaf to concerns she'd raised in the past regarding the magazine's visual and literary content; and both racist and patronizing. That Lorde had decided what poetry *Chrysalis* should feature several issues beyond her departure made for a messy separation. She expected her decisions to be sovereign, even as she allowed she was no longer the poetry editor. She was outraged they continued to distort her own "persistent vision of what *Chrysalis* could become" when the poetry she'd selected for Issue #8 "was trimmed to exclude the contribution of the one woman of color represented, Toi Derricotte." She was furious they'd distorted "the shape of the poetic comment"[1] she envisioned for that issue when they featured a poem in tribute to her by Mary McAnally, an Oklahoma-based poet.[2] The editors saw McAnally's poem as a way to thank Lorde for her "priceless contribution to *Chrysalis*."[3] But Lorde was enraged by the exclusion of Derricotte's poem and the inclusion of a poem she hadn't selected. And she did not wish to have her name associated with a work over which she had no control. Lorde insisted once again that her name be removed from the masthead, and she closed her letter by threatening to take legal action if they did not do so by the next issue.[4] It was months before she heard from them.

It was also months before she got a reply from Mary Daly. Daly's letter, dated September 22, 1979, was courteous, and began by thanking Lorde for sending her *The Black Unicorn*, stating she'd read several of the poems many times. "Many of them moved me very deeply—" Daly commented, "others seemed farther from my own experience. You have helped me to be aware of different dimensions of existence, and I thank you for this." Daly also sought to explain the "long delay" in responding to Lorde's letter: ". . . by no means indicates that I have not been thinking about it—quite the contrary. I did think that by putting it aside for awhile I would get a better perspective than at first reaction. I wrote you a note to that effect which didn't get mailed since I didn't have your address. . . ." Though Daly left open to speculation how she got hold of Lorde's address, she defended her analyses while acknowledging Lorde's issues with *Gyn/Ecology*:

> . . . I wrote <u>Gyn/Ecology</u> out of the insights and materials most accessible to me at the time. When I dealt with myth I used commonly available sources to find what were the controlling myths and symbols behind judeo-christian myth. . . . You have made your point very strongly and you most definitely have a point. I could speculate on how <u>Gyn/Ecology</u> would have been affected had we corresponded about this before the manuscript went to press, but it doesn't seem creativity-conducing to look backward. There is only <u>now</u> and the hope of breaking the barriers between us—of constantly expanding the vision.

Daly closed by proposing the two of them meet the Friday she was to be in New York for an upcoming conference honoring the work of Simone de Beauvoir, "The Second Sex—Thirty Years Later: A Commemorative Conference on Feminist Theory," which was to be held at New York University (NYU), in Manhattan, on September 27–29. As an alternative, she suggested they could meet in Boston if Lorde planned to be in the area any time. Finally, she said she'd called and left a message on Lorde's answering machine, offered her own telephone number, and hoped to see Lorde and talk with her soon. In a handwritten postscript, Daly added that she hoped Lorde was feeling well: "May the strength of all the goddesses be with you."[5] Daly's willingness to meet with Lorde at the conference was brokered in part by Adrienne Rich's efforts to encourage a meeting between the two.

Daly's presence at the conference's Friday afternoon panel on "Developing Feminist Theory" situated her within contending and shifting truths confronting white feminist academics: success, promotion, acceptability within academe depended largely upon white male approval. Even as they sought to subvert and reframe its culture, to distance themselves from "the Land of the Fathers," privileges accorded to whiteness enabled white feminist academics to negotiate inside academe. While struggling within an "ole boys network" from which they wrested a degree of power, white feminist academics were the main distributors and consumers of that power, as the managers of women's studies programs and, later, departments; constituting, in ensuing decades, an "ole girls network" and becoming, in effect, "the new boys." It was the very paradigm Daly railed against in *Gyn/Ecology*: dependent upon legitimation from men and assimilation of male models for validating women's knowledge, the feminist movement had "merged with 'the human (men's) community.'"[6]

Lorde was also in the academy and subject to white male approval for promotion within its ranks. Yet she claimed a larger world "outside the circle of this society's definition of acceptable women; those of us who have been forged in the crucibles of difference—those of us who are poor, who are lesbians, who are Black, who are older,"[7] with which she openly identified and in which she was ideologically grounded. This larger world glorified Lorde's persona as outsider, and was wedged between herself and the academy, particularly as the academy was being reconfigured then by white feminist theory. In the institutional milieu of black feminist and black lesbian feminist scholars—which was to crystallize in the late 1980s—and within the context of conferences sponsored by white feminist academics, Lorde stood out as an angry, accusatory, isolated black feminist lesbian voice.[8] This enhanced her notoriety on the one hand, and provided an expanding platform from which she both agitated and courted controversy on the other.

At NYU, Lorde and Mary Daly met in a private space beyond earshot of the public. Their meeting proved comparatively trival. Although Lorde was more willing than Daly to risk a public confrontation between them, Daly was wary of even a private one.[9] Lorde found the moment "disappointing" because she hadn't expected Daly "to be so out of emotional touch with herself."[10] That Mary Daly appeared unemotional or unfeeling at that point might be explained, in part, by a letter from Rich to Lorde a couple of months after the conference. Assessing the complexity and depth of the friendship between herself and Daly, Rich wrote:

> I know Mary's rigidities, her self-protections, her tendency to see all criticism as onslaught, as pure attack (so that she could not really read your letter as written). But also I know that . . . nothing comes easy for Mary nor does she make anything easy; "false transcendence" was her phrase and she is repulsed by glib "feelings."[11]

Lorde had agreed—and expected—to comment upon papers discussing difference in American women's lives; this presupposed, in her mind, a discussion of race, sexuality, class, and age as specific indices of difference. But the papers did not address these issues and Lorde publicly denounced them at the Saturday afternoon panel on "The Personal and the Political," noting that the "absence of these considerations weakens any feminist discussion of the personal and the political." She castigated papers written by the other panelists—Linda Gordon, Camille Bristow, Bonnie Johnson, Manuela Fraire, and the conference coordinator, Jessica Benjamin—as embodying the limitations of the conference's scope, lashing out at "a particular academic arrogance" that would assume it legitimate to discuss feminist theory "without examining our many differences, and without a significant input from poor women, Black and Third World women, and lesbians." Lorde's essay, "The Master's Tools Will Never Dismantle the Master's House," framed a guerrilla-tactics moment in which she struck at the unsuspecting "mistresses" of the master's house.[12]

"The Master's Tools" was an attack on the parochialism of feminist theory, its underlying racism, and racist feminist practice as unexamined dependence upon the patriarchy. As Lorde perceived it, by denying or excluding a forum for difference, white feminist academics duplicated rather than transformed systems of oppression: "the master's tools." The use of those tools, she warned, "may allow us to temporarily beat him at his own game, but they will never enable us to bring about genuine change. And this fact is only threatening to those women who still define the master's house as their only source of support." Linking white middle-class women's interests with those of "the master," Lorde exposed the dialectic of color-blind feminism and feminist practice as it was stratified by class: "If white american feminist theory need not deal with the differences between us, and the resulting difference in our oppressions, then how do you deal with the fact that the women who clean your houses and tend your children while you attend conferences on feminist theory are, for the most part, poor women and women of Color? What is the theory behind racist feminism?"[13] she asked.

The notion that middle-class white women's intellectual and personal freedom was inflected with metaphors of bondage and depended on a modern-day version of the mistress/indentured servant/slave relationship implicated contemporary white academics as accomplices in the historic narrative positioning white men (masters), white women (mistresses), and black people (slaves). Further, this took place at just the moment when they were celebrating their own emancipation as configured by the impact of feminist analysis thirty years after Simone de Beauvoir's *The Second Sex*, a book many saw as shaping the modern age of feminist thought.[14] The comparison of white women to white men as agents of oppression was a scathing one.

Lorde's critique spared white feminist academics little or no wiggle room to justify the absence—or bare visibility—of black women at academic gatherings, in feminist culture, and of black women's books on reading lists for courses. Ignorance of women of color was a "cop-out," Lorde argued, and she referred her audience to a recent talk by Adrienne Rich to make the point that "white feminists have educated themselves about such an enormous amount over the past ten years," but they had been unable to educate themselves about black women. Nor should black women be called upon to educate white women about black women's existence; just as women should not be called upon to educate men about women's existence, because that was "an old and primary tool of all oppressors to keep the oppressed occupied with the master's concerns."[15] From Lorde's perspective of the academy-as-plantation, its house was supported by deeply flawed, suspect means on the part of feminists.

"The Master's Tools" identified and prophesied a new feminism—black feminism—that mainstream feminism could not see coming, or was ignoring. It exercised a vision of women's liberation that was glaringly absent in white feminist analyses, which lacked any consciousness of class. And Lorde was unrelenting in her insistence on a feminist movement that was race- and class-conscious. Her articulation of class consciousness further separated her from white feminists, the majority of whom led comfortable, middle-class existences.

"The Master's Tools" inflamed many conferencegoers. The organizers felt especially wounded by it. On behalf of several who served on the program committee, Jessica Benjamin sent a letter to Lorde a month later, citing Lorde's public anger at the failures in their vision as legitimate but essentially divisive. The organizers admired her as a poet and activist but they felt betrayed and disappointed. As they saw it, Lorde had acted out, disrupting a self-congratulatory moment for them and others. To their ears, she'd privileged her identities as black and lesbian, embodying differences that framed boundaries around assumptions of sameness as feminists. In so doing, she had assumed a moral authority based on suffering; but suffering was a condition of all women, as they saw it, and they had envisioned a discussion that would push beyond the guilt-producing politics that so often arise from powerlessness. They asserted that accusations of racism paralyzed, rather than permitted, any comfortable discussion of the topic.[16]

Benjamin's letter underlined a conspicuous reality within and beyond the conference: it was near to impossible to raise the subject of racism without rupturing comfort levels. White women were slow to put forward an articulated analysis of race or racism, generally speaking. Black women who did so were seen as betraying the calm to cause guilt in whites. But the "feminist sisterhood" was now more than a decade old.

Throughout its time, the paralysis of white women's guilt, and the imperviousness of black women's anger as it was frustrated by that guilt, had become like oil and water.

Yet Lorde felt her anger at the conference was justified. One of her priorities now was publicly to confront white women's racism. Reviewing the moment in a letter to Adrienne Rich, she explained that "to be a black woman dealing emotionally on any but the most prescribed and defended levels with white women who I do not know intimately, means for me to be constantly vulnerable to racial incidents of varying degrees, the possibilities of racial incidents of varying degrees, and the racial interpretation of other incidents which may or may not be so." Lorde added that she believed she'd "refined those prescribed and defended levels to such a degree" now that they served rather than worked against her. Her response to Jessica Benjamin's letter had been anger, not hurt, as she was to admit, "I had hoped for, but not expected, anything different."

Daly had not been present to hear "The Master's Tools." Lorde told Rich, "I'm sorry Mary wasn't there to hear it; it might have made our conversation easier." Given the content and tone of Lorde's comments, however, it is difficult to imagine how their conversation might have been made "easier." Having met with Daly on principle, Lorde felt that she'd done what she had to do, and there was no further reason to expose herself to what she'd seen in Daly's face as they talked. "I have no more business with her," Lorde wrote. "She is not my enemy, but it would be dishonest not to tell you that the fact of your loving protects her."[17]

Rich did not define her allegiance to Mary Daly as protecting Daly. At the same time, Adrienne was unwilling to forego a certain pragmatism in relation to Mary; believing she and Mary had work to do, as friends and as white feminists. Those bonds precluded distancing herself from Daly and were outside Lorde's control—much to Lorde's open displeasure. Ultimately, the fated meeting between Lorde and Daly compounded a failed personal dialogue between two eminent feminists, especially as it was shaped by the earlier silence in the time lapse between Lorde's letter to Daly in May and Daly's response four months later.

Lorde claimed not to have received a reply to her letter to Daly; a claim she did not revise before or after publishing the letter as "An Open Letter to Mary Daly" in 1980 and 1984, prefacing it with the statement:

"The following letter was written to Mary Daly, author of *Gyn/Ecology*, on May 6, 1979. Four months later, having received no reply, I open it to the community of women."[18] Viewing what was between her and Daly as "a public matter" and the letter as "useful" because "it helped to focus my rage," Lorde remained resolute that she was right publicly to call into question what she believed was Daly's racist theorizing. But in an 1982 interview, she deftly allowed, "I had no response that had any satisfaction to it," while admitting that "We talked." And then she modified her statement of "no response that had any satisfaction to it" with, "If I had had a response, I don't think I would have made the letter open."[19]

Lorde knew that "the community of women" hailed herself and Mary Daly amongst its icons. And she certainly knew the letter's publication would spark controversy. By now, her theory of difference was a cross-fertilized position from which she publicly wrestled white feminists for intellectual space, competed with them for that space, and individuated herself as black icon within their midst. She both embraced and rubbed against the movement's need for royalty, acting contrary, at times, to expectations of the very audience that conferred royalty upon her. She refused to play "house nigger," risking her status within the feminist movement even as she courted attention from white feminists and was the center of their attention as celebrated black feminist. The challenge to Daly's work pitted Lorde against the movement's valorization of white feminist intellectuality, and she "was risking being seen as a leader."[20] But Lorde had an inherently insecure position "as a leader." In an essentially white, heterosexual movement, she was black and lesbian; she articulated identities that remained marginal and problematic to the mainstream feminist agenda.

Still, the existence of Daly's letter amongst Lorde's papers, and with Daly's last name handwritten by Lorde in the bottom corner,[21] appears as an insoluble fact. It is less so when juxtaposed against several possible, interconnected explanations for Lorde's public claim she'd received "no reply" from Mary Daly. When the hoped-for reply in terms of recognition from Daly did not come as a result of their meeting, Lorde wrote Daly off. There was an element of "sibling rivalry" in her view of the sisterhood between Rich and Daly that Lorde found herself outside—insecure and intensely jealous. Lorde's love-hate-competitive relationships with white women informed an unresolved anger toward them and raised deeper questions unresolved by her theory of the "creative uses of difference" as to why she'd chosen them as lovers, allies, or enemies. She felt no desire to protect Daly, as she believed Rich did. Rules of civility, including recanting that claim, no longer applied, since in her mind Daly's disregard for her as a feminist was racially motivated. Mary Daly the person, then, ceased to exist.

But as an icon, Daly was an easy, if unwilling, target. While a real focus of Lorde's anger, Mary Daly became symbolic of that anger as it was particular to white feminist racism. Daly's work was the catalyst which made it possible for Lorde to challenge the imperialist nature of white feminist thought as it was embedded in Western cultural and historical frameworks, and as it presumed to speak for a global sisterhood. In the long run, Lorde's "open letter" served notice to the feminist community that the fixation on gender oppression, as reality and theory, obscured and skewered knowledge by women whose identities were informed by cultural and historic contexts beyond those of the West. That fixation also derailed opportunities for true solidarity between differing women and denied the movement the potential to be revolutionary rather than reformist. And it helped to reconfigure mainstream feminism as a social justice project which, while it might produce enormous change within American society, would not change the basic structures undergirding America.

But to that extent, America *had* changed. The first National March on Washington for Lesbian and Gay Rights took place in Washington, D.C., on Sunday, October 14, 1979. As an activist, Lorde was no stranger to Washington. Over the course of her life, she'd participated in several demonstrations and protests there. In the sixteen years since she had gone to the celebrated March on Washington in 1963, the nation's capital had come to symbolize the country's eventual embrace of the rhetoric and tactics of the civil rights struggle. Lorde's prominent return to Washington now mirrored the impact of lesbian and gay rights as civil rights issues.

Two days before the march, the first National Third World Gay and Lesbian Conference convened at the Harambee House Hotel in D.C. for four days of workshops, panels, and caucuses. Organized by the

National Coalition of Black Gays, the conference goals included the hope of establishing a national network for Third World lesbians and gays; establishing educational and communication networks for Third World lesbian and gay organizations; and confronting issues of racism, sexism, and heterophobia among Third World lesbians and gays, as well as homophobia directed at them.[22] On Friday morning, October 12, Lorde delivered the keynote address.

Speaking to literally hundreds of black, Hispanic, Asian, and Native American lesbians and gay men, Lorde opened the conference with her address, "When Will the Ignorance End?" The speech recognized this moment as profound, impossible in the thirty years earlier, and only possible now because of "the power of vision" that called them together as a community. Lorde's own vision of community linked the past, the present, and the future: an understanding of community rooted in an African epistemology. As an oratorical strategy, it invoked for her audience the historic price paid by those who had not lived to see this moment; those who were presently closeted because of fear; and those for whom mitigating conditions such as imprisonment, existence in mental institutions, and debilitating illness prevented their presence. Her identity as mother not spelled out specifically, though it was normally part of her standard introductory statement, Lorde made reference to this in linking children to the future of community. At different moments, she remarked upon making real a commitment to social change that would include commitment to children; the need of younger people for role models so that they would not be "alone in daring to define themselves outside the approved structures"; and the fact that all children, not just those "we may have mothered and fathered ourselves," are "our joint responsibility and our joint hope," with the right to grow free from "the diseases" of social "isms" and "the terror of any difference."[23]

Much of Lorde's address focused on the theme of difference. She encouraged the notion that the fight for freedom as homosexuals was tied to freedom for all members of their respective ethnic communities. Thus, in order to bring about a world free of any oppression, it was necessary to "see ourselves within the context of a civilization that has notorious disrespect and loathing for any human value, for any human creativity or genuine human difference." Noting the diversity of the groups in attendance and differences within those groups, Lorde warned of the necessity to resist the divide-and-conquer tactics that historically segregated differing communities from each other and homosexuals from their communities, creating the ignorance of each other that prevented solidarity between oppressed peoples. She foresaw that homosexuals had to perceive themselves, not just heterosexuals, as agents of oppression in the lives of other oppressed people; after all, they had been programmed to view difference with suspicion. The address was a sweeping vision of "a future which is not yet" as Lorde momentarily rested on the point of the difficult questions they would face over the weekend.

Perhaps the most poignant point she addressed was the isolation and lack of support she'd lived with herself, as a black lesbian, for most of her life. Lorde noted its cost to her and to others in the room who'd suffered similarly. "And for me," she told the audience, "it was only the consciousness, the vision, of a community somewhere, someday, it was only my vision of the existence and possibility of what it is, in fact, here tonight, that helped to keep me sane. And sometimes not even that did. . . ."[24] The fact of the conference, the hope for a national network of Third World lesbians and gays, was emblematic of the spiritual home she'd longed for but suffered without; yet the spiritual homelessness her isolation engendered had been eased, to some extent, by engagement with white lesbians and the feminist movement.

In sum, Lorde's address recognized a meeting point between her life as "an only" black lesbian feminist within particular white feminist lesbian circles, the emergence of younger, organized black lesbian feminists, and the possibility of a larger movement of Third World lesbians and gays she could identify with and be celebrated within. A veteran of many social wars, she understood the fight for lesbian and gay liberation as one of the last frontiers upon which social justice, in America, would be fought. And she concluded her speech by urging Third World lesbians and gay men, "the most despised, the most oppressed and the most spat upon people within our communities," to see their survival in the face of that oppression as testament to their strength. That strength was, Lorde insisted, useful to implementing "a future free from the mistakes of our oppressors, as well as from our own."[25]

Lorde's presence at the conference before the march was politically important to its organizers and her audience. She was, after all, the most well known black lesbian feminist, and her appearance was inspirational. Being there had an emotional effect on her, too, that was gratifying in one respect and new in another. Several days afterwards, Lorde noted in her journal: "The National Conference was so important & generative to me. The collective energy of 250 3W dykes was tremendous; healing and provocative." The presence of so many Third World ("3W") lesbians was like a psychic balm, underscoring how much her life—and survival—depended upon recognition from and bonds with women of color. What was new, however, was the connection she now felt to gay black men. Of that, she wrote: "I felt a connection to certain men I'd never found before—black men I never knew existed. I'd like to send Jonathan off to some of them. . . . They were saying things I'd never heard any men say before, about the father land."[26] That consciousness of gay black men was pivotal, as Lorde would later feel especially close to Essex Hemphill and Joseph Beam—two gay black writers who credited her work as inspiring their own.

On October 14, more than one hundred thousand people descended on the nation's capital to "end all social, economic, judicial, and legal oppression of Lesbian and Gay people." The march recognized 1979 as the tenth anniversary of the Stonewall Riots, the historic rebellion that helped to launch the contemporary wave of lesbian and gay liberation, and the visible impact of lesbian and gay organizing at local levels nationally. And it came in the wake of challenges by the New Right to hard-won lesbian and gay rights.

At the decade's midpoint, eighteen states had repealed sodomy laws and several cities had passed ordinances forbidding discrimination on the basis of sexual orientation. Openly lesbian and gay public officials such as Harvey Milk of San Francisco, and Kathy Kozachenko and Elaine Nobel of Michigan and Massachusetts, respectively, represented a sign homosexuals were becoming a major political force within the Democratic Party. However, by 1977, the New Right formed a loose, well-organized, well-financed coalition of religious and secular social conservatives and antiregulation business interests intent on rolling back gains made by social movements for justice in preceding decades. Opposing civil rights protections for homosexual people, the New Right coalesced around antiabortion and antipornography campaigns, among other issues. As the New Right saw it, the nation's tolerance for sexual permissiveness and a federal government that was assuming increasing regulatory powers threatened traditional family structures, gender relations, and conservative notions of reproduction, sexuality, and capitalism.

With the political climate against homosexuals becoming an increasingly hostile one nationally, organizers of lesbian and gay groups had reason to fear the march would spawn a right-wing backlash. That backlash would materialize, in fact, during the 1980s.[27] But on this October Sunday in 1979, the first National March on Washington for Lesbian and Gay Rights helped to shape a national movement.

As one of the speakers at the march, Lorde's remarks were brief and written on both sides of one page. Yet speaking to the "sea of people"[28] stretched before her beyond the podium, Lorde represented an ideological link between the civil rights, feminist, and lesbian and gay liberation movements. In recalling her first trip to Washington, D.C., and the humiliation endured by her family at the ice cream parlor some thirty years before, she spoke of the history of racial injustice suffered by black Americans.[29] As a presence on the stage, she personified the struggle lesbian feminists had waged to be voiced within the feminist movement, giving what Blanche Cook called a "galvanizing, terrific speech."[30] And she spoke to the larger history of lesbian and gay activism, noting there were familiar faces from other marches she'd attended in the crowd. In doing so, Lorde countered the myth of lesbian and gay activism as historically separate from multiple social justice issues, "for lesbians and gay men," she said, "have always been in the vanguard of struggle for liberation and justice in this country and within our communities."[31]

Beyond Lorde's remarks, there was personal significance to the moment. This was the largest audience she'd ever spoken before. As the center of attention, even briefly, she embodied the national cause. This enlarged her persona as warrior, the audience for her books, and her impact as a public intellectual. When the weekend was over, Lorde's keynote address at the National Third World Gay and Lesbian Conference and her remarks at the first National March on Washington for

Lesbian and Gay Rights were crowning personal and political achieve-ments in the war against sexual repression.

BACK HOME, there were other wars.

Too much time elapsed before any of the *Chrysalis* editors responded to Lorde's July 20 letter. In the interim, she'd communicated her fury at them to friends and associates. By the time Deborah Marrow wrote to her on November 1, a series of letters to *Chrysalis* from Patricia (Spears) Jones, Adrienne Rich, June Jordan, and Charlotte Sheedy supported Lorde's rage.

In response to letters received from Lorde, Adrienne Rich, and June Jordan, Patricia (Spears) Jones wrote to the editors that October. Jones was one of several emerging black poets who owed their publication in *Chrysalis* to Lorde, and her letter set the stage within the larger social debate: "That there is still a continuing refusal to allow black and other women of color a complete and integral participation in the philosophi-cal, psychological and public elements of the women's movement is an indictment of the movement. . . . Chrysalis reflects not only the limita-tions of the current movement, but also a limited vision of a 'women's culture.' "[32]

Adrienne Rich found herself situated amidst the whirling dervish that was Lorde's anger, validation of that anger, complicated friendships with Susan Griffin and Kirsten Grimstad as women associated with *Chrysalis*, and serving her own interest in "that work within one's own community which is slow, often thankless, and which brings us face to face with all in ourselves that needs changing as well as what must change in others." Rich's letter to the *Chrysalis* editors, in support of Lorde, incurred criticisms from Grimstad, Griffin, and Lorde. As con-veyed by Rich in a subsequent letter to Lorde, the friendship with Grim-stad had been an "unequal" one in which Rich "played Good Mother," but Grimstad had now "cast" her "as the Bad Mother, the spoiler and destroyer—her way of denying the real issue." Griffin "presumably" agreed that the magazine's policy was racist, yet found fault with Rich's style of criticism and felt Rich was "abandoning" her.

Meanwhile, Lorde wanted an undivided loyalty from Rich, and was angry that Rich's letter had not permanently severed her connection to the women who represented *Chrysalis*; later, she admitted to an insensitivity "because I wanted you [Rich] to write my letter so they could hear it, which of course is not possible." Rich defended "any continuing connection" she might have with the magazine or Susan Griffin or any white feminist as politically motivated. She held firm to her belief that it was possible for white women to change and refused to forego acknowledging other white feminists and lesbians she knew of who were engaged in concrete, antiracist work.[33]

But Lorde's problems with *Chrysalis* and its editors went beyond the personal. She was also serving now as a policy panelist for the Literature Program of the National Endowment for the Arts, reviewing applications from small presses and literary magazines. In this capacity, she was privy to efforts in communities of color and other underfunded communities to gain a foothold in the publishing arena. Feminist writers of color, especially those who identified as radical lesbians, had fewer sympathetic venues in which to publish their works outside the uneven appearance of publications they created, and the "special Third World women's issues" of white feminist publications. Publishing had become a crucial and desired feminist tool; but, given disparities in organizational and financial resources, black and Third World women lagged behind white feminists in terms of a viable, sustainable means by which to do so.

In her letter to Lorde, Deborah Marrow admitted to being hurt and stunned; noting that she'd put Lorde's letter aside and now realized doing so was a mistake. Marrow pleaded for understanding, on the grounds that she was worried the *Chrysalis* editors might appear insensitive to women of color, since they took seriously the scarcity of black and Third World material in the magazine. As its managing editor, she accepted personal responsibility for the disparity between how the editors felt and what was actually published in *Chrysalis*. Marrow did not want Lorde to disassociate herself from the magazine. She felt that the editors needed Lorde's support, energy, and criticism if *Chrysalis* was to become the kind of publication they all envisioned.[34] But Marrow's appeal had no impact. Lorde was through with *Chrysalis*.

. . .

BY NOVEMBER 10, Lorde was in residence at the MacDowell Colony in Peterborough, New Hampshire, having left Frances and the children at home for the four weeks she would stay there. Beth and Jonathan were now sixteen and fifteen years old, respectively. Time away from her family was becoming routine; the demands of a public life increasingly competed with her domestic roles as mother, co-parent, and lover. Her public life rested upon her identity as an artist, and Lorde wanted time to nourish that identity, away from Frances and the children. While she could not imagine life without them, she also couldn't conceive of compromising her career to spare more time with them. Now more than ever, she was compelled by a conviction that her needs had to come first, however selfish exercising those needs appeared.

At MacDowell, writers, composers, and artists occupy individual one-room cabins, equipped with fireplaces, strategically isolated within the colony's pristine acres of woods; this provides a sense of virtual solitude free from the distractions of others. Essentially bare but comfortable, the cabins anticipate needs for a desk, table, bookcase, and easy chair. Adding a personal touch to her otherwise naked walls, Lorde decorated them with pictures of Frances, Beth, and Jonathan. There were no telephones or televisions in the cabins and armylike cots served as beds. Prepared by the staff, breakfast and dinner were served in the main cabin, and provided opportunities to socialize. Lunch was delivered in wicker baskets discreetly left on the screened-in porches. The colony's aim was to privilege artistic endeavor in a near-monastic environment unhampered by the mundane.

While Lorde was there she noted that most of the other artists in residence were women, including the poets May Swenson and Jean Boudin. To her, the other women acted as if they were at a girls' school and complained a lot. She wondered why they were there, and could not understand why all they talked about was getting away, going into town for a movie or Chinese food, being bored, and experiencing sensory deprivation. Of Swenson, she observed: "May plays pool all evening after dinner, but is really nicer than I thought, in a Swedish tight assed way."[35]

Much of the time Lorde kept to herself, noting how others seemed to resent her self-sufficiency, which she cared little about since she was "quite pleased" to be there and felt "full of possibility."[36] She walked alone in the pinewoods, taken in by the area's manicured natural beauty—its damp, hilly textures and a well-gnawed log by a drainpipe under a road she believed to be the workshop of a beaver. She noted her sense that MacDowell brought in a great deal of money, making art "big business here." That notion of the colony as well funded prompted the observation, "Next time I'll try & not pay," alluding to the fact that people were encouraged to contribute financially to their stay if they could afford to. Even so, she noted in her journal, others she knew should have the same opportunity to spend a month there.

Away from the wars of her public life, Lorde used the time to further flesh out the stories of what would become *Zami*. With that came journal notes reflecting upon some of the women, friends, and former lovers she included in it: Ginger, Eudora Garrett, Ruth Baharas, Genny, "The Branded." Of those she'd been intimate with, she wrote: "These women of my youth are all so different—it is as if I slept with & made love to all the——[37] parts to me within each one of them, and came together in Afrekete." She also made notes on pivotal memories: crawling into her parents' bed to lie next to her sleeping mother one Saturday morning after her father had gotten up to make breakfast; Mexico; times when she was out of work or looking for work; her abortion.[38] One lengthy journal entry recorded glimpses of emotional wars within herself and at home.

The emotional war within was a battle between opposing voices—should she go back into therapy or not? Therapy had benefited her in the past. But she dreaded its emotional upheavals, "the fear & despair & uselessness" it wrought in the process. In subsequent sentences, she suggested reasons why therapy was on her mind. Though she was participating as fully as possible in her life, the breast cancer and ensuing amputation of her right breast had left her fighting "the endless battle of despair." Attendant to her despair was a fear her rage could become self-destructive unless directed otherwise: "I am afraid I will damage my self in rage and without other target." That despair waited "like a pale cloud" to "engulf" and "consume" her "into cells of itself." No matter how well she hid or mediated it, her despair was "ever present," waited to drown her, and threatened her hold on life and her health. "That," Lorde wrote, "means destruction for me."[39]

Without Frances Clayton to care for the children and household, Lorde could not have gone to MacDowell so easily. She recognized that while there, "untangling the strands" of her life. She also recognized "the enormity of the tasks" before Frances and herself in raising two teenagers now; thinking "of the pleasures and the wonder of discovery of the past 12 years," yet wondering, "is there really still more to be discovered in the next twelve?" and deciding, in that moment, she didn't "feel too equal to the task." Having left Frances to manage their domestic scene, Lorde was furious that Frances now expressed some resistance to the role of housewife at what she saw as a vulnerable time in her life.

According to several pages of Lorde's journal in which she reviewed their life together, she'd seen Frances through a hellish period of some three to four years after Clayton left Brown University during which Clayton had weathered some personal struggles. From Lorde's perspective, she'd been a supportive, loving partner, who'd given Clayton two loving, admiring, accepting children. All of which had, in her book, carried Clayton through the hard times. "Now I'm in my hard times," Lorde wrote, "and I've got a body that carrys its own death around inside & blind and 2 adolescents who want & can't give, and a lover who's doing her journey actively now & says I don't have anything for you right now & I need room from you while I find out the things you've wanted me to find out all these years."[40]

Not only did Lorde not know if she could imagine another twelve years with Frances Clayton, she felt the "shit storm" was childish. She'd felt similarly during a period of her marriage to Ed Rollins when she'd viewed his emotional acting out as inconsistent with being an adult. Then, she'd thought of herself as having to raise three children. Now she thought of her responsibility for "3 adolescents." And she prayed to Seboulisa that she might remember what she'd paid so much to learn.[41]

THIRTEEN

A T THE START of 1980, Lorde's priorities were to find publishers for "The Cancer Journals"—the three previously published essays on her cancer experiences she now wanted to turn into a book—and for the autobiographical manuscript, "I've Been Standing on This Street Corner a Hell of a Long Time!" which she'd driven herself for months to produce and thought of as a novel. She had other priorities, too: to connect with women representing communities beyond the United States, and to keep her fear of a cancer recurrence at bay. Although she'd survived breast cancer, Lorde believed her body retained the potential to reproduce cancer elsewhere. Propelled by that belief, she shifted into high gear.

In spite of a five-year relationship with her agent, Charlotte Sheedy, Lorde bullheadedly maintained the position that her work was her own to negotiate, disregarding, at her discretion, more conventional professional obligations Sheedy expected between them. She continued to make decisions independently, submitting work to feminist presses run by women she'd befriended. Though she gave the manuscript of her novel to Sheedy to find a publisher for, Lorde now took the matter of "The Cancer Journals" into her own hands, submitting the book to Spinsters Ink, a feminist press co-founded by two friends of hers, Maureen Brady and Judith McDaniel.

Lorde told Brady and McDaniel no one wanted to publish it, and that she'd tried to place it with other publishers who'd turned her down. Without Sheedy's knowledge, she negotiated and signed a contract with Spinsters Ink. As *The Cancer Journals* went to press, Lorde insisted on the "bright and sunny" yellow cover of its first paperback edition, and that there be no picture of herself on the book.[1]

ON FEBRUARY 22, 1980, a group of writers met in New York in response to a growing perception of their underrepresentation, as members of communities of color, in the allocation of public monies dispensed by literature programs under the National Endowment for the Arts (NEA). Among the writers and poets present at that meeting were Patricia (Spears) Jones, Wesley Brown, Jessica Hagedorn, Thulani Davis, Fay Chiang, Walter Dean Meyers, Maurice Kenny, and Akua Leslie Hope. In their view, the problem stemmed from systemic racism, evidenced by the paucity of the NEA's prestigious Creative Writing Fellowships awarded to writers of color, in particular, and the Endowment's failure to solicit the participation of representative numbers of writers of color to serve on its literature panels. An ad hoc steering committee drafted a letter to David Wilk, director of the NEA's Literature Program, and Mary MacArthur, assistant director.

Lorde was not at the initial meeting, but she was present at the second general meeting on March 7 when the steering committee's draft and notes were handed out. High on the agenda were discussions on amendments to the letter to Wilk and MacArthur, membership in a group "dedicated to addressing the needs of Third World Writers in the United States," and voting on a name—the National Association of Third World Writers (NATWW). When the letter to Wilk and MacArthur went out near the end of the month, Lorde was one of thirty-three writers whose handwritten signatures endorsed it.[2]

Wilk and MacArthur's lengthy, expository response of April 14 acknowledged receipt of the NATWW's letter of April 7. As evidence of their willingness to begin "an ongoing dialogue," they proposed a meeting with the NATWW on the afternoon of Monday, May 12, at the Fifth Avenue offices of Teachers and Writers Collaborative, just above the Village.[3] Lorde attended this May 12 meeting, which fell far short of rectifying the NATWW's perception of institutional discrimination against Third World writers. Two months later, the NATWW issued a press release, which cited "historic neglect, censorship, or worse" as reasons to emphasize that "access to public opinion and consciousness" was "a political" and "cultural necessity" long denied to Third World writers, who had now joined together to put an end to the "whiteout of Third World perspectives and values in mass media, generally."[4]

Lorde's involvement with the NATWW was decidedly different from the intensity she felt participating in the black feminist retreats. By definition and mission the NATWW was not a vehicle for promoting her own identity as lesbian, nor was she singularly important to it. In spite of the participation of several women writers of color with strong feminist leanings, those leanings were underarticulated within the organization; and the presumption of heterosexuality precluded an articulation of problems specific to Third World lesbian and gay writers. The organization addressed the problems faced by Third World writers as race-based, primarily—a limited, retrograde analysis in Lorde's mind. In short, the NATWW was not big enough for Lorde ideologically and her participation in subsequent activities fell off.

Yet her fleeting association with the NATWW mirrored an intellectual shift that was significant. The "historic neglect, censorship, or worse" described in the NATWW's press release was also borne by Third World women writers who, by virtue of gender and/or their sexuality as lesbians, suffered a particular lack of "access to public opinion and consciousness." This access was also "a political" and "cultural necessity" for them, as Lorde had begun to see, and was at the center of their struggles to be published, to put an end to the "whiteout" which "sexed out" of the mainstream Third World women's writings and openly lesbian and gay literature by writers of color.[5] As the first out black feminist lesbian to break into the mainstream, she well knew those struggles, being still dependent, in part, upon small and alternative presses for publication, as were so many. At the time, there was no group within which she could exercise links to Third World women writers specifically; nor was there a press run by Third World women targeted to their audiences. Such a group and such a press would have to be created.

By the summer, Lorde was struggling with the introduction to *The Cancer Journals* and saw herself "having grave trouble."[6] She'd drafted several approaches in her journal, but felt uncomfortable with them. Lorde's discomfort was rooted in having to describe her fears, revisit them, and confront a sense that she had neither conquered them nor had they ever completely disappeared—lying, as they did, just beneath the surface and testifying against her in her sleep. She wrestled with her emotions: in the eighteen months since her mastectomy, she'd recovered from the surgery but not the loss. She'd made the decision to live without a prosthesis with passionate resolve. That resolve separated her from what she knew of most breast cancer survivors, shaping both her ongoing pain and bravery.

"Sometimes," she wrote early in April, "I miss my right breast acutely and furiously, and I feel the utmost empathy & compassion for those women who, believing this pain might last forever, chose illusion of conformity." Admitting to her loss was an acknowledgment of the pain, and made suffering it sufferable: "The pain becomes familiar and gradually proof of redefinition of self, tempered and assertive."[7] Her bravado—the public construction of herself as a warrior nobly wounded in battle—did not erase the impact of lingering fear, and she yearned to be remembered, as a model, for battling it.

> When you finger fear and move onward
> remember me
> refusing to honor it
> more than your self
> remember me.[8]

There were moments she felt hopeful: "The richness of my life in retrospect serves to spur me on into the future full of promise."[9] Then she'd lapse into questioning that hopefulness, wondering if her good moments were "a hoax," a "narcissistic indulgence," some "subtle form of the flaccid opptimism [*sic*] that characterizes stupidity and blindness"¹⁰ and shielded her from a more true despair. She searched for a language to name the power she drew strength from, and to define "the clarity that comes with restraint."

Sexual intimacy between herself and Clayton tested perceptions of herself as still desirable ("I hunger for Frances, & hope she does not turn away from me") and illuminated, from her perspective, Clayton's physical uneasiness with her: "When I come to her my heart & body full & burning sometimes she is afraid, masked as hidden anger and the need for denial."¹¹ That she hadn't prevented her own cancer, somehow, or that getting cancer had resulted from something she'd done, haunted Lorde, even as she publicized and politicized the links between cancer, the environment, social attitudes affecting women's bodies, and access to (or lack of) medical knowledge. She fought her anxiety, treating her high tides and low tides with visualization and deep relaxing exercises she culled from books. These self-treatments were episodically effective and made her feel less anxious, which she viewed as a change from living in constant fear of the cancer's recurrence.¹²

She was also dealing with some resentment having to do with an absence of attention to the importance of her work compared to the revived interest in the lives of Zora Neale Hurston and Billie Holiday. The reissue of Hurston's classic novel, *Their Eyes Were Watching God* (first published in 1937), and Robert Hemenway's biography, *Zora Neale Hurston: A Literary Biography* (1977), and the publication in 1979 of Alice Walker's reader on Zora Neale Hurston, *I Love Myself When I Am Laughing . . . and Then Again When I Am Looking Mean and Impressive*, all helped to shape Hurston's literary revival. Holiday's popularity lasted throughout her lifetime, and her blues and jazz remained singular. As music diva and pop culture icon, Holiday came to symbolize a female version of Charlie "Bird" Parker and other black jazz musicians whose lives were considered tragic because of their addictions to drugs. Early in June 1980, as Lorde wrote in her journal, the absence of attention to her work sent her into a fit of rancor: "If bitterness were a whetstone I would be sharp as grief." This "bitterness" was driven, in part, by a sense of being "convinced nobody will attend my work with the passionate dare & precision it deserves & needs until I am dead." Lorde perceived the attention afforded to Hurston and Holiday as "safe" because "they no longer threaten the women who'd have spat on them in the street or more likely looked the other way from their pain."[13] The fact that Hurston and Holiday were long dead underscored her assessment her own work would merit attention only when she too was dead.

None of this explains her resentment fully, but it does explain a fear of dying without the satisfaction of significant popular or critical attention to her work. The fear of obscurity is deeply human and understandable, in retrospect, in the context of Lorde's pioneerism: she lived by her own dreams and volitions. She did the things she had to do, often without models or encouragement.[14] Her multiple identities both troubled and parted waters as she "held the world by the tail and tried to change it." As time went on and Lorde's writings became more widely known, growing numbers of black and white feminists, lesbian and gay activists—indeed, writers and activists of varying stripes—used her work in the service of their own. They often credited her as visionary, but not always.

Subsuming all this emotional turmoil was Lorde's struggle to bring order to the chaos of life-threatening illness, to wrest her life from that chaos, and to empower other women whom she hoped would benefit from *The Cancer Journals*. With her introduction still unwritten by mid-July, she left for Copenhagen, Denmark.

Lorde spent ten days there, attending and reading, as an invited poet, at the International Festival of Women Artists; she returned to the United States on July 24. She made no day-by-day notes of those ten days in her journal, summarizing them in one entry dated on her last day. She indicates she didn't find being in Copenhagen exceptional. It was only in the last two days that she'd thought the city and her experience of it beautiful, and then it was "as if a pall has been lifted from me and from the face of this city."[15] But there were significant dimensions to that Copenhagen trip.

The festival's forum on lesbian identity and politics was the first international panel at which Lorde explicitly presented herself as black feminist lesbian, offering instructive analyses for defining one's self as "other" in an oppressive society.[16] By doing so, though, she believed that she'd alienated some of the European and American women when she introduced racial issues, and she'd alienated some of the African women when she discussed the historic realities of lesbians.[17] Even so, Lorde felt a sense of connection—across racial and sexual differences—to other women who'd spoken during the forum.[18] As a representative of America's oppressed citizens, her identity as black lesbian shaped the emergence of yet another identity: that of the secular itinerant preacher, willing to travel the globe to preach the gospel of social justice.

There were two other notable dimensions to this trip. First, she flirted with a new mythology of herself. In a self-ridiculing moment in her journal, Lorde noted wanting to write about "being almost blind and one breasted and how in some wonderful tragedicomic way that makes me the perfect amazon seeress!!!" The idea that she could reinvent these bodily traumas as tragicomic and herself as mythic woman, gifted with powers of sight, pleased her. But even as she wasn't yet sure how to write about herself in that way,[19] she'd opened a space *to be* that way. Second, being away from home for a while gave her some needed distance from struggling with writing the introduction to *The Cancer Journals*. After returning home, she went back to it, drafting and redrafting the language, and finishing it in August.

WHEN THE SEMESTER began at John Jay, Lorde returned to the campus reluctantly. In mid-September 1980, she recorded the following journal entry: "First autumn day—it is 94 degrees. I am in John Jay where I don't want to be."[20] Teaching remained an important, expressive aspect of who she was, as did her $35,000-a-year salary. But after four years, she was growing tired of working at an institution where the emphasis was on criminal studies, and she was outgrowing its provincial atmosphere.

The Cancer Journals was published by Spinsters Ink early in the fall.[21] It was a landmark that had a seismic effect on its readers. No earlier work had explored the impact of breast cancer on a black feminist lesbian's life. Though singular in perspective, *The Cancer Journals* pioneered wider public discourse on the disease within feminist circles. It gave women a precedent to speak about both the disease and their fear of it. At the same time, Lorde explored spiritual aspects of loving women—the notion of women's culture and community as redemptive, healing forces in her life. As word of *The Cancer Journals* circulated and it began to appear on the shelves of feminist bookstores, Lorde received letters from other lesbian women who'd also had mastectomies; who knew women friends with breast cancer; whose mothers had had breast cancer; and who understood the culture of silence framing the disease. As the writer and activist Elly Bulkin shared in a letter,

> I most wanted to thank you for breaking the silence around breast cancer and mastectomies. I say this as the daughter of a woman who died while I was in my early teens after having two mastectomies. The word cancer was never spoken in my house and no information was ever shared with my brother or me about the exact nature of her hospitalization, surgery, etc. From this perspective, I see your book as a wonderful gift to . . . those of us who do not see breast cancer as necessarily happening only to other women and who greatly need the sound of voices that place it within a framework that is life-affirming and political.[22]

Lorde was "very pleased" with the first edition of *The Cancer Journals*, but some owners of feminist bookstores became increasingly worried. Even customers who knew the work by name said they had difficulty spotting it in a stack of books. The yellow cover was pale rather than "sunny" and it lacked an eye-catching design. At the Second Women in Print Conference in Washington, D.C., in 1981, many of them shared their concerns about this lack of visibility with Spinsters Ink's co-founders. McDaniel and Brady then passed on these concerns to Lorde, who agreed to have a photograph of herself on the cover of the second edition.[23] This marked for her an increasing consciousness of her books as visual products.

The black-and-white photograph Lorde chose for the cover showed a smiling, confident, larger-than-life Audre Lorde in an African gele and top. The photo asserted Lorde's African heritage. It was cropped above the breasts and did not visually exploit her one-breastedness. But a single, dangling earring in the right earlobe and two studded earrings in the left one pointed up both her lesbianism and the asymmetry of her single breast.[24]

Susan McHenry remarked on this in her review of *The Cancer Jour-*

nals for *Ms.* magazine the following year: "Lorde . . . dares to acknowledge her radically altered body image 'in the name of grand asymmetry,'
and with it embraces a radically altered self-one even more vital and
whole than before." Her concluding comment resonated with Lorde's literary intention: "This book transcends the specific tragedy of its subject
matter to extend a powerful example of self-healing useful to anyone
working through a crisis of any sort. . . ."[25]

As an acknowledged breast cancer survivor, Lorde defined new territory of the personal-as-political. "I am who the world and I have never
seen before,"[26] she stated in *The Cancer Journals*. That statement underlined the flirtation with a reinvented self she'd entertained in Copenhagen. If the publication of *The Black Unicorn* expressed a poetic
embracing of African mythologies, for spiritual sustenance, then *The
Cancer Journals* signaled Lorde's self-styled transfiguration as Seboulisa
incarnate. She became a living version of the one-breasted warrior goddess, central to her spiritual links to a reimagined, mythic Africa. Surviving breast cancer and living with fear of a recurrence became the
"pervasive, central modus operandi"[27] driving her forward from then on.
But it was not simply that Lorde had breast cancer or a mastectomy; it
was what she did with those facts.

Although pleased with the debut of *The Cancer Journals*, Lorde was
not pleased with responses from mainstream editors to the manuscript
of her novel "I've Been Standing on This Street Corner a Hell of a Long
Time!," which she was adding to and revising even as it was circulating.
Between March 19, 1980, and April 29, 1981, editors at nearly a dozen
trade houses rejected the work, including W. W. Norton, Houghton Mifflin, Random House, Viking Press, Seaview Books, Delacorte Press,
Macmillan, Dutton, and G. P. Putnam's Sons. Though most of the editors especially praised the early childhood sections and Lorde's writing,
the collective response was that the book lacked focus; suffered from
being neither a traditional autobiography nor a traditional novel; was
structurally flawed, overdependent on chronology for its narrative progression, unevenly written; lacked an ability to show, rather than tell, the
main character's growth; and generally was not ready for consideration
by their editorial boards.[28]

None of the editors explicitly objected to the book's lesbianism, although Charlotte Mayerson at Random House thought Lorde's work was similar to that of Maya Angelou.[29] The comparison to the protagonist's brief encounters with lesbians in the first of Maya Angelou's autobiographies, *I Know Why the Caged Bird Sings*, was a misreading of themes both common and different in black women's literature, given that Angelou, though black, was neither a lesbian nor writing of coming-of-age as a black lesbian. Nor did there exist at the time a plethora of similar works. Ann Allen Shockley's novel, *Loving Her* (1974), was "the first sympathetic black lesbian novel."[30] Published in 1974 by Bobbs-Merrill, Shockley's book remained singularly distinguished, albeit obscure to the mainstream. The senior editor at Macmillan, Marion Wheeler, did not comment directly on Lorde's overt lesbianism in the manuscript, yet managed at the same time to imply that the topic was taboo in the mainstream. Wheeler flatly stated she thought Lorde's manuscript would be difficult for a trade house to publish. But she diplomatically suggested an alternative: one of the feminist presses, with the right distribution outlets and an identifiable reputation for publishing similar works, would be a better option.[31] Of all the rejection letters, the one from Lorde's editor at W. W. Norton carried the most emotional weight.

John Benedict admitted in his letter: "There are few things I've done more reluctantly in my publishing life than this, but I'm afraid I must return the manuscript of Audre Lorde's I'VE BEEN STANDING ON THIS STREET CORNER. . . ." Although he thought "Much of the manuscript is extraordinary, in that it gives a number of deep—almost visionary—insights into the life of an extraordinary woman and poet, and many of these insights are rendered in a uniquely compelling form and style," he viewed the work as an anthology of insights that did not hold together for him as a book or move him to a richer understanding. Benedict also noted his disappointment with the final sections in which he felt Lorde hadn't "given us the depth of vision into the later events in her life that she gave into the earlier events, particularly in the passages about her mother." Additionally, he acknowledged, and thought "entirely justifiable," Lorde's resistance to working on the manuscript further without a contract. Having already discussed with Sheedy her search for a publisher for another collection of Lorde's poems, Benedict proposed instead that Norton publish a book of selected poems drawn from *Coal*,

The Black Unicorn, her earlier small press publications, and new work. He noted that the editors at Norton thought she was at a point in her poetic career where she was ready for a book that collected the best of the past and looked forward to the future.[32]

Lorde took Benedict up on his suggestion she compile a selection of poems, going to work on the project soon after. By late September, he had an initial manuscript of "Chosen Poems—Old and New."

As Sheedy saw it, the editors at Norton turned the novel down because they didn't know how to read it and judged it, wrongly, by European standards. Lorde was "so hurt" by the Norton rejection, and Sheedy infuriated at their rejection of "a brilliant novel."[33] Nevertheless, Sheedy understood, better than Lorde, that a manuscript could be rejected many times before it struck a nerve with a receptive editor.

At St. Martin's Press, Michael Denneny had earned a reputation for publishing books by gay and lesbian writers. A gay man himself, and an activist within publishing circles, Denneny sought to normalize the publication of gay and lesbian literature in mainstream publishing,[34] and he was ideologically receptive to Lorde's work. But several months passed before he responded to Sheedy. In the interim, Denneny had not returned any of Sheedy's phone calls. Exacerbating that silence was his reputation for being disorganized.[35] In a letter written well after the fact, Denneny confessed to his reputation: "By the way, I know my reputation for tardiness is abysmal, but . . . I have spent the last year getting the office backlog under control and can now guarantee a speedy response on any submissions. . . ." At any rate, Denneny sincerely wanted to publish Audre Lorde, and, after Lorde called him, he met with her for lunch on October 7.

Back at his office that afternoon, Denneny immediately dispatched a letter to Charlotte Sheedy. In a detailed account which began with an apology for not responding sooner, he explained: "I delayed writing because I couldn't quite get clear in my mind what I wanted to say. I love parts of it, but thought that as a whole it didn't quite come into focus; unfortunately I was having trouble trying to come up with concrete criticisms and suggestions." He described the meeting with Lorde as a long and "profitable" lunch during which he'd been able to articulate a fundamental critique: "the book needs a whole new draft." Despite his concerns over the organization and a feeling that "too much of the story had been related rather than dramatized right there on the page," Denneny expressed his confidence in the book and in Lorde: "I think it is very important for Audre to work this book up into something astonishingly good, which I am absolutely sure she is capable of." At the same time, he was concerned that being a poet, black, and a lesbian ("and quite honestly that means she's got three strikes against her to begin with") positioned Lorde—and the work—in "an uphill struggle. . . . To get this book through the editorial meeting," he emphasized, "I need the best possible book she is capable of writing."

Denneny conceded it was unfair to suggest "that blacks, or women, or lesbians, have to be twice as good as anyone else to get recognized," but that was the reality of mainstream publishing, and he wanted to wait until Lorde had revised the manuscript before trying to secure a contract for it. Still, he was unwilling to relinquish an opportunity to publish her; so he suggested that if his position was unacceptable to Sheedy, and if Sheedy wanted to continue to shop the manuscript around, he would try to get a contract for it even though he was not optimistic he could do so with the current draft. Also, he was concerned that if it were turned down now, it would be harder to sign up later when a revised version surfaced.[36]

The day after her lunch with Denneny, Lorde flew to Washington, D.C., for meetings of the NEA's Literature Program policy panel. Having served for a year, her term was officially drawing to a close. Two days later, as other panelists whose terms were also ending gave statements summarizing their experiences, Lorde resisted doing so but was awash with a sense of feeling "sentimental." Despite having been "furious with some of the decisions made," she'd come to better understand the positions of others "and their commitment to their causes as opposed sometimes to their interests." She'd seen herself as exercising that same sense of commitment. Moreover, she'd come to understand that panelists and NEA staff members alike were caught working within a system with a life of its own that seemed to limit progressive vision or movement, except in prescribed ways.[37] That understanding temporarily shaped her decision to serve another year as a policy panelist.

When Lorde returned to New York, she found a copy of Denneny's letter to Sheedy waiting for her. His letter sounded like another rejection, and Lorde could not tolerate rejection. She flew into a rage. She felt he'd flirted with her, made a lot of promises, hadn't responded in a timely fashion, and had been untruthful.[38]

The day after Michael Denneny wrote his letter, Gloria Greenfield, of Persephone Press, sent her own letter to Lorde. Greenfield's communiqué of October 8 was all of one paragraph and to the point: "This is a quick note to remind you that there is a lesbian-feminist publishing house in Watertown, Massachusetts that would be absolutely thrilled to receive literary submissions from Audre Lorde . . . seriously, Pat [McGloin] and I are admirers of your writings, and would be honored to be your publisher. Please consider us for your next (and next, and next . . .) manuscript."[39]

The timing of the two letters was fortuitous, but Greenfield's letter resonated with the earlier suggestion made by Marion Wheeler, at Macmillan, that one of the women's presses might be a better fit for Lorde's manuscript. Her rage and rejection fueling her, Lorde decided to send the manuscript of her novel to Persephone Press without telling Charlotte Sheedy beforehand. When she did eventually call Sheedy to inform her the novel was being published by Persephone and that she wanted Sheedy to review the contract she'd already signed, Sheedy was stunned—there was nothing she could do about a signed contract.

By the end of October, Lorde was preparing for a trip to Boston where she was to participate in a poetry reading by black women on October 31. Other poets scheduled to read included Hattie Gossett, also from New York City, and Kate Rushin, who lived in Boston. Before leaving, Lorde had a telephone conversation with Barbara Smith in which she told Smith they had to do something about publishing. The context for Lorde's remark was a shared perspective developed over many conversations and several years of comparing notes on the racism each had experienced as writers dealing with white women's presses and periodicals. Smith understood Lorde to have "something more concrete in mind." As the conversation ensued, she volunteered to organize a group of women to meet and discuss the issue further while Lorde was in Boston.

On Saturday, November 1, a meeting was held at Smith's Roxbury apartment. A second was held that Sunday. Most of the women at the initial meeting were from the Boston area, except for Lorde and Gossett, and were predominantly of African American or African Caribbean descent.[40] Agreeing on the need for an "autonomous publishing resource,"[41] the group decided at the very first meeting to found a press for all women of color.[42] That decision ran counter to the historic separation between groups of color; they recognized that as women, feminists, and lesbians of color, they had experiences and work to do in common, even though they also had differences. Despite these differences, a commonality between them was their identity as writers and activists, as women of color who had minimal access to power (including the power of media) and who were determined to provide an alternative to white-dominated publishing venues. Not until a year later, when it was officially founded, did they choose a name for their press, Kitchen Table: Women of Color Press. The name signified its location as a grassroots organization, established by women who felt they could not rely on the benefits of class privilege to do what had to be done.[43]

The group held subsequent meetings to clarify details about the new press they hoped to build. A discussion arose as to whether they should publish a magazine as well as books. While there was no disagreement on the question of publishing books, some, like Smith, were opposed to publishing a magazine because periodicals were expected to appear on a regular basis.[44] A persuasive argument against publishing a periodical was that most published by women and lesbians of color suffered brief lifetimes before disappearing; from the outset, the collective pledged to make their press an institution.[45] That meant, in part, raising funds to support its longevity. They began to write grants for funding. Smith had a friend in Boston, a fund-raiser, who helped them secure a significant contribution from a private donor. Within a couple of months of starting, they had money in the bank.[46] With Lorde and Smith as its co-founders, the group began working as a collective. It would grow to include an array of women of color, among them, Hattie Gossett, Helena Byard, Susan Yung, Ana Oliveira, Rosie Alvarez, Alma Gomez, and Leota Lone Dog.[47]

Barbara Smith's lover at the time, Cherríe Moraga, moved to Boston in December 1980 and also became one of the original members of the collective. When Smith and Moraga decided to move to New York City in the summer of 1981, they took the press with them. The decision to relocate was precipitated, in part, by a recognition that the major energy for building and sustaining Kitchen Table lay in New York.[48] With Smith and Moraga living in Brooklyn then and Lorde based in Staten Island, not only were the co-founders close to each other, but by virtue of being reestablished in New York, the press was better positioned within an even more dynamic women's cultural scene.

In time, Kitchen Table: Women of Color Press became the first press run by women of color for women of color in the United States and actively supported the cultural struggles of all lesbians of color. It considered itself an activist publisher with the goal to educate a target audience not solely comprised of women or lesbians of color, but of readers across categories of race, nationality, age, gender, sexuality, and economic status.[49]

As a co-founder, Lorde became a significant asset. She gave critical financial support to Kitchen Table's operating funds, donating substantial earnings from her readings.[50] In New York and elsewhere, she was the main attraction at benefits. Her literary reputation drew other women of color to dedicate themselves to its goals. When traveling, she promoted the press and urged women writers of color to consider it as a potential publisher. The editorial responsibilities she assumed, as a member of the collective, enabled her to exercise the same power assigned to mainstream and white feminist publishers: as representative of a literary institution, she would help shape its markets and the reading public. " 'The table,' "[51] as Lorde referred to Kitchen Table Press, filled a void that the National Association of Third World Writers could not. It synchronized the cultural and political necessity for feminists and lesbians of color to acquire autonomy in the publishing arena, and coincided with Lorde's widening personal network of contacts, both in the United States and abroad.

Lorde sent a letter to David Wilk and the NEA at the beginning of November 1980, giving notice that she had now decided she would not serve another term and was resigning from the policy panel. Being a policy panelist had afforded her a measure of power—to assist the Literature Program in formulating policy, developing and revising its guidelines, determining future programs, and making recommendations on grant applications. Yet her brief stint working for change within a federal bureaucracy only proved it ideologically and structurally opposed to radical engagement. Still, she was leaving with valuable insights on the Literature Program's processes; she added that she'd come to a point where the demands of her own work, her financial responsibilities, and responsibility to her health made it impossible to continue serving.

Lorde concluded by strongly urging the NEA to fill her vacancy with one of the women artists of color whose names and addresses she supplied.* Though she recognized the decision was not solely hers to make, she trusted that "my reappointment means that my suggestions will carry some weight." Finally, she acknowledged that although there had been "some vigorous disagreements" between them, working together had been a pleasure.[52]

Before the month was out, David Wilk wrote back accepting "with great regret" her resignation from the panel. Wilk said he hoped Lorde would remain a resource for informal advice and counsel in the future and that she would continue to communicate her concerns to the Literature Program. He thanked her for her suggestions for future panelists, noting panelists for the upcoming year had been selected already (he enclosed a list with his letter) but promising to keep her suggestions on file. He ended by thanking her for her service as a panelist and saying that, "in disagreement or in harmony," he'd found working with her an exceptional experience.[53]

As the Christmas season approached, Lorde felt disheartened. She remarked upon the winter solstice as "a day of strength and hard beginnings." That night, she and Frances went out to greet the full moon, but what was a ritual between them was marred, for her, by an emotional struggle. As she noted in her journal: "We are for & close as only women who love each other but battle alone can be. We each want the other to help but cannot define the aid we are seeking." Also, Beth and Jonathan were making their own plans for the holidays. "I will always remember this Christmas as the year the children left," she wrote. She felt Frances didn't understand how emotionally difficult it would be for her to be without the

---

* Lorde named June Jordan; Janice Mirikitami, a San Francisco–based Japanese American poet; and myself as the three women of color she urged on the NEA as possible replacements.

children on Christmas, and she was uncomfortable with Frances's efforts to make the separation easier. The emotional distance between herself and Frances, the thought of Christmas without Beth and Jonathan, and the realization they were no longer little children bewitched by Christmas, all combined to feel "so hurtful, even if it is in the nature of things."[54]

EARLY IN FEBRUARY 1981, Lorde received a brief letter from Phyllis G. Moe, chair of the Department of English at Hunter College. Moe informed Lorde she'd been suggested as someone who might be interested in a position the department had advertised in *The Chronicle of Higher Education*, the full text of which was enclosed. The college had an opening for a poet to teach poetry workshop courses in the English Department's Creative Writing Program. The course load would include a course in literature or expository writing, and the tenure-track position was to begin in September 1981. "Should you find the position of interest," Moe encouraged, "we would be very pleased to hear from you."[55] Phyllis Moe's invitation came as a possible solution to Lorde's increasing dissatisfaction with teaching at John Jay. Within days of receiving the letter, she wrote back expressing her interest in the position, enclosing, as required, a copy of her curriculum vitae, and hoping for the best.

Gloria Joseph also wrote to Lorde at the beginning of the year to invite Lorde's participation in the Women Writers Symposium she was organizing in St. Croix, in the U.S. Virgin Islands. Joseph was a native of St. Croix and had spent much of her life in the States teaching, having earned a PhD in education and sociology from Cornell University. Joseph's family had immigrated from the Caribbean to New York City; she'd grown up in a Catholic, West Indian household. Joseph was a respected social scientist whose publications on black women were widely regarded, an athlete, and a committed black feminist activist. Three years later, she would convene a number of black feminist scholar-activists to discuss strategies for offering support and showing solidarity to black women of South Africa. The women she convened included Zala Chandler, Johnnetta Cole, Andrée McLaughlin, Barbara Riley—and Lorde. As a result of Joseph's initiative, the organization Sisterhood in Support of Sisters in South Africa (SISA) was formed.

SISA's immediate goals included recognition of the emerging South African women's self-help movement as a form of political resistance to apartheid;[56] developing relationships with two significant sister grass-roots organizations, the Zamani Soweto Sisters and the Maggie Magaba Trust; encouraging personal bonds between North American women of the African diaspora and black South African women; and promoting the responsibility of African American women to share economic and political resources far more available to them in the West with women of the African diaspora. Both Lorde and Adrienne Rich gave major poetry readings around America as benefits in support of SISA. Lorde's involvement ultimately led to a friendship with the South African writer-activist Ellen Kuzwayo, and to a link with a black women's movement in South Africa; it signified a powerful, contemporary example of the international links between the quest for black liberation in America and in Africa.

At the time, Joseph did not know Lorde well. They'd only been in each other's company on a couple of occasions, during one of the black feminist retreats and briefly during the late 1970s. A professor at Hampshire College in Amherst, Massachusetts, Joseph had secured a small sum to invite black women writers and intellectuals—including Toni Cade Bambara, Mari Evans, and Dr. Betty Shabazz—to the college to speak before her class on black women, "Insurgent Sisters." Lorde was one of the invited speakers.

The symposium was to take place in March 1981. Michelle Cliff and Adrienne Rich were also invited, on the basis of their international reputations and their friendships with Joseph. Lorde was invited because of her connections to Rich and Cliff.[57] Discussing the upcoming event in a letter to Rich, Lorde supposed the event and travel weren't as hectic as it all sounded, but on a personal level she felt Joseph was communicating conflicting messages of apprehension and anticipation. And Lorde was disturbed about the financial arrangements. Cliff was being offered less money than Rich, Bambara, and herself. Lorde felt they should all receive equal honorariums, particularly since she'd never forgotten how unjust it felt to be paid less. She thought paying Cliff less was not only unfair but an underestimation of Cliff's worth as writer.[58]

. . .

On February 12, Lorde accompanied her sister, Helen, and her mother to a funeral home to get a feel for the kind of coffin Mrs. Lorde wanted to be buried in.[59] Mrs. Lorde was now in her mid-eighties. She'd developed Parkinson's disease, suffered two heart attacks during the 1970s, and had been blind since 1976. She still lived in the 152nd Street walk-up apartment building into which Lorde's family had moved four decades earlier. After losing her eyesight, she'd sought help from the Center for Independent Living and learned how to navigate the apartment alone, to distinguish between different denominations of paper currency, and to boil water for tea. In spite of impairments to her mobility, she maintained the practice of going to church.[60]

The visit to the funeral home was difficult for the two sisters, but Lorde felt it was harder on Helen.[61] Although she assumed responsibility for accompanying her mother to appointments with doctors from time to time, it was Helen who visited Mrs. Lorde every evening after work, religiously, sitting with her, sharing a cup of tea, doing what she could to make her mother comfortable, making sure the home attendant had what she needed. When Mrs. Lorde's food supplies ran low, she'd replenish them. Oftentimes, Helen slept over at her mother's apartment and left from there for work the next morning.[62] And it was Helen who felt unprepared, by their mother, for life as a woman.

According to Lorde's journal, after the three women returned to Mrs. Lorde's apartment, Helen, "realizing again that mother was not going to live forever, or even give her the answer, asked again why mother had never prepared her for the world, taught her how to be a woman."[63] Having been raised in a household in which education was stressed but relations between men and women were not discussed, Helen had fulfilled her parents' expectations; she'd graduated from Adelphi University with a master's degree in social work in the 1960s and eventually landed a job with the Agency for Child Development in Manhattan. But her own expectations for personal happiness never quite came to fruition. An expensive dating service she registered with provided a stream of potential suitors for two years, but nothing came of them. Then the same agency paired her with a handsome, bright African from Liberia who was going to school and working in the States. In her thirties and lonely, she fell head over heels for him immediately. Although the relationship had lasted ten years on and off, Helen still hoped it would lead to marriage. But the Liberian, who was married and claimed to be divorcing his wife, proved to be interested only in a mistress—one who could provide a sexual relationship without need for conversing about politics or current events. When it was finally over, he'd broken her heart; years later, she still could not bring herself to speak his name.

Helen had often wondered why her life had not been like Phyllis's or Audre's, both of whom had married and had children. Later in life, she'd likened their differing lives to three ships sailing from one port in different directions. In retrospect, Audre appeared to her to have sailed away from the port more able, "doing everything under the sun, getting married, having female lovers."[64] Lorde did not tell Helen that, for her, lack of preparation had been a blessing which left her free to choose and to define herself.

In Lorde's journal entry, she remembers the elderly Mrs. Lorde referring to Helen as "darling child," professing, "I loved among you three children the best I knew how. . . ." It was considered improper, her mother explained, to discuss sexual relations between men and women in those days, and she did not know what she could have done differently. She asked Helen to leave her alone and not to torment her by bringing up the past. As Helen cried, Audre held her, feeling there was nothing else she could do. Though frail, Mrs. Lorde had retained an imposing authority as mother. But her dependence on Helen compelled her to ask if Helen would still take care of her.

Although she treated that day's events largely as an observer and cited little about her own feelings, Lorde empathized with both her sister and her mother. She'd come to understand their mother as being "from a different culture"[65] in far less romanticized terms than those she'd understood as a child. Though younger than Helen, Audre was the more worldly of the two. Her trip to Grenada in 1978 had yielded a more sympathetic, expanded view of the narrow world Mrs. Lorde came from and remained rooted to. Moreover, the mother-daughter intimacy Helen desired had been emotionally impossible for Mrs. Lorde, who did not have a language to communicate that intimacy. And Audre understood that.

.   .   .

THE DAY OF HER birthday, Lorde noted in part: "I am 47 years here. Good living. I lay in the yard and felt the sun affirm the beginning of this new season. Doing old things in a new way. Pressed by necessity into finding beginnings where endings are standard. . . ."[66] Six days after her birthday, she began some notes for a piece on the murdered children of Atlanta.

Between 1979 and 1981, more than two dozen black children in Atlanta mysteriously disappeared from the city's streets or their homes. Their strangled, beaten bodies were found along riverbeds and in the woods. These seemingly unexplained murders terrorized black Atlantans, and focused media attention on Atlanta and its first black mayor, Maynard Jackson. In time, the FBI was called in to solve the case and Wayne Williams, a twenty-three-year-old black man, was convicted, largely on circumstantial evidence, of killing two of the children and sentenced to two life terms in prison. Throughout his trial, and for years afterwards, Williams maintained he was innocent of the crimes.[67]

Lorde's "Notes for Atlanta" were shaped as a poem and revisited a preoccupation with the lives of black children as expendable:

> . . .
> these are the children
> found beaten and silenced
> muzzled and buried
> in the schoolyard, the rock heap
> and we dismiss them under the stamp
> street-children . . .

She threaded images of Atlanta to those of the civil rights movement,

> . . . the force of this silent hatred trained upon them
> like a hose. . . .

and to media reports of police brutality:

> . . .
> broken childs body falling
> into the news from a rooftop the

side of a building a policeman's
jerking pistol falling into
the news & out as quickly as
a dark bag of bones becomes
onerous refuse in the straight
beam of media
light . . .[68]

Ultimately, Lorde did not formalize these "Notes" on the Atlanta child murders into a specific poem. But the horror of unfolding events there stayed on her mind, linked to daily news of drought victims in Africa, the U.S. government's support of repressive forces in El Salvador, Nicaragua, and Guatemala, the impact of U.S. foreign policy on Haiti, and the liberation struggle in South Africa. The Atlanta child murders came to represent, for her, only one aspect of the calculated destruction of people of color worldwide.

An accomplished poet now, her poetry was the measure of who she was as a writer. That her "Notes for Atlanta" did not materialize into a poem frustrated Lorde. She began to feel she wasn't concentrating enough on her poetry. As an atypically highly productive writer, unaccustomed to poetic droughts, this frightened her. A journal entry dated April 24, 1981, while she was in Minneapolis on a speaking engagement, offers this hopeful note: "I had one beautiful afternoon in Minneapolis when I knew I would write poems again."

John Benedict thought the manuscript of "Chosen Poems" was "an extraordinary and resonant manuscript," but he now understood it as too long for Norton to publish at a reasonable price. In a letter to her at the end of February 1981, he maintained his and the publisher's enthusiasm for publishing it, but underscored the necessity to drastically reduce the number of pages by excluding some of her selection. He referred to a version of the work in which she'd rescinded her earlier position on not including poems from *The Black Unicorn*; their addition lengthened the midsection of the book considerably. Benedict explained that he understood such an editing process would be painful for her; at the same time, he encouraged her to consider a less-is-more approach that "might make the great poems of your career stand forth in more splendor." To resolve the problem of lengthiness, he gingerly suggested two alternatives: he could edit the manuscript for her approval, which, even as "an affectionate and admiring outsider," not only made him apprehensive but also he felt sure would not please her, to have someone else fiddling with her work; or, he could return it to her and she could edit it.[69] In closing, Benedict left the decision as to how to proceed up to her, reiterating his desire to publish her book. With that dilemma looming, Lorde now had to revisit the project.

In addition, she was invested in a new direction as prose writer and was still in the throes of fine-tuning the manuscript of her autobiographical novel, encouraged not only by the contract with Persephone but also by Adrienne Rich's support, for one, throughout the process. Rich believed in the inherent importance of the work and had urged Lorde forward. In one letter to her in which she described Lorde's manuscript as "becoming a very, very important autobiography," she'd suggested, "I feel you have been mistressing some new power in the process of writing this book which for a long time you would not even identify as a book. You will have to go back when you are finished and revise the earlier work in tone with what you know now that you didn't know when you began to write. . . ."[70] Rich's independent take on the work's problems was not totally dissimilar from the generalized critique of mainstream editors who'd read and responded to it: she was both moved by parts of it and found other parts lacking. At the same time, Rich shared with Lorde a perspective as lesbian-feminist writer and a shared desire to be heard and understood by "listening" readers, real and imagined.[71] As elements of their friendship, this would prove critical both to how Lorde received Rich's comments on her work and her sustained engagement with it.

LORDE ARRIVED IN St. Croix at the beginning of March for the Women Writers Symposium. Running March 7 through March 9, the symposium was the first of its kind in the Virgin Islands, funded by a $3,000 grant from the Humanities and Arts Council there which partially covered expenses.[72] Like Toni Cade Bambara and Bambara's daughter, Karma, Cliff, and Rich, she stayed at Joseph's home—85 Judith's

Fancy—in Christiansted. Bambara and her daughter were living in Atlanta at the time, and because Bambara was a community activist who was recording the stories of several of the murdered victims' mothers, the two had intimate knowledge of what became known as the Atlanta Murdered and Missing Children's Case.[73] In St. Croix, there was a brief respite from the events enveloping them back home.

The symposium was held at the Little Theater, on the St. Croix campus of what was then known as the College of the Virgin Islands (CVI). Over the course of several days, there were nightly readings, formal presentations, or slide shows.[74] One of the readings featured Bambara and Lorde, with Bambara reading from her work-in-progress on the Atlanta murders and Lorde reading some poetry.

Lorde expressed mixed feelings about being in St. Croix. The posters Joseph had printed announcing the symposium listed Adrienne Rich's name first. Rich found that upsetting, because there was an unwritten rule in the feminist movement in the States to list names in alphabetical order, eschewing the hierarchal practice of making one person more important than the next. As Rich, Cliff, Lorde, and Bambara discussed the posters one night on Gloria Joseph's porch, Lorde was protective of Gloria, who, she argued, knew best how to handle things in St. Croix.[75] Although Lorde appeared to be spending more time focused on Gloria than on symposium events,[76] in her journal she complained Gloria was only partially attentive to her.[77]

The cultural climate was different in St. Croix. Used to acting out her sexuality in a more visible, politicized lesbian community, Lorde was unaccustomed to being in a culture that accepted women's bonds and friendships, and the implication of sexuality within them, yet not a public discourse on "lesbianism." Joseph recognized that homophobia, as well as racism and sexism, existed in St. Croix as it did throughout the Americas,[78] but she became upset when the issue of lesbianism was raised at the symposium by Lorde and Rich. As she'd often explained to Cliff and Rich, sexual intimacy between black women in the Caribbean was subsumed within the structures of the community[79] and thus was not distinct—or articulated as distinct—from the larger island life.

Gloria Joseph embodied the culture of "Zami-ness"—of women who lived and worked together as friends and lovers—that Lorde was later to

accept as her own lived experience and as a "new spelling" of her lesbian self. But in the moment, she thought that Joseph was "entirely
cocooned" in her importance as the symposium's organizer, leaving
Lorde to feel dissatisfied with the shifting dynamic between them and
wanting to go home. Neither the celebrated lesbian nor the center of
attention she expected to be, at one point Lorde wrote of "feeling left
out." At another, all she could see were "impassive differences" between
herself and Joseph.[80]

Lorde's mixed feelings in St. Croix had much to do with seeing and
experiencing Gloria Joseph in her own cultural milieu for the first time.
Heretofore, she'd encountered Joseph only in the States. Though a formidable personality wherever she was, Gloria Joseph's formidability was
heightened on her own terrain. She had status amongst others on the
island where, being highly educated aside, she was known as one of
them. In retrospect, Joseph reminded Lorde of Pat Parker, whom Lorde
felt was "the hardest person I can connect to and the most important,"
and she often thought of the two together.[81] Parker's refusal to behave
like a doting fan, or treat with Lorde as anything but a peer, confounded
her; yet it was also the deeper reason Lorde respected Parker. As the
friendship between Lorde and Joseph developed, Joseph acted similarly,
resisting falling under the spell of Lorde's public persona as celebrated
lesbian.[82]

The commonalities in their personal backgrounds and complementary political interests, as well as Joseph's own sense of an achieved life,
shaped a parity between the two women that Joseph insisted on. Further, Joseph's academic, activist, and social ties in the United States
brought highly visible personalities to the island who often stayed at her
house, giving rise to a view of her as a woman with power and connections. With respect to the symposium, she was seen as someone who'd
had "the foresight and spunk" to do what needed to be done. More
broadly speaking, she was looked upon as a "catalyst."[83] Neither a doting
fan nor easily seduced, Joseph presented Lorde with the challenge of
relating to a mature, self-possessed Caribbean black woman, other than
her mother, for the first time in her life.

At the last formal session, on Sunday, March 9, Toni Cade Bambara
gave "a marvelous speech" embracing the men in attendance and "com-

passionately" urging them, as brothers, to examine the behavior of themselves and other men in relation to the issues raised by the women
present and in their lives.[84] Bambara's comments were part of the
discussion following Adrienne Rich's presentation on "Sexism and
Racism in the Women's Movement." Near the close of the discussion,
Roberta Knowles, a professor of English at CVI, asked the gathering
what should be done now, in the face of the stories shared by many of
the women present. Lorde immediately stood up and responded, urging
a pencil and sheet of paper be passed around so that those interested
could sign up for a meeting to continue what had been started. Subsequently, a meeting was held and the Women's Coalition of St. Croix was
formed. The Coalition's mission was to act as an advocate for women's
rights and to fight against oppressions engendered by racism, sexism,
and physical abuse.[85] Its creation defined a significant step toward articulating veiled aspects of women's lives in St. Croix and Lorde's engagement with Caribbean women's communities.

Although she'd jump-started the Coalition's birth by suggesting a
tried and true organizing tool familiar to feminists stateside, Lorde was
not unmindful of the distinct conditions shaping U.S. feminism. Rather,
she used her knowledge of women's struggles in America—and her particular struggles within those struggles—to encourage a flow of information and mutual support across cultural and national borders. She began
to reposition her multiple identities as doorways for women—and
women of color, in particular—outside the United States. At the thresh-
olds of these doorways, she met them as sister outsiders: as women who
articulated some, if not all, aspect of those identities, and who understood themselves as historicized either by colonialism, or apartheid, or
slavery, or imperialism. However different the specifics of their historic
oppression, she and they shared resistance to those oppressions and the
aftermath of them: racism, sexism, homophobia, and disenfranchise-
ment as women. Her association with Gloria Joseph, and the later shift
between them from friends to intimate companions, encouraged a
reflective, articulated sense in Lorde of herself as Afro-Caribbean. This
ideological decentering of the West allowed her to claim a historicized
self beyond America. As she came into more contact with an international movement of women activists, the exchange between them would

prove essential to redefining notions of community and to building connections between women's movements overseas.

In less than a year and a half, Lorde had realized her priorities: *The Cancer Journals* had been published and Persephone Press was poised to publish her autobiographical novel. She'd connected with an international community of women in Copenhagen, and with Caribbean women in St. Croix. And she hadn't allowed her fear of a recurrence of the cancer to overtake her life.

FOURTEEN

"**S**O IT IS BETTER to speak/remembering/we were never meant to survive," Lorde closed her poem "A Litany for Survival."[1] Now, speaking became defined by her singular position: she had clout no other black lesbian feminist had. There were times when her speaking out was not only controversial, it was timely. At times, her writings spoke for her to audiences far and wide. Other times, she had to undo the speaking she'd done; to repair aspects of her private life, both in person and in her journals. In the mid-1980s, Lorde's speaking—in person and on paper—provoked more complex interpretations of black women's lives.

In mid-March 1981, Lorde received a report there was blood in her stool sample. The medical report indicated the possibility of cancer of the colon.[2] It turned out to be a scare, but the incident underscored the ever present fear of a cancer recurrence. It also highlighted, just weeks later, her belief that *The Cancer Journals* were not finished. Lorde felt she had to continue writing them, because so much of her energy was still focused on how to wait through moments such as this, and as she reminded herself, "I am still involved with cancer."[3]

On March 25, she was invited to a meeting with representatives of the English Department at Hunter College to be interviewed for the position of resident poet. As Lorde walked the familiar halls of her alma mater, she wanted to return to teach there and found that her constant fear felt less important at Hunter. Lorde thought a new challenge awaited her in the opportunity to run a poetry workshop for students of a higher caliber than those at John Jay.[4]

Lorde called John Benedict early in April to inform him she was willing to edit the manuscript of "Chosen Poems," which was now 284 pages, and get it down to approximately 128 pages; she planned to take the summer to do so. Benedict was delighted with her decision and offered to investigate the possibility of increasing the page allowance for the book. He was pleased she understood the difference in production costs and price a shorter book would make, gently urging against her thoughts of cutting out all of the poems from The Black Unicorn as a solution.[5]

By late April, the English Department at Hunter had eagerly recruited Lorde. On April 23, Phyllis Moe sent Lorde a letter, thanking her for lunching a few days earlier and for the opportunity to discuss the content of the courses she would be teaching.[6] By the time Moe's letter came in the mail, though, Lorde was on her way out of town, and she didn't respond until two weeks later.

In the two weeks she was gone, Lorde appeared at readings and speaking engagements in Minneapolis, Minnesota; Charlottesville, Virginia; Detroit, Michigan, and Boston. In Minneapolis, in particular, the size of the women's community there and the response to her was overwhelming. Lorde felt she had to consider her responsibility to speak honestly in light of the numbers of women who listened to her.[7]

She characterized the reading in Boston, which was sponsored by Persephone Press, as "a real high" because it brought together women she admired and loved: Pat Parker, Judy Grahn, Michelle Cliff, Adrienne Rich, and Paula Gunn Allen—the last a Laguna/Pueblo Sioux Native American writer-scholar she felt an immediate connection to and hoped to correspond with.[8] Yet there was a blight on the occasion when a white woman in the audience hissed as Julie Blackwomon read one of her poems, "Revolutionary Blues."[9] Blackwomon's poem prioritized racial solidarity between black women and men over their gender differences as necessary to black revolutionary struggle. The incident infuriated Lorde, who saw it as racist. Though tired of having to address white women's racism, she felt compelled to speak and write about it, even as she felt others would rather she didn't. She was anticipating her appearance at the National Women's Studies Association Convention, in Storrs, Connecticut, in June: she and Adrienne Rich were to deliver the two keynote addresses, and she wanted to tackle anger and racism as subjects of her remarks.[10]

Upon her return home in May, Lorde sent a letter to Phyllis Moe apologizing for the delay because she'd been out of town. Lorde described the course she would teach on "American Fiction and Poetry Since World War II" as a "study of the writer as Outsider in postwar America."[11] She expected her poetry workshop to develop her students' creative and critical skills. Over the next five years, Lorde's workshop at Hunter would become the hallmark of her legacy there[12] and would nurture the talents of a legion of budding poets and writers; some of them would establish literary careers, and all of them would find their voices as women and writers under her exacting, generous tutelage.

As the month drew to a close, Lorde divided her writing energies between editing "Chosen Poems" and drafting and refining the text of her keynote speech for the National Women's Studies Association Convention; wondering, at the same time, if the racism and rage she was writing about was just a useful means of avoiding other things, namely, her daughter's approaching departure, in September, for her first year at Harvard. She anticipated the separation between them as "My loss of Beth."[13]

The National Women's Studies Association (NWSA) Convention was held on the campus of the University of Connecticut at Storrs in June[14] and coincided with the Berkshire Women's History Conference at Vassar College that same month. The program of the Berkshire Women's History Conference sought to focus on broad interpretations of women's history and women's studies, and on the hostility of the world beyond the Berkshires to attempts by feminists to assume their rightful place in academe. The NWSA Convention chose as its focus the theme "Women Respond to Racism," a theme that invited acknowledging the necessity for a political struggle and set the stage for several days of confrontational sessions and debates. As Adrienne Rich put it in her keynote address, the NWSA "chose . . . to address the estrangement, ignorance, fear, anger and disempowerment created by the institutional racism which saturates all our lives."[15] Thus focused on racism within the feminist movement, the convention began in controversy.

Arguing from different but compatible positions, Rich and Lorde set the tone of that controversy. Rich's address, "Disobedience Is What NWSA Is Potentially About," identified white women's "disobedience" to patriarchy as essential to an engaged examination of racism in order to understand their obedience to and complicity in their own oppression as well as that of women of color. In summing up, Rich pointed to her own self-examinations, "which have to do with living in a white skin," as part of an evolving feminist politics, a "political literacy,"[16] critical to the liberation of all women.

The second keynote address, by Lorde, was entitled "The Uses of Anger." She began by defining racism, then elaborating on the notion of women responding to racism in anger. Citing a list of anecdotal exchanges so as to preclude any perception of her remarks as theoretical, Lorde emphasized specifically her anger at white women—and white feminist academics. She questioned whether white academic women truly sought a dialogue on racism, given the attendant class assumptions of the NWSA in its refusal to waiver the registration fee for poor women and women of color. As Lorde allowed, both white women's anger and the anger of women of color were more useful when "expressed and translated into action." Moreover, any discussion among them as women about racism necessitated recognizing their anger; fear of that anger could deflect from "the hard work of excavating honesty."

Among additional points Lorde addressed was the recognition that use of the term "women of color" did not refer to black women only: she too was learning to honor the right of women to be identified by their own ethnicity and not to conflate differing struggles with racism as identical to her own. In closing, Lorde described herself as "a Lesbian woman of Color."[17] Not as particularized as her usual longer definition ("black, lesbian, feminist, mother, poet warrior"), the shorter statement reflected both a "continuing quest for new spellings of her name"[18] and shifting engagements with her other identities.

With that description, Lorde situated herself within a wider community of women whose faces were "other faces" of her own: unemployed mothers who could not feed their children; victims of home abortions or state-sanctioned sterilizations; lesbians who'd chosen not to have children; those closeted within homophobic communities which served as their only life support; women who'd chosen silence over other forms of death; those who were terrified her anger might trigger an explosion of their own. As "other faces" of herself, all were reminders that the pursuit of individual freedom, as feminists, harbored the dangers of "unquestioned privilege."[19] Speaking from within that broader community, Lorde assumed her more recent persona as itinerant-preacher, interpreter of the gospel of social justice. Both interpreter and witness as a black woman writer, she spoke in and through multiple tongues to multiple audiences. Lorde's "speaking in tongues"[20] projected simultaneous discourses of a multiple self, which in turn linked her to black community, especially poor black women; to communities of women of color; to a lesbian community, which separated her from heterosexual black and white women and men; to a discourse as woman, linking her to the gender issues of white women; and to a discourse of racialized gender that separated her from white women.

The reactions to Rich's and Lorde's addresses were mixed. Though generally viewed as necessary preparation for the activities to come, some in attendance were demoralized by the speeches. In a political climate in which the New Right and its partner movement, the Moral Majority, were gaining ground opposing women's agendas, they felt it important to show feminist solidarity against that external hostility. Expressions of anger amongst women who were, for all intents and purposes, allies was, they felt, a luxury feminists could ill afford. Others viewed the two speeches as essential analyses of the complex relations between women of color and white women, which had to be articulated now not only as an aspect of the convention but in terms of the larger goals of feminism and women's studies.[21]

After the conference, Lorde noted in her journal: "The anger talk went well, fraught with the emotions of my other lives. I must amend it to make the connections between this anger and the w of c pain with each other."[22] In subsequent undated journal entries, Lorde began to explore even deeper contours of anger as she recalled difficult memories of exchanges between herself and other black women. Her pronouncement at the NWSA Convention that women of color should be identified by their own ethnicities and not have their identities conflated with those of black women came back to haunt her; in the past, she now realized, she'd often meant black women when speaking of women of color.[23] The specificity of her anger thus more clearly identified, Lorde began sculpting notes on black women's anger.

IN THE MEANTIME, she finished her work on "Chosen Poems" and sent it to John Benedict at the end of June. He wrote back on July 13, congratulating her on editing the manuscript down to 120 pages and promising to mail her full advance of $500 to Charlotte Sheedy. But Benedict was bothered by the fact she'd now resolved the question of length by entirely excluding poems from *The Black Unicorn*. He gently reminded her of their agreement to cut back on some but not all of those poems. He was concerned new readers of her work might be disturbed by the gap their absence would create. Once again, he offered two solutions: she could revisit the manuscript, deleting a few poems in order to include a short number of poems from *The Black Unicorn*; or she could add a prefatory note explaining why that work was not represented.[24] An admitted nit-picker,[25] Benedict wanted the best for the book; but Lorde was now determined that *The Black Unicorn* was an entity unto itself. As she wrote in the prefatory note to *Chosen Poems* (1982), "There are no poems included here from *The Black Unicorn* because the wholeness of that sequence/conversation cannot yet be breached."

That month, Lorde also received a letter from Dagmar Schultz, a German woman she'd met and spoken with briefly in Copenhagen who had attended the NWSA Convention. Schultz wanted Lorde to know the impact of her speech at the NWSA Convention, testifying that Schultz represented of one of the multiple audiences Lorde had spoken to, and in a language she'd understood. "I want to tell you how deeply moved I was by your address at the NWSA," Schultz wrote, "that is, by your honesty, your willingness to confront and share and, of course, by the beauty and strength of your language, your voice, your presence." Schultz outlined her own personal history as a young woman who came to the United States in her twenties and stayed ten years, during which her involvement in the civil rights struggle—especially working for the Mississippi Freedom Democratic Party in the North—and her teaching experience led to a deeper political consciousness of the complexity of American racism. Upon her return to Germany, Schultz's evolving sensitivities to racism, anti-Semitism, and homophobia as an impact of German nationalism became integral to her present personal and political work.

The writer reminded Lorde she'd wondered whether Lorde might be interested in teaching at the John F. Kennedy Institute for North American Studies, at the Free University of Berlin. The earliest opportunity would be the summer of 1983, given the women's studies committee's efforts to persist despite a shortage of funds. The summer semester ran from mid-April to mid-July. Schultz was certain Lorde would attract women from the Afro-German community, the black American, and white American communities.

As one of the editors of Sub Rosa Frauenverlag, a women's publishing house in Berlin, Schultz also wanted permission to translate and publish in pamphlet format both Lorde's keynote address and her essay, "Uses of the Erotic: The Erotic as Power." Finally, Schultz urged Lorde to let her know if she could consider the invitation to teach in Germany, even though it would mean a commitment far in advance.

Lorde did not respond immediately, so Schultz wrote to her again two months later, urging a reply.[26] In time, Lorde did agree to the German publication of "The Uses of Anger" and "Uses of the Erotic" and accept the offer to teach in Berlin. This set in motion the development of a deep friendship with Schultz throughout Lorde's remaining years; a significant relationship between Lorde and a group of Afro-German women; and Lorde's gradual awareness of the contemporary manifestations of racism, anti-Semitism, and homophobia in Germany as imperialist in nature. Lorde's friendship with Schultz would also ultimately lead her to explore alternative medical treatments available in Europe but not in the United States, and to her introduction to Manfred D. Kuno, a German naturopath.

In the meantime, Lorde and Frances Clayton vacationed in Vermont in August.[27] Intent on editing the autobiographical novel she now called her "biomythography," Lorde rented a typewriter and corresponded with Barbara Smith and Cherríe Moraga, who were assisting her with the editing.[28] Being in Vermont encouraged a healthier lifestyle, her weapon as a deterrent to cancer. She cooked vegetarian meals and began a jogging routine, rising at dawn to run before breakfast.[29] In spite of the fact that running every day was difficult, Lorde was pleased by the aftereffects and determined to keep going.[30] Although Frances was the more enthusiastic fisherwoman of the two,[31] when the weather permitted, they went fishing together in nearby ponds and rivers.

According to Lorde's journal, the dynamics between the two women shifted between moments of intimacy and distance, almost from the start. As Lorde experienced their interactions, both were, at times, at differing ends of an emotional spectrum. Whereas she took joy in being in Vermont, she found "Frances' joylessness very depressing. . . ." So much so, she felt, that "if there's anything that will make me leave her it will be that." "At other times," she wrote, "our warmth is enough to remind us we are 2 crotchety women trying not to take it out on each other in a place we both love."[32] After several days together, she became "hungry to communicate about something other than wild flowers, birds and shopping chores."[33] As a point of fact, Clayton had always been a bird lover— an aspect of her personality Lorde was attracted to when they first met. Lorde had never been for a walk in the woods before she met Frances,[34] who was, in that sense, a conduit for Lorde's real, rather than imaginative, connection to the natural world. Yet the ways Frances expressed herself had grown bothersome, mundane.

Toward the end of the month, Adrienne Rich and Michelle Cliff came for a brief stay. Audre had been anticipating their arrival for several days, and the time spent with them temporarily countered the mood swings between herself and Frances: "we restored each other and talked good meaningful things & examined the different paths." But after they were gone, and she was watching a sunset, she felt "lonely for someone to share it with"[35] in spite of the fact that Frances was with her.

For Lorde, these moments of emotional uncoupling continued after she and Clayton returned home to Staten Island. On a handwritten sheet of paper inserted into her journal and dated early September,

Lorde tried to turn what she was feeling into poetry. The first stanza appeared as one try:

> The august sky is ripening
> we enter each others landscapes—(vanish)
> a cloud in the background
> darkening speck just below
> the horizon.

But the second stanza underwent two versions before, in the third, Lorde rendered, definitively, the clarity she was seeking:

> There is no crucial lens bearing your face
> no broad base lurks beneath having
> to vibrate my name
> like a mantra of direction
> We are no longer central
> to each other.[36]

In a journal entry the following day, Lorde returned to the emotional separation from Frances that she was feeling: "Isn't it possible to do this thing for each other & go on separate and together? This is what I'm reaching for with Frances—that sharing does not mean being untrue to self—that we do not have to give up ourselves to get each other." Overarching this experience, however, was Lorde's sense of being "curiously happy." Although the reality of teaching at Hunter seemed scary to her now, she looked forward to that engagement, and to what the fall season would produce, determined not to let anyone or anything take from her "this sense of goodness."[37]

As autumn came and matured, Lorde was energized by that "sense of goodness." Between September and October, the day-to-day business of helping to establish Kitchen Table Press kept her happily busy.[38] Early in October, she attended the Second Women in Print Conference, in Washington, D.C. She was one of several women of color—mostly black—who were invited, in recognition as active participants in the women-in-print movement, and for Lorde in her capacity as one of the founding editors of Kitchen Table, where its formation was officially announced. Though the conference occasioned a bitter debate between black and white women over charges of racism, several of the white women were committed to antiracist feminism and agreed to provide whatever technical and emotional assistance to Kitchen Table would be helpful, which included soliciting contributions from the conference floor.[39] Afterwards, Lorde thought of the conference as "wonderfully energizing, just what we all needed. I think both new action and sustained vision will result from some of the work there."[40]

Very probably, Lorde met Nancy Bereano at this conference. Bereano, who'd cut her political teeth as an anti–Vietnam War activist and welfare rights organizer, was the mother of a son and came out as lesbian in her late thirties. At the time, she was working as a part-time editor at The Crossing Press—a small, alternative press based in Trumansburg, New York, where she took over the position of editor of the press's Feminist Series. Lorde and Bereano's paths continued to cross at poetry readings and other cultural events marking the intersections between lesbian literature and politics. Bereano was in awe of Audre Lorde, who appeared to her goddesslike. She was intimidated by Lorde's public persona and hypersensitive about offending Lorde with her own issues as a white woman.[41] In time, the two women would develop a cordial knowledge of each other, balancing in the early years of their association a significant professional relationship.

Shortly after Lorde returned to New York, John Benedict sent her an advance copy of Adrienne Rich's new collection of poems, *A Wild Patience Has Taken Me This Far: Poems 1978–1981* (1982). In her letter back, Lorde began with heartfelt thanks for the advance copy, calling Rich's new work "a strong, beautiful book." In answer to Benedict's lingering concerns, she provided information on the copyrights to *From a Land Where Other People Live* and *New York Head Shop and Museum*, and gave a patient rationale for citing all the periodicals in which some of the poems in *Chosen Poems* had been published previously. Lorde had never recognized these small press and feminist publications and now wanted to give credit to those she felt indebted to.[42]

But the advance copy of Rich's newest book underscored moments of unraveling confidence about her own poetry. A poem-in-progress,

"Outlines"—eventually a long narrative about herself and Frances Clayton—eluded Lorde's ear as she fought with different versions.[43] Work on the manuscript of her autobiographical novel was more satisfying. She'd redrafted "I've Been Standing on This Street Corner a Hell of a Long Time!" four times by now and had changed the title at one point to include the subtitle, "A New Spelling of My Name."[44] By the time she completed the final, fifth version in October, she'd come to believe that the word "zami" defined it. In a journal entry dated early in April 1981, Lorde recorded a brief context for this word: "Zami—the women who love each other—friends, lovers. The men came home and found themselves attended but besides the point of power—In Carriacou the women outnumber the men sometimes 5 to 1."[45]

She'd come across it by chance, after discovering a small scholarly pamphlet which cited "the unusually vibrant, loving relationships among the *zami* of Carriacou—calling them 'the women who work and love together' " and who "were left on the island by seafaring men." That information—in particular, the friendships formed between these women who were left to themselves—shaped a maternal heritage, specific to Carriacou, that Lorde had only imagined existed until then. After her book was published, she was to recall that the word was one she'd heard her mother and aunts use to describe a female friend, though she did not then know its origin or its root meaning. She'd assumed it was African, until she met a young Trinidadian who, in speaking of her book, told her he'd recognized the word *zami* as something heard on his island. He ascribed the origin as French patois for *les amies*, "women friends," pronounced "lay-zami." Now she chose a new title: *Zami: A New Spelling of My Name*.[46] Renamed, the work recognized a different impetus. As it progressed, Lorde saw it become more than a response to an absence or negation of black lesbian narratives. It became a testament to her own life, to loving, to the women who'd nourished her in essential ways; and it rearticulated connections to African ways of raising children, to the knowledge of Caribbean foremothers, the roots of her own identification as Caribbean woman—specifically "those Grenadian dykes running around the hills calling themselves, Zami."[47]

By November, Lorde was deeply depressed and wrote in her journal, at length, of experiencing "so many pains." An essential sense of herself as being alone, an outsider, had prevented her from ever calling her life into question. Now, she felt she had to reexamine everything she believed had nourished her throughout the three years following her breast cancer. She felt she was "falling through the clash" of her own days. "It's not simply power & control," she reasoned, "it's knowing how close to the brink I live—meanwhile, the land has extended itself—like tides and floods have laid down a delta until I am far from shore, yet I still feel I can drown at any moment." There was the paradoxical pain of consciously fending off death and fighting to stay alive—feeling she'd done the best writing of her life in the past six years, but that perhaps that work had been achieved at the cost of her own survival.

There was the pain of thinking the knowledge illuminated by her words had come from weakness, not strength; whatever their source, her words seemed more available to other women than to her. As Lorde understood herself, she was not afraid of pain—she'd both run from it and based her life upon walking through it. Between feeling "self-obliterating" and "like killing," she felt she could not live a "pleasant empty life."

Not wanting to live that kind of life meant addressing a painful truth in relation to Frances Clayton. If the wifely order and domesticity she needed from Frances and which Frances had provided could now be read by Lorde as a "pleasant empty life," then blaming Frances alone for that life was insufficient. Her passivity as "feminist-husband," as "feminist-father figure," was the other half of the equation between them. "It's always been so simple to blame her—anyone other than myself—my real self," Lorde confessed. "I could blame the doer—but she only serves the real Audre—the one who sits & looks & runs things—who is responsible and who MUST NEVER BE WRONG."

In her depression, she lashed out at herself: she was guilty of not loving Jonathan enough, or of not loving Ed Rollins at all but wanting to use Rollins to pay for a belief that she did. She was guilty of not really caring about anything except being right and of acting godlike, doing what she pleased, because she'd felt beyond death, but she was not. And there was the episodic depression she experienced about her ability to write poetry. A sign that hung over her desk read: " 'The reason that I cannot write/is because I am/has to do with being black & white.' "

At the end of this lengthy journal entry, Lorde began an unfinished letter to Adrienne Rich, asking, "do you have a little room inside yourself right now? Cause I need to lean a little—" and then acknowledging, "I've never admitted aloud that I've not been able to write poetry for two years. That I bought life with life and its [sic] not a bargain I can make—afford to make—want to make."[48] Poetry was an essential source of Lorde's erotic power, the practice of which was life-giving. She needed poetry to arouse her energy; to sustain her, as a shadowy cancer thing followed her, threatening to return, some day, in some form. To have felt she'd bargained for one form of life (living) at the expense of another (her poetry), and with regret, added further dimension to her depression—a dilemma articulated in her statement, "poetry is not a luxury."[49]

The publication of *The Black Unicorn* in 1979 had not only marked the production of a significant body of work, it presented a challenge. She had viewed the poems as awesome,[50] and she was still wondering if she could produce work of that quality again. Was she stymied by her own achievement? Was there an implicit "or if" in her wondering which now loomed, but obscured the actuality that she was writing and publishing new poems, albeit in spurts markedly different from the more sustained, prolific burst defining *The Black Unicorn*?

Of the new poems, "Need" (1979) was published four times between 1979 and 1981.[51] The magazine *Sinister Wisdom* published "Afterimages," an epic poem she'd begun in 1979 that was later included in her collection *Chosen Poems: Old and New*.[52] Using the brutal murder in 1955 of young Emmett Till, who was found floating in Mississippi's Tallahatchie River, "Afterimages" wove together resounding images of the fourteen-year-old Chicago-born youth accused of whistling at a white woman while visiting family in Mississippi that summer; the overflow of the Pearl River as it flooded Jackson, Mississippi, in 1979; and the televised account of a white woman who'd lost her home as a result of the flood. Though Lorde was empathetic toward the last woman (". . . This woman would tear your heart out. The pain, you couldn't be impervious to it"), she postulated the devastated woman could have been an older version of the younger white woman whose southern womanhood Emmett Till had "dishonored," for which he was punished by being castrated and drowned.[53] Having spent two years crafting the work, was she now underestimating its historic value? Had she simply forgotten about, or dismissed, these new poems? Was her mood so dark she could only focus on a quantitative absence rather than on the qualitative assertions of these intricate, weighty narratives?

The present moment was also configured by the impending publication of Rich's new book. *A Wild Patience* was her thirteenth book, only two of which—*Of Woman Born: Motherhood as Experience and Institution* (1976) and *On Lies, Secrets, and Silence: Selected Prose, 1966–1978* (1979)—were not collections of poems. Lorde had to compete with Rich's literary output. Despite suffering through stages of rheumatoid arthritis, Rich remained prolific and seemingly had not "bought life with life,"[54] as Lorde believed she had. Yet there was something else shaping her present sensitivity to Rich's new work: she'd written in her journal, "I have been afraid to read Adrienne's new book—afraid I will stumble across something that will destroy me—shatter this fragile peace—the sanctity of the waiting place."[55] The fear that there was something in Rich's work—something literally "to do with being black and white"— that might destroy her was certainly grounded in the principled differences that surfaced and submerged between them. But Lorde's enduring admiration for Adrienne Rich as woman and poet, and for "that part that is most tender & vulnerable in strong women,"[56] moved her to recognize that the time had come not only to embrace Rich's new book but to embrace a deeper sense of willingness "to learn and re-learn admitting error."[57] Thus she resolved, "this piece I will love without question teach me what you know that I do not."[58]

Lorde and Rich appeared at a benefit on Saturday evening, December 5, for the Astraea Foundation—a New York City–based, multiracial, multiethnic organization founded by feminists in 1977 to raise and distribute monies to support women's projects. The event was billed as "Poets in Conversation" and was held at the Hunter College Playhouse on East 68th Street. In anticipation of their "Conversation," Rich proposed in a letter beforehand, if Lorde were agreeable, that the two should each select a recent poem of theirs to read and discuss its history as a way of encouraging the other in a dialogue about poetry arising out of their particular emotional and political needs as poets. While not wanting to direct what Lorde might read, she'd thought of "Afterimages" "because of its moral complexity" and because she'd understood the struggle Lorde was engaged in in "writing harder and harder poems."[59] On the night of the reading, both poets made opening remarks.

As the first speaker, Lorde's comments included recognizing that this "Conversation" was as much for the two of them as for the audience, though they often had opportunities to converse as poets. She stressed that she and Rich were "not icons" with ready-made answers or solutions to the compelling issues confronting women of color and white women, and the country. This disclaimer of their objectification as "icons" spoke to Lorde's desire to entertain a different subjectivity now, having already achieved iconic status. It also underlined further comments about both of them as women who'd struggled with each other to be friends, and recognized there had been difficult moments between them that were aspects of both love and poetry.

The evening was a blend of commentary and poetry as Lorde and Rich examined personal and political perspectives—talking to each other, refining each other's statements on the meanings of poetry. Reading several poems between them, they broached a number of topics, including the genesis and evolution of specific poems, the uses of poetry, their power as poets, art as a function of social change, the erotic as inseparable from poetry, and poetry as inseparable from life. At one point, Lorde openly admitted to her private struggle in writing poetry.[60]

In a letter dated December 7, 1981, John Benedict took an opportunity to gently nag Lorde about the copyedited manuscript of *Chosen Poems*, which he'd sent to her to go over only two weeks before but was anxious to get back. Benedict had informed Lorde of the production schedule at every step, and patiently awaited a new poem Lorde wanted to include but had not yet delivered.[61] He enclosed a Xeroxed sketch of the jacket, and in a postscript noted that the photograph was one taken by himself ("your humble servant in one of his more experimental phases") of a section of red cabbage, up close, which others at Norton thought was effective and he hoped she would think so too.[62]

Although Lorde and Benedict continued to work together throughout the proofreading process and consult on the jacket and design, Benedict didn't discover what Lorde actually thought of his photograph as the image for her book until several months after *Chosen Poems* was published. He found himself the subject of Lorde's rage in mid-December 1982.

Over the period that he was her editor at Norton, Benedict's letters to Lorde generally reflected a deepening appreciation for her poetry, aesthetics, politics, and sensitivities. Their differences were obvious from the start: he was an older white male, she was black and lesbian. While performing the expectations required of him as a vice president and editor at an established trade house, he'd come to think of himself as a strong champion of her work there and an affectionate admirer. He called her a "dear friend."[63] Yet his posture toward her also could be viewed as paternalistic, and Lorde was privately ambivalent about working with him. But why she stewed over the jacket of *Chosen Poems* for so long is unclear.

After learning by telephone from Sheedy just how offensive Lorde found his photograph, and of her demand the jacket be redesigned, Benedict wrote to Sheedy on December 20, informing her that Norton was looking into all aspects of the expense of redesigning *Chosen Poems* once the current printing had run out. He also noted, "I must confess to being a little surprised by all of this, in view of the fact that I was under the impression, while working with Audre on the proofreading and on the jacket, that, after we'd made the changes she asked for, she was satisfied. Apparently I was wrong."[64] Ending his brief note on a tone that barely veiled his hurt and humiliation, Benedict said he had not realized that his willingness to be Lorde's "humble servant"—and to expose his own artistic nature in doing so—could be viewed as literally "covering" her work with his, something white artists had done to black artists historically. In an even briefer note to Lorde dated the same day, Benedict appeared clueless as to whom he had offended, noting, "If it's you, I'm deeply sorry. I really did think we'd gotten things worked out," before wishing her the best for the coming holidays.[65] But it would be months before they communicated again.

LORDE WENT TO Harvard University in February 1982, to deliver a talk. Beth was now in her second semester there. The occasion was a weekend celebration of the legacy of Malcolm X and part of activities for

Black History Month. Lorde's talk, entitled "Learning from the 60s," began by boldly linking herself as a black lesbian feminist to Malcolm X's legacy. Even more bold was her statement that, as "an inheritor of Malcolm and his tradition," the ghost of Malcolm's voice spoke through her mouth to ask a new generation of black people what they were prepared to do in the name of black survival and black liberation. She told the Harvard students that had Malcolm X lived, his expanding vision of black liberation would have set him on a course of "inevitable confrontation with the question of difference as a creative and necessary force for change."

The substance of Lorde's talk summed up personal and historical perspectives on the activism of the 1960s, while calling into question a revival of black nationalist ideology that would lead a new generation both to misread Malcolm X's true legacy and to blindly repeat unlearned lessons from the past. As well as speaking to the need for new visions of black unity rather than unanimity, Lorde's address linked black feminist analyses to the ongoing black liberation struggle as defined by the realities of the 1980s, the feminist and gay liberation movements, and the impact of American foreign policies on people of color—especially in Latin America and the Caribbean.[66] Lorde informed her audience of young, privileged listeners of a contemporary black history more complex than prevailing representations would have it. She stood before them as one who'd lived and resisted aspects of that history, and laid claim to the most revolutionary black iconic figure to have shaped that history.

Early in April, Lorde left for California and a series of readings there. On the flight west, she spent some time trying to craft a poem linking environmental issues in urban America, the struggle in South Africa, black labor as historically essential to the development of Western civilizations, and poetry. But none of it was as coherent as her thoughts on South African women engaged in the freedom struggle:

> . . .
> How many of the small-boned
> dark women wearing gun belts . . .
> who

activated the plastique
bombs behind the oil refineries
outside Cape Town . . .
write poems
are lesbians lie with other women
in wonder and the flesh affirmation
history is not kind to us
but we rekindle their story
living our own . . .[67]

On the West Coast, Lorde read at venues in San Francisco, Oakland, Los Angeles, Stanford, and San Diego. In her journal, there are lapses in days between entries; most give annotated lists of the names of a host of women she met and spoke with in one place or another, and support her feeling that she wanted to remember the trip as being about people.[68] She did not record any details about her readings or audience responses to them.

Back east, while waiting in the airport in Syracuse for her flight to New York, Lorde chastised herself in her journal for having made what she now saw as "a foolish bargain"—one made in desperation and in which she'd bartered "one death for another" in terms of her life and her poetry. The nearly three weeks in California had given Lorde the space to realize that speaking for herself was her power and her glory; living with the possibility of a cancer recurrence was a condition, not her central focus or purpose.[69] Acknowledging that condition rather than focusing on it freed her to speak.

At some point, Nancy Bereano approached Lorde to ask if Lorde had ever considered putting together a collection of her essays. Since the Second Women in Print Conference in 1981, Bereano's work as editor for the Feminist Series at The Crossing Press had become increasingly important, a personal mission. Bereano also felt the analytic aspects of the conference had made clear to her the need to actively pursue manuscripts by women of color and not wait for those manuscripts to come to her. In addition, when her son was at the stage between boyhood and teenhood, she'd read Lorde's essay, "Man Child: A Black Lesbian Feminist's Response," in *Conditions* and found it deeply moving and helpful.

When Bereano first raised the subject of an essay collection to Lorde, the latter was cool to the idea. Bereano was convinced of the political importance of Lorde's essays, but Lorde wanted time to think about such a collection.[70]

IN 1982, AUDRE LORDE published two major works within months of each other. Her eighth collection of poems, *Chosen Poems: Old and New*,[71] was published in June, and her first and only full-length work of autobiographical fiction, *Zami: A New Spelling of My Name*, in October, defining that year in her converging and expanding literary ambitions. That *Chosen Poems* was published by Norton and *Zami* by Persephone Press also outlined Lorde's appeal as a writer who could disrupt both the hegemonic discourse of mainstream publishing and the antihegemonic discourse within much of white feminist lesbian publishing. As Lorde saw this nearly synchronous publishing moment during an interview several months later, she noted: "Sometimes I have a feeling that *Zami* is a frame upon which the poems of *Coal*, *The Black Unicorn* and *Chosen Poems: Old and New* are set like jewels. Many of the poems take off from places within those stories."[72] *Chosen Poems* consolidated works from five previous publications, and Lorde's awareness of the symbiosis between the "frame" and the "jewels" set upon that frame sparkled most particularly within several of the poems in the book's final section, "New Poems."

In "The Evening News," a poem addressed to Winnie Mandela, Lorde uses the work to link the deaths of children fighting for survival in black communities in South Africa and New York City as representative of a reconfigured, or transbordered, Third World, which includes black populations in the United States and a new generation of resistance fighters:

> . . .
> in the streets of Soweto and Brooklyn
> (what does it mean
> our wars
> being fought by our children?) . . .

At the same time, the poem is replete with references to and images of this reconfigured Third World as female:

> . . . the moon in Soweto is mad
> is bleeding my sister into the earth . . .
> while the Ganvie fisherwomen with milk-large breasts
> hide a fish with the face of a small girl
> in the prow of their boats.

While still addressing Mandela and recognizing an absence of even ritualized connection between them ("Winnie Mandela . . . We have never touched shaven foreheads together . . ."), it was the imagistic "face of a small girl" hidden by West African "fisherwomen with milk-large breasts" which served as Lorde's underlying intent to recover the history, the names, of that hidden girl:

> . . .
> yet how many of our sisters' and daughters' bones
> whiten in secret
> whose names we have not yet spoken . . .[73]

Again, in the poem "Za Ki Tan Ke Parlay Lot," Lorde shows that she is thematically concerned with the deaths of black children. The children in this poem also live in cities, and the inhabitants of these cities are deaf to, and pointedly responsible for, their deaths:

> . . .
> there is no metaphor for blood
> flowing from children
> these are your deaths
> or your judgments . . .[74]

The poem also situates the speaker as bilingual—alternating between English and the patois of Carriacou, where the poem's refrain, *za ki tan ke parlay lot* ("you who hear tell the others"), is called out in the streets before a funeral or burial.[75] As a speaker linguistically situated both in the United States and in Carriacou, Lorde laid claim to two mother tongues, two national identities.

The world of the poem "October" also reimagines the Third World as female ("the heroically dead"), as Lorde first enters a non-Western cosmos of creation and recreation,

> Spirits
> of the abnormally born
> live on in water
> of the heroically dead
> in the entrails of snake.[76]

then poses the present as a question of "life" after life,

> Now I span my days like a wild bridge
> swaying in place
> caught between poems like a vise
> I am finishing my piece of this bargain
> and how shall I return?[77]

before she calls upon Seboulisa, her spiritual mentor, to guide her toward this reconfigured female world. Speaking to Seboulisa, Lorde now rereads the ugly duckling self of childhood, the "shadow-self" who was "fat, black and ugly," as a welcome recovered self.[78] As Seboulisa incarnate, she accepts her spiritual mentor, and herself, as embodying the traditional African view of black women as "fat and beautiful." She implores Seboulisa to assist her out of the poetic "vise" she is "caught between," to give her the wings of new poems, new stories:

> Seboulisa, mother of power . . .
> fat and beautiful . . .
> help me to attend with passion
> these tasks at my hand for doing.[79]

Not only does Lorde want to be guided toward this reconfigured Third World—which in actuality becomes Gloria Joseph's house in St.

Croix/the Caribbean—she also seeks a name for herself there, a home within it, that will end her spiritual homelessness:

> Carry my heart to some shore
> that my feet will not shatter . . .
> Do not let me die
> still
> needing to be stranger.[80]

As points of departure within the stories shaping *Zami*, these poems signify a larger journey: Lorde's psychic journey toward a reconfigured Third World that is woman-identified, where she will have "a new spelling" of her name, a place to belong and to be accepted.

Zami originated a new discursive space for more complex renderings of black women's lives. It began with the poet's entry into a world of Caribbean black women embodied by her immigrant maternal history, and ended on her brief affair with the symbolic black lesbian, "Afrekete." Significantly, Lorde's story of coming-of-age as the daughter of Caribbean immigrants also reframed her identity as black woman into one as Afro-Caribbean. In the Epilogue, Lorde's spiritual connection to the "zami" women of Carriacou contextualized her lesbianism within a "new living the old in a new way." With this reframed identity at its center, then, *Zami* posed Lorde's identity and sexuality as fluid aspects of her transnational blackness, rooted both in the migration between "there" and "here" ("We carry our traditions with us") and in the "there" ("There it is said that the desire to lie with other women is a drive from the mother's blood").

Unlike more traditional articulations of the immigrant narrative as "settler" experience, in which the narrator is physically severed from home and attempts to recreate home, culture, and community in a new and different national space, *Zami* proposes notions of home, culture, and community as unbordered, deeply female spaces. The flow between them disrupts the binaries imposed by "settler in" and "returnee to," metaphorically scripting her dual citizenship in the United States and the Caribbean.[81] Thus, as a new frontier within Afro-Caribbean women's literature produced in the United States, *Zami* reflects traditional migration narratives of displacement and simultaneously disrupts them, undermining the traditional with a gendered historical perspective.[82]

In a review for *The New York Times Book Review* of the double debuts of *Zami* and *Chosen Poems*, Rosemary Daniell remarked that readers who began with a journey through *Zami* would find in *Chosen Poems* "recognizable markers for that journey." Calling *Zami* an "evocative autobiography" and Lorde "a poet of her time, her place, her people," Daniell was the only mainstream reviewer to publish a critique of both books, ultimately finding throughout each "the author's growth toward an unusual autonomy."[83] Other mainstream reviewers at the time concentrated on *Chosen Poems*.

Of these, the reviewer for *Publishers Weekly* (PW) hardly disguised a truculent contempt for the author. The anonymous reviewer wasted little time distinguishing between an elite, mainstream, white "we" and Audre Lorde. This "we" supposed that for Lorde, "poetry is an expression of whatever happens to be on your mind at any given time." Even worse, in this reviewer's mind, "since Lord [sic] is by and large unconcerned with the mechanics of poetry, her voice is undistinguished." The PW reviewer made the analogy that Lorde's "school" of poetry compared to mainstream poetry as jazz did to classical music—stressing spontaneity and a natural, raw emotional energy over tradition, order, and craft.[84] The implicit stereotype of black people as naturally rhythmic, atraditional, and primitive rather than civilized emerged from the review like a rerun of the 1950s sitcom, *Amos 'n' Andy*.

Lorde was appalled by the *Publishers Weekly* write-up, seeing it as not a review at all but a "vicious attack on Black poetry in general."[85] Adrienne Rich also saw through the reviewer's barely veiled racism and spearheaded a tidal wave of written protests on Lorde's behalf.[86] Between late May and late June 1982, the editors at *Publishers Weekly* were the focus of letters from a range of Lorde's friends and supporters, including Marge Piercy, Nancy Bereano, John Benedict, Jan Clausen, Elly Bulkin, Barbara Smith, and Adrienne Rich. The letters collectively charged that the review was a racist attack upon Lorde, a major, influential poet of her time.

Two other reviewers, neither of whose names or genders were cloaked in anonymity, offered more supportive perspectives. In *Contact*

II, Sally Jo Sorensen's review, peppered with excerpts from Lorde's poetry, recognized her as "one of the few American poets read widely outside of the narrowly confined poetry community" and *Chosen Poems* as an illustration of "both her growth as a writer and a woman, and the astonishing range and complexity of her many 'chosen' voices." As Sorensen put it, "Lorde also excels as one of the nation's most capable urban poets." Toward the end of her review, Sorensen urged critics and scholars to heed Barbara Smith's call for a black feminist criticism and to see Lorde's work as an excellent place to begin. She also declared "essential" a definitive collection of essays and criticism by Lorde, urging even casual readers to view *Chosen Poems* as a book to see them "through our winter of Reaganomics."[87] Rochelle Ratner's review for the *Library Journal* was also specific and informed. Ratner discussed individual poems in *Chosen Poems* as well as contextualizing Lorde's thematic impetus as spanning a thirty-year period: "From the first, Lorde has been writing directly of her love for women, and such daring has remained the trademark of her work."[88]

Meanwhile, *Zami* captured the lasting attention of reviewers in the black feminist, white feminist, and lesbian literary communities precisely because it was a significant, timely first. Susan McHenry commented in *Ms.* magazine: "She has assembled language and myth . . . creating new combinations and contexts in order to apprehend . . . her own life as well as to appreciate what she has in common with others."[89] Gloria Joseph's review for *Sinister Wisdom* recognized that in creating a new literary term ("biomythography"), Lorde had entered an arena in which new words "are often curiously intriguing in that they open new vistas." Pinpointing that "the soul of the book" resided in its Carriacou namesake—which Joseph defined as including African, Caribbean, and Afro-American women—she summarized *Zami* as a quest for love, identity, and the soul's fulfillment that recognized the poet's Caribbean heritage.[90] For Lorde, coming to terms with that Caribbean heritage, as Joseph and other reviewers allowed, meant coming to terms with a complex of identities on an arduous journey toward acceptance of her "Caribbeanness." In a much later review of *Zami* by Regenia Gagnier in *Feminist Studies*, that complex of identities conditioned a sense of Lorde as "one of the first to articulate what has since come to be called 'feminist post-modernism,' the theory of the diverse components of complex modern identities."[91] And mirroring the sentiments of an up-and-coming generation of black lesbian feminist writers for whom Lorde was the standard-bearer, Jewelle Gomez, a former member of Lorde's poetry workshop at Hunter, wrote in *Conditions* that "Her tale reveals the enduring traditions of women, their place in history and how they can see us through our journey."[92] That "journey" had shaped *Zami* into Lorde's master work.

Without a doubt, *The Black Unicorn* and *The Cancer Journals* were firsts in Lorde's literary career: each established multiple dimensions of new terrain; new prophetic insights into Lorde as lesbian/woman/artist/intellectual. In fact, Lorde's second life produced a series of literary firsts, including *Zami*. But *Zami* came closest to distinction as her masterpiece in several significant ways. For one, the work was both timely and ahead of its time. It coincided with the beginning of the emergence of a distinct black lesbian and gay movement of the 1980s—a movement largely articulated by black lesbian and gay writers and other artist-activists—and was, visibly, the vanguard of a Third World lesbian and gay cultural movement in the United States. A uniquely radical project, it both constructed and opened the door through which it entered into the lexicon of contemporary black American and feminist literary histories; personifying, in the process, Lorde's long resistance to the suppression of black lesbian narratives within African American community and literary discourse generally, and the marginal attention accorded them within white feminist/lesbian community and literary discourse.

At the same time, Lorde broke new ground as a black woman writer, creating a new genre—"biomythography"—and recovering from existing male-dominated literary genres (history, mythology, autobiography, and fiction) whatever was inextricably female, female-centered. Moreover, *Zami* was Lorde's most comprehensive treatment of her identities: it illustrated that, however much these identities were shaped by living in America, they were deeply non-Western in concept. The singular impact of *Zami* was—and remains—its ability to connect with multiple racial and ethnic populations of lesbian, gay, heterosexual, and academic readers in and beyond the United States.

In August 1982, Jonathan was due to go off to his first year at Vassar, just days before his eighteenth birthday. Audre and Frances, who'd been vacationing in Vermont, drove back to Staten Island, helped him pack, and then drove him to the Vassar campus. In the process, they had "a huge fight" which he saw as a separation fight, essentially, and the anger expressed between them covered and made easier that separation.[93] But the fight occurred within a larger context.

While in Vermont, Audre and Frances had disagreed about sharing their life and home with the children still, now that both were off to college. According to Lorde's journal, after years of sharing Lorde with children she'd come to love and co-parent, Frances had recently expressed her desire for a life distinctly separate from the children now. Lorde neither wanted to act as if Beth and Jonathan were unimportant aspects of her life nor live in a house her children could not come home to, if they needed. As Lorde understood it later, she and Clayton had different needs in relation to the children: Clayton needed to impose boundaries on them, whereas she wanted to indulge them.[94]

NANCY BEREANO continued to push the necessity for a collection of Lorde's essays, maintaining her belief in their singular political importance to lesbian literature. She insisted on The Crossing Press's ability to publish such a collection.[95] In time, Lorde came to see the merit of the idea. She'd written a number of essays—some published in a spread of journals, others talks or speeches she'd given. This writing represented her persona as sister outsider and the nexus of her social activism: her challenges to multiple audiences to ask of themselves, as she did, the difficult questions of survival and liberation. A collection of both published and unpublished pieces in one volume would denote her emergence as a major literary figure. After thinking it through, Lorde agreed to let The Crossing Press publish a book of her essays.

On November 19, 1982, she signed a contract with The Crossing Press, which projected as publication date May 31, 1984.[96] At that point, she became the first major lesbian feminist author the press was to sign, and *Sister Outsider* was the first book Bereano initiated at The Crossing Press.[97] The Crossing Press had a policy of not doing books represented by an agent. Once again, Lorde signed a book contract without letting Charlotte Sheedy review it in advance; negotiating, though, a provision requiring the publisher to consult with Lorde on the book's jacket and typographical design. Although *Sister Outsider* was ultimately "a big money maker"[98] for The Crossing Press, the contract Lorde signed provided for an advance against royalties of a mere $100. Nevertheless, she felt rushed into signing the contract on November 19 and told Bereano so.

That day, Lorde celebrated *Zami*'s publication with a book party given by Frances Clayton. Lorde described her gratitude for this loyal, caring act in her journal as "the great happiness of Nov 19. . . ."[99] Their private battles notwithstanding, the two partners still loved each other, and Frances remained by Audre's side. The party she gave was held at the Eleanor Roosevelt House, on Hunter's campus. Frances oversaw the preparations on the second floor and the arrival and comfort of Audre's guests.[100]

That night, Lorde was ecstatic—partly because of "the wonder and joy" she felt now that *Zami* was a reality, and partly because the fact of its existence was "a richness" she felt she could "draw from for a long time. . . ." The festive evening was more gala than book party. The hundred or so guests included her old friend from the East Village, Ruth Baharas (Gollobin); her sister Helen; Beth and Jonathan; scores of other friends; and members of the publishing and media communities—among them Charlotte Sheedy, the Persephone Press women, Martha Nelson from *Ms.* magazine, and Nancy Bereano.[101]

Two days later, she fought to hold onto the euphoria of that evening. On Sunday, November 21, Lorde appeared at a benefit reading for Persephone Press at the Boston YWCA. The press was experiencing financial problems, as was much of the country at the lower end of the economic stratum in Ronald Reagan's America. A campaign to encourage women to invest capital in Persephone had not panned out, and it was hoped a benefit would raise money in more immediate fashion.[102] Introduced by Adrienne Rich, the reading also featured another Persephone Press author, the poet Irena Klepfisz, a lesbian feminist activist who was becoming known for her examinations of the historic and contemporary realities of Jewish people.

The occasion marked the publication of their new works—Lorde's *Zami* and Klepfisz's second book of poems, *Keeper of Accounts* (1982).

Lorde read excerpts from *Zami*, but in reading to the largely white female audience, she felt their racism was palpable. Just days before, she'd been the center of attention, celebrated and catered to. Here, it seemed to her, "there was no support—no context, no kindness anywhere."[103] At one point after the reading, a woman rose to comment upon her delight with the publication of the anthology *This Bridge Called My Back*,[104] as it now meant she could address the issue of racism outside of black women's anger. The remark infuriated Lorde. She privately vowed not to speak in personal terms for the balance of the event, feeling ill-received; the reading was the most unpleasant experience she'd had in a long time.[105]

Two days before Christmas, the personnel office at Hunter College sent Lorde a memo informing her her request for leave had been granted. The special leave of absence, without pay, covered six months off in 1983 for research and writing purposes. The prospect of not having her base salary to depend on, even temporarily, was less frightening now that Beth and Jonathan were grown and in college. Even so, this would mean an adjustment for Clayton, since it took both their salaries to make their household economy work.

THE YEAR 1983 began with Lorde free from teaching responsibilities for the first time in fourteen years. The sense of time as her own now both excited her and made her anxious. She was anxious because she worried she might not be able to "shake loose those poems" which were within but elusive. Thinking of them, in one moment, as "those poems which ride me through the night," in another she rethought them as "there, as surely as the shadows of the South African women are there, the pain of their displacement, their emptiness and their resolve."[106] The beginning of her journal for that year suggested Lorde's deepening shift toward the black women of South Africa as embodying the struggle against apartheid.[107] Though she'd specifically addressed Winnie Mandela in her poem "The Evening News," and the iconic figure of Winnie Mandela remained a recognizable symbol of black South African women in the liberation struggle, Lorde was turning her attention now toward the conditions of the less celebrated, contemplating their lives not just as romanticized revolutionaries but as women who might be poets and lesbians[108] suffering and resisting a deeply dehumanizing existence akin to, in a contemporary sense, African enslavement.

On January 23, 1983, Nancy Bereano sent Lorde galleys of the first installment of *Sister Outsider* for proofing, along with a black and white rough of the jacket design. The rough featured a well-placed photo submitted by Lorde of herself, looking fully sagacious and philosophic, peering over her glasses at the camera, a strip of kente cloth the only adornment softening her tailored lapels. As with the photograph of herself on the jacket of the second edition of *The Cancer Journals*, this image scripted Lorde's conscious intent to project and market her own, clearly defined demeanor. In the proposed design, the photo complemented Lorde's name, prominently displayed. Having consulted others at The Crossing Press, Bereano said she was "absolutely convinced that the photograph works both as part of the design and as a selling device."[109] In time, both Lorde's intent and Bereano's conviction would prove correct. The essays in *Sister Outsider* underscored Lorde's identity as a mature black lesbian feminist thinker, and the visual association between Lorde's photograph and name enhanced the book's marketability.

The early months of her journal for 1983 also suggested an ongoing examination of the root sources of black women's anger—a strongly personal subject. "I want to write about an anger so huge and implacable, so corrosive," Lorde noted, "that it must destroy even what it needs for its own resolution." As she'd been considering it, black women's ingrained self-hatred produced their rage and silence. "Not only do we use this rage this engendered fury against the beloved image of our hate, the problematic self painfully mirrored, but we do it at the mercy of an awful silence within which we annihilate each others help, each others connection, each others possible answer to the corrosive aloneness that fuels the anger while it appears to help by keeping anger under control."[110] She understood the necessity to connect her experiences to those of other black women—specifically, as those experiences defined the ways black women had been taught to disrespect both themselves and each other. Black women's anger was, metaphorically then, an unevenly cobblestoned path of unexpressed fear, internalized race hatred, lack of knowledge of each other, and a sense of never being good enough.[111]

The issue of black women's anger was, Lorde foresaw, crucial to examining within the larger context of a growing contemporary black women's movement. Early in January 1983, she commented upon that movement during a talk show hosted by the writer Judy Simmons in the studios of WLIB, one of New York City's black radio stations. Simmons's morning talk show served a constituency of black and Caribbean listeners and had a call-in segment. Lorde's appearance as that morning's guest was intended to promote *Zami*, but it was also an opportunity to clarify distinctions between the black and white women's movements. As Lorde informed Simmons and her listeners, the growing black women's movement signaled the existence of more than one women's movement in America: it was neither identical to the white women's movement nor an imitation of it, nor had the black women's movement progressed in the same way as the white women's movement.

Moreover, Lorde's statements on black women's anger stressed that such anger was an unattended aspect of black community life necessary to understanding black women's development as psychological beings. As survivors of slavery and generations of racist and sexist oppression, black women had become conditioned to being resilient, mean, and angry. These traits were an advantage to their resistance in a white world, but often pitted them against each other. In a moment clearly addressed to the radio show's black female listeners, Lorde posed the question: "why is it, for instance, that we find it so easy to shed each other's psychic blood, why do we go for the jugular, so often, black woman to black woman?"[112] Neither Simmons nor any of her listeners attempted an answer and Lorde did not provide one; but by airing the question, she'd instigated a consideration of black women's interpersonal dynamics as political realities.

In March, Lorde returned to the MacDowell Colony, this time for six weeks, with an ambitious, efficient plan for writing. She had three projects she wanted to work on, and made a detailed schedule: two weeks on the piece on anger (3/7–3/21); two weeks on *Sister Outsider* (3/21–4/3); two weeks on her poetry (4/3–4/17).

Working on the anger piece, Lorde found herself tracing the threads of her own rage back to the white hatred of blackness her parents had to learn to cope with in order to survive. As a child, she realized, she'd both interpreted and internalized that hatred of blackness as her parents' hatred of her. Now, she understood that they'd loved her and that their love was the reason she'd survived.

She appreciated what internalizing all that hatred meant: every human interaction she had was tainted by the negative passions and intensity of its byproducts, namely, anger and cruelty. She'd come to value the hatred of her enemies more than the love of her friends, because that hatred was the source of her anger, and that anger fueled great strength. Even more, anger alone, it seemed, kept her alive. But if that were true, Lorde reasoned, then ridding herself of the hatred of her enemies might diminish the source of her power—which was anger. She saw anger as more useful than hatred, but limited.[113]

Judy Simmons, an admirer of Lorde's work, both shepherded and edited Lorde's essay on black women's anger for *Essence* magazine. Published for the first time as "Black Women's Anger," it was an excerpted version of the longer essay, "Eye to Eye: Black Women, Hatred, and Anger," later included in *Sister Outsider*.[114] *Essence* delivered Lorde's message to a wide audience of black women for whom the popular magazine was essential reading and who might not have previously read Lorde's work. It also signified a mutual moment for Lorde and *Essence* magazine within a nascent black women's self-help/self-recovery movement. In the coming decade, that movement would focus on healing aspects of black women's psychological, emotional, physical, and spiritual lives. As the magazine's editor in chief, Susan L. Taylor increasingly promoted this focus in her monthly columns, "In the Spirit." Lorde's essay on anger was a groundbreaking contribution to the black women's self-help/self-recovery movement that her work preceded.

UNLIKE DURING Lorde's first stay at MacDowell, this time there was evidence of Frances Clayton's own take on what was going on at home while Lorde was away. In a five-page letter posted from Staten Island, Frances described missing Audre deeply, planning to visit her the weekend of March 25, and occupying herself with her therapeutic practice in the meantime. Frances's letter indicated their communication by telephone was mutually desired. She relayed some news about a car repair, spring bulbs that were starting to bloom inside and outside the house, and the activities of seasonal birds. The letter also relayed intimate, emotional details about Frances herself: she hadn't yet taken time to be more self-reflective; she'd been eating so much she gained five pounds and knew she was avoiding something, but honestly did not know what. When moments of reflection presented themselves, she thought of things she had to do instead. In closing, Frances assured Audre things with the kids would work out as long as they continued to accommodate change. As she signed off, she reiterated the depth of her love for Lorde. In another note, she commented lovingly on Lorde's absence, yearning to be physically close.[115]

By March 20, Lorde concluded she'd been overeating, too: "I am eating too much here at MacDowell because I am not writing poems."[116] She attempted some. One, untitled, began: "There is a timber of voice that comes/from not being heard . . ." A second, "Letting the Blood Run," tried to capture the story of a woman named Belinda whose daughter had been murdered and whose urban life was a living death. The third, "In Soho," also tried to capture the impact of urban life upon a mother and daughter.[117] As drafted in her journal, they remained unfinished. During a walk near the beaver trail that same day, the first of spring, Lorde heard a nearby thawing stream "begin to speak." Its "speaking" struck her as a metaphor for an opening of words; the mud she encountered as she walked was another sign of productivity to come.[118]

Lorde did not leave MacDowell until some time around mid-April, but she was ready to go. She'd spent a lot of time thinking about her first residency there, "that bleak and yet calmer (depressed?) November of 1979,"[119] when she'd escaped from the cacophony of her public and personal lives to devote herself to the stories of *Zami*. Then, she'd thought she could never get enough of the solitude and seclusion at MacDowell; this time she thought six weeks of it was just about enough.[120]

Lorde's journal notes and Clayton's letter suggest reasons for Lorde's desire to go home aside from the boredom of solitude. However beneficial to her productivity, the monastic arrangement at MacDowell meant adjusting to working out of context. Lorde's context was proximity to other women she was intimate with, and her physical space at home in

322 • WARRIOR POET

Staten Island. Now, for the first time, she could rethink the possibilities of such physical and psychic space. Though she wanted Beth and Jonathan to have a place to come home to, she also saw there could be other uses for their third-floor rooms—especially Jonathan's, a coveted spot overlooking the bay. Equally important, Lorde saw Clayton's busyness with her own professional life as a measure of the self-sufficiency she expected of Clayton. It had its practical benefits, financially, for one. Clayton supported Lorde's time away at MacDowell. She performed within a certain domesticity Lorde expected of her, and was willing now to accept still sharing Lorde and their home with Beth and Jonathan.[121] In comparison to November 1979, life at home was good. Lorde no longer felt responsible for "3 adolescents."[122] Within the context of her leave from Hunter, this second residency at MacDowell was an extension of a sense of freedom from demanding, "mothering" responsibilities, and textured the meaning of "a new living the old in a new way."[123]

It wasn't surprising that Lorde was both emotionally attached to her home and emotionally distant from it, particularly as her intimate relationship with Gloria Joseph evolved. Lorde's ability to compartmentalize her worlds and relationships factored into this emotional splitting, and was aided, on the one hand, by the emotional uncoupling she felt with respect to Frances Clayton, though she still needed and acknowledged what love had built between them. It helped that Joseph believed Clayton was Lorde's problem, and simply wasn't interested in the longtime lovers' relationship.[124] Also, as the relationship between Lorde and Joseph matured, it proved more private and not subject to scrutiny by Lorde's public life.

BACK AT HOME, Lorde became embroiled in a battle with Persephone Press. The financial problems of the press had progressively worsened, and eventually it went bankrupt. Lorde had not received any royalties for *Zami*, even though the first edition of five thousand copies sold out. By April 1983, the book was out of print. Lorde secured the services of an attorney, Theodore N. Kaplan, who wrote to Persephone Press, citing these reasons as breaches of contract and notifying the press that all contractual rights now reverted to his client.[125]

Nancy Bereano was following unfolding events and was in communication with Charlotte Sheedy. In a letter to Lorde dated May 2, Bereano stated her commitment to Lorde's work and willingness to do whatever she could to get *Zami* into readers' hands.[126] She then pursued the possibility of getting a contract for *Zami* with The Crossing Press.

On July 15, Lorde signed a contract with The Crossing Press for republication of *Zami* by October 1, 1983, again agreeing to an advance against royalties of $100 and grateful to Nancy Bereano "for picking up the pieces."[127]

After months of silence between them, Lorde now had a change of heart over John Benedict. She called him that July and invited him to lunch. In a letter afterwards, Benedict expressed his "thankful joy at our good lunch and its outcome. It was strongly straight of you to suggest our reunion; thanks." As well as initiating a reconciliation between them, the gist of the lunch was a conversation about redesigning the type for *Chosen Poems* in the next printing. Benedict reiterated their agreement on aesthetic concerns aired at the lunch, agreeing both of them should review the book and indicate where the type appeared crowded, as a guide for the designer.[128] Benedict's habit of recording conversations and decisions between Lorde, Charlotte Sheedy, and himself in follow-up letters confirms the speculation that Lorde did not make the fact of his photograph on the original jacket an issue for the next printing. Benedict's photo remained.[129]

IN AUGUST, Lorde and Clayton were, as usual, secluded in Vermont. They'd been spending summers there consistently since 1978, but Lorde felt this one might be her last. As she reflected on previous summers, she recalled that her memories of endless rain were partly rooted in fact, but were actually reflections of an acute depression. For her, the low point had been August 1980. As she remembered, it had rained nearly every day; things between her and Frances were going sour; and she was furious with Frances because she didn't respond to Lorde's needs and loved being in such a bleak, rainy place.[130]

Beyond the secluded environs of Vermont, that summer marked the twentieth anniversary of the historic 1963 March on Washington; on

August 27, the March on Washington for Jobs, Peace and Freedom was held. The organizers—including representatives of prominent civil rights organizations—had conceived it as a commemoration and extension of the 1963 march, and developed an agenda linking race, sex, class oppressions, and world peace. They felt the time had come to call upon Americans to address "Three critical conditions in our society—insufferable unemployment; an escalating arms race; and the denial of basic rights and programs which ensure freedom. . . ."[131] This call also announced the formation of the New Coalition of Conscience, a broad-based alliance of civil rights, religious, peace, women's, labor, and other groups that endorsed the march[132] and was brought together by a common dream of restoring a sense of goodwill and conscience to American domestic and foreign policies. The New Coalition of Conscience claimed not to aspire to a monolithic ideology, but in the days before the march, its ideological limitations surfaced, exposed by lesbian and gay activists in D.C. who protested the organizers' unwillingness to include a representative of the lesbian and gay movement as one of the platform speakers.

Unlike the first March on Washington, lesbian and gay activists openly opposed a civil rights agenda bent on silencing them. In the twenty years between the two marches, the lesbian and gay liberation movement had become a significant, visible social movement; within that movement, lesbian and gay people of color had also established themselves as an organized, critical mass to be reckoned with. The National Coalition of Black Gays (NCBG), which was based in D.C., led the effort to include a lesbian or gay speaker on the platform; determined to subvert both the general public's perception of the gay community as exclusively white and male and the invisibility of gay people of color within the gay community.[133]

As the most prominent black lesbian feminist activist, Lorde was the NCBG's candidate of choice. Gil Gerald, director of the NCBG, contacted her in Vermont by telephone to ask if her name could be submitted as a representative speaker, and she agreed. But at a press conference on August 23, Representative Walter Fauntroy, a Democrat, longtime civil rights advocate, and the national director of the march, commented that the issue of gay rights was a divisive one within the New Coalition of

Conscience. He also worried publicly that an official endorsement of gay rights might be viewed as advocating homosexuality.[134]

A former chairman of the Congressional Black Caucus, Fauntroy was, paradoxically, a sponsor of a gay rights bill now before the U.S. House and Senate and another that would ban anti-gay discrimination by U.S. immigration authorities. Gerald called Lorde again, informing her of the activists' resolve to press the issue and that Judy Goldsmith, president of the National Organization for Women (NOW), had threatened to pull NOW out of the march if a dialogue between gay activists and march organizers did not take place.[135] The day after Fauntroy's press conference, seven activists, organized by the NCBG, attempted to meet with Fauntroy at his office to discuss the matter. When Fauntroy proved unavailable, the activists staged a sit-in and refused to leave. Four were subsequently arrested by the Capitol security police.

The protestors were still in jail when a conference call took place, in the wee hours of August 25, between leading gay rights activists and several co-chairs of the march. Communicating by telephone were Gil Gerald; Virginia Apuzzo, executive director of the National Gay Task Force; Coretta Scott King, now head of the Martin Luther King Center for Non-Violent Social Change; Reverend Joseph Lowery, head of the Southern Christian Leadership Conference (SCLC); Reverend Benjamin Hooks, director of the National Association for the Advancement of Colored People (NAACP); Judy Goldsmith; and Representative Fauntroy.[136] That the call between high-level civil rights leaders and representatives of the lesbian and gay liberation movement took place at all indicates the political clout lesbian and gay activists and their supporters now wielded. Gerald and Apuzzo pressured the civil rights leaders over several demands. When the call was over, the civil rights leaders had agreed to allow an openly lesbian or gay speaker as part of the "Litany of Commitments to Jobs, Peace and Freedom," a segment at the end of the official program slated for representatives of multiple social change movements. They also agreed to let the gay contingent be repositioned from the back to the center of the march, and to continuing dialogue between the two movements. However, they felt they could not agree to an official endorsement of the gay rights bill. The reason they cited was that as the only representatives of the New Coalition of Conscience (which comprised more than seventy diverse groups), it was too late to guarantee such an endorsement.[137]

On the morning of August 26, a press conference was held in Mayor Marion Barry's office and a compromise agreement was announced: Audre Lorde, representing a renamed National Coalition of Black Lesbians and Gay Men, would speak at the march. Coretta Scott King, Walter Fauntroy, Reverend Lowry, Judy Goldsmith, and Reverend Cecil Williams of Glide Memorial Baptist Church all agreed to pledge their individual support for the gay rights bill. Fauntroy retreated from his earlier statement that gay rights was a divisive issue.[138]

Getting Lorde included as a platform speaker was only half the battle. As Gerald told her on the phone, the march organizers wanted to script her remarks and Lorde told Gerald she never read anyone else's lines.[139] After she'd flatly refused to do so, Lorde was informed she could write her own statement, but it had to be cleared with the march officials in advance, to ensure conformity to expectations of the "Litany" speakers.[140] Lorde agreed to allow her statement to be edited, if necessary, before reading it.[141]

The March on Washington for Jobs, Peace and Freedom drew a crowd of more than a quarter million, who marched to the Lincoln Memorial protesting the impact of "Reaganomics" at home and American militarism abroad. Lorde arrived in Washington midmorning on the 27th, with instructions to proceed to the staging area at the Lincoln Memorial. She was scheduled to speak in the third segment of the "Litany," the theme of which was freedom. Because of her eleventh-hour designation as a speaker, she had no official credentials and spent the entire afternoon trying to gain access to the speaker's platform. This left her feeling invisible and with a sense of being thwarted by some who would have preferred that she not be present.[142] She discovered also that none of the other speakers scheduled to participate in the "Litany" had been required to submit their speeches beforehand.[143]

When it was her turn to address the massive crowd, Lorde had three minutes to deliver her eight-line statement. She began by introducing herself by name and as speaking for the National Coalition of Black Lesbians and Gay Men. As she cited the common goals of the civil rights and gay liberation movements in the quest for jobs, health, peace, and freedom, some marchers heckled her while others applauded and cheered.[144] "We marched in 1963 with Dr. Martin Luther King," Lorde told the crowd, "and dared to dream that freedom would include us, because not one of us is free to choose the terms of our living until all of us are free to choose the terms of our living." Denying representatives of the march any wiggle room, she flatly stated: "Today the black civil rights movement has pledged its support for gay civil rights legislation."

Lorde also linked the gay civil rights struggle in America to the struggles of oppressed people in the Middle East, Central America, the Caribbean, and South Africa. In closing, she invoked the spirit and words of Martin Luther King, Jr., embracing the quarter million or more present in a universal "we" that recognized difference, diversity as power, and the possibility to "join hands across the table of our differences" because, she concluded, "then we will in truth all be free at last."[145] Afterwards, Lorde told a reporter for the *New York Native* she felt her three minutes were a defining moment for the black civil rights movement, the lesbian and gay movement, and for the recognition of lesbians and gay men of color.[146]

Lorde often spoke and wrote of wanting her work, her self, to be used by others. That day, the lesbian and gay movement of color had used her as its greatest political symbol. She was their only representative with the stature and reputation to pull the moment off, bringing glory to the movement. But back in Vermont, she admitted to herself she'd felt victimized by the homophobia of others and had struggled not to feel like a victim through it all. There had been moments of great highs, countered by lows. She felt both nostalgia and bitterness, hope and weariness.[147]

THAT FALL, Lorde followed up on Dagmar Schultz's ongoing efforts to bring her to teach at the Free University of Berlin. In a draft of her letter of acceptance for a guest professorship during the university's summer semester 1984, she explained to Dr. Hartwich, at the Free University, the need for a feasible financial arrangement since she would have to take a leave from Hunter College without pay, and her family and household obligations required a salary equivalent to at least half her annual salary at Hunter. She hoped the financial aspects could be clarified as soon as possible; she needed to confirm her schedule for 1984 by the end of the year, particularly if she was to take a leave from Hunter in order to fulfill her public obligations.

She also drafted a letter to Schultz, reiterating the need to have the details settled by December's end. She thought it probable she might be in Nicaragua in early to mid-November and said she hoped to hear from the university before leaving or soon after her return. Lorde addressed Dr. Hartwich's expectation that she would teach three courses. She thought it impossible for her to prepare three separate courses in one term and do justice to each subject and the students. Instead, she proposed teaching two courses: one on "The Poet as Outsider," and a second on "Contemporary Women's Poetry," a proposal that recognized her strengths and would maximize upon them.

The probability Lorde would be in Nicaragua early to mid-November faded when, by the latter part of October, she was consumed by events in Grenada. On October 25, the United States led an invasion of the island—assisted by military personnel from several Caribbean nations.[148] That day, Lorde wrote in her journal: "They have invaded Grenada. I feel like that island, trampled on and mashed up. And who will say—you have killed my country—what does a conquered people tell their tormentors, clothed & armed & buckled. . . ."[149] For the Reagan administration, the day celebrated the notion of peace maintained by force.

As news of the invasion-turned-occupation came to light in the American media and Lorde learned Carriacou was captured without resistance, she grew even more solemn:

> Grenada Grenada I could cover the page with your tears. With my tears and your cries of outrage. 6000 soldiers. 700 captured Cubans. 1500 militiamen and women. The snipers in the hills are protecting their nutmeg trees, their banana plants, their own plot of land. . . . My heart feels like it is bursting.

The thought of Grenada as "trampled on and mashed up" incited Lorde's hopes for Grenada, loyalty, and outrage: "The revolution will continue. Oh Grenada sweet Carriacou we are staying close to you. The anger is monstrous. The pain is harder to swallow."

The racial text undergirding the U.S. occupation of her beloved island-homeland prompted Lorde to observe, "If Grenada was white this would never have happened. Never allowed. We must not allow this to disappear."[150] Several pages of her journal suggest she was increasingly engaged by black and Caribbean protests against the invasion in the streets and in the media, and by the U.S. government's spin on the invasion as a rescue mission.

Gloria Joseph, who had close friends in Grenada, actively opposed the invasion, and while she was on a trip to New York visiting relatives, she and Lorde discussed the situation. Their shared concern for the Third World revealed an essential worldview that shaped the relationship between them. They agreed on the necessity to assess the situation firsthand and decided then and there to travel to Grenada on an independent fact-finding mission.

The two women arrived in Grenada, via a flight from Barbados, on December 16, barely two months after the invasion. Over the following week, they stayed at the Hibiscus Hotel, a small establishment off Morne Rouge Bay, in St. George's. There was an eeriness about the place, since there were no other guests on their floor and there were moments when they had no electricity. The aftereffects of the invasion were apparent as they witnessed the movements of soldiers, wire fencing along the beach, and people everywhere trying to repair their lives.[151] Lorde noted in her journal: "We found reports of welcome true but they had no water, food, dead soldiers—Aerial attack on St. Georges—Bodies still found in hospital. No evidence of Cuban soldiers. . . . Slight stench of death. . . ." In a subsequent entry she questioned the irony of having come "home" to stay at a hotel where the cuisine was geared to Euro-American tastes: "what does it mean to find your home too late, invaded, raped, and you still eating the food of its marauder?"[152] Lorde's concern with events on the island was more than nostalgic: she had living relatives there. While trying to find out how they were doing, she learned that the army had commandeered a fleet of taxis belonging to an uncle of hers and crashed several of them.[153] The economic disruption to her uncle's life was multiplied in the faces and stories of others, and by the "trampled on" landscape.

Lorde and Joseph witnessed firsthand the terrorizing, warlike conditions under which Grenadians had been traumatized and were now struggling to recover. Lorde urged herself to write about what she'd seen "in a way that is useful."[154] Their week's stay over, they left Grenada on December 23.

BACK HOME, before the month was out, Lorde went to Hampshire College in Amherst, Massachusetts, at the invitation of *Essence* magazine to participate in a prearranged "Conversation" with James Baldwin. The idea was originally Gloria Joseph's. At the time, Baldwin held a visiting professorship at Hampshire. Lorde and Baldwin were familiar with each other's work, but had not met. As a professor there, Joseph had used work by both writers in her classes. After meeting John Stoltenberg, managing editor for *Essence* magazine, some time before, she'd pitched the idea of a possible dialogue between the two to him. Stoltenberg took to it immediately: Lorde and Baldwin were legendary figures. Each had spent decades, as socially conscious artists, condemning the evils of American society and redefining black sexuality in American literary traditions. They were quintessential outsiders and groundbreaking voices of dissent, representing a radical edge within black activism and thought. Greenlighted by the magazine's other editors, Stoltenberg oversaw arrangements for the meeting to take place, to be taped and edited for publication. Before the formal conversation, Lorde and Baldwin met first at a dinner, each eating little and taking stock of the other courteously.[155]

The actual conversation totaled five hours,[156] consisted of two separate sessions, and was held in a comfortable lounge area of a residential house managed by Charles Frey, a professor at Hampshire. There was a small group of witnesses to the conversation, including Skip Stackhouse, Baldwin's secretary; Charles Frey and a male student of Frey's who was visiting with him; and Gloria Joseph.[157]

As excerpted and published in *Essence*, the gist of the dialogue, "Revolutionary Hope: A Conversation Between James Baldwin and Audre Lorde," allowed a vicarious reading of the meeting of two intellectual perspectives on race, America, the challenges of black womanhood and black manhood, and the responsibilities of each to future generations. In the introduction to the piece, Baldwin and Lorde were identified as "revolutionaries and visionaries" who "bravely, subversively" rendered truth and in whom readers could "hear the voices of Every Black Man and Every Black Woman." That distillation of two extraordinarily complex personalities served the triple purpose of popularizing Lorde and Baldwin for the *Essence* readership, connecting them to the theme of "revolutionary hope" between black women and black men that was the context of their conversation, and catering to the magazine's heterosexual orientation. The fact that Lorde was a lesbian and Baldwin homosexual, and that they had discussed black sexualities, was not revealed in the *Essence* version of their conversation.[158]

In the published article, the writers' complexity as thinkers is evidenced in moments of agreement and extreme disparity during what the magazine editors identified as a "passionate, compassionate, and sometimes vehement conversation."[159] Lorde came off as unwilling to digest notions of "easy blackness" and grounded in the current scene in America as shaped by the sexual politics between black women and black men threatening black communal life. At one point she tried to tell Baldwin how violence against black men had a domino effect on black women. When Baldwin said he did not understand the point, Lorde broke it down: "Okay, the cops are killing the men and the men are killing the women. I'm talking about rape. I'm talking about murder."[160]

By comparison, Baldwin came off as philosophical, abstract. He addressed those dynamics through the lens of what American racism had done to black men, black masculinity, historically: "A Black man has a prick, they hack it off. A Black man is a nigger when he tries to be a model for his children and he tries to protect his women."[161] Whereas Lorde sounded in the moment, he did not, which lent credence to an oft-heard criticism that years of living abroad in France had rendered Baldwin out of sync with day-to-day America, in spite of his periodic trips back. At times, the two writers sounded as if they were listening to each other. At other times, the they sounded like two fighters engaged in a battle royal during which they traded blows until the last round and, with no declared winner, settled for a draw.

The publicized conversation showcased Lorde's stance as black feminist within the context of a popular black women's magazine. It also lent legitimacy to a growing perspective: though black women and men shared a racial history, they had different gendered histories. If there was to be any "revolutionary hope," it lay in coming to terms with those different realities. Lorde and Baldwin spoke to a larger discourse preoccupying black Americans: the social and economic realities of the 1980s that threatened black survival. As Lorde made clear, the assumption of homogeneous blackness was equally threatening. Although readers of *Essence* were not privy to any thoughts the two writers shared on being lesbian or gay, those who were familiar with their literary careers could recognize the space for representative lesbian and gay voices the magazine periodically allowed.[162] In the end, Lorde's participation in that conversation afforded her another opportunity to speak to legions of black women who faithfully read *Essence* magazine, and with whom she shared a sense of sisterhood and history despite different sexual identities. In reaching out to them a second time now, she found a way of interpreting black women's sisterhood within a new history of "black women organizing across sexualities."[163]

PART TWO

"The Marvelous Arithmetics of Distance"
(1984–86)

FIFTEEN

L ORDE TOOK HER first trip to Grenada nearly a year before Maurice Bishop and a new generation of radical intellectuals seized power in pursuit of reversing the poverty of their country's people. Then, she'd gone in search of the Grenada exalted in her mother's stories of "home." That home had been colonized and kept poor, first by the French and later by the British, for centuries. The Grenada she saw in 1978 was independent by British decree but still living out a colonized history. In the years between her first and second trips, Grenada had attempted to decenter its relationship to the West in a bid for true independence, basing its relationships on those regions of the world that shared its worldview and critique of Western hegemony.

In those same years, Lorde had done the same thing, psychically. In *The Black Unicorn* (1979), she'd established a spiritual relationship to Africa. In *Zami* (1982), she'd reconciled with a self that was Caribbean. In the essay she wrote upon returning from post-invasion Grenada, "Grenada Revisited: An Interim Report,"[1] Lorde launched her most explicit, studied critique of America, gazing at it as a citizen of the Third

336 • WARRIOR POET

World, as a transnational who claimed both a "there" and a "here" as home. "Grenada Revisited" was written as *Sister Outsider* was being typeset. Despite its final-hour inclusion, its placement as the last essay in the collection was a potent conclusion to nearly a decade of work representing multiple selves as an outsider—book-ended between her 1976 trip to Russia and her report on Grenada.

From the location as outsider, Lorde criticized U.S. hegemony in the Americas and its hypocrisy as a democracy. While offering up a scathing counternarrative to "the lies and distortions of secrecy"[2] surrounding the American-led invasion, "Grenada Revisited" set the invasion of Grenada as emblematic of American foreign policy in the region and as an aspect of its chief export: racism. As Lorde examined it, U.S. foreign policy was the flip side of its domestic culture. In America, racism made acceptable the continuing dehumanization of black people. Racism, then, at home and abroad, made acceptable to white America the crushing blow to Grenada's attempt at self-definition and independence. An independent Grenada would set "a bad example, a dangerous precedent"[3] for Caribbean, Central American, and black American peoples. Lorde's essay bore witness to popular support for "the Grenadian Revolution" and defended the People's Revolutionary Government which was its brief spark, citing documented socioeconomic differences between pre-revolutionary and revolutionary Grenada.

Lorde's treatment of U.S. democracy as hypocritical was scathing. She denounced an America that purported to be interested in seeing democracy take hold in the Caribbean yet supported repressive governments in Haiti and the Dominican Republic.[4] That hypocrisy extended to the Reagan administration's engagement with the white minority–run government of apartheid South Africa. She believed that America stood "on the wrong side of every single battle for liberation taking place upon this globe. . . ."[5] Throughout, Lorde's tone toward the United States was as unforgiving as it was anti-imperialist.

In the essay, she clarified her identity as Caribbean, as specifically "Grenadian-american." It was a significant clarification, primarily because it furthered the link to Grenada and Carriacou Lorde had established in *Zami* as not just her maternal history (the past) but her own (the present). This second trip to Grenada, then, marked incremental stages of consciousness and reclamation of home as she first searched for physical evidence of the "home" in her mother's memories; they identified an erotic link to women's friendships "at home" which shaped a personal and contemporary bond for her; and finally came to terms with examining how to construct a "legitimate position as a concerned Grenadian-american toward the military invasion of this tiny Black nation by the mighty U.S."[6] It was not the first time she'd employed a lowercase "a" when writing about America. Over time, Lorde had made a habit of doing so because she was "angry about the pretenses of america." When traveling abroad now, she identified herself as African-Caribbean-american.[7]

As "Grenadian-american," Lorde both decentered her American identity and proclaimed herself kin to Grenadians with whom she shared a blood history, but not a lived history. For them, the island was indeed physically home, and its future was up to them, not outsiders—including herself. She'd gone to Grenada the second time to be reassured Grenada had survived the American war, and it had. She'd found the island and its people "bruised but very much alive" and felt "proud to be of stock from the country that mounted the first Black english-speaking People's Revolution in this hemisphere." Having reclaimed Grenada in the context of her mother's memories, a personal, eroticized bond, and the political present, she was now fully free to acknowledge Grenada as homeland—although careful not claim it as home space (". . . Grenada is their country. I am only a relative")—adopting the Caribbean itself as her spiritual home.[8]

THOUGH SHE'D CHANGED her diet severely and monitored what she ate for years now, at the start of 1984 Lorde was having problems digesting food. She was in pain and unable to eat anything except raw fruits and vegetables. In February, she went for some tests and was diagnosed as having had an acute gall bladder attack.[9] A little over two weeks before her fiftieth birthday, she was informed by her oncologist, Peter Pressman, that the CAT scan she'd had to assess her gall bladder revealed a tumor in her liver, and there was a possibility she might have liver cancer. If so, it had more than likely metastasized from the breast cancer for which she'd had her right breast removed six years earlier. A biopsy would confirm or refute the diagnosis. Except for a problematic gall bladder, she was asymptomatic. The fear of a cancer recurrence that she'd fought ever since her mastectomy was now intensely real. Secondary liver cancer was incurable.

On February 18, Lorde's fiftieth birthday, Blanche Cook and Clare Coss threw her a party at their Long Island home. Lorde thought of the evening as "sparkling," but the celebration was shadowed by the fact she had "a bad gallbladder."[10] She could hardly digest anything and barely ate.[11]

Lorde did not want to believe she had metastatic liver cancer,[12] and she and Frances decided to go to Mexico for a few days of escape at the beginning of March.[13] They returned to New York on March 9; soon after, she kept an appointment at Memorial Sloan-Kettering Cancer Hospital with a Dr. Kurtz, a specialist in liver tumors.

Kurtz urged an immediate biopsy of the liver to determine whether the tumor was malignant or benign. To Lorde, he seemed dismissive and unpleasant, and trivialized the fact she needed to listen to her own body first. Kurtz's manner was such that her "deepest & not necessarily most useful suspicions were aroused"; but long afterwards, Lorde credited him with turning her fear and fury into the hours of research she did at the library and the books on the liver and gastrology she bought at Barnes & Noble.[14] Lorde felt Kurtz was trying to scare her into having a biopsy. But she did become afraid when she saw the image of the tumor in her liver on the CAT scan. Then she had to face the realization that even with treatment, metastatic liver cancer could only be arrested. Nevertheless, she decided to forego a biopsy for the moment.

It was a risky decision—she knew that. As she reasoned, if she submitted to a biopsy and the tumor proved malignant, that would mean submitting to radiation treatments and chemotherapy, courses of action that would deplete her physically. There were things she wanted to do still, including the impending trip to Europe and her teaching job in Berlin. If the tumor was benign, invasive surgery could precipitate a malignant process.[15]

In mid-March, she went to St. Croix to visit with Gloria Joseph. Lorde spent four days there, soaking up the tropical weather and considering her options. In spite of not wanting to believe in the possibility of liver cancer, she had to confront what that possibility meant. "I suspect I shall have to concentrate upon how painful it is to think about dying all the time,"[16] she wrote while on the plane back to New York.

Sometime in March, Joseph Beam called Lorde at home early one morning and, as prearranged, interviewed her by telephone. He'd been asked to do the interview by Sidney Brinkley, the publisher of *Blacklight*, a popular black gay and lesbian magazine published in Washington, D.C., for which Beam worked as a contributing editor. Though he was living in Philadelphia at the time, Beam was well known to D.C.'s black gay community as a social figure, gay rights activist, and writer. In addition to *Blacklight*, he wrote for other gay publications, including *Au Courant*, *The Advocate*, *New York Native*, Philadelphia's *Gay News*, the *Gay Community News*, and *Blackheart*.[17]

Beam did not need any prompting to do the interview. Like many black gay men of his generation, he greatly admired Audre Lorde as a writer, black lesbian, and pioneering activist. He was impressed with the emergence of black lesbians in the publishing arena and believed more black gay men could and should do likewise. At the time of the interview, he'd already envisioned the project that would become *In the Life*, the first anthology of black gay men's writing in the United States, which he edited and which was published two years before his death, in 1988, from a heart attack related to AIDS. Beam's interview with Lorde was never published in *Blacklight*, and Brinkley later guessed the reason it was shelved was an oversight, given the swirl of projects both he and Beam were involved in.[18] But Beam oversaw its publication in April 1985 as a columnist for *Au Courant*, Philadelphia's largest gay and lesbian newspaper.

During the 1984 telephone interview, Lorde and Beam discussed her perspective on a number of subjects: the invisibility of black lesbians in mainstream and gay publications in general, her work with Kitchen Table Press as creating an institution for women of color, the importance for gay men of color to create their own institutions. Lorde also told Beam of her desire to start a second work of fiction, about which she was admittedly vague because, at that point, she wasn't sure what shape the work would take.[19] She'd made some fragmentary notes on it at the beginning of the year,[20] but it was still much more an idea than a sustained work. As an idea, though, this second work of fiction was to be a novel situated in the 1970s and the emerging Black Studies movement. The protagonist of the novel, Deotha Chambers, was a divorcée and musician whose interracial marriage, lesbianism—and life as mother of two children, revolutionary, and college professor at a public college in New York—patterned her own.[21]

Toward the end of March, Lorde felt herself about to slide into depression, what she called "a real downer," but she wanted to "abort this slide if possible."[22] As planned, she went to Europe, arriving in Germany in mid-April.

The move did help to allay her depression. After her first week in Berlin, she noted, "I have been here a week, and already a whole new life has begun which I wish to keep in balance. . . ."[23] Lorde's journal notes paint her initial adjustment to Berlin and details about Germany's history she recorded from conversations with Dagmar, and from listening to Raya Lubinetzki, Katharina Oguntoye, and several other Afro-German women in her classes there. She was conscious that these women's stories did not blot out "the fear of fear," or her own: "each woman I approach becomes some other place to hide."[24] Early in her stay, she wrote a brief vignette about her novel's protagonist, Deotha Chambers. The one-page manuscript describes a scene in which Deotha is driving an old black Rambler through Central Park to Fifth Avenue, headed toward 82nd Street[25] and an upper-class neighborhood to which Lorde had referred in her first vignette.[26] In this piece, Deotha is concerned about getting to an unspecified destination on time and not being late.

As her stay in Europe lengthened and she kept prearranged engagements in other European cities, Lorde's notes reflected her deepening perspectives on hyphenated racial identities: Afro-British, Afro-Dutch, Afro-Asian, and Afro-German. The globalization of her consciousness of women of color came in her second life. Increasingly, her physical passport reflected that consciousness as shaped both by international requests for her presence and the tasks of mediating her cancer: ". . . being in the world was her instrument of power, her great bargaining chip, her means of negotiating her daily living with chronic and terminal illness. . . ."[27]

On May 24, Lorde arrived in Zurich. While there, she gave a poetry reading at a women's bookstore and found it difficult to respond to questions afterwards about *The Cancer Journals*, particularly since the possibility of liver cancer loomed, and she felt she needed all her strength to fight that possibility, to negotiate the moments of despair.[28] She also found the Swiss women insular, curiously removed from the strife of the world, more interested in gazing at the lives of black women in America than focused upon the need for change in their own environment, and ignoring, therefore, the fact that cancer was on the rise in the cities of Basel and Zurich. Responding to questions about *The Cancer Journals* may not have been what she wanted to focus on just then, but the book had the status of a feminist bible on the subject. Lorde may have been too critical of the Swiss women's attempts to make the link between the rise of cancer there and her book as a model for dealing with it.

By the time Lorde was back in Berlin, she was more determined than ever to fight, and felt she could arrive at a broader definition of "winning" her fight to live that would mean she could not lose. "What I mean by that," she clarified for herself, "is I want desperately to live—and am ready to fight for living, at the same time as I recognize how lucky I am to have lived to this point in my life even if I were to die shortly."[29] She was also heartened by news from home of a forthcoming favorable *Booklist* review of *Sister Outsider*. The review couldn't have been more complimentary. It recognized her as "one of the foremost black feminist voices of our time" and *Sister Outsider* as deserving "to be widely distributed." It also took note of "Lorde's central position in contemporary literature, in the feminist movement, in lesbian politics, and in the ongoing struggle against racism. . . ."[30] That praise had been long desired and linked a lifetime of making the road by walking it. The review confirmed Lorde's sense that her work now had enough stature to survive her.

In unpublished journal entries written in Europe, Lorde neither mentioned nor detailed the decline in health she began to suffer while there. But in *A Burst of Light*—a second book largely devoted to journal entries on living with cancer published four years later[31]—Lorde charted that decline in Berlin. The possibility of liver cancer was one thing, and could be fought against with denial. Acceptance of its actuality was another, and had to be lived with. She did not want to believe that she had metastasized liver cancer, nor was she able to accept the fact until more than a year later.

As Lorde reconstructed it in *A Burst of Light*, she wasn't in Berlin long before she couldn't eat cooked food, began to feel sicker, and began rapidly losing weight. Her liver was so swollen she could feel it under her ribs. Dagmar Schultz suggested she see a Dr. Rosenblum, a homeopathic doctor in Berlin who specialized in the treatment of cancer and believed in surgery only as a last resort. Rosenblum was also an anthroposophic doctor, disciple of the Austrian occultist and social philosopher Rudolf Steiner, who founded a school of thought in 1912 based on the notion of explaining the world in terms of human spiritual nature (anthroposophy). Before leaving for London, she made an appointment to see Rosenblum upon her return.[32]

At the beginning of June, she went to London for a week; there she read at and attended the First International Feminist Book Fair. She'd anticipated making connections with numbers of black feminists (both straight and lesbian) living in England. At her first reading, though, there were only a handful of black women in attendance. Lorde wasted no time publicly questioning the issue of the absence of greater numbers as a function of the racism of white feminists who'd organized the fair. Afterward, she learned some black women felt the organizers had not publicized the fair efficiently in London's black communities and bookstores and many black women who might have attended did not even know Lorde was in London. She was furious no provisions had been made for her to do book signings or to meet with black women in smaller forums to discuss her books, specifically *Zami* and *Sister Outsider*. She was only scheduled to participate in the larger readings and a forum on lesbians, and to conduct a workshop; all of which she felt served the white feminist community, not her or the women she'd come to London to meet, for whom she was writing and whom she needed to hear from.[33] Despite the organizers' view that they'd gone to great lengths to include women of color, she felt used by the London book fair.[34]

During an interview, Lorde did have an opportunity to converse, at length, with some women of color, creating in that moment the forum unavailable to her at the fair. The interview appeared several months later in *Spare Rib*, a white feminist magazine with a wide readership, published in London. The interviewers were Dorothea, a black feminist of Afro-Caribbean descent who lived in South London; Jackie Kay, a black feminist writer from Glasgow; and Uma, a black feminist of Indian descent and political activist from the South Pacific, involved in indigenous struggles and based in London.

While acknowledging the magazine's primary readership as white and their differences with it, the three interviewers reasoned it was a useful vehicle through which to reach if only one black woman in the Welsh countryside, the Pacific, or some other part of the world. This reasoning appealed immensely to Lorde. Over the course of the interview, she got from them what she could not at the Feminist Book Fair: a sense of her legacy as role model in an international context of women of color; the adoration of representative members of that context; and the sense of women of color reading and being nourished by *Zami*, *The Cancer Journals*, and *The Black Unicorn* not only in London but in the Pacific islands, in Aotearoa,* Australia, Scotland, and other places around the world. Lorde needed these ego-gratifying moments as she faced the inevitable aspects of metastasized liver cancer. She'd already admitted to wondering about a past littered with less than gracious selves, pondering whether the ghosts of her "crueler selfs" would return, believing she'd be kinder to them now that she saw her time, her season, as finite.[35]

Lorde returned to Berlin to keep her appointment with Dr. Rosenblum, who agreed with Lorde's decision not to have a biopsy. She recommended Lorde begin injections of Iscador, an herbal compound made from mistletoe reputed to strengthen the immune system and fight the growth of malignant cells. In addition to using two other herbal therapies credited with stimulating liver function, Lorde started injections of Iscador three times a week; and she began to feel less weak. Within days of starting these alternative treatments, Rosenblum confirmed the diagnosis of possible liver cancer and respected Lorde's decision not to have surgery. Lorde remained in denial of that possibility, even as she submitted to alternative treatments which seemed to be working. She was thankful to Dagmar Schultz for introducing her to Rosenblum. She felt

---

*Aotearoa is the indigenous Maori name for the country that was renamed New Zealand by the white colonial invaders.

reassured communicating with a medical doctor who agreed with her view that a biopsy had the potential to accelerate an existing or dormant malignancy. And despite her dislike for having to self-inject the Iscador, she was convinced doing so shielded her from the possibility of liver cancer.[36]

In Holland in mid-July,[37] Lorde found herself once again having to rethink her definition of blackness after she'd met and spoken with immigrant women from Indonesia, Suriname, and the Netherlands Antilles. While identifying as Dutch, these women disliked the term "women of color" and also chose to identify as black—a way of fostering solidarity between them as Dutch people who also recognized themselves as outsiders. But Lorde found their use of the term "black" troubling because, to her, "black" was not only a symbolic term. As she'd come to think of it and be invested in it, "black" connoted culture rooted in Africa first, no matter where else it was also rooted. Any disregard for those "cultural" facts seemed to her to obscure socioethnic differences. Yet she conceded that she might be archaic[38] in defining blackness so narrowly.

After three months in Europe, Lorde returned to the States on July 29, 1984. She'd found Berlin an easy urban environment to live in, but the depths of its horrific past nearly impenetrable. German history, she believed, camouflaged truths about the wholesale slaughter of Jews, concentration camps, the campaigns against Gypsies, homosexuals, blacks, and other "enemies" of the German state. This falsely protected German children from their history and humanity, and provided the potential for Germany as a whole to repeat its history of genocide upon new "enemies," perhaps those who were Turkish, or Afro-German.[39] She'd gone to Germany with strong reservations, but found a mutuality in the women she met there. Lorde left with the feeling of having made a difference in the lives of Afro-German women, many of whom articulated a new sense of self and community.

They had made a difference in her life, too. They helped her to understand what it meant to claim a consciousness as Afro-European, which was neither conceptually "African European" nor defined by a scripted blackness.[40] These were women she now saw as real, rather than imagined, allies in global struggles for social change, and she was excited about working with them on their idea for a book.[41] She also left feeling that German non-Jewish feminists had a critical role to play in the battle to make anti-Semitism a feminist issue, as much as did German Jewish lesbians. This she saw as a necessary battle—one she wanted to participate in. Throughout her life, she'd associated with American Jewish women as allies, lovers, friends, even adversaries, and her feelings about them were decidedly complex. Even so, she empathized with the "killing polite silence" that greeted Jewish women's attempts to address anti-Semitism, in much the same way that silence greeted black women's anger in the United States, and served to render the observations of either inauthentic. In Europe, she'd witnessed an attention to her work and a seriousness toward it that brought new affirmation. She'd gotten a taste for a simpler life, which she hoped to duplicate once back in Staten Island, in part by moving into Jonathan's room and converting it into her office.[42]

Shortly after she returned from Europe, Lorde underwent a second CAT scan, which showed the tumor in her liver unchanged. That news led her to believe that either the Iscador injections were working or the tumor was not malignant. It brought relief, vindication, and hope. The pain was controllable as long as she stayed on a diet of fruits and vegetables; a course of action she could live with in light of her feeling she'd been handed a second chance.[43]

Lorde and Clayton went to Vermont in August, despite her suspicion the summer before that she would never return. She realized this was the first visit during which she did not write in her journal daily. Yet she was reconciled that absence of habit would still give a qualitative importance to what she did write.[44] While in Vermont, Lorde recorded fragments and stanzas of untitled, unsettled poems.[45] She also recorded reflections on a perceptible difference she felt between the time she began a conscious war against breast cancer and the present moment. Back then, as she recalled, everything she'd read—whether it bolstered or disparaged her concerns and precautions—imparted some message that spoke to her and gave her something to hold onto, even though much of what she read was indirectly related to battling cancer. By comparison, it seemed everything she read now spoke directly to her of women reaching a certain age and, in one way or another, divesting themselves of the trappings of other people's lives.[46] She'd reached "a certain age," and that message resonated with wanting a simpler life.

Between that summer and late fall, *Sister Outsider* met with resounding praise and was lauded as a significant statement of her analytic impact. The reviewer for *Publishers Weekly* (once again anonymous) called Lorde "a convincing, powerful writer" and the work "an eye-opener."[47] Thulani Davis and Cheryl Everette's joint review for *Essence* magazine singled out the essay "Grenada Revisited: An Interim Report" as "the most powerful" of the fifteen in the collection, and pronounced the whole work as adding up to "a personal, thought-provoking portrait of a multifaceted artist."[48] In *The Women's Review of Books*, Barbara Christian's lengthy examination of Lorde's prominence in contemporary African American women's literature noted that *Sister Outsider*, in conjunction with *Zami*, traced "important concepts in Lorde's development as a black feminist thinker . . . reflected in her emphasis on the erotic and her analysis of the concept of difference."[49] Kate Walter's review for the *Village Voice* was hip and gutsy, and assumed "most readers already know the politics of this erudite black lesbian feminist." But she thought Lorde's focus on difference as a path toward creative social change left unclear exactly how women and men could transcend oppressions ingrained in childhood. That critique aside, Walter hailed much of Lorde's analysis, noting that the ideas shaping *Sister Outsider* were intentionally provocative.[50] Barbara Christian and Tana Love had less trouble with Lorde's perception of the significance of difference. Writing for *New Directions for Women*, Love gushed over this, observing that Lorde's essay on Grenada applied her theory of difference to countries as well as to people.[51]

IN MID-NOVEMBER, Lorde received a letter from Susan Hawthorne of Melbourne, Australia.[52] Hawthorne was the writing and theatre coordinator for the "Women 150" Women Writer's Week. She was inviting Lorde to be the keynote speaker there in Melbourne during the first week of September 1985 as part of the 150th Women's Festival. The capital of Victoria, the city of Melbourne was poised to celebrate its one hundred fiftieth anniversary. "Women 150" had been designed to heighten and focus upon the achievements, aspirations, and needs of Victoria's women; to call attention to the fact of women's inequality, the undervaluation of women's achievements in history; and to stress the need for social change in the future.[53] As Hawthorne explained, the theme for that week, "The Language of Difference," was inspired by the essays in *Sister Outsider* and the forthcoming program was structured around the notion of difference. As well as her invitation to be the keynote speaker, Lorde was invited to conduct a workshop on writing, and to participate in a community writing program that would travel to suburban and rural centers.

After the Thanksgiving break, Lorde returned a call to Hawthorne and accepted the invitation to Melbourne. In a letter dated January 1, 1985, she confirmed the dates for the Women Writer's Week, her participation in activities for the following week, and stated her need to be back in New York by September 16.[54] The prospect of being in Melbourne in August began a year largely spent in travel during which she felt her health was generally stable, but delicate. As Lorde noted in *A Burst of Light*, beyond her injections of Iscador, restricted diet, and diminished energy physically, her thoughts about cancer were constant but not dominant.[55]

At the beginning of January 1985, Lorde went to Cuba for a week, as part of a delegation of black women writers. The group included Toni Cade Bambara, Jayne Cortez (who'd organized many of the details), Mari Evans, Verta Mae Grosvenor, Rosa Guy, Gloria Joseph, Mildred Pitts Walter, and Mel Edwards—a sculptor and close male friend of Cortez's. The trip was sponsored by *The Black Scholar*, the Cuban government, and the Union of Cuban Writers. The purpose was to allow the delegation to experience cultural aspects of postrevolutionary Cuba. The week spent there meant one less week in New York's winter, and Lorde found the weather an antidote to a developing sense that her body needed heat. As time went on, though, she had unresolved questions about Cuban society.[56] Lorde never wrote publicly of her perspectives on being in Cuba, but privately she reflected: "It is a vital and encouraging socialist society. As a black lesbian feminist, I found contradictions there, but they were contradictions, meaning there is another basic truth. In this country . . . we do not speak of contradictions, we merely live them, too often in rage or silence, unnamed and unused."[57]

· · ·

IN SOME LATE-FEBRUARY notes, Lorde at age fifty-one addressed the subject of menopause. She was thinking about hot flashes, mood swings, and a heightened sexuality she connected to her own hormonal changes and menopausal fluxes.[58] She wanted to write about menopause as an aspect of black lesbian sexuality. At the same time, she did not want to deal with her own sexuality as a black lesbian either in the abstract or as a pathology, but rather as a means of heightened perception and insight.[59] But other projects—including a new book of poems, the novel, her travels, the will to live in spite of diminished energy—took precedence over that one.

In February as well, she went to St. Croix once again, spending some time there with Gloria Joseph. She'd wanted to stay longer, and upon leaving early in March felt that doing so was becoming harder.[60] As Joseph later reflected, with each trip Lorde would leave behind a few of her personal things. Thus her physical move to St. Croix was part of a gradual dissociation from New York. Both she and Joseph accepted this within the context of their evolving intimacy, Lorde's disentanglement from Frances Clayton, from the stress of living in New York; and within the context, too, of Joseph's open-door policy, which allowed for a flow of people who'd lived with her for varying lengths of time over the years.[61]

Between travels, Lorde attended to notions of travel as a literal subject within her work. For the novel she was writing, she'd sketched out a new scene in which Deotha arrives late at the private school that her two children[62] attend, and feels guilty explaining herself to Pia Murillo, her son's teacher. Murillo is a white woman of indeterminate age. In the scene, a sexual tension surfaces between them as they discuss Deotha's plans to take the children to Rhode Island that weekend on a skiing trip.[63] Lorde also began to think about the poems she'd been working on, not as individual works but in book form, reflecting that the title of one, "On My Way Out I Passed Over You and the Verrazano Bridge,"[64] felt more and more like a general title for the book, but did not seem as much like the title poem as did "Sisters in Arms." A poem about bonds between women as comrades, in the context of an intimate encounter with a black South African freedom fighter who was compelled to return home, she felt "Sisters" was the work around which the other poems, as a book, coalesced.[65] Eventually, it became the poem which yielded the book's title, *Our Dead Behind Us*:

> . . .
>
> we were two Black women touching our flame
> and we left our dead behind us . . .[66]

Her four years at Harvard over, Beth was now graduating, with plans to enter medical school. Lorde and Clayton left for Cambridge, Massachusetts, toward the end of May; they joined Blanche Cook, Clare Coss, and Ed Rollins there and stayed through the commencement exercises the first week in June. By Lorde's own account, the first half of the year was spinning past.[67]

What might have seemed a brief respite came in June, when she and Frances went to Vermont. But being there held little joy for her now. In a journal entry dated mid-June, she began: "What a long & wearisome week and yet time flies. I feel all the time I am waiting—for mail, a conversation, some final reckoning." Further along in that entry, she noted she'd raised with Clayton the issue of what each of them wanted out of life now, and Clayton agreed they should discuss the subject, but that conversation had not yet taken place. Lorde felt it would happen only if she pushed the matter; but she was caught between worrying about initiating the conversation and actually being responsible for doing so. She felt the situation was futile. She didn't want to spend the rest of her life taking month-long vacations in Vermont. It was just as possible to have her work, and the few brilliant, beautiful days Vermont offered, at home. Furthermore, she felt claustrophobic in the house they shared there and that she had no privacy except when Frances was out fishing. She wanted more freedom in her life—freedom to be close at some times and distant at others.[68]

They returned to New York in July and spent some time visiting with Blanche Cook and Clare Coss at their home on Long Island. By this point, Cook was facing a diagnosis of cancer, though it was undetermined still what type she had. Lorde thought Cook was "bearing very well what is unbearable,"[69] sympathetically noting in her journal how her dear friend was now facing her same fears and uncertainties.[70]

At the same time, Lorde was firming up plans for a stop in New Zealand before going on to Melbourne. She wrote to Donna Awatere, a Maori writer whose work she was familiar with, introducing herself and saying she hoped they would have an opportunity to discuss similarities and differences between black women's struggles in America and those of Maori women.[71]

There was an understated excitement to her letters and travels plans, but by mid-July, Lorde felt that a "curious lethargy has settled upon me." The novel, Deotha in particular, seemed farther and farther away[72] as she was turning greater attention toward the immediacies of the moment. Spontaneous eruptions in the black townships of South Africa were increasing. The apartheid regime was responding to the black human rights struggle there with even more repressive tactics; South African police had state-sanctioned license to kill black South African children, women, and men. A slate of black deaths in New York claimed the lives of Michael Stewart, a young black artist beaten to death by transit policemen; Eleanor Bumpers, an elderly black resident of the Bronx who defended herself against eviction with a butcher knife and was killed by the housing police; and Edmund Perry, a seventeen-year-old black graduate of exclusive white schools, home in Harlem for the summer, who was shot down by an undercover New York City cop. In Philadelphia, police bombed a black community whose residents included members of an eclectic counterculture group known as MOVE; they killed eleven of the group's members, including five children, and left two hundred fifty black people homeless.[73]

The wanton killings of black South Africans, the killings of black Americans, government neglect of the social needs of black communities, the precarious nature of black survival against the backdrop of struggles for power on the world stage, were all emblematic of connecting political realities, and Lorde felt "the urgency to unearth the connections between these assaults." That "urgency" drove her to write the essay "Apartheid U.S.A.," a stinging condemnation of those and other connections maintained by white supremacy in America and South Africa. Kitchen Table: Women of Color Press published it in 1986, along with an essay by Merle Woo, "Our Common Enemy, Our Common Cause: Freedom Organizing in the Eighties," as the second pamphlet in its Freedom Organizing Series. Before its publication she made some corrections on a copy and signed it: "For Adrienne & Michelle/with love & a lot of energies/Audre 8/1/85."[74]

As planned, Lorde left New York on August 11 on a flight for San Francisco; from there she caught a flight to Hawaii and then another on to Auckland, New Zealand.[75] Once in New Zealand, her eleven-day stay was a combination of informal fact-finding mission, vacation, and cultural exchange. She did not get a chance to meet Donna Awatere while in Auckland as she'd hoped. But before she left New Zealand, Lorde had talked, danced, read poetry, and feasted with Maori and Pacific Island women, many of whom were lesbians who'd read *Zami* or *Sister Outsider*. When she left for Melbourne, she took with her their names and addresses; the hope that she'd given back something as useful as what she'd received;[76] and a more nuanced understanding of the intersections between the struggles of women of color in and beyond the West, despite their differences.[77] She also took with her some of their poetry, books, and other materials, and a desire to assist their introduction to feminist and lesbian feminist literary outlets she was known to back in the States.

Lorde arrived in Australia, as scheduled, on August 26. She wrote in her journal that she didn't care for Melbourne, which seemed "bland & racist and hectic as NY with a brash English overlay." She sensed something sad and flat about white women. Within days of being there, she was conscious that the native black population had all but disappeared in Victoria, and was attuned to the Aboriginal struggles for land rights.[78]

Early Saturday morning, August 31, Lorde delivered her keynote address, "The Language of Difference," at the start of the week devoted to women writers. Her solidarity with Aboriginal women as members of an oppressed, indigenous population was evident; having read that morning's newspaper, she'd inserted into her remarks notice of a report stating that only one in four white Australians favored any Land Rights legislation for Aboriginal attempts to reclaim ancestral lands.[79] The issue was an emotionally charged one,[80] and Lorde linked it to examinations of the language of difference "as a necessity of self-conscious living" for writers. "What does this mean for Black Australian women?" she confronted the largely white female audience. "What influence do you have upon those other three who do not favor Land Rights? Or are you, perhaps, one of them? . . ." Lorde's remarks implicated white Australian women in the oppression of Aboriginal women. Afterwards, she was viewed by some as assuming a self-righteous, inflammatory stance.[81]

Before she left Melbourne, Lorde took a walk through a nearby park one morning. Although it was damp from rain, the spring weather was reason for the joy she experienced and could only attribute to that season of beginnings. At the same time, she felt her "body & strengths waxing" and thought all the traveling she'd done in the last few years was readying her to move, and live, someplace else where she could still enjoy the change of seasons but not follow them with the same kind of rigidity.[82]

SOMETIME BETWEEN late October and early November 1985, the pain in her midsection returned and Lorde began to feel weaker. She'd lost a noticeable amount of weight since returning from Australia. She underwent another CAT scan. The results were undeniable: there was a second tumor in her liver, and the first one was spreading.[83] By mid-November, she'd found a doctor in Spring Valley, New York, Gerald Karnow, whose medical philosophy as an anthroposophic doctor was similar to that of Dr. Rosenblum. On November 18, Karnow confirmed the diagnosis of liver cancer. Yet Lorde still did not want to believe this.[84] Karnow suggested she go to the Lukas Klinik at Basel in Switzerland, a private clinic known for its primary research on Iscador and other alternative cancer treatments.[85] Traveling to Switzerland for treatment was not outside the realm of possibility, given the fact she found unacceptable the medical views of doctors like Dr. Kurtz. "I will go to the Lukas Klinik," she wrote in her journal, "as soon as they will take me, & see what they say."[86] That she could consider Switzerland at all was due, in part, to feeling she'd already found in Europe a medical approach more sympathetic to her beliefs, one that paired the power of spirituality with medical science.

The fall semester at Hunter was drawing to a close as Lorde mustered the energy to keep up with her teaching responsibilities. At the same time, she made arrangements to go to Switzerland with Frances Clayton.[87] Over the Thanksgiving break, she formally responded to Gloria Joseph's invitation, on behalf of the St. Croix women's group, Sojourner

Sisters, to attend another conference there on "Caribbean Women: The Historical and Cultural Ties That Bind." The invitation gave her something to look forward to, especially now. In keeping with her policy of accepting lower fees for events organized by grassroots women, she informed Joseph the proposed honorarium was acceptable, "and the prospect of five days in beautiful St. Croix in April is just too fine to let slip away."[88] Lorde was not well off and often could not afford to be financially generous. Had it not been for friends who willingly gave her money to cover the trip to Switzerland,[89] she would not have been able to go. Long after she returned from Switzerland she thought about her life as privileged, relative to that of other black women with cancer, and felt convinced she would have died sooner without that financial support.[90]

ON DECEMBER 13, the Audre Lorde Women's Poetry Center was dedicated at Hunter College, where it would be housed on the fifth floor of the Eleanor Roosevelt House—a site on the Hunter campus Lorde's life kept returning to. That evening, she could not have been happier. As one of those "occasions in life too special to dissect," it was, for her, "the sum of unexpected fantasies and deep satisfactions all come together at one point in time."[91] The event was organized by students of the Hunter College Women's Poetry Center Club and others, and marked an occasion to shower Audre Lorde with living proof of the singular contribution she'd made to the lives of a new generation of women poets, and of her legacy—at and beyond Hunter. Amidst the celebrants and well-wishers were several who connected the tissue of her life: Beth, Jonathan, Frances, Charlotte Sheedy, Clare Coss, Blanche Cook, Gloria Joseph, Johnnetta Cole, Yolanda Rios Butts, her sister Helen, many of her current students, and Mabel Hampton.[92]

Lorde was presented with a plaque naming the Women's Poetry Center in her honor, followed by younger poets reading from their work in tribute to her. Even more moving was listening as Beth and her old friend, Yolanda, read from her own work, "my words coming out of their mouths illuminated exactly by who they are themselves . . . these women I love so dearly." Whatever was to be the outcome of her trip to Switzerland, it didn't matter that night. What mattered most was the recognition accorded her work; the women who embodied that work in their own; and the sense of a future that would take them to places she'd only dreamed of.[93]

Two days later, on December 15, Lorde and Clayton arrived in Basel. Lorde checked into the Lukas Klinik and Clayton checked into a nearby hotel. Settling in, Lorde felt hopeful and wrote in her journal: "So here I am, at the Lukas Klinik in Switzerland while my body decides if it will live or die now. I intend to fight fiercely to make it live. The anthro way seems promising, & I am here. I will commit myself to this way for a while. . . ."[94] She spent nearly three weeks at the secluded, private clinic; there with some fifty other patients, attended by a dozen or so staff doctors and several visiting doctors and trainees from other countries. She was the only American among the predominantly Swiss and German patients and two French women. All of the patients either had or were suspected of having cancer.[95]

She'd brought a copy of *The Cancer Journals* with her. Rereading it recalled a sense of her work as prophetic, and of herself as always having planted in it, unknowingly, what she needed to harvest later. She felt that was true of her new book of poems, *Our Dead Behind Us*, which was at the production stage and soon to be published by Norton.[96]

The Klinik's philosophy treated with body, mind, and spirit. Though a part of her wanted to dismiss aspects of the program, in the main Lorde felt it important to give herself over to it while she was there—particularly since she was willing to undergo anything except surgery. That meant taking painting classes, color therapy, oil dispersion baths, massage, scheduled rest periods, and liver compresses; she also took curative eurhythmy, which combined sustained rhythmic body movements and controlled breathing based on consonant and vowel sounds.[97] It meant, too, submitting to sonograms, X-rays, other tests, and medical consultations.[98]

Upon her arrival, Lorde had constructed being at the Lukas Klinik as an either/or: life or death. But almost immediately she discovered there a book on active meditation, in which she "found something interesting."[99] In addition to identifying several steps toward self-control, the author dispelled the idea of living or dying, replacing this with the notion of life as both/and, as composed of simultaneous forces: growth and decay, living and dying, sprouting and withering.[100] Reading these words prompted her to write: "As a living creature I am part of two kinds of forces . . . and at any given moment of our lives, each one of us is actively located somewhere along a continuum between these two forces."[101]

During those three weeks, Frances Clayton was Lorde's main physical and emotional support. She acknowledged the fact she was not allowed to stay at the Klinik by taking meals with Audre there.[102] One night during the standard communal dinner, several other patients at the table wanted to discuss New York City's bad neighborhoods. The conversation smacked of a genteel racism Lorde found infuriating. But she didn't have to handle the situation alone, as "Frances, good old trooper that she is, brought up the rear magnificently."[103] Frances's hotel room was Audre's escape from the kind but strange European atmosphere of the Lukas Klinik. She went there for quick cuddles between scheduled liver compresses and temperature readings. They went sightseeing in the village of Arlesheim, and on walks about the countryside, affirming each other's courage, contemplating the future.[104] However that future would be defined, in the isolated distance of winter in Switzerland during those crucial three weeks, Frances acted as what she'd always been in Audre's life—her partner.

The isolation of distance helped Lorde to accept what she had earlier always denied. On the morning of December 23, she was informed by one of the doctors, a Dr. Lorenz, that the results of a liver sonogram and crystallization test were positive. The tumors in her liver were malignant. She had liver cancer. She was alone when that news came and wished Frances were with her.[105] Lorde wrote in her journal:

> I have liver cancer—metastasized breast cancer. They will do iscador and hormone medication now. Well it helps to know. Somehow I still don't believe it but I might as well not waste time doubting. I said if they believed it here I'd accept the diagnosis so I do. Now the question to be decided is what to do."[106]

Of immediate concern was how to treat the liver cancer once she was back in the States. She wasn't sure if she should opt for chemotherapy now or just continue with the Iscador injections, or if she could do both.

She was also concerned about selling 207 St. Paul's Avenue, the house in Staten Island. Much later she wrote of extricating herself from it, from the life it represented: "Sometimes we cannot heal ourselves close to the very ones who love us most—because it is also close to the very places and smells that went along with the habits we are trying to break—altering my life means altering the atmosphere internal & external within which I decide what direction the alteration must take." Selling the house was, by her reasoning, significant to healing and altering her life. "I want to put it up for sale now," she determined, "200,000. Possession fall 1987. Take or leave. I don't want us rushed into anything."[107] But even a slow process of dispossession meant putting in motion the physical separation between herself and Clayton. In spite of Frances's commitment in the moment, Lorde had long felt she could not allow what had drawn her to Clayton from the start, what she loved, to drown her.[108] Even as she still wanted, needed, Frances in her life, Frances embodied some of those "habits" polluting her "atmosphere internal & external." Frances smoked cigarettes, was not diet-conscious, and, in general, not health-conscious.[109]

On Christmas Day, Lorde tried to break through the insularity at the Lukas Klinik isolating her from the outside world, only to meet with the staff's resistance to allowing outgoing telephone calls.[110] The next day, however, calls were put through to her from Adrienne Rich, Michelle Cliff, and Gloria Joseph; Joseph was visiting with the other two in California, where they now lived. Though she'd spoken with Gloria at least once several days earlier,[111] in general Lorde had been feeling cut off from people she loved. She felt she needed to speak with Gloria, who was increasingly significant to her. Hearing Gloria's voice was reassuring and uplifting. Though Lorde recognized that Clayton was being wonderful despite how wearying the situation was, speaking with Joseph aroused a feeling of wanting to reserve her energies in order to be in the Virgin Islands come April[112] with Joseph, and at the conference on Caribbean women.

She planned to call Blanche Cook and Clare Coss later that morning, admitting in her journal: "I am avoiding plunging directly into liver cancer as a fact but I'm edging in, & my friends too."[113] Later, in *A Burst of Light*, she elaborated on how she approached the subject with her friends, noting that although they shared in this experience, and mutual support drew them closer to each other, "there is some that they will have to deal with on their own, just as there is some fury and grief that only I can meet in a private place."[114] In that "private place," she would rephrase the earlier question to herself in her journals, "how will I be allowed to live my own life the rest of my life,"[115] into a "Better question how do I want to live the rest of my life," and answer it: to have as much joy as possible, to do the things she wanted to do and with women she wanted to do those things with.[116]

It was an answer which meant she did not have to accept anyone else's expectations or restraints. In light of the lifetime she'd shared with Frances Clayton, however, it seemed self-centered; especially since Clayton was devoted to her, imperfect as that devotion may have been. But self-centeredness kept Lorde alive well beyond medical expectations for someone with liver cancer. She could justify being self-centered: she had terminal cancer; what life she had left was hers alone to live and define.

Lorde and Clayton remained in Switzerland through the first days of the New Year, suffering through, as Lorde recounted it, feeling ostracized during the New Year's Eve dinner at the Klinik. She was particularly galled that in a place where socializing and community were encouraged, they were surrounded that night by empty chairs on each side of them, an island unto themselves.[117] On January 4, 1986, they arrived back in New York.

Lorde spent a good part of January consulting her primary oncologist in New York City, Peter Pressman; Dr. Charlotte Cunningham-Rundles (whom she referred to as "Dr. C."); and Dr. Karnow in Spring Valley,[118] gathering information on approaches to treating liver cancer. Dr. Pressman suggested she consider chemotherapy, an injection of drugs via the hepatic artery into the liver, as well as surgery to remove her gall bladder,[119] which would end her gall bladder attacks. He also wanted to confer with an oncologist at Manhattan's Mt. Sinai Hospital, a Dr. Holland, and to check on the possibility she could undergo chemotherapy at Beth Israel Medical Center as an outpatient. Chemotherapy would probably require a liver biopsy first, and Dr. Cunningham-Rundles advised against surgery. Pressman agreed chemotherapy necessitated submitting to a biopsy, which had to be carefully done. In addition, he recommended she contact Dr. Bernard Kruger,[120] a specialist in internal medicine and oncology with a practice on East 78th Street. Kruger eventually took her on as a patient.

She was also advised to consider hyperthermia—raising the body temperature to an extremely high, feverish level as a treatment for advanced cancer—but she wanted to ask Dr. Karnow about that. Karnow thought it important to find out the size of her tumors and how many hyperthermia treatments were being suggested. He also told her chemotherapy was incompatible with Iscador,[121] and prescribed chelidonium, an herb, and hepatodoron, an anticancer drug used in the treatment of liver cancer.[122] Not only was there no cure for secondary liver cancer; anticancer drugs could only slow the progress of the disease.

In her journal notes for a conversation with Dr. Kruger, Lorde itemized several key concerns shaped by her consultations with Pressman and Cunningham-Rundles, including the Iscador injections, the prognosis, the best way of monitoring liver cancer, how often she should be tested, and undergoing hyperthermia.[123] Kruger told her the prognosis was maybe five years, but it was hard to say as prognoses were so highly individualized. He also encouraged her not to be stoic and to be attentive to her body's signs.[124]

IN FEBRUARY 1986, Lorde and Joseph took a trip to Anguilla in the British West Indies, arriving there on the 19th and staying two weeks. She'd heard her homeopathic doctors refer to cancer as a "cold" disease and came to feel her bones "quake sometimes in their desire for heat—sunlight."[125] In Anguilla, there was not only the heat of the sun, there was the sea—with its tides, fish, sounds, beaches, fossilized sand dollars, and fishermen gathering at dawn at Crocus Bay.[126] Being close to "the infuriatingly inviting but cold clear water,"[127] listening to it speak to her, was what Lorde's body, mind, and spirit needed; and it reminded her of occasions when her mother took her and her sisters to gaze at another body of water, the dirtier Harlem River. The sea touched an essential part of her, in a place where her past and future intersected with the present.

Joseph introduced Lorde to Anguilla, an island she hadn't known of before. It felt "like a piece of home" and reminded her of Carriacou. She believed that its sun and sea were helping to save her life; the water there was in sharp contrast to the waters surrounding New York City. In Anguilla, away from "that line of stress and connection and performance"[128] emblematic of life in the city, she began to draft a poem,[129] the central metaphor of which was the difficulty of surviving in a concrete landscape:

> . . .
> You cannot make love to concrete
> if you care about being
> non-essential   wrong or worn   thin
> in the rub   you cannot make love to concrete
> if you fear being
> diamonds or lard
> if you cannot pretend
> concrete needs your loving. . . .[130]

As Lorde spent more time in the Caribbean, and she and Joseph took a subsequent trip to Anguilla,[131] she grew to feel that being in the Caribbean with Gloria Joseph was especially affirming—not simply because she felt like a Caribbean woman at home, but because she was there with a black woman who was also at home, and more so than she. Joseph's ease in the Caribbean, her familiarity with island peoples and customs, shaped Lorde's own sense of being familiar, of being taken for local. And the Caribbean became a place where she felt, "I am one among many."[132] Gloria embodied the spiritual medicine she needed: sunlight, laughter, healthy living, a shared political life, a black female-centered emotional space that was soul-satisfying.

That sense of bliss and belonging, however, could not blot out the fact of her cancer. At some point during the two weeks in Anguilla, a song recorded by the Beatles in the late sixties, "Let It Be," came to her. Where or how she heard it is unclear. But the song's message reflected how terribly painful it was, and would be, to have to live (". . . I tremble because I do not know how many birthdays I will see again and then my tears fall")[133] while letting life go.

Lorde and Joseph left Anguilla on March 3. Before returning to New York in mid-March, Lorde spent a few days with Joseph in St. Croix. By the first week of April, she was back participating in the conference on "Caribbean Women: The Historical and Cultural Ties That Bind."

The four-day conference convened some two hundred women from ten different countries. It offered presentations and workshops; remarks were made by Dessima Williams, former ambassador from Grenada to the Organization of American States, Johnnetta Cole, and the Trinidadian writer-lecturer Merle Hodge. A sizable undertaking, the conference highlighted its organizers' efforts to instigate solidarity between Caribbean women as citizens of the Caribbean diaspora.

Lorde's published perspectives on the conference, in *A Burst of Light*, mirrored those in her journal.[134] She felt more genuine excitement about the conference than she had about any such gathering in years. It was an opportunity to interrogate transnational questions about Caribbean women's identities, what she called "the correct relationship between our differences." She was particularly impressed by the wide range of community involvement and support as evidenced by the differences in age, educational background, political interest, and philosophy of those in attendance.[135] That the conference happened at all was a tribute to Gloria Joseph and several others who had had the vision to plan and finance it.

Beyond the intellectual aspects, being in St. Croix engaged Lorde at a deep-rooted emotional level. There, the language she heard spoken, flavors of foods that signified home, the trade winds, beach, and sea, the sense of healing within a network of black women, all shaped what she felt was "a loving context within which I fit and thrive."[136] After the conference there were several days when chest pains, shoulder aches, an upset stomach, and tiredness bothered her.[137] Though she would return to New York several times before the year was out, she spent much of spring 1986 combing the beaches in the place she now thought of as home.

FRANCES CLAYTON continued to live in the house on Staten Island. Over the next two years, she and Lorde saw each other primarily during Lorde's visits to New York. By then, however, Lorde was fully involved in her new life with Gloria Joseph—a bitter pill for Clayton to swallow after a seventeen-year partnership. When the house was sold in 1988, the relationship between them was formally severed. Clayton eventually moved to California.[138]

The elusive protagonist of Lorde's still-unnamed novel, Deotha Chambers, returned to her in St. Croix, absorbing Lorde more and more[139] as she set about crafting Deotha's story of juggling the demands of motherhood, a long-distance relationship with a white woman Deotha had met at a peace march in Washington, D.C., who lived in Rhode Island, and the politics of creating a Black Studies Department at a city college in the 1970s.[140] With a few details disguised, it was to be, after *Zami*, the next chapter of Lorde's own story.

In St. Croix, Audre Lorde found the spiritual home she'd spent a lifetime searching for. And it was outside the United States. For what time she had left now, Lorde planned to live as fully as her health would allow. In one of her last poems, "Today Is Not the Day," which she dated April 22, 1992, Lorde bravely asserted:

> *I can't just sit here*
> *staring death in her face*
> *blinking and asking for a new name*
> *by which to greet her*
>
> *I am not afraid to say*
> *unembellished*
> *I am dying*
> *but I do not want to do it*
> *looking the other way.*

> Today is not the day.
> It could be
> but it is not . . . [141]

EPILOGUE

ORDE HAD HALF sisters she'd never met. The twins, Mavis and Marjorie, were the offspring of Daisy Jones, a young, single Grenadian woman, and Lorde's father, Byron Lorde. They were born in Grenada in 1923, the same year Lorde's parents married. The existence of the twin girls was a well-known fact in Grenville, the small coastal community located on Grenada's eastern shore in the parish of St. Andrews. Lorde's mother knew of the twins too, but after she and Mr. Lorde emigrated to Harlem, her husband's twin daughters were a secret guarded by her culpable silence. Though Byron Lorde died in 1953, Linda Lorde maintained his secret, and took to her grave in October 1988 what she knew about the twins.

Known to family in Grenada and to relatives living in the United States, the twins remained unknown to Lorde and her sisters, Phyllis and Helen, until 1991. With Linda and Byron both dead now, Lorde's cousin Hilda Wells broke the family silence. During one of Helen's visits to her Brooklyn home, Hilda casually mentioned that she'd seen Helen's sister while on a recent trip to Grenada. Helen knew neither Phyllis nor

Lorde was in Grenada then, and she was confused. By the time she understood what Hilda was saying, she was shocked. When Helen got back to her Upper Manhattan apartment, she called Phyllis in Seattle and Audre in St. Croix.

Once her own shock wore off, Lorde was determined to establish a bond of sisterhood. She sent a letter to Mavis, introducing herself.[1] Within no time, Mavis wrote back. Yes, she wanted to meet Lorde, too. Lorde was excited by the possibility of meeting the sister whose fraternal twin now lived in Texas.

Even before the news of her twin sisters, Audre and Gloria Joseph had planned a vacation trip to Grenada and Carriacou. When they arrived in Grenada, Audre called Mavis from the hotel. With a meeting arranged, Audre and Gloria agreed Audre should go to her sister's house alone the first time. Dressed in one of her signature African outfits, Audre sped off in the cab that would take her to Mavis's front door.

When the cab approached the small Grenadian house on Sendall Street in Grenville, Mavis came out to greet it. Seeing Audre emerge, she came down the porch steps, flinging open her arms wide. The embrace between them left Lorde speechless. She confided to Joseph later, it was like meeting "a long lost older sister who really loved me."

Peeling away membranes of silence and separation between them, Audre and Mavis talked about learning of one another's existence, and about the half brother Lorde also did not know she had. Mavis talked of how their father never once answered letters the twins wrote asking for money to pay the costly tuition required by middle-grade schools modeled on the British system of educating only those who could afford it. As Mavis talked, Lorde noted how much Mavis looked just like Byron Lorde. How she had his build and, more important, that darker brown skin coloring Lorde had, which she'd always seen as separating her from her "creamy fine-boned sisters."[2]

A couple of days later, Audre visited with Mavis a second time, bringing Gloria with her. She took Mavis gifts and copies of her books, and they talked some more. A sweet, soft-spoken woman, Mavis showered Audre with the tenderness of an older sister. It was a tenderness Lorde had long hungered for and had felt, as a child, was missing from her two full sisters. Before the visit was over, they took lots of pictures, documenting what was for Lorde a loving, emotional encounter.

Lorde wrote to but never met the other twin, Marjorie. She did for Mavis what their father had not: she sent money to help her out, since Mavis, despite her age and without benefit of a Social Security system, was still working a few days a week. Lorde spent eight months crafting the poem "Inheritance—His"[3] for her final collection, *The Marvelous Arithmetics of Distance*.[4] Published posthumously, the book was dedicated to her "blood sisters," including Mavis and Marjorie. "Inheritance—His" chronicled the silences of Byron Lorde's life, particularly as the father who was as elusive to her as he was to her twin sisters. It was one of the last silences she would address.

Within fifteen months of meeting Mavis, Lorde died, at age fifty-eight. On November 17, 1992, her fourteen-year battle with cancer ended. A year earlier, she'd been designated New York State Poet, the first African American and first woman to be awarded that distinction.[5] She'd also taken on an African name, Gamba Adisa—"she who makes her meaning known."[6] The transparent, moonlit night she died in St. Croix, Audre Lorde closed her eyes on the trees she loved, the watching stars, and the sea just footsteps away from the comfortable home she'd shared with Gloria Joseph. The last six years of her life she'd lived there, ensconced in a community of Caribbean women where the "lines between lesbian and straight are a lot more blurred" and where, admittedly, she'd missed "an *articulated* black lesbian community."[7] Still, life on the small Caribbean island satisfied her deepest longings for home, history, peace. By her bedside were the filmmaker Ada Griffin; Dagmar Schultz; Ika Huegel and May Opitz, two Afro-German women; and Gloria Joseph, who'd become Lorde's companion and a significant caretaker in the final years. Lorde's children had been with her earlier in the week. The women then began the work of letting the world know she was gone, dividing up lists of names they'd agreed upon that week when it became apparent the end was near.

In St. Croix, news of Lorde's passing came over the radio, in the local newspaper, and by word of mouth. She was remembered as the beloved poet who'd chosen to live amongst them, as at home with the local people as she was with an international audience; who'd shared with them the triumph of surviving Hurricane Hugo, the worst hurricane in U.S. history.[8] Beyond the waters insulating St. Croix, condolences and tributes poured in from South Africa, Berlin, Cuba, Hawaii, New York, Canada, New Zealand, London, throughout the United States, and the Caribbean; and from the hundreds of organizations and individuals her revolutionary work for social justice supported and spawned.

Lorde's body remained in St. Croix overnight, then was flown to Puerto Rico, where it was cremated. When Gloria, Beth, and Jonathan went to the funeral home in St. Croix where Lorde's ashes were stored until they were claimed, the funeral home director remarked she'd never seen ashes perform the way Lorde's had.[9] Although sealed with tape, the bag containing them kept popping open, mysteriously. After the third attempt to seal the bag, the funeral director concluded, "these ashes just don't want to be sealed up."[10]

Lorde had spent a lifetime defying socially imposed boundaries, and she wanted her ashes scattered in several places: Buck Island in St. Croix, the underwater trails of which she loved to swim; Krumme Lanke, a lake in Berlin where she'd canoed across the cool water easing her mind between experimental treatments; Hawaii, where she, Joseph, Blanche Cook, and Clare Coss went in 1990 just to witness the eclipse. She also wanted some ashes strewn in the yard of what was once her home in Staten Island, and in Washington Square Park in Manhattan, a symbol of the artistic and sexual freedom of Greenwich Village.

She was honored with memorials internationally. In New York City's Cathedral of St. John the Divine, upward of four thousand people from around the globe gathered in the massive, stained-glass gallery. In front of the pulpit stood a grand, larger-than-life altar, sumptuously dressed with the icons of Lorde's spiritual bonds to the natural world: flowers, seashells, nuts, rocks, and fruit. At the conclusion of those services, her admirers were instructed to take of the "living body" symbolized by this altar. The predominance of the altar—its resurrection theme of life beyond death—at the memorials in St. Croix and Berlin also testified to Lorde's near-messianic public persona.

At the Berlin memorial, her German naturopath, Manfred D. Kuno, noted in his remarks: "Audre Lorde did not die of cancer, Audre Lorde died with cancer." Having spent thirteen years of intensive work with cancer patients and dying persons, and convinced that "cancer is a response to a deep wound," Kuno told the gathered, "She lived with and suffered from a deep wound, caused by the brutal discrepancy between the knowledge of the possibility of human existence and love on the one hand and the experience of human coldness and cultural destruction on the other hand."[11]

She'd called herself "black, feminist, lesbian, mother, poet warrior." Over the course of her life, Lorde used these multiple identities as passports between an array of sisterhoods, declaring within each of them, "I am your sister."[12] In her family and in the larger world, she'd connected women to a knowledge of themselves, and to other women as sister images of the self. Audre Lorde was more than her own politicized constructions; as (Akasha) Gloria Hull noted, her "seemingly essentialist definitions of herself as black/lesbian/mother/woman [were] not simple, fixed terms." She was a woman who constructed a complex self,[13] its parts irreducible from the whole.

NOTES

Introduction

1 I owe a debt to June Jordan and her essay, "The Difficult Miracle of Black Poetry in America or Something Like a Sonnet for Phillis Wheatley." In rereading it, I came to appreciate even more clearly the difficulties black women poets have faced historically as we've sought self-defined freedom in America. See June Jordan, *On Call: Political Essays* (Boston: South End Press, 1985), 87–98.

2 The argument for this approach comes from insights offered by Phyllis Rose, who has written biographies of Charles Dickens, Virginia Woolf, and Josephine Baker. In her essay, "Confessions of a Burned-Out Biographer," Rose notes the subjective nature of biography, distinguishing the "school of literary biography" from "the objective school," in which the "truth" can be known, codified, exists apart from the biographer's own biases, and can be served up in copious detail. See Rose, "Confessions of a Burned-Out Biographer," *Civilization* (Winter 1995), 72–74.

3 Ibid., 72.

4 See Victoria Glendinning, "Lies and Silences," in Eric Homberger and John Charmley, eds., *The Troubled Face of Biography* (New York: Macmillan, 1988), 60.

5 Ibid., 53.

The First Life
Part One
Chapter 1

1 Prior to the 1920s, most African Americans who lived in Manhattan lived in what were known then as the Tenderloin and San Juan Hill districts in midtown. When African Americans began to move into Harlem in the early decades of the twentieth century, white Americans met their presence with reluctance. That reluctance was reinforced in a racial divide demarcated by Eighth Avenue. From Eighth Avenue west to the Hudson River, Harlem was white. East of Eighth Avenue to the Harlem River, and from 130th to 145th Streets, was black Harlem. See David Levering Lewis, *When Harlem Was in Vogue* (New York: Vintage Books, 1979).

2 Marcus Garvey's impact on the cultural, social, and political life of Harlem in the 1920s and 1930s, his "Back to Africa" movement and the reasons for its failure have been widely documented. For further discussion, see Lewis, *When Harlem Was in Vogue* and *Marcus Garvey, Life and Lessons. A Centennial Companion to the Marcus Garvey and Universal Negro Improvement Association Papers*, ed. Robert A. Hill (Berkeley: University of California Press, 1987).

3 Lewis, *When Harlem Was in Vogue*, 89–103.

4 Irma Watkins-Owens, *Blood Relations: Caribbean Immigrants and the Harlem Community, 1900–1930* (Bloomington: Indiana University Press, 1996), 1.

5 I am employing Watkins-Owens's analysis of the sociopolitical encounter between Caribbean immigrants and African Americans in Harlem, which she defines as one of both cooperation and conflict, debating previous scholarship which views that encounter as defined chiefly by conflict.

6 See Watkins-Owens, *Blood Relations*, 6.

7 Ibid., 4.

8 Ibid., 2.

9 Ibid., 3.

10 Ibid.

11 Ibid., 7.

12 Ibid., 3–4.

13 The following is part of the oral history of Grenada I learned while at a conference of Caribbean writers and scholars there in May 1998: For nearly a century and a half, the Carib peoples of Grenada repulsed all attempts by first the Spanish, then French and British invaders to colonize them until a French expedition from Martinique succeeded in purchasing large tracts of land for the price of a few beads, knives, and hatchets. Hostilities between the Caribs and the French broke out almost immediately, as the French sought to extend their control over extensive tracts of land and thus the whole island. Determined not

to submit to French rule, Carib resistance prevailed, in spite of a succession of losing battles. Rather than be enslaved, the last surviving Caribs jumped to their death off a steep cliff, north of the island, known today as "Carib's Leap" and "Leaper's Hill." The exact spot is now a cemetery.

14 According to Lorde's cousin, Hilda Wells, Elizabeth and Peter Belmar had seven daughters, as well as a son who was shipped out in World War I and never heard from again.

15 Phyllis Lorde Blackwell, personal interview, 12 December 1995.

16 Phyllis clearly remembers her mother's story of Ma-Liz's objections to Byron as a prospective son-in-law, when it became clear Linda wanted to marry him. It was a story she'd heard more than once and that had been passed on to her as her mother's truth. Whatever the private conversation that story represented, publicly the family behaved otherwise. As Hilda Wells recollects, the Belmars loved Byron and had no objections to his color or the fact of his earlier children.

17 Audre Lorde, "Inheritance—His," in *The Marvelous Arithmetics of Distance* (New York: W. W. Norton, 1993), 15–19.

18 Ibid., 16.

19 Watkins-Owens, *Blood Relations*, 173.

20 John Jacob Astor IV built the original Astoria Hotel next door to the Waldorf Hotel, which was owned by William Waldorf Astor, son of John Jacob Astor III. The two luxury hotels were run as one until 1929, when they made way for the Empire State Building. The new Waldorf-Astoria was erected on Park Avenue in 1931.

21 Phyllis remembers her mother telling stories of passing for white when her parents first came to New York, because whites weren't offering jobs to blacks. Phyllis's recollection of these stories is corroborated by Helen Lorde's.

22 Watkins-Owens, *Blood Relations*, 167.

23 Ibid., 4.

24 Ibid., 5.

25 Ibid., 172.

26 Pauline E. Hopkins, an African American playwright, novelist, and journalist, published a mystery story, "Talma Gordon," in the *Colored American Magazine* in 1900. As a story whose plot pivoted on Talma—a mulatta who passed for white—Hopkins's fictional account stands at the beginning of twentieth-century explorations of the theme of passing in African American literature. For more contemporary accounts, see Nella Larsen, *An Intimation of Things Distant: The Collected Fiction of Nella Larsen*, ed. Charles R. Larson (New York: Anchor Books, 1992); Valerie Smith, "Reading the Intersection of Race and Gender in Narratives of Passing," *Diacritics*, 2 (1994); Judy Scales-Trent, *Notes of a White Black Woman: Race, Color and Community* (University Park, PA:

Pennsylvania State University Press, 1995); Gregory Howard Williams, *Life on the Color Line* (New York: Plume Books, 1994); Toi Derricotte, *The Black Notebooks* (New York: W. W. Norton, 1996); and Adrian Piper, "Passing for White, Passing for Black," in Elaine K. Ginsberg, ed., *Passing and the Fictions of Identity* (Durham, NC: Duke University Press, 1996).

27 I am indebted to my graduate student and research assistant, Anne Borden, whose conversations with me about her master's thesis on passing reminded me that I'd read and remembered Griffin's, *Black Like Me.*

28 Lewis, *When Harlem Was in Vogue*, 89–118.

29 Ibid., 109.

30 Watkins-Owens, *Blood Relations*, 44–45.

31 For a discussion of Father Divine's life and work, see Robert Weisbrot, *Father Divine* (Boston: Beacon Press, 1983).

32 Aishah Rahman, "'Wanderin' and Wonderin': Home in the Imagination of Black Women Artists," *Black Renaissance/Renaissance Noir*, 1:2 (1997): 8–14.

33 Elizabeth Alexander, "Coming Out Blackened and Whole: Fragmentation and Reintegration in Audre Lorde's *Zami* and *The Cancer Journals*," *American Literary History*, 6:4 (1994): 695–715. For a discussion on the linkages between literature and history in African American fiction and autobiography, see Roger Rosenblatt, "Black Autobiography: Life as the Death Weapon," in James Olney, ed., *Autobiography: Essays Theoretical and Critical* (Princeton: Princeton University Press, 1980), 169–80.

34 James Olney, "Autobiography and the Cultural Moment: A Thematic, Historical and Bibliographical Introduction," in ibid., 3–27.

35 Toni Morrison, "The Site of Memory," in William Zinsser, ed., *Inventing the Truth. The Art and Craft of Memoir* (Boston: Houghton Mifflin, 1987), 103–24.

36 See Audre Lorde, *Zami: A New Spelling of My Name* (Boston: Persephone Press, 1982).

37 Clarissa Pinkola Estes, *Women Who Run with the Wolves. Myths and Stories of the Wild Woman Archetype* (New York: Ballantine Books, 1992), 165.

38 Rosenblatt, "Black Autobiography," 171.

39 Helen Lorde, personal interview, 2 October 1995.

40 St. Mark's Academy was founded in Harlem in 1912 by Mother Katherine Drexel and the Sisters of the Blessed Sacrament, a Catholic order of nuns whose missionary duty, subsumed within the racialized dogma of Catholicism, was selfless dedication to the education of "America's Indians and Coloured People." St. Mark's Academy (now St. Mark's the Evangelist School) opened first on the ground floor of a leased tobacco factory on 134th Street, and was only large enough then to accommodate seventy students. It was New York's first all-black Catholic school—save for the whites who ran it. In 1914, it moved

to 138th Street and Lenox Avenue. At the height of the depression, the school claimed to have educated and fed more than five hundred of Harlem's mostly poor, black American and Caribbean children—St. Mark's Academy brochure.

41 Phyllis Blackwell and Helen Lorde, personal interview, 29 July 1996.

42 Blackwell interview, 12 December 1995.

43 Hilda Wells, telephone interview, 9 February 1998.

44 Helen Lorde interview, 3 October 1995. When interviewed alone, Helen spoke briefly of the years of therapy she underwent to understand the emotional and psychological impact of her upbringing. I have honored her request not to reveal the details of those years.

45 Helen recalls that Mr. Lorde had several offices out of which he and her mother managed rooming houses, rented properties, and leased buildings. One was at 357 Lenox Avenue at 128th Street, the boarded-up remains of which still exist.

46 Audre imagined her sisters were more intimate than they actually were, according to both Helen and Phyllis. Phyllis recollects some resentment that she and Helen were always lumped together, in an enforced inseparability engineered by their parents (the one bedroom they shared, going to the same schools). Helen recalls that their mother insisted she and Phyllis do chores, pitting one against the other and fueling the tensions of their growing up.

47 Helen Lorde interview, 2 October 1995.

48 I am deeply indebted to my colleague at the State University of New York at Buffalo, Professor Monica Jardine, who developed this idea for me and generously allowed numerous conversations on the Caribbean, migration discourse, and Caribbean women's experiences.

49 Blackwell interview, 12 December 1995. I am indebted to the scholar Ann Czvetskovich, whose visit and lecture at the State University of New York at Buffalo, 2 March 1998, pieced together for me the psychic and physical impact of immigration and migration on communities of color.

50 Cited in James P. Draper, "Audre Lorde," *Black Literature Criticism*, vol. 2 (Detroit: Gale Research, 1992), 1275.

51 St. Mark's Academy school records, 11 September 1939–7 February 1944.

52 I use the term "wildish" because it suggests Estes's discussion on the wild woman archetype as instinctive nature, which is another way to read Lorde as a young girl. For a fuller discussion, see Estes, *Women Who Run with the Wolves*, 4–21.

53 Adrienne Rich, "An Interview with Audre Lorde," *Signs: Journal of Women in Culture and Society*, 6:4 (1981): 713–36.

54 Estes, *Women Who Run with the Wolves*, 171.

55 Rich, "An Interview with Audre Lorde," 722.

56 Blackwell interview, 12 December 1995. Lorde was not a dark-skinned

woman, but she was the "darkest" of her sisters and darker than her mother. The issue of intraracial attitudes toward "light" and "dark" skin is a leitmotif undergirding much of African American life; it stems from an internalized racism (and color consciousness) established in the nineteenth century during enslavement, but persists today. For contemporary treatments of the theme, see Spike Lee's *School Daze* (1988); Alice Walker, "Embracing the Dark and the Light," *Essence* magazine (July 1982); Bonnie Allen, "It Ain't Easy Being Pinky," *Essence* magazine (July 1982); Kathy Russell, Midge Wilson, and Ronald Hall, eds., *The Color Complex: The Politics of Skin Color Among African Americans* (New York: Anchor Books, 1992); Angela Neal and Midge Wilson, "The Role of Skin Color and Features in the Black Community: Implications for Black Women and Therapy," *Clinical Psychology Review*, 2 (1989): 329; and Bertrice Barry, "Black-on-Black Discrimination: The Phenomenon of Colorism Among African Americans," unpublished dissertation, Kent State University, 1988.

57 In the documentary film *A Litany for Survival: The Life and Work of Audre Lorde*, directed by Ada Griffith and Michelle Parkerson (Third World Newsreel, 1995), Lorde boasts of her "bad girl" persona as a young girl, rejuvenating both herself and her image at a time when she was physically battling cancer.

58 Helen Lorde, personal interview, 3 October 1995.

59 Blackwell interview, 12 December 1995.

60 Helen Lorde interview, 3 October 1995.

61 Although Bryon Lorde was unquestionably man of the house, and was sometimes present when punishment was metered out by his wife, according to all three daughters he rarely beat his children.

62 Blackwell interview, 12 December 1995.

63 Ibid.

64 My sense of the Lorde daughters as trophies comes from interviews with Helen and Phyllis, whose memories suggest that their parents were proud of them only when they embodied their parents' accomplishments as good parents.

65 Karla Hammond, "Audre Lorde: Interview," *Denver Quarterly*, 16 (1981): 10–27.

Chapter 2

1 Lorde, *Zami*, 3.

2 I thank Dr. Virginia Batchelor-Robinson, a graduate of the Graduate School of Education, State University of New York at Buffalo, who shared with me critical insights on African American women's Catholic school experiences as she was completing her dissertation.

3 Largely as a result of "white flight" and its attendant socioeconomic fac-

tors, Washington Heights is today home to diverse populations of the African American, Caribbean, Hispanic, and Asian American working class.

4 Lorde, *Zami* 59–60.

5 Keats, Byron, Shelley, and other Romantic poets of the nineteenth century espoused belief in a return to nature, exaltation of the senses, and emotions over reason and intellect. They also promoted an admiration for the heroic, the individual, and the imagination of the artist. As a young poet, Lorde was indelibly—and largely—shaped by ideas inherent to their poetry.

6 Hammond, "Audre Lorde: Interview," 20.

7 Unpublished journal, ca. 1949.

8 Hammond, "Audre Lorde: Interview," 19.

9 Rahman, "Wanderin' and Wonderin'," 14.

10 Diane di Prima, telephone interview, 25 October 1997.

11 Ibid.

12 Ibid.

13 Audre Lorde, cf. p. 36, Audre Lorde Papers, Spelman College, Atlanta, Georgia (cited hereafter as Audre Lorde Papers).

14 Unpublished journal, Thursday, 5 January 1950.

15 di Prima interview, 25 October 1997.

16 Hammond, "Audre Lorde: Interview," 18.

17 Ibid.

18 Joan Sandler, personal interview, 7 October 1995.

19 di Prima interview, 25 October 1997.

20 Unpublished journal, Tuesday, 10 January 1950.

21 Unpublished journal, Tuesday, 7 March 1950.

22 Unpublished journal, undated entry, 1950.

23 Unpublished journal, Sunday, 1 January 1950.

24 Unpublished journal, undated entry, 1950.

25 Unpublished journal, Sunday, 8 January 1950.

26 Sandler interview, 7 October 1995.

27 di Prima interview, 25 October 1997.

28 Sandler interview, 7 October 1995.

29 Unpublished journal, undated entry, 1950.

30 Judy Simmons, "Audre Lorde, The Many Faces of . . . ," *Contact II Poetry Magazine*, 5:27 (1982): 44–47.

31 Sandler interview, 7 October 1995.

32 Ibid.

33 di Prima interview, 25 October 1997.

34 Sandler interview, 7 October 1995.

35 Ibid.

36 Ibid.

37 di Prima interview, 25 October 1997.

38 Sandler interview, 7 October 1995.

39 Ibid.

40 I owe the suggestion of this question to Judy Simmons, who extends the point in her article, "Audre Lorde, The Many Faces of . . . " In the 1950s, the terms "homosexual" and "homoerotic" were defined by the medical establishment as synonymous with aberrant sexual behavior. Because of the social implications, many homosexuals became alcoholics, masked their homosexuality in heterosexual relations and marriages, or committed suicide. Contemporary data on teenaged homosexuals reveals that teenagers too often resort to suicide when they discover their own homoerotic desires.

41 Certificate of Baptism, Church of St. Mark the Evangelist, 65 West 138th Street, New York City, dated 15 July 1934.

42 Unpublished journal, 16 March 1951.

43 Unpublished journal, 28 December 1950.

44 Unpublished journal, 16 March 1951.

45 Unpublished journal, 15 March 1951.

46 Unpublished journal, 16 March 1951.

47 Audre Lorde, 22 September 1950, Audre Lorde Papers. The quotes that follow are taken from this unpublished piece.

48 Simmons, "Audre Lorde, The Many Faces of . . . ," 47.

49 Unpublished journal, 17 February 1951.

50 Blanche Cook and Clare Coss, personal interview, 24 June 1998. Cook recalled meeting Burstein years later while in Lorde's company and remembered Burstein as "an old school dyke" who was very "butch."

51 Unpublished journal, undated entry, 1951.

52 Rich, "An Interview with Audre Lorde," 730.

53 Unpublished journal, 14 December 1951.

54 Unpublished journal, 26 June 1951.

55 Unpublished journal, 25 June 1951.

56 Unpublished journal, 30 June 1951.

57 Unpublished journal, 3 March 1951.

58 Unpublished journal, 12 July 1951.

59 While unspecific in her journal as to why she admired Countee Cullen's poetry, Lorde shared with Cullen (whose sexuality has been the focus of recent debate) an admiration for the lyric poetry of John Keats and Edna St. Vincent Millay. He was particularly fond of Keats, believing poetry should align itself more with emotion than with intellect. Considered an important poet of the Harlem Renaissance and the themes of its "black awakening," Cullen struggled with the tensions between race consciousness and the romantic strain in his poetry. Although many of his poems spoke to the agony of being black in Amer-

ica, he was not a protest writer by nature. Cullen once suggested "Negro" poets should align themselves with English and (white) American literary traditions rather than with African ones. Unable to escape the theme of racial identification in his work, he sought to subsume it within his goal of writing poetry that was beautiful and musical. See James A. Emanuel and Theodore L. Gross, eds., *Dark Symphony: Negro Literature in America* (New York: Free Press, 1968), 172–75.

60 Unpublished journal, 28 June and 2 July 1951.

61 Unpublished journal, 30 July 1951.

62 I am indebted to my friend, the poet Jimmie Gilliam of Buffalo, NY, who generously gave me a copy of Vivian Gornick's *The End of the Novel of Love* (Boston: Beacon Press, 1997) to read, in which I discovered a discussion of Radclyffe Hall's novel *The Unlit Lamp* (1924). Gornick analyzes the struggle of a bright, talented young woman wanting to lead a life of her own and the demands of a mother emotionally indifferent to those talents.

63 I borrow this term and its discussion from Gornick's chapter, "Ruthless Intimacies." See also Lorde's eroticized descriptions of her mother in the early chapters of *Zami*.

64 Wald founded the Henry Street Settlement House and fought to improve living conditions for immigrant families surviving their ghettoization as outsiders. See Blanche Wiesen Cook, "Female Support Networks and Political Activism: Lillian Wald, Crystal Eastman, Emma Goldman," in Linda K. Kerber and Jane Sherron De Hart, eds., *Women's America. Refocusing the Past*, 4th ed. (New York: Oxford University Press, 1995), 303–20.

65 Unpublished journal, 28 August 1951.

66 Unpublished journal, 9 September 1951.

67 Unpublished journal, 15 September 1951.

68 Ibid.

69 Hammond, "Audre Lorde: Interview," 16

70 Unpublished journal, October 1951.

71 Unpublished journal, 23 September 1951.

72 Ibid.

73 Unpublished journal, 21 October 1951.

74 Unpublished journal, 28 October 1951.

75 Unpublished journal, 9 November 1951.

76 Sandler interview, 7 October 1995

77 Unpublished journal, undated entry, 1951.

78 Unpublished journal, 13, 14, and 21 November 1951.

79 Lorde, *Zami*, 107–15.

80 This note was found by Gloria Joseph six years after Lorde's death, amongst undiscovered papers at their home in St. Croix.

81 Sandler interview, 7 October 1995.

82 Lorde, *Zami*, 119.

83 Simmons, "Audre Lorde, The Many Faces of . . . ," 47.

84 See Sharon M. Howard, "Harlem Writers Guild," *Encyclopedia of African-American Culture and History*, vol. 3 (New York: Simon & Schuster, 1996), 1219–20.

85 Rich, "An Interview with Audre Lorde," 722.

86 Lorde, *Zami*, 125–26.

87 Ibid., 135–36.

88 Sandler interview, 7 October 1995.

89 Many homosexual and bisexual people in the 1950s were forced to conceal same-sex relationships. Prior to the "Stonewall Rebellion" of 1969—which came about as a response to police harassment of homosexuals at the Stonewall Bar in New York's Greenwich Village and which historians of lesbian and gay community life pinpoint as the pivotal moment of the gay liberation movement—homosexual identity, culture, and community life existed in a closeted reality without benefit of an articulated collective political consciousness. See John D'Emilio, *Sexual Politics, Sexual Communities: The Making of a Homosexual Minority in the United States, 1940–1970* (Chicago: University of Chicago Press, 1983), and Martin Duberman, Martha Vicinus, and George Chauncey, Jr., eds., *Hidden from History: Reclaiming the Gay and Lesbian Past* (New York: New American Library, 1989).

90 Lorde, *Zami*, 146.

91 I am encouraged in posing this question by the work of Dr. Harold P. Freeman, director of the Department of Surgery, Harlem Hospital Center, New York City. Formerly national president of the American Cancer Society and chief architect of the society's initiative on cancer in the poor, Dr. Freeman is a leading authority on the interrelationships between race, poverty, and cancer. His public lecture, "Race, Poverty and Cancer," delivered in collaboration with the Roswell Park Cancer Institute of Buffalo, NY, on 13 February 1998, strongly suggested the importance of examining the intersection between race, behavior, culture, poverty, and science in combating incidences of breast, prostate, and colon cancer (among others) in African American communities. For a decidedly more critical discussion, see Freeman's address to the President's Cancer Panel, National Cancer Institute, "The Meaning of Race in Science—Considerations for Cancer Research, Concerns of Special Populations in the National Cancer Program," Herbert Irving Comprehensive Cancer Center, Columbia University, New York, 9 April 1997 (National Cancer Institute, 31 Center Drive MSC 2473, Building 31, Room A48, Bethesda, MD 20892–2473).

92 Sandler interview, 7 October 1995.

93 Ibid.

94 Ruth Baharas, telephone interview, 29 March 1998.

95 Ibid.

96 Sandler interview, 7 October 1995.

97 Baharas interview, 29 March 1998.

98 See Howard Zinn, *A People's History of the United States* (New York: Harper & Row, 1980), 424–25.

99 Shortly after Lorde's trip to Washington on behalf of the Rosenbergs, President Dwight D. Eisenhower (who'd refused the Rosenbergs clemency) signed an executive order desegregating the nation's capital. The bitterness with which Lorde embraced that news was embedded in the humiliation her family suffered as a result of having been refused service at an ice cream parlor years before.

100 Lorde, *Zami*, 149.

101 Sandler interview, 7 October 1995.

102 Ibid.

103 Lorde, *Zami*, 149.

104 Unpublished journal, undated entry, 1954, 1.

Part Two
Chapter 3

1 Lorde's unpublished journal recording the months she spent in Mexico starkly contrasts with the autobiographical, fictionalized account she published in *Zami* thirty-odd years later. The critical literature on autobiography and memoir offers some insights. Roger Rosenblatt argues that black autobiography and black fiction intersect when the expressed desire to live as freely as possible and the criticism of external sociopolitical conditions oppressing or impeding that desire are represented; both share a historic authenticity and both explain each other. Toni Morrison recognizes similarities and differences between memoir and fiction, as well as an embrace between the two crafts that is symbiotic. Stephen Butterfield establishes the point that the self in black autobiography is inextricably tied to community. Joanne Braxton has argued that black women's autobiographies represent "a tradition within a tradition," and presents individual black women in relation to others with whom they share "emotional, philosophical, and spiritual affinities, as well as political realities." Whether the written accounts of Lorde's trip were "fact" or "fiction," both her journal and aspects of *Zami* serve as primary sources for interpreting the significance of her experiences in Mexico. See Roger Rosenblatt, "Black Autobiography: Life as the Death Weapon," in Olney, ed., *Autobiography: Essays Theoretical and Critical*, 169–80; Toni Morrison, "The Site of Memory," in William Zinsser, ed., *Inventing the Truth: The Art and Craft of Memoir* (Boston: Houghton Mifflin, 1987), 103–24; Stephen Butterfield,

Black Autobiography in America (Amherst: University Press of Massachusetts, 1974); and Joanne Braxton, *Black Women Writing Autobiography: A Tradition Within a Tradition* (Philadelphia: Temple University Press, 1989).

2 Unpublished journal, undated entry, 1954, 2.

3 Ibid.

4 Unpublished journal, undated entry, 1954, 3.

5 Rich, "An Interview with Audre Lorde," 716.

6 Lorde, *Zami*, 154.

7 Unpublished journal, undated entry, 1954, 3.

8 The actual letter was lost over the years, but Baharas distinctly remembered this phrase as Lorde's description of her initial feelings once in Mexico.

9 Unpublished journal, undated entry, 1954, 7.

10 Unpublished journal, undated entry, 1954, 8.

11 Lorde, *Zami*, 154.

12 Rahman, "Wanderin' and Wonderin'," 14.

13 Hammond, "Audre Lorde: Interview," 24.

14 Lorde, *Zami*, 155.

15 Ibid., 158.

16 Unpublished journal, undated entry, 1954, 4.

17 Unpublished journal, undated entry, 1954, 5.

18 Unpublished journal, undated entry, 1954, 27.

19 Audre Lorde, "Poetry Is Not a Luxury," in *Sister Outsider*, 36.

20 Hammond, Audre Lorde: Interview," 24.

21 Lorde, *Zami*, 160.

22 Unpublished journal, Thursday, 5 January 1950.

23 Rich, "An Interview with Audre Lorde," 717.

24 Lorde, *Zami*, 160.

25 Unpublished journal, undated entry, 1954, 17.

26 Unpublished journal, undated entry, 1954, 32.

27 Lorde, *Zami*, 161–76.

28 Lorde's journal of her experiences in Mexico makes no mention of the detailed story of the affair between herself and Eudora as constructed in *Zami*.

29 Audre Lorde, *The Cancer Journals* (San Francisco: Spinsters Ink, 1980), 35.

30 Lorde, *Zami*, 170.

31 Lorde, *The Cancer Journals*, 35.

32 Unpublished journal, undated entry, 1954, 37.

33 Unpublished journal, undated entry, 1954, 41.

34 Unpublished journal, undated entry, 1954, 38.

35 Unpublished journal, undated entries, 1954, 38–40; 42–43.

36 Unpublished journal, undated entry, 1954, 46.

Chapter 4

1 Lorde, *Zami*, 7.

2 Unpublished journal, undated entry, 1958, 1.

3 Joy James's discussion of African philosophy, theory, and "living thinkers" asserts the relationship of African American epistemological perspectives to the health and well-being of community—chosen as well as cultural, and rooted in activism. See Joy James, "African Philosophy, Theory and Living Thinkers," in Joy James and Ruth Farmer, eds., *Spirit, Space and Survival: African American Women in (White) Academe* (New York: Routledge, 1993), 31–46. I have also embraced Clarissa Pinkola Estes's discussion on creativity as a force capable of changing shape—from one art form to another, for example; or, as in Lorde's case, from one literary genre to another and integral to her social activism. I am extending Estes's discussion to include Lorde's intellectual shape-shifting as creative and evolutionary—see Estes, *Women Who Run with the Wolves*, 297–33.

4 Elizabeth Lapovsky Kennedy and Madeline D. Davis, *Boots of Leather, Slippers of Gold. The History of a Lesbian Community* (New York: Routledge, 1993), 69–70.

5 Ibid., 5.

6 Lorde, *Zami*, 177.

7 Ibid., 180–81.

8 Kennedy and Davis, *Boots of Leather*, 5.

9 Ibid., 212–13.

10 Lorde, *Zami*, 208.

11 Ibid., 210–13.

12 Ibid., 198.

13 Baharas interview, 29 March 1998.

14 Unpublished journal, undated entry, 1958, 7.

15 Lorde, *Zami*, 224.

16 Staff was also chair of the editorial committee for *Psychoanalysis*, a quarterly published by the National Psychological Association for Psychoanalysis (NPAP), founded in 1948 by Dr. Theodor Reik, a pupil, friend, and colleague of Sigmund Freud. Clement Staff was on the faculty of the NPAP school at 66 Fifth Avenue, which housed the Theodor Reik Clinic for Mental Health and Research. He was affiliated with the clinic—Obituary, *The New York Times*, 27 March 1958.

17 Unpublished journal, undated entry, 1958, 6.

18 Unpublished journal, undated entry, 1958, 5.

19 Edwin Rollins, personal interview, 9 December 1995.

20 Unpublished journal, undated entry, 1958, 8.

21 Unpublished journal, undated entry, 1958.

22 Before her death, Lorde requested that Gloria Joseph conduct interviews of her to be used as primary sources for a future biography. The interviews took place at their home in St. Croix and in Germany, and were spread over many months in 1990–91; several audiotapes were later transcribed by Annie Avery. As specific dates of individual sessions were not recorded, and are recorded unevenly on the tapes and in the transcripts, all references to these interviews are cited as Audre Lorde, personal interviews, 1990–91.

23 Judith C. Kohl, "Blanche Cook, American Historian," in Michael Tyrkus, ed., *Gay & Lesbian Biography* (Detroit: St. James Press, 1997), 126–28.

24 See Sale Kirpatrick, *SDS* (New York: Vintage Press, 1973); see also Arthur Liebman, *Jews and the Left* (New York: John Wiley & Sons, 1979). For more on the FBI's surveillance of SDS, the Black Panther Party, the American Indian Movement (AIM), and other New Left radical organizations, see Ward Churchill and Jim Vander Wall, *Agents of Repression: The FBI's Secret Wars Against the Black Panther Party and the American Indian Movement* (Boston: South End Press, 1988).

25 Blanche Cook, personal interview, 24 June 1998.

26 See Kerber and De Hart, eds., *Women's America, Refocusing the Past.*

27 For more on Hansberry's complex persona, see Jean Carey Bond, ed., *Lorraine Hansberry: Art of Thunder, Vision of Light.* Special issue of *Freedomways,* 19:4 (1979): 183–304.

Chapter 5

1 Audre Lorde, "Learning from the 60s," in *Sister Outsider,* 134–44.

2 Documentary, *A Litany for Survival: The Life and Work of Audre Lorde.*

3 Audre Lorde, personal interviews, 1990–91.

4 Elizabeth Lorde-Rollins, telephone interview, 24 November 1995.

5 Elizabeth Lorde-Rollins, telephone conversation, 9 April 1996.

6 Audre Lorde, personal interviews, 1990–91.

7 Lorde-Rollins interview, 24 November 1995.

8 Edwin Rollins, personal interview, 9 December 1995.

9 Martha Einson, telephone interview, 22 March 1999.

10 Elizabeth Lorde-Rollins, telephone interview, 21 March 1999.

11 Ed Rollins had been working for the local campaign on his own. He'd met Margie Gumpert in 1960, and his friendship with her grew along with their mutual political work. Both were part of a generational split in the Democratic Party in which old guard Democrats favored nominating Senator Lyndon B. Johnson and many younger Democrats supported the more youthful, charismatic John F. Kennedy. As they saw it, Kennedy had the potential to usher in a new Amer-

ica—one different from that defined by Eisenhower's eight years of Republican leadership, or by Johnson, who was a Texan with close ties to the South.

12 Lorde-Rollins interview, 21 March 1999.

13 Einson interview, 22 March 1999.

14 Cook interview, 24 June 1998; also Audre Lorde, personal interviews, 1990–91.

15 Elizabeth Lorde-Rollins, personal interview, 21 March 1999. While initially agreeing, Yolanda Rios later declined repeated efforts to interview her. This made it necessary to construct the details of her relationship with Lorde from secondary sources, including Lorde's daughter Elizabeth, and her ex-husband, Ed Rollins.

16 Audre Lorde, personal interviews, 1990–91.

17 Edwin Rollins interview, 10 April 1996.

18 Lorde-Rollins interview, 21 March 1999.

19 Einson interview, 22 March 1999.

20 Lorde-Rollins interview, 21 March 1999.

21 Audre Lorde, personal interviews, 1990–91.

22 Ibid.

23 Ibid.

24 Ibid.

25 Ibid.

26 Zinn, *A People's History of the United States*, 444–45.

27 Edwin Rollins, personal interview, 10 December 1995.

28 Clare Coss, personal interview, 24 June 1998.

29 Cook interview, 24 June 1998.

30 Neal and Martha Einson, personal interview, 8 May 1996.

31 Rollins interview, 10 December 1995.

32 Ibid..

33 Edwin Rollins, letter to Audre Lorde, 10 November 1961.

34 Paul R. Spickard, *Mixed Blood: Intermarriage and Ethnic Identity in Twentieth Century America* (Madison: University of Wisconsin Press, 1989), 278–79.

35 Rollins interview, 10 December 1995.

36 Edwin Rollins, letter to Audre Lorde, 10 November 1961.

37 Rollins interview, 9 December 1995.

38 Ibid.

39 Audre Lorde, personal interviews, 1990–91.

40 Ibid.

41 Rollins interview, 9 December 1995.

42 Audre Lorde, personal interviews, 1990–91.

43 Rollins interview, 10 December 1995.

44 Einsons interview, 8 May 1996.

45 Rollins interview, 10 December 1995.

46 Rosey E. Pool, ed., *Beyond the Blues: New Poems by American Negroes* (Lympne, UK: Hand and Flower Press, 1962).

47 This version also appears in Lorde's first collection, *The First Cities* (New York: The Poets Press, 1968).

48 Audre Lorde, *Coal* (New York: W. W. Norton, 1976), 4–5.

49 Audre Lorde, personal interviews, 1990–91.

50 Neal Einson interview, 8 May 1996.

51 Lorde, *The First Cities.*

52 They are "Oaxaca," "To a Girl Who Knew What Side Her Bread Was Buttered On," "Nymph," "How Can I Love," "Suspension," "Moon minded the sun . . . ," "Father, Son and Holy Ghost," and "Father, the Year . . ."

53 Paul Breman, Preface to *Sixes and Sevens: An Anthology of New Poetry* (London: Paul Breman Ltd, 1962), 6–8.

54 Ibid., 40.

55 Kohl, "Blanche Cook," 126–27.

56 Coss interview, 24 June 1998.

57 Audre Lorde, personal interviews, 1990–91.

58 Elaine Shelly, "Conceptualizing Images of Multiple Selves in the Poetry of Audre Lorde," *Lesbian Ethics* (Winter 1995): 88–98. I thank Professor Bahati Monica Kuumba, formerly of Buffalo, New York, and now at Spelman College, for her careful reading of Elaine Shelly's article.

59 Audre G. Lorde, "Suffer the Children," *Negro Digest*, 10:3 (1964): 15.

60 Faith Berry, *Langston Hughes: Before and Beyond Harlem* (Westport, CT: Lawrence Hill & Co., 1983) 322.

61 Hughes actually began soliciting materials from Lorde for the anthology in 1960, according to three letters he wrote to her between April 1960 and October 1960. As his letters suggest, the publishing process was a slow one, and the original manuscript was edited several times. In one version, Lorde's poems were edited out—Audre Lorde Papers.

62 Sandler interview, 7 October 1995. Sandler remembered the letter and its contents, although she was no longer sure she possessed it.

63 Baharas interview, 29 March 1998.

64 Jonathan dropped "Lorde" from his name when he enlisted in the U.S. Navy in the mid-1980s, as it was not the name on his birth certificate. According to Gloria Joseph, Lorde was deeply hurt by this. In a will, dated 20 November 1991 (which was not her last will), Lorde stipulated, in part, that in the event of death while her estate was still producing income, "If Jonathan Rollins reassumes my name, then his share shall descend to his heirs per stirpes. If he does not reassume my name, then upon his death his share shall go to his sister, Elizabeth Lorde-Rollins, if alive, or otherwise descend to her heirs per stirpes."

65 Gwendolyn Brooks, Foreword to Langston Hughes, ed., *New Negro Poets, USA* (Bloomington: University of Indiana Press, 1964), 13–15.

66 Audre Lorde, "And Fall Shall Sit in Judgment," *New Negro Poets, USA*, 20.

67 Audre Lorde, "Pirouette," *New Negro Poets, USA*, 106.

68 Adrienne Rich, in documentary, *A Litany for Survival: The Life and Work of Audre Lorde*.

69 See Audre Lorde, *Coal*, and Audre Lorde, *Chosen Poems: Old and New* (New York: W. W. Norton, 1982).

Chapter 6

1 Lorde-Rollins interview, 24 November 1995.

2 Lorde-Rollins interview, 21 March 1999.

3 Unpublished journal, 5 March 1974–13 June 1974.

4 Lorde-Rollins interview, 21 March 1999.

5 Unpublished journal, 5 March 1974–13 June 1974.

6 Audre Lorde, personal interviews, 1990–91.

7 Ibid.

8 Lorde-Rollins interview, 21 March 1999.

9 Edwin Rollins, personal interview, 10 April 1996.

10 Unpublished journal referencing the year 1972. In the original, untitled draft of what became the poem "Journeystones I–XI" (which was later published in *The Black Unicorn*), Lorde began section VII of the poem with "Dear Yolanda;" reinventing Yolanda as "Isabel" in the draft and final version. In the poem Lorde expressed the confusion she felt having to grapple with Yolanda's needs.

11 See Larry Neal, "The Black Arts Movement," in Addison Gayle, Jr., ed., *The Black Aesthetic* (New York: Doubleday, 1971), 272–90.

12 Don L. Lee, Introduction to Woodie King, ed., *Black Spirits: A Festival of New Black Poets in America* (New York: Vintage Books, 1972), xxv–vii.

13 Hoyt W. Fuller, Introduction to Gayle, ed., *The Black Aesthetic*, 3–12.

14 Charles L. James, "Gwendolyn Brooks," *Contemporary Poets*, 5th ed. (Detroit: St. James Press, 1991), 102–04.

15 Ibid., 104.

16 Lorde-Rollins interview, 24 November 1995.

17 Diane di Prima interview, 25 October 1997.

18 Gretchen H. Munroe, "Diane Di Prima," *Dictionary of Literary Biography*, vol. 5. (Detroit: Gale, 1980), 202–05.

19 Ibid., 202.

20 While later rejecting his own avant-garde poetry as that of a pre-black-consciousness period, Jones was deeply attracted to the bohemian lifestyle of the predominantly white countercultural community of the East Village, and was a

well-known fixture at coffeehouses and clubs. Between 1958 and 1962, Jones and his first wife, Hettie Roberta Cohen, co-edited the offbeat literary magazine *Yugen*. Although the magazine appeared irregularly, it featured the work of New York Beat poets such as Allen Ginsberg, Gregory Corso, and di Prima, as well as the black poet A. B. Spelman. The relationship between Diane di Prima and LeRoi Jones was both literary and personal. See Floyd Gaffney, "Amira Baraka (LeRoi Jones)," *Dictionary of Literary Biography*, vol. 38 (Detroit: Gale, 1985), 22–41.

21 Rich, "An Interview with Audre Lorde," 719–20.

22 Ibid., 720.

23 Ibid., 721.

24 Audre Lorde, personal interviews, 1990–91.

25 Juan Williams, *Eyes on the Prize: America's Civil Rights Years, 1954–1965* (New York: Viking/Penguin, 1987), 60–63.

26 Lorde-Rollins interview, 21 March 1999.

27 Ibid.

28 Ibid.

29 Ibid.

30 Audre Lorde, personal interviews, 1990–91.

31 Rich, "An Interview with Audre Lorde," 723.

32 Lorde-Rollins interview, 24 November 1995.

33 Unpublished journal, 1968.

34 Edwin Rollins interview, 9 April 1996.

35 Audre Lorde, personal interviews, 1990–91.

36 Rich, "An Interview with Audre Lorde," 723.

37 Dudley Randall, "White Poet, Black Critic," *Negro Digest*, 14 (1965): 46–48; "Ubi Sunt and Hic Sum," *Negro Digest*, 14 (1965): 73–76.

38 See Baxter R. Miller, "Dudley Randall," *Dictionary of Literary Biography*, vol. 41 (Detroit: Gale, 1985), 266–73.

39 Dudley Randall, *Negro Digest*: 17 (1968): 13.

40 Audre Lorde, personal interviews, 1990–91. According to Lorde, Rollins changed his initial position on the war in Vietnam after they separated.

41 An acronym for Search for Education, Elevation and Knowledge, SEEK was a pre-baccalaureate program instituted by the City University of New York. During the 1960s and 1970s, its aim was to identify and assist urban students whose high school educational records did not indicate true academic potential.

42 Audre Lorde, "Martha," *Cables to rage* (London: Paul Breman Ltd., 1970), 14.

43 Lorde-Rollins interview, 21 March 1999.

44 Lorde-Rollins interview, 24 November 1995.

45 June Jordan, telephone interview, 23 August 1997.

46 Rich, "An Interview with Audre Lorde," 724.

47 This version originally appeared in *Cables to rage*. It was revised when Lorde included it in *Chosen Poems: Old and New*.

48 Adrienne Rich, personal interview, 17 July 1998.

49 Anne Newman, "Adrienne Rich," *Dictionary of Literary Biography*, vol. 5 (Detroit: Gale, 1980), 184–88.

50 Elizabeth Meese, "Adrienne Rich," *Dictionary of Literary Biography*, vol. 67 (Detroit: Gale, 1988), 232–40.

51 Ibid., 233.

52 Rich interview, 17 July 1998.

53 di Prima interview, 25 October 1997.

54 Jordan interview, 23 August 1997.

55 Ibid.

56 Ibid.

57 Lorde-Rollins interview, 24 November 1995.

58 Audre Lorde, personal interviews, 1990–91.

Part Three
Chapter 7

1 Audre Lorde, "Uses of the Erotic: The Erotic as Power," in *Sister Outsider*, 53.

2 Ibid., 58.

3 Unpublished journal, 7 November 1972.

4 Unpublished journal, 5 and 6 January 1970.

5 Rich, "An Interview with Audre Lorde," 725.

6 Unpublished journal, 4 May 1970, and undated class notes.

7 Unpublished journal, 14 October 1969.

8 Rich, "An Interview with Audre Lorde," 725.

9 Edwin Rollins interview, 9 April 1996.

10 Angela Bowen, "Who Said It Was Simple: Audre Lorde's Complex Connections to Three U.S. Liberation Movements, 1952–1992," unpublished dissertation, Clark University, 1997.

11 Gloria Joseph, audiotape to the author, 19 May 1999.

12 Audre Lorde, "After a first book," *Cables to rage*, 9.

13 Mike Doyle, "Made in Canada," *Poetry*, 69:6 (1972): 357.

14 Ibid., 356–57.

15 Ibid., 361.

16 Statement of the editors, "A Portfolio of Poetry," *Negro Digest*, 17: 11–12 (1968): 53.

17 Audre Lorde, "Naturally," *Negro Digest*, 17: 11–12 (1968): 71.

18 Rich, "An Interview with Audre Lorde," 726.

19 Unpublished journal, undated class notes, 1972.

20 Handwritten pages, 26 November 1970, 1.

21 Handwritten pages, 26 November 1970, 2.

22 Ibid.

23 Handwritten pages, 26 November 1970, 1.

24 Handwritten pages, 26 November 1970, 1–2.

25 Handwritten pages, 26 November 1970, 2.

26 Ibid.

27 Handwritten pages, 14 December 1970, 1.

28 Handwritten pages, 14 December 1970, 1–2.

29 Handwritten pages, 14 December 1970, 3.

30 Handwritten pages, 14 December 1970, 4.

31 An outgrowth of the civil rights struggle and campus unrest bridging the decades of the sixties and seventies, the demand for black studies programs and departments ushered in one of the most significant reform movements in higher education. The Black Studies movement was led by black students, faculty, and community leaders and confronted the absence or distortion of African American experiences in higher education curricula. Initially, the movement called for the hiring of black faculty and staff; the creation of black programs; increased enrollment opportunities for black students and financial aid to support them; and black history courses. As the movement matured, the demand for courses focused on a more comprehensive demand for interdisciplinary offerings with black history at their center. The Black Studies movement gave increased visibility to black male scholars and scholarship produced by them, little of which critically addressed the ways in which race, gender, and sexual oppression impact black women. See Delores P. Aldridge, "Black Studies," in *Black Women in America: An Historical Encyclopedia*, ed. Darlene Clark Hine, 2 vols. (New York: Carlson, 1993), 136–37.

32 Lorde-Rollins interview, 24 November 1995.

33 Ibid.

34 Audre Lorde, personal interviews, 1990–91.

35 Audre Lorde, "Who Said It Was Simple," *Woman: A Journal of Liberation*, 2:3 (1971): 13.

36 Rich interview, 17 July 1998.

37 Lorde, *Zami*, 226.

38 See Alexander, "Coming Out Blackened and Whole," 695–715.

39 Ultimately, the desires of a white, middle-class heterosexual majority helped shape the movement as reformist in nature. Even as it sought change in the status of women, the feminist movement lacked an analysis of the relation of capitalism to patriarchy, of racism to both capitalism and patriarchy, and of multiple oppressions affecting the lives of women who were not white, middle-class, or heterosexual. Those analyses were asserted by women like Frances Beale, Florence Kennedy, Barbara Smith, Audre Lorde, and other blacks—lesbian and heterosexual—who questioned notions of "universal sisterhood" based solely on demands for gender equity.

40 Lorde-Rollins interview, 24 November 1995.

41 Audre Lorde, personal interviews, 1990–91; also, Lorde-Rollins interview, 24 November 1995.

42 Ibid.

43 I am indebted to a telephone interview with Michelle Cliff, 23 November 1998. While discussing her novel *Free Enterprise* (1993), Cliff spoke of the "unofficial record" as a counternarrative to the "official record," which often deletes or denies the centrality of black women to historic events. I am extending Cliff's point to include women of other racial/ethnic groups, and the significance of women's social and working relations with each other. The official record of Clayton's academic career as a behavioral scientist is a brief entry in *American Men and Women in Science*. Yet Clayton reinvented herself as a psychotherapist who helped many other women.

44 Lorde-Rollins interview, 24 November 1995.

45 Hammond, "Audre Lorde: Interview," 22.

46 Cliff and Rich interview, 18 July 1998.

47 Cliff interview, 18 July 1998.

48 Unpublished journal, 7 November 1972.

49 A number of white feminists did theorize about the biological and cultural meanings of the centrality of motherhood to women's lives. By the end of the decade, feminist analyses shaped several significant publications. See Linda Gordon, *Woman's Body, Woman's Right: A Social History of Birth Control in America* (New York: Grossman, 1976); Adrienne Rich, *Of Woman Born: Motherhood as Experience and Institution* (New York: W. W. Norton, 1976); and Nancy Chodorow, *The Reproduction of Mothering: Psychoanalysis and the Sociology of Gender* (Berkeley: University of California Press, 1978).

50 Adrienne Rich, interview with Alexis De Veaux, *Spoken Words*, WBFO, Buffalo, 30 March 1998.

51 Rich interview, 17 July 1998.

52 Lorde-Rollins, telephone conversation with author, undated notes.

53 Cook interview, 24 June 1998.

54 Huey P. Newton, chairman of the Black Panther Party, once deviated from the prevailing rhetoric. At the party's Philadelphia convention in the summer of 1970, Newton called upon black Americans to view the struggles for gay liberation and women's liberation as the struggles of allies and friends, asserting the necessity for coalition building with other radical movements beyond racial identification. See Neil Schlager, ed., *St. James Press Gay and Lesbian Almanac* (Detroit: Gale, 1996), 281.

55 Bayard Rustin's homosexuality was often used as a weapon against Martin Luther King, Jr., by white opponents of the civil rights movement and by some black leaders—including New York congressman Adam Clayton Powell, Jr. Before the 1963 March on Washington, civil rights leaders debated whether or not Rustin should be allowed to continue his public work with the organizing committee. King and A. Phillip Randolph were in support but blacks were con-

flicted. As some saw it, the movement could ill afford to lose numbers of supporters if it appeared to openly condone homosexuality; and yet it relied on the
commitment of Rustin and other known homosexuals, whose energies and leadership infused the movement without drawing attention to themselves, or to the
hidden homosexual communities of the South. Rustin did not publicly admit to
being homosexual until 1983. See "Local and Regional Views," *St. James Press
Gay and Lesbian Almanac*, 631–47, and Lou Chibarro, "Civil Rights Activist
Rustin to Speak," *Washington Blade*, 11 October 1985: 1.

56 During the Harlem Renaissance, for example, the lesbian entertainer
Gladys Bentley became a cult figure in Harlem clubs and night spots. Bentley
was famous for her on-stage and off-stage penchant for wearing men's clothing.
Though the more repressive late 1940s and 1950s forced her to deny her lesbianism in order to work, and she never regained her earlier fame, Bentley's cross-
dressing, gender-bending presentation made her one of the first black drag
kings. See Kathleen Thompson, "Gladys Bentley," *Black Women in America: An
Historical Encyclopedia*, 110.

57 Audre Lorde, "Love Poem," 1971.

58 Rich, "An Interview with Audre Lorde," 727.

59 Joan Larkin, "Frontiers of Language: Three Poets," *Ms.* (1974): 38–40. See
also *Choice* (July–August 1974): 755.

60 Kalamu ya Salaam, "Sonia Sanchez," *Dictionary of Literary Biography*, vol.
41 (Detroit: Gale, 1985), 295–306.

61 Sonia Sanchez, telephone interview, 13 July 1999.

62 Sonia Sanchez, in documentary, *A Litany for Survival: The Life and Work
of Audre Lorde*.

63 Sanchez interview, 13 July 1999.

64 Copy of Statement, Audre Lorde Papers.

65 Miller, "Dudley Randall," 268.

66 Unpublished journal, 1972–73.

67 Ibid.

68 Handwritten pages, Thursday, 19 April 1973.

69 Handwritten pages. Lorde dated this "Friday April 4/21" (the actual date
was 20 April).

70 Ibid.

71 Handwritten pages, Saturday, 21.

72 Handwritten pages, Sunday.

73 Handwritten pages, Thursday.

74 Rich interview, 17 July 1998.

75 Rich, "An Interview with Audre Lorde," 728.

76 Rich interview, 17 July 1998.

77 Ibid.

78 In the mid-1970s, many lesbian and gay academics began to organize against the sexual discrimination that excluded lesbian and gay realities from higher education curricula and silenced them as homosexuals. According to Blanche Wiesen Cook, who also taught at John Jay, Lorde may not have been at the first meeting of the Gay Academic Union at John Jay, but she became affiliated with it. The Union's formation in 1974 helped to reshape the emotional arena in which Lorde and other lesbian and gay faculty at John Jay College worked; most of them had not been out before.

79 Audre Lorde, "Blackstudies," *New York Head Shop and Museum* (Detroit: Broadside Press, 1974), 52–56.

80 Audre Lorde, "A Sewer Plant Grows in Harlem Or I'm A Stranger Here Myself When Does the Next Swan Leave," *New York Head Shop and Museum*, 9.

81 Lorde, "Blackstudies," *New York Head Shop*, 55.

82 Lorde, "New York City 1970," *New York Head Shop*, 1.

83 Lorde-Rollins interview, 24 November 1995.

84 Unpublished journal, 13 July 1974.

85 Unpublished journal, 15 July 1974.

86 Telegram from Audre Lorde to Helen Lorde, Lome, West Togo, 15 July 1974.

87 Unpublished journal, 15 July 1974.

88 Unpublished journal, 18 July 1974.

89 Unpublished journal, 15 July 1974.

90 Unpublished journal, 17 July 1974.

91 Unpublished journal, 18 July 1974.

92 John Picton and John Mack, *African Textiles* (New York: Harper & Row, 1989), 165–66.

93 Lorde-Rollins interview, 24 November 1995.

94 The ideological architect of what became known as the civil rights movement in America, Du Bois had chosen to leave America, living out his last years in Ghana. He died in Accra on 27 August 1963, one day before the famed March on Washington. For more on Du Bois's later life, see David Levering Lewis, *W. E. B. DuBois: The Fight for Equality and the American Century, 1919–1963* (New York: Henry Holt, 2000).

95 Ibid., 8.

96 Unpublished journal, undated notes written on page opposite entry dated 2 August 1974.

97 Jonathan's journal, Friday, 2 August 1974. Audre Lorde Papers.

98 Lorde-Rollins interview, 24 November 1995.

99 Unpublished journal, Friday, 2 August 1974.

100 Unpublished journal, Wednesday, 24 July 1974.

101 Unpublished journal, Wednesday, 31 July 1974.

102 Unpublished journal, Wednesday, 24 July 1974.

103 Jonathan's journal, Monday, 22 July 1974, 9. Audre Lorde Papers.

104 Basil Davidson, *Africa in History*. Rev. ed. (New York: Macmillan, 1991), 215.

105 Robert Farris Thompson, *Flash of the Spirit: African and Afro-American Art and Philosophy* (New York: Vintage Books, 1983), 176.

106 Ibid., 164.

107 Ibid., 167.

Chapter 8

1 Audre Lorde. "New York City 1970," *New York Head Shop*, 1.

2 Unpublished journal, undated entry, 1974–75.

3 Jonathan Rollins, telephone interview, 28 August 1999.

4 Unpublished journal, undated entry, 1974–75.

5 Audre Lorde, "School Note," *Between Our Selves* (Point Reyes, CA: Eidolon Editions, 1976), 4–5.

6 Audre Lorde, "125th Street and Abomey," *The Black Unicorn* (New York: W. W. Norton, 1978), 12–13.

7 Judgment of Divorce, Part 5A, New York State Supreme Court. County Courthouse, 21 March 1975.

8 Lorde's name appeared as Audre Lorde on the covers and title pages of her first two books, but on the copyright pages of her second two collections the work was copyrighted as Audre Lorde Rollins.

9 Non-archived papers, dated 4/75.

10 Charlotte Sheedy, telephone interview, 15 June 1999.

11 Ibid.

12 Ibid.

13 Lorde, dedication, *Between Our Selves*.

14 Ibid., 6–8.

15 Unpublished journal, undated entry, 1975–76.

16 Lorde, *Between Our Selves*, 15.

17 According to accounts in *The New York Times* (30 April 1973–13 June 1974), Clifford was accompanying his stepfather, Add Armstead, to Armstead's job at the Pilot Automotive Wrecking Company yard, 112th Avenue and New York Boulevard, just blocks from their home. Officer Shea and his partner, Walter Scott, responded to a report of a robbery of a taxi driver by two black men an hour earlier. The driver described the two men he'd picked up as passengers as both approximately twenty-four, about 6 feet tall, one weighing 155 and the other 180 pounds. The policemen claimed they stopped Clifford and his step-

father because they resembled the description of the hold-up suspects. Clifford Glover, at ten, was 4 feet 11 and weighed 90 pounds. Initially, the officers maintained that after they identified themselves, Clifford aimed a gun at them, then gave it to his stepfather as the two suspects fled. Shea fired three shots, striking Clifford once in the right shoulder and once in the chest. The boy died an hour later at a Queens hospital. His stepfather asserted the officers had not identified themselves, were verbally abusive, and that he and Clifford ran away out of fear of the two white men.

18 Rich, "An Interview with Audre Lorde," 734.

19 Laurie Johnston, "Jury Clears Shea in Killing of Boy," *New York Times*, 13 June 1974.

20 Audre Lorde, "Power," *Between Our Selves*, 2.

21 Sheedy interview, 15 June 1999.

22 Ibid.

23 Unpublished journal, 4 January 1976.

24 Unpublished journal, 1 January 1976.

25 Jonathan Rollins interview, 28 August 1999.

26 Sheedy interview, 15 June 1999.

27 Ibid.

28 Audre Lorde, "Notes from a Trip to Russia," in *Sister Outsider*, 14.

29 Unpublished journal, undated entry, 1976–77.

30 See David Magarshack, *Pushkin: A Biography* (New York: Grove Press, 1969). Pushkin's maternal great-grandfather was Abraham Petrovich Hannibal, also known as "The Negro of Peter the Great." The fact that Pushkin—who had kinky hair, dark skin, and full lips—was of African ancestry was so well known in Russia, it was taken for granted. Pushkin took his ancestry seriously, referred to it often, and felt his African blood gave him a unique position in Russian society. Even so, he suffered a complex about his looks and just as often remarked upon his ugly, Negroid features. See J. A. Rogers, *World's Great Men of Color*, vol. II (New York: Collier, 1972), 79, and E. J. Simmons and Samuel Cross, eds., *Centennial Essays for Pushkin* (Cambridge: Harvard University Press, 1937).

31 Unpublished journal, Monday night, 1976.

32 Unpublished journal, 28 Tuesday?, 1976.

33 Unpublished journal, Wednesday, 1976.

Chapter 9

1 Bowen, unpublished dissertation, 144.

2 Ekua Omosupe, "Pat Parker, African-American Poet," *Gay and Lesbian Biography*, 353–54.

3 Pat Parker, *WomanSlaughter* (San Francisco: Diana Press, 1978), 53–54.

4 Omosupe, "Pat Parker," 353.

5 Bowen, unpublished dissertation, 145.

6 Pat Parker, "For Audre," *Movement in Black* (New York: Firebrand Books, 1999), 201–03. Originally published by Diana Press in San Francisco in 1978, *Movement in Black* was reissued in 1983 under The Crossing Press Feminist Series imprint. It was published for a third time by Firebrand Books shortly after Parker's death.

7 Audre Lorde, letter to Pat Parker—though undated, the contents approximate a time frame between 1974 and 1975. Audre Lorde Papers.

8 Audre Lorde, letter to Pat Parker, 16 February 1983. Audre Lorde Papers.

9 I am indebted to Nancy K. Bereano, publisher of Firebrand Books, for releasing copies of these letters to me. The originals were sent to Bereano as she prepared to publish the expanded edition of *Movement in Black*. Of course, Parker's letters in response would certainly flesh out the contours of the friendship. However, Parker's letters are the private property of her estate.

10 Audre Lorde, letter to Pat Parker, 1974–75. Audre Lorde Papers.

11 Audre Lorde, letter to Pat Parker, 12 October 1974. Audre Lorde Papers.

12 Bowen, unpublished dissertation, 145.

13 Unpublished journal, 7 November 1976.

14 Alex Poinsett, "FESTAC '77," *EBONY*, 32 (1977): 33ff.

15 Unpublished journal, 13 January 1977.

16 Valerie Maynard, telephone interview, 17 July 1999.

17 Ife Enohoro, "The Second World Black and African Festival of Arts and Culture: Lagos, Nigeria," *The Black Scholar: Journal of Black Studies and Research*, 9:1 (1977): 27–33.

18 Poinsett, "FESTAC '77," 35.

19 Maynard interview, 17 July 1999.

20 Unpublished journal, 1 February 1977.

21 Unpublished journal, undated entry, 1977.

22 Ibid.

23 Unpublished journal, 18 January 1977.

24 Unpublished journal, undated entry.

25 Cedric Dover, *American Negro Art* (Greenwich, CT: New York Graphic Society, 1960), 31.

26 Joanne Harris, "Thompson, Mildred, American sculptor, painter, and printmaker," in Thomas Riggs, ed., *St. James Guide to Black Artists* (Detroit: Gale, 1997), 525.

27 Unpublished journal, 25 January 1977.

28 Audre Lorde Collection, Lesbian Herstory Archives, Brooklyn, NY. The four poems were "Time piece," "Fog Report," "Recreation," and "Ghost."

29 Maynard interview, 16 July 1999.

30 Sheedy interview, 15 June 1999.

31 Unpublished journal, undated entry,

32 Audre Lorde, letter to Kirsten Grimstad and Susan Rennie, 5 December 1976. Audre Lorde Papers.

33 June Jordan, "Poem About My Rights," *Passion: New Poems, 1977–1980* (Boston: Beacon Press, 1980), 86–89.

34 Alexis De Veaux, "June Jordan: Creating Soul Food," *Essence* magazine (April 1981): 68ff.

35 Jordan interview, 23 August 1997.

36 Sheedy interview, 15 June 1999.

37 Unpublished journal, letter to June Jordan, 23 March 1977.

38 Jordan interview, 23 August 1997.

39 June Jordan, "I Must Become a Menace to My Enemies" and "MetaRhetoric," *Chrysalis: A Magazine of Woman's Culture*, 3 (1977): 62–63.

40 Michelle Cliff, personal interview, 17 July 1998.

41 I am indebted to my colleague, Professor Judy Scales-Trent, School of Law, State University of New York at Buffalo, for her insightful book, *Notes of a White Black Woman* (Philadelphia: Pennsylvania University Press, 1995).

42 Michelle Cliff, "If I Could Write This in Fire I Would Write This in Fire," in Barbara Smith, ed., *Home Girls: A Black Feminist Anthology* (New York: Kitchen Table: Women of Color Press, 1983), 15–30.

43 Cliff interview, 17 July 1998.

44 It was published by Out & Out Books, Brooklyn, NY, in 1977.

45 Cliff interview, 18 July 1998.

46 Audre Lorde, letter to Michelle Cliff, 3 October 1979.

47 Ibid.

48 Cliff interview, 18 July 1998.

49 Unpublished journal, 20 February 1979.

50 Barbara Smith, Introduction, *Home Girls*, xix–lvi.

51 Smith, "Home," *Home Girls*, 68.

52 Smith, Introduction, *Home Girls*, xx.

53 Jerome Szymczak, "Barbara Smith, African-American writer and activist," *Gay and Lesbian Biography*, 409–10.

54 Barbara Smith, "Toward a Black Feminist Literary Criticism," in Gloria T. Hull, Patricia Bell-Scott, and Barbara Smith, eds., *All the Women Are White, All the Blacks Are Men, But Some of Us Are Brave* (Old Westbury, NY: Feminist Press, 1982), 157–75.

55 Lorde was poetry editor for *Amazon Quarterly* during a brief stint between 1974 and 1975. Published out of Oakland, CA, and Somerville, MA, it was in existence from fall 1972 until March 1975. In its short life, *Amazon Quarterly* strove to provide publishing opportunities for a number of women and les-

bians, most of whom were white. Lorde's brief stint as poetry editor was marred by friction with the publishers. Given the brevity of that experience, and its overall insignificance compared to other events in Lorde's life during the same period, I chose not to treat with it here.

56 Barbara Smith, telephone interview, 11 June 1999.

57 Ibid.

58 Audre Lorde in *A Litany for Survival: The Life and Work of Audre Lorde*.

59 Smith interview, 11 June 1999.

60 For oral histories of some retreat participants and more comprehensive analyses of both the Combahee River Collective and these black feminist retreats, see Duchess Harris interview, "All of Who I Am in the Same Place: The Combahee River Collective Retreats," *Womanist Theory and Research*, 2:1 (1999): 9–21.

61 Smith interview, 11 June 1999.

62 Unpublished journal, 11 November 1977.

63 Unpublished journal, 12 November 1977.

64 Unpublished journal, 15 November 1977.

65 An excerpt from Clare Coss's poetic journal, *Daughter of Alistene Melpomene Thalia: A Play Within a Play*. See *Chrysalis*, 5 (1978): 59–69.

66 Unpublished journal, 17 November 1977.

67 Ibid.

68 Unpublished journal, 1 December 1977.

69 First published in *Chrysalis*, 7 (1979): 9–27.

70 Rich, "An Interview with Audre Lorde," 735.

71 First published in *Sinister Wisdom*, 6 (1978): 11–15.

The Second Life
Part One
Chapter 10

1 Unpublished journal, 1 January 1978.

2 Barbara Smith, letter to Audre Lorde, 10 January 1978. Audre Lorde Papers.

3 Audre Lorde in *A Litany for Survival: The Life and Work of Audre Lorde*.

4 Unpublished journal, 30 December 1977.

5 Unpublished journal, 11 January 1978.

6 Ibid.

7 Unpublished journal, 27 July 1977.

8 Lorde, *Zami*, 78.

9 Audre Lorde, "My Mother's Mortar," *Sinister Wisdom*, 8 (1977): 54–61. My Mother's Mortar" was not the first work of fiction Lorde published. Back in

1956, her short story, "La Llorona," appeared under the pseudonym Rey Domini, in a small magazine, *Venture*. Essentially a story about the relationship with her mother, it is based on a legend Lorde heard in Mexico: La Llorona was a haunting riverwoman who was fertile, poor, breathtakingly beautiful, rich in soul and spirit. But she kills her three sons in retaliation for her husband's adulterous behavior. Lorde's short story reinterpreted the legend to address a mother figure who "killed" the spirit of her children not out of a sense of evil, but out of a sense of wanting her own life and having lived a distorted one.

10 Nancy Bereano, Introduction to *Sister Outsider*, 7–11.

11 Unpublished journal, 13 February 1978.

12 Ibid.

13 Audre Lorde, letter to Adrienne Rich, ca. 1978. Though this letter is undated, Rich catalogued it as one she received in 1978. The full text corroborates this time frame.

14 Unpublished journal, undated entry, 1978.

15 Hammond, "Audre Lorde: Interview," 14.

16 Ibid., 15.

17 Unpublished journal, 17 July 1978.

18 Ibid.

19 Unpublished journal, undated entry, 1978.

20 Audre Lorde, "Man Child: A Black Lesbian Feminist's Response," *Conditions: Four*, 2:1 (1979): 30–36. The essay was revised when it was later published in *Sister Outsider*—see *Sister Outsider*, 72–80.

21 Unpublished journal, 17 July 1978.

22 Lorde, *Conditions: Four*, 33.

23 Unpublished journal, 17 July 1978.

24 Jonathan Rollins in *A Litany for Survival: The Life and Work of Audre Lorde*.

25 Audre Lorde in ibid.

26 When Lorde included this essay in *Sister Outsider*, she extended her initial perspectives to include significant anecdotal remarks on black men she'd met by the mid-1980s who were gay or raising families or with whom she felt she shared strategies for survival as black people.

27 Audre Lorde, "Scratching the Surface: Some Notes on Barriers to Women and Loving," *The Black Scholar: Journal of Black Studies and Research*, 9:7 (1978): 33–35.

28 Unpublished journal, 17 February 1978.

29 Lorde, "Scratching the Surface," *The Black Scholar*, 33–34.

30 Unpublished journal, 18 February 1978.

31 Lorde, "A Litany for Survival," *The Black Unicorn*, 31–32.

32 Unpublished journal, 30 April 1977.

398 • *Notes to pages 207–14*

33 Lorde, *The Black Unicorn*, 32.

34 Unpublished journal, 10 May 1978.

35 Audre Lorde, "Of Sisters and Secrets," in Margaret Cruikshank, ed., *The Lesbian Path* (Monterey, CA: Angel Press, 1980), 186–95.

36 Unpublished journal, 24 February 1978.

37 Unpublished journal, 7 March 1978.

38 The *I Ching* affirms, rather than abandons, individual agency, offering advice on how to face the future in the best possible manner. It also acts as a guide to the mysteries of the unconscious self by shedding light "on the hidden world behind appearances." See Alfred Douglas, *How to Consult the I Ching* (New York: Berkley Medallion Books, 1971), 133–35.

39 Unpublished journal, 18 March 1978.

40 Unpublished journal, undated entry following entry dated 21 March 1978.

41 Unpublished journal, 18 March 1978.

42 Ibid.

43 Ibid.

44 Unpublished journal, 21 March 1978.

45 Unpublished journal, entry dated "Tuesday," 1978.

46 Unpublished journal, undated entry following entry dated "Tuesday," 1978.

47 Unpublished journal, 22 March 1978.

48 Unpublished journal, undated entry following entry dated 22 March 1978.

49 Ibid.

50 Audre Lorde, letter to Kirsten Grimstad, 30 October 1977. Audre Lorde Papers.

51 Audre Lorde, letters to *Chrysalis* editors, October 1977–May 1978. Audre Lorde Papers.

52 Audre Lorde, letter to Kirsten Grimstad, 30 October 1977. Audre Lorde Papers.

53 Audre Lorde, letter to Kirsten Grimstad. 13 May 1978. Audre Lorde Papers.

54 Kirsten Grimstad, letter to Audre Lorde. 6 January 1978. Audre Lorde Papers.

55 Lorde, "Scratching the Surface," *The Black Scholar*, 33.

56 As an out black lesbian feminist, Lorde paved the way for several notable black lesbian writers to emerge after her, among them Cheryl Clarke, Jewelle Gomez, Akasha (Gloria) Hull, Kate Rushin, and Barbara Smith.

57 Rich, "An Interview with Audre Lorde, 733–34.

58 Unpublished journal, undated entry, 1977.

59 Ginny Vida, Introduction to Vida, ed., *Our Right to Love: A Lesbian Resource Book* (Englewood Cliffs, NJ: Prentice-Hall, 1978), 222.

60 Hammond, "Audre Lorde: Interview," 26.

61 Audre Lorde, letter to Kirsten Grimstad, 1 September 1978. Audre Lorde Papers.

62 Audre Lorde, letter to Adrienne Rich, ca. 1978.

63 Hammond, "Audre Lorde: Interview," 26.

64 R. B. Stepto, "The Phenomenal Woman and the Severed Daughter," *Parnassus, Poetry in Review* (Fall–Winter 1979): 312–20. Audre Lorde Papers.

65 Lorde, "From the House of Yemanjá," *The Black Unicorn*, 6.

66 Pamela Annas, "A Poetry of Survival: Unnaming and Renaming in the Poetry of Audre Lorde, Pat Parker, Sylvia Plath, and Adrienne Rich," *Colby Quarterly*, 18:1 (1982): 23–24.

67 Lorde, "The Black Unicorn," *The Black Unicorn*, 3.

68 See Geoffrey Parrinder, *African Mythology* (London: Hamlyn Publishing Group, 1967), 28, and Jan Vansina, *Art History in Africa. An Introduction to Methods* (London: Longman, 1984), 146.

69 Elsy Leuzinger, *The Art of Africa* (New York: Crown Publishers, 1960), 78–80.

70 Lorde. "A Woman Speaks," *The Black Unicorn*, 5.

71 Lorde. "Poetry Is Not a Luxury," *Sister Outsider*, 37.

72 Joan M. Martin, "The Notion of Difference for Emerging Womanist Ethics: The Writings of Audre Lorde and bell hooks," *Journal of Feminist Studies in Religion*, 9: 1–2 (1993): 39–51.

73 Andrea Benton Rushing, review of *The Black Unicorn* in *Ms.* magazine, 7:7 (1979): 43.

74 Assata Shakur escaped from prison and fled to Cuba, where she continues to live free and in exile. The late Toni Cade Bambara once characterized Shakur's autobiography, *Assata*, as a "postmodern slave narrative" because it resonates with themes found in nineteenth-century writings by many African Americans who chronicled their own coming-to-consciousness and eventual escape from bondage.

75 Lorde. "For Assata," *The Black Unicorn*, 28.

76 Lorde. "Fog Report," *The Black Unicorn*, 70.

77 *Booklist*, 75:2 (1978): 148.

78 Rochelle Ratner, *Library Journal*, 103:17 (1978): 1987.

79 *Kirkus Reviews*, 46:19 (1978): 1129.

80 *Choice*, 16:1 (1979): 80.

81 Hayden Carruth, "A Year's Poetry," *The Nation*, 227:22 (1978): 712.

82 Rushing, review in *Ms.*, 43.

83 Stepto, "The Phenomenal Woman," *Parnassus*, 316.

84 Unpublished journal, 22 July 1978.

85 Harris interview, "All of Who I Am in the Same Place," 9–21.

86 Unpublished journal, 22 July 1978.

87 Barbara Smith, letter to Audre Lorde, 23 June 1979. Audre Lorde Papers.

88 Barbara Smith, letter to retreat participants, 31 July 1979. Audre Lorde Papers.

89 Audre Lorde, letter to Adrienne Rich, ca. late July–early August 1978.

90 Audre Lorde, "Tar Beach," ed. Lorraine Bethel and Barbara Smith. Special issue of *Conditions*, 2:2 (1979): 47.

91 Unpublished journal, 18 August 1978.

92 See http://www-berks.aas.duke.edu/history.html

93 Judith Schwarz, letter to Barbara Smith, undated. Audre Lorde Papers.

94 Barbara Smith, letter to "Dear," 14 August 1978. Audre Lorde Papers.

95 Schwarz, letter to Barbara Smith, undated. Audre Lorde Papers.

96 Farah Jasmine Griffin, "Textual Healing: Claiming Black Women's Bodies, the Erotic and Resistance in Contemporary Novels of Slavery," *Callaloo*, 19:2 (1996): 519–36.

97 Lorde, "Uses of the Erotic," in *Sister Outsider*, 58.

98 Griffin, "Textual Healing," 526.

99 Audre Lorde, letter to Barbara Smith, 1 September 1978. Audre Lorde Papers.

100 Unpublished journal, 4 September 1978.

101 Unpublished journal, undated entry following entry dated 20 September 1978.

102 Lorde, *The Cancer Journals*, 33.

103 Unpublished journal, 20 September 1978.

104 Unpublished journal, undated entry following entry dated 20 September 1978.

105 Unpublished journal, 21 September 1978.

106 Unpublished journal, 22 September 1978.

107 Audre Lorde, "Breast Cancer: A Black Lesbian Feminist Experience," *Sinister Wisdom*, 10: (1979): 51.

Chapter 11

1 Unpublished journal, 22–23 December 1978.

2 Jonathan Rollins in *A Litany for Survival*.

3 Unpublished journal, 9 October 1978.

4 Kirsten Grimstad, letter to Audre Lorde, 16 October 1978. Audre Lorde Papers.

5 Audre Lorde, letter to Kirsten Grimstad, 1 September 1978. Audre Lorde Papers.

6 Kirsten Grimstad, letter to Audre Lorde, 16 October 1978. Audre Lorde Papers.

7 Audre Lorde, letter to Kirsten Grimstad, 25 November 1978. Audre Lorde Papers. *Uses of the Erotic: The Erotic as Power* was published in pamphlet format by Out & Out Books, the feminist press based in Brooklyn, NY, in October 1978.

8 Unpublished journal, 4 November 1978.

9 Rich, "An Interview with Audre Lorde," 736.

10 Unpublished journal, 11 November 1978.

11 Sheedy interview, 15 June 1999.

12 Unpublished journal, 7 November 1978.

13 Rich, "An Interview with Audre Lorde," 735–36.

14 Unpublished journal, 22–23 December 1978.

15 Unpublished journal, 11 November 1979; 10 November 1980; 9 April 1981.

16 Unpublished journal, 22–23 December 1978.

17 Audre Lorde, undated notes. Audre Lorde Papers. Lesbian Herstory Archives, Brooklyn, NY.

18 Unpublished journal, undated entry, 1978.

19 Unpublished journal, undated entry, 1979–80.

20 Unpublished journal, undated entry, 1978.

21 I am indebted to my friend and colleague, Professor Monica Jardine. Professor Jardine made this statement during a session of the conference, "You've Struck a Rock," held at Buffalo State College, Buffalo, NY, in March 2000. In explaining social movements in the Caribbean, and Caribbean women's participation, she proposed that the women's activism was shaped by ordinary realities—including labor, family ties, and patterns of migration—and that these realities were defined by Caribbean women's gendered notions of themselves as social actors.

22 Audre Lorde, undated notes. Audre Lorde Papers. Lesbian Herstory Archives, Brooklyn, NY.

23 Unpublished journal, undated entry, 1979–80.

24 Audre Lorde, interview with Gaye Williams, "A Vision of Our Past," *Sojourner, The Women's Forum*, 8:5 (1983): 15–19.

25 Unpublished journal, undated entry, 1979–80.

26 Lorde, "A Vision of Our Past," *Sojourner*, 15.

27 Ibid., 15–16.

28 Ibid., 16.

29 Unpublished journal, 1 July 1979.

30 Unpublished journal, 9 January 1979.

31 Deborah Marrow, letter to Audre Lorde, 11 January 1979. Audre Lorde Papers.

32 Audre Lorde, letter to Kirsten Grimstad, 15 January 1979. Audre Lorde Papers.

33 "The Transformation of Silence into Language and Action" was published first by *Sinister Wisdom* in Spring 1978.

34 Lorde, *The Cancer Journals*, 55–57.

35 Ibid., 64–65.

36 Audre Lorde, letter to Sue Edmiston, 31 March 1980. Audre Lorde Papers. The essay was published under the title "Warrior, Not a Victim: The Politics of Breast Cancer."

37 Unpublished journal, 3 May 1979.

38 See Hester Eisenstein, *Contemporary Feminist Thought* (Boston: G. K. Hall & Co., 1983), 107, and "Daly, Mary," in *Completely Queer. The Gay and Lesbian Encyclopedia*, ed. Steve Hogan and Lee Hudson (New York: Henry Holt, 1998), 167.

39 Rich interview, 17 July 1998.

40 "Daly, Mary," in *Completely Queer*, 167.

41 Lisa Loutzenheiser, "Mary Daly, American theologian and feminist philosopher," Tyrkus, ed., *Gay and Lesbian Biography*, 141.

42 "Daly, Mary," in *Completely Queer*, 167.

43 Eisenstein, *Contemporary Feminist Thought*, 108–15.

44 See "Daly, Mary," in *Completely Queer*, 167, and Eisenstein, *Contemporary Feminist Thought*, 108.

45 Unpublished journal, 3 May 1978.

46 Mary Daly, *Gyn/Ecology: The Metaethics of Radical Feminism* (Boston: Beacon Press, 1978), 43–72.

47 Unpublished journal, 3 May 1978.

48 Daly, *Gyn/Ecology*, 111. According to Daly, the other four atrocities perpetrated upon women and which women participated in were Chinese foot binding, European witch burnings, the Indian practice of suttee, and American gynecology.

49 Ibid., 154–55, 109-12.

50 Interestingly, nearly fifteen years later, Alice Walker and Pratibha Parmar collaborated in England on a film, *Warrior Marks* (1993), that addressed the cultural and political issues of female genital mutilation. It included interviews with women from Senegal, Burkina Faso, Gambia, the United Kingdom, and the United States. This sparked an international debate in the 1990s between Western and non-Western feminists.

51 Unpublished journal, 3 May 1978.

52 Lorde. "A Sewer Plant Grows In Harlem Or I'm A Stranger Here Myself When Does The Next Swan Leave." *New York Head Shop and Museum*, 9.

53 Unpublished journal, 3 May 1978. Daly used an excerpt from Pat Parker's poem, "there is a woman in this town," in addition to excerpts from other

women writers, at the beginning of her ninth chapter, "Sparking: The Fire of Female Friendship."

54 Unpublished journal, 3 May 1978.

55 Cover note attached to copy of Lorde's letter to Mary Daly.

56 Daly, *Gyn/Ecology*, xvi–vii.

57 Rich interview, 17 July 1998.

58 Unpublished journal, 25 August 1978.

59 Adrienne Rich, letter to Audre Lorde, 22 November 1979.

60 Rich interview, 17 July 1998.

61 Audre Lorde, letter to Kirsten Grimstad, 20 May 1979. Audre Lorde Papers.

62 Lorde, letter to Deborah Marrow, 31 May 1979. Audre Lorde Papers.

63 Jaime M. Grant, "Who's Killing Us?", in Jill Radford and Diane E. H. Russell, eds., *Femicide. The Politics of Woman Killing* (New York: Twayne Publishers, 1992), 145–60.

64 Barbara Smith, in "All of Who I Am in the Same Place: The Combahee River Collective Retreats," interview with Duchess Harris, *Womanist Theory and Research*, 2:1 (1999): 16.

65 Grant, "Who's Killing Us?", 149.

66 Harris interview, 15–16.

67 Ibid.

68 Jill Radford, Introduction to Radford and Russell, eds., *Femicide*, 3–12. According to Radford and Russell, in more recent years the issue of femicide—the killing of women by men—has been studied by feminists as a cross-cultural phenomenon, extending feminist analyses to address varying expressions of male violence.

69 Harris interview, 17.

70 Ibid.

71 Smith and Harris concur that the *Boston Globe* hardly acknowledged these murders. According to Smith's comments to Grant, there was no national media coverage.

72 Barbara Smith, letter to Audre Lorde, 26 May 1979. Audre Lorde Papers.

73 Grant, "Who's Killing Us?", 147. Combahee River Collective pamphlet, *Six Black Women, Why Did They Die?* Audre Lorde Papers.

74 Grant, "Who's Killing Us?", 149.

75 Unpublished journal, 25 June 1979.

76 Smith interview, 11 June 1999.

77 Barbara Smith and Beverly Smith, "Dear Sisters" letter to black feminist retreats participants, 31 July 1979, and Notes: Closing Discussion Fifth Black Feminist, 8 July 1979, attached to "Dear Sisters" letter. Both in Audre Lorde Papers.

78 List of indications of the growth of the black feminist movement in the year between the Fourth and Fifth Black Feminist retreats, attached to Notes from the Fifth Black Feminist Retreat. Audre Lorde Papers.

79 Smith's letter of 31 July 1979 to participants in the retreats specifically mentioned the murders of twelve black women in Boston but did not mention the one white woman Grant cites in her essay.

80 Kate Rushing, "Clearing a Space for Us," *Radical America*, 4:4 (1993): 85–88.

81 An aspiring actress who lived in Detroit and mother of a four-year-old son, Cowan auditioned for the lead role in a play, *Hammer*. While enacting a scene in which an argument ensued between a married couple, she was bludgeoned to death by the playwright; a black man who struck her repeatedly in the head, from behind, with a five-pound sledgehammer. Cowan's son, who'd accompanied his mother to the audition, witnessed the incident and was hospitalized as a result of injuries suffered in a hammering attack upon him as well. In a letter to Barbara Smith, Lorde commented on subsequent news regarding Cowan's attacker: "On June 26th he pleaded not guilty by reason of insanity but was found not able to stand trial and now is in the bin for the criminally insane." See Audre Lorde, letter to Barbara Smith, 1 September 1978. Audre Lorde Papers.

82 I am indebted to my research assistant, Shelby Crosby, for her frank discussion of the brutality surrounding these deaths, and of the further brutality engendered by the silence that made researching them difficult.

83 Lorde. "Need: A Choral of Black Women's Voices," *Chosen Poems: Old and New*, 111–15.

84 Smith interview, 17 June 1999. Barbara Deming was a noted poet, peace activist, and essayist who was known for her participation in the civil rights and peace movements between the 1960s and 1980s. In the mid-1930s, Deming had no audience for her poems about lesbians and suffered from self-hatred. Later, she found a new awareness of her own oppression and that of lesbians as a class of people. Deming died of ovarian cancer in 1984.

85 In her discussion on the sexual politics of black womanhood, Patricia Hill-Collins, a leading black sociologist, notes a significant effect of the legacy of sexual violence against black women is reflected in their absence from anti-rape movements. See Patricia Hill-Collins, *Black Feminist Thought: Knowledge, Consciousness, and the Politics of Empowerment* (Boston: Unwin Hyman, 1990), 163–79.

Chapter 12

1 Audre Lorde, letter to the Editors of *Chrysalis*, 20 July 1979. Audre Lorde Papers.

2 See Mary McAnally, "For Audre Lorde," *Chrysalis*, 8 (1979): 66.

3 Editors' statement, ibid.

4 Lorde, letter to the Editors of *Chrysalis*, 20 July 1979. Audre Lorde Papers.

5 Mary Daly, letter to Audre Lorde, 22 September 1979. Audre Lorde Papers.

6 Daly, Introduction and Preface, *Gyn/Ecology*, 19, xvi.

7 Audre Lorde, "The Master's Tools Will Never Dismantle the Master's House," in *Sister Outsider*, 112.

8 Though black feminist scholarship began to appear in the 1970s, the mid- to later 1980s saw a significant rise in the number of black female academics identifying as black feminists. Many credit the emergence of scholarship to the publication in 1982 of the anthology, *All the Women Are White, All the Blacks Are Men, But Some of Us Are Brave*, edited by Gloria T. Hull, Patricia Bell Scott, and Barbara Smith. Other developments include Alice Walker's introduction of the term "womanist" in 1983, as well as feminist writings published by Kitchen Table Press; the founding of *Sage: A Scholarly Journal on Black Women*; Barbara Christian's *Black Feminist Criticism, Perspectives on Black Women Writers* (1985); and bell hooks's *Talking Back: Thinking Feminist, Thinking Black* (1989). The 1994 conference, "Black Women in Academe," held at the Massachusetts Institute for Technology, brought together more than 2,000 participants with academic and non-academic affiliations.

9 Rich interview, 17 July 1998.

10 Audre Lorde, letter to Adrienne Rich, ca. 1979.

11 Adrienne Rich, letter to Audre Lorde, 22 November 1979.

12 Lorde, "The Master's Tools Will Never Dismantle the Master's House," in *Sister Outsider*, 110.

13 Ibid, 112.

14 See Simone de Beauvoir, *The Second Sex*, trans. H. M. Parshley (New York: Knopf, 1953; *Le Deuxième Sexe*, 1949).

15 Lorde. "The Master's Tools Will Never Dismantle the Master's House," in *Sister Outsider*, 113.

16 Jessica Benjamin, letter to Audre Lorde, 23 October 1979. Audre Lorde Papers. Seven of the eight other women for whom Benjamin spoke were Margaret Honey, her assistant; Serafina Bathrick; Kate Ellis; Carol Ascher; Muriel Dimen; Harriet Cohen, and Sara Ruddick.

17 Lorde, letter to Adrienne Rich, 1979.

18 Audre Lorde, "An Open Letter to Mary Daly," in *Sister Outsider*, 66–71. This was first published in the anthology, eds. Gibbs and Bennett, *Top Ranking: A Collection of Articles on Racism and Classism in the Lesbian Community* (New York: February 3rd Press, 1980), before Lorde included it in *Sister Outsider*.

19 Audre Lorde, "Audre Lorde: Lit from Within," *off our backs*, 12:4 (1982): 2–3.

20 Rich interview, 17 July 1998.

21 The handwritten inscription of Daly's last name is consistent with all other examples of Lorde's handwriting. See Mary Daly, letter to Audre Lorde, 22 September 1979. Audre Lorde Papers.

22 See Conference Brochure, http://www.milleniummarch.com/1979MOW brochure.html.

23 Lorde, "When Will the Ignorance End?", *off our backs*, 8. In identifying as a "black lesbian feminist warrior poet" but not "mother" during this keynote address, Lorde may have simply committed a slip of the tongue.

24 Ibid.

25 Ibid., 22.

26 Unpublished journal, 18 October 1979.

27 See "Chronology," *Gay and Lesbian Almanac*, ed. Neil Schlager (Detroit: St. James Press, 1998), 13–14. The first AIDS cases were reported in 1981, when what became the AIDS pandemic initially struck gay men in California and New York. Because these first cases seemed limited to gay men, AIDS was popularly nicknamed the "gay plague." The social conservatism of the Reagan administration shaped the general public's ignorance of the causes of AIDS, treatment and prevention strategies, and the spread of the disease in other social categories.

28 Jewelle Gomez in *A Litany for Survival*.

29 Audre Lorde in ibid.

30 Blanche Wiesen Cook in ibid.

31 Audre Lorde in ibid.

32 Patricia Jones, letter to the Editors, 12 October 1979. Audre Lorde Papers.

33 Adrienne Rich, letter to Audre Lorde, 22 November 1979.

34 Deborah Marrow, letter to Audre Lorde, 1 November 1979. Audre Lorde Papers.

35 Unpublished journal, 10 November 1979.

36 Ibid.

37 Unpublished journal, 11 November 1979. I tried several approaches to figuring out the word Lorde has at the end of this sentence. Months later, I decided to leave a blank, acknowledging that every question truly does not have an answer.

38 Unpublished journal, 13 November 1979.

39 Unpublished journal, 26 November 1979.

40 Ibid.

41 Ibid.

Chapter 13

1 Judith McDaniel, "Audre Lorde and Spinsters Ink," e-mail to the author, 12 March 2001.

2 Notes of Steering Committee, 28 February 1980, and National Association of Third World Writers (NATWW) press release, 28 April 1980. Both in Audre Lorde Papers, Spelman College, Georgia. The other endorsers included a number of writers who were critical to the organization or influential as it evolved: Wesley Brown, Ntozake Shange, Fay Chang, Imogunla Alakoye, Lois Elaine Griffith, Jessica Hagedorn, Akua Lezlie Hope, Patricia (Spears) Jones, Thulani Davis, Mbembe Milton Smith, Fatisha, Ed Bullins, William Demby, Sekou Sundiata, Lori Sharpe, Judy Simmons, and this author.

3 David Wilk and Mary MacArthur, letter to Members of the National Association of Third World Writers, 14 April 1980. Audre Lorde Papers.

4 NATWW press release, 28 July 1980. Audre Lorde Papers.

5 The writing of James Baldwin stands as an exception. An early essay, "Preservation of Innocence" (1949), which was not included in *Notes of a Native Son* (1955), addressed the notion that homosexuality was unnatural. His novel *Giovanni's Room* (1956) and later works such as *Just Above My Head* (1979) treated openly with gay sexuality. Though he had male lovers throughout his life, Baldwin resisted identifying as "gay" publicly for complex reasons. See Fred L. Standley and Louis H. Pratt, eds., *Conversations with James Baldwin* (Jackson, MS: University Press of Mississippi, 1989); David Leeming, *James Baldwin, A Biography* (New York: Henry Holt, 1994); and Quincey Troupe, ed., *James Baldwin: The Legacy* (New York: Simon & Schuster, 1989).

6 Unpublished journal, 16 June 1980.

7 Unpublished journal, 9 April 1980.

8 Unpublished journal, 10 April 1980.

9 Unpublished journal, 30 April 1980.

10 Unpublished journal, 28 April 1980.

11 Unpublished journal, 30 April 1980.

12 Unpublished journal, undated entry, 1980.

13 Unpublished journal, 5 June 1980.

14 In an article covering the scope of Sidney Poitier's achievements as "America's first black movie star" by Jeff Simon, Poitier spoke of the public's propensity to forget the importance of pioneers. See Jeff Simon, "Call Him Mr.," *Buffalo News*, 11 March 2001: E6.

15 Unpublished journal, 24 July 1980.

16 Audre Lorde, audiotape #9, Copenhagen, 1980. Audre Lorde Papers.

17 Unpublished journal, 24 July 1980.

18 Lorde, Copenhagen, audiotape #9.

19 Unpublished journal, 24 July 1980.

20 Unpublished journal, 21 September 1980.

21 Spinsters Ink was originally located in Argyle, NY. Some years later, the founders sold the press to a Californian feminist, Sherry Thomas. After Thomas

merged Spinsters Ink with another small feminist press, the Aunt Lute Book Company in 1986, Lorde became enraged her work was now being published by strangers who'd bought the original publishing house and its assets, including *The Cancer Journals*. She insisted Charlotte Sheedy get her work back. But Sheedy had not had an opportunity to review the contract with Spinsters Ink in advance and Lorde had unknowingly passed on her work to new publishers. *The Cancer Journals* was lucrative, as Sherry Thomas admitted in a letter to Lorde on 21 May 1986: "*The Cancer Journals* made all of Spinsters continued existence possible and I've always been very grateful for your support of small women's presses, despite some terrible experiences."

22 Elly Bulkin, letter to Audre Lorde, 25 December 1980. Audre Lorde Papers.

23 McDaniel, "Audre Lorde and Spinsters Ink," 12 March 2001.

24 Although widely accepted in heterosexual circles today, the practice of wearing two earrings marked lesbian identity in the 1980s. In the 1970s and 1980s, the culture of bodybuilding defined a homoerotic aesthetic in gay and lesbian communities and came to symbolize challenges to stereotypes of gay men as effeminate and an opportunity for lesbians to recast stereotypes of the female body. Today, the muscular bodies of beautiful male fashion models and powerful female athletes help to sell products, trading on a heterosexual fascination with homoeroticism.

25 Susan McHenry, review of *The Cancer Journals* in *Ms.* magazine, 9:10 (1981): 42.

26 Lorde, *The Cancer Journals*, 48.

27 Sheedy interview, 15 June 1999.

28 These responses were detailed in numerous letters written to Charlotte Sheedy.

29 Charlotte Mayerson, letter to Charlotte Sheedy, 2 May 1980. Audre Lorde Papers.

30 Shockley, Ann Allen," in *Completely Queer*, 506–07.

31 Marion Wheeler, letter to Barbara Held/Charlotte Sheedy Literary Agency, Inc. 5 August 1980. Audre Lorde Papers.

32 John Benedict, letter to Charlotte Sheedy, 2 April 1980. Audre Lorde Papers.

33 Sheedy interview, 15 June 1999.

34 Ellen R. Greenblatt, "Michael Denneny, American editor," in *Gay and Lesbian Biography*, 146–47.

35 Sheedy interview, 15 June 1999.

36 Michael Denneny, letter to Charlotte Sheedy, 6 April 1981. Audre Lorde Papers.

37 Unpublished journal, 10 October 1980.

38 Sheedy interview, 15 June 1999.

39 Gloria Greenfield, letter to Audre Lorde, 8 October 1980. Audre Lorde Papers.

40 Smith interview, 11 June 1999.

41 Barbara Smith, Introduction to *The Truth That Never Hurts* (New Brunswick, NJ: Rutgers University Press, 1998), xi–vi.

42 Smith interview, 11 June 1999.

43 Barbara Smith, "A Press of Our Own: Kitchen Table: Women of Color Press," in Ramona P. Rush and Donna Allen, eds., *Communications at The Crossroads: The Gender Gap Connection* (Norwood, NJ: Ablex Publishing Corp., 1989), 202–07.

44 Smith interview, 11 June 1999.

45 Smith, Introduction, *The Truth That Never Hurts*, xv.

46 Smith interview, 11 June 1999.

47 Except for Cherríe Moraga and Hattie Gossett, these writers (and Smith and Lorde) all appear in a photograph taken in November 1983, reproduced in the catalogue accompanying the exhibition "Transcending Silence: The Life and Poetic Legacy of Audre Lorde." The exhibition was organized by the Franklin H. Williams Caribbean Cultural Center African Diaspora Institute, New York, May 12–September 1994. Mora J. Byrd, director of special projects for the Caribbean Cultural Center, was the curator.

48 Smith interview, 11 June 1999.

49 Publicity flyer, Kitchen Table: Women of Color Press, 1993.

50 Smith interview, 17 June 1999.

51 Publicity flyer, Kitchen Table: Women of Color Press, 1993.

52 Audre Lorde, letter to David Wilk and Mary Ann Tighe, 1 November 1980. Audre Lorde Papers.

53 David Wilk, letter to Audre Lorde, 24 November 1980. Audre Lorde Papers.

54 Unpublished journal, 21 December 1980.

55 Phyllis G. Moe, letter to Audre Lorde, 2 February 1981. Audre Lorde Papers.

56 Gloria I. Joseph and Audre Lorde, "In Memory of Our Children's Blood," *Sage: A Scholarly Journal on Black Women*, 3:2 (1986): 41–43.

57 Gloria I. Joseph, audiotape to the author, 23–24 July 2001, and telephone conversation, 20 October 1997.

58 Audre Lorde, letter to Adrienne Rich, "Wednesday, 3:30pm," hand-dated by Rich "1981."

59 Unpublished journal, 12 February 1981.

60 Elizabeth Lorde-Rollins, "In Emergency," in Evelyn C. White, ed., *The Black Women's Health Book. Speaking for Ourselves* (Seattle, WA: Seal Press, 1994), 342–51.

61 Unpublished journal, 12 February 1981.

62 Helen Lorde interview, 2 October 1995.

63 Unpublished journal, 12 February 1981.

64 Helen Lorde interview, 2 October 1995.

65 Unpublished journal, 12 February 1981.

66 Unpublished journal, 18 February 1981.

67 Williams was convicted on the basis of mostly circumstantial fiber evidence. In 1992, his lawyers sought a new trial, arguing that police officials withheld evidence linking members of the Ku Klux Klan to twenty of the killings. At a hearing to determine whether Williams deserved a new trial, Billy Joe Whitaker, described as a reliable police informant for eighteen years, testified that he was asked by a detective to wear a body bug and gave permission to have his phone tapped after Charles Saunders, a Klan member, vowed he would kill Lubie Geter, a fourteen-year-old black. Whitaker claimed he asked Saunders about the boy's death and Saunders admitted, on tape, to killing him. For other perspectives on this case see James Baldwin, *The Evidence of Things Not Seen* (New York: Holt, Rinehart & Winston, 1985); Toni Cade Bambara, "What's Happening in Atlanta?", *Race and Class*, 24(2): 111–24; and Bernard Headley, *The Atlanta Youth Murders and the Politics of Race* (Carbondale and Edwardsville, IL: Southern Illinois University Press, 1998).

68 Unpublished journal, 24 February 1981.

69 John Benedict, letter to Audre Lorde, 27 February 1981. Audre Lorde Papers.

70 Adrienne Rich, letter to Audre Lorde, 11 January 1980.

71 I thank my graduate student, Jenna Rossi, doctoral candidate in American Studies, SUNY at Buffalo, for this idea. During my Women's Studies seminar on "Black Women Writers and the Re-imagination of American Culture," Jenna introduced me to Carla Kaplan's *The Erotics of Talk: Women's Writing and Feminist Paradigms* (New York: Oxford University Press, 1996), in which the idea is expanded.

72 Joseph audiotape, 23–24 July 2001.

73 I am using the language that Toni Cade Bambara used in her novel, *Those Bones Are Not My Child*, (published posthumously, 1999), which took more than ten years to research and write. Bambara describes the terror many black Atlantans experienced during the disappearances of more than two dozen black children. She died of colon cancer in 1995; Toni Morrison, her close friend, edited the novel.

74 Joseph audiotape, 23–24 July 2001.

75 Rich interview, 17 July 1998.

76 Cliff interview, 17 July 1998.

77 Unpublished journal, St. Croix, VI, 8 March 1981.

78 Gloria I. Joseph, "Audre: My Partner and Companion," in "Transcending Silence: The Life and Poetic Legacy of Audre Lorde," exhibition catalogue, 6.

79 Cliff interview, 18 July 1998.

80 Unpublished journal, St. Croix, VI, 8 March 1981.

81 Unpublished journal, 10 November 1980.

82 Gloria Joseph in *A Litany for Survival*.

83 Roseann P. Bell, letter to Audre Lorde, 15 March 1981. Audre Lorde Papers.

84 Rich interview, 18 July 1998.

85 Joseph audiotape, 23–24 July 2001.

Chapter 14

1 Lorde, "A Litany for Survival," *The Black Unicorn*, 32.

2 Unpublished journal, 25 March 1981.

3 Unpublished journal, 2 April 1981.

4 Unpublished journal, 25 March, 1981.

5 John Benedict, letter to Audre Lorde, 9 April 1981. Audre Lorde Papers. Benedict acknowledged her call to him in this letter.

6 Phyllis G. Moe, letter to Audre Lorde, 23 April 1981. Audre Lorde Papers.

7 Unpublished journal, 29 April 1981.

8 Unpublished journal, 9 May 1981.

9 Julie Blackwomon, *Revolutionary Blues and Other Fevers* (Philadelphia: self-published, 1984), 6–8.

10 Unpublished journal, 9 May 1981.

11 Audre Lorde, letter to Phyllis G. Moe, 12 May 1981. Audre Lorde Papers.

12 Dedication of Audre Lorde Poetry Center, Hunter College, 13 December 1985, audiotapes #28–30, Audre Lorde Papers.

13 Unpublished journal, 20 May 1981.

14 For more in-depth analyses of the convention, see the *Women's Studies Quarterly*, 9:3 (Fall 1981).

15 Adrienne Rich, "Disobedience Is What NWSA Is Potentially About," ibid., 4–6.

16 Ibid. Rich's address evokes a useful interpretation by Margo V. Perkins, *Autobiography as Activism* (Jackson, MS: University Press of Mississippi, 2000).

17 Lorde, "The Uses of Anger," ibid., 7–10.

18 Susan McHenry, "Audre Lorde's Biomythography," review of *Zami: A New Spelling of My Name*, in *Ms.* magazine, 11 (February 1983): 26.

19 Lorde, "The Uses of Anger," *Women's Studies Quarterly*, 10. I am grateful to Mae G. Henderson for deepening my understanding of Lorde's work and the oratorical tradition underpinning much of black women's writing. See Mae G.

Henderson, "Speaking in Tongues: Dialogics, Dialectics, and the Black Woman Writer's Literary Tradition," in Sidonie Smith and Julia Watson, eds., *Women, Autobiography, Theory* (Madison: University of Wisconsin Press, 1998), 343–53.

20 See ibid., 344–49.

21 Deborah S. Rosenfelt, "An Overview of the Third Annual NSWA Convention," *Women's Studies Quarterly*, 10.

22 Unpublished journal, 1 June 1981, "w of c" was Lorde's shorthand for "women of color."

23 Unpublished journal, undated entry, Anger, 1981.

24 John Benedict, letter to Audre Lorde, 13 July 1981. Audre Lorde Papers.

25 John Benedict, letter to Audre Lorde, 29 September 1980. Audre Lorde Papers.

26 Dagmar Schultz, letter to Audre Lorde, 12 September 1981. Audre Lorde Papers.

27 Unpublished journal, entries dated between 1–21 August 1981.

28 Unpublished journal, 13 August 1981. The fact that Lorde called the work a "biomythography," speaking publicly to its blending of truth, mythmaking, and social history, seems to get lost in her readers' desires for an iconic Lorde.

29 Unpublished journal, 4 August [8:15am–8:45] 1981.

30 Unpublished journal, 5 August 1981.

31 Unpublished journal, 11 August 1981.

32 Unpublished journal, 5 August 1981.

33 Unpublished journal, 7 August 1981.

34 Unpublished journal, second entry, dated 20 March 1983.

35 Unpublished journal, 21 August 1981.

36 Unpublished journal, 11 September [10:30am] 1981.

37 Unpublished journal, 12 September 1981.

38 Unpublished journal, undated notes, 1981.

39 Nancy Bereano, telephone interview, 13 July 1999.

40 Lorde, letter to John Benedict, 9 October 1981. Audre Lorde Papers.

41 Bereano interview, 13 July 1999.

42 Lorde, letter to John Benedict, 9 October 1981. Audre Lorde Papers.

43 Unpublished journals, fragments of undated entries, 1980, 1981. "Outlines" appears in *Our Dead Behind Us* (New York: W. W. Norton, 1986), 8–13.

44 Original mss, Lesbian Herstory Archives, Brooklyn, NY.

45 Unpublished journal, 3 April 1981.

46 Audre Lorde, "Zami—A Journey of Strength and Survival," interview with Amanda Powell. This interview originally appeared in *Equal Times* on January 2, 1983, and was later reprinted by Persephone Press as part of the publicity materials for *Zami* (no vol. no. or page refs given for this interview). Lesbian Herstory Archives, Brooklyn, NY.

47 Lorde, "Audre Lorde: Lit from Within," *off our backs*, 11.

48 Unpublished journal, 11 November 1981.

49 Lorde, "Audre Lorde: Lit from Within," *off our backs*, 2.

50 Lorde, letter to Adrienne Rich, 1978.

51 According to Lorde's unarchived papers, "Need" was published in *Heresies: A Feminist Publication of Art and Politics* (1979); *The Black Collegian* (Spring 1980); *The Black Scholar* (May 1981); and *Fight Back!*, an anthology published by Cleis Press in Minneapolis.

52 Audre Lorde, "Afterimages," *Sinister Wisdom*, 17 (1981): 53–56; Lorde, *Chosen Poems*, 102–05.

53 Lorde, "Audre Lorde: Lit from Within," *off our backs*, 2.

54 Unpublished journal, 11 November 1981.

55 Unpublished journal, 12 November 1981.

56 Unpublished journal, written below entry dated 12 November 1981.

57 Unpublished journal, 11 November 1981.

58 Unpublished journal, below entry dated 12 November 1981.

59 Adrienne Rich, letter to Audre Lorde, 7 November 1981, and original Hunter College flyer.

60 Audre Lorde and Adrienne Rich, audiotapes #1–2, 5 December 1981, Astraea Benefit, Audre Lorde Papers.

61 John Benedict, letter to Audre Lorde, 7 December 1981. Audre Lorde Papers.

62 Ibid.

63 John Benedict, letters to Audre Lorde, 7 and 20 December 1980, 27 February, and 13 July 1981. Audre Lorde Papers.

64 John Benedict, letter to Charlotte Sheedy, 20 December 1982. Audre Lorde Papers.

65 John Benedict, letter to Audre Lorde, 20 December 1982. Audre Lorde Papers.

66 See Audre Lorde, "Learning from the 60s," in *Sister Outsider*, 134–44.

67 Unpublished journal, 10 April 1982.

68 Unpublished journal, 24 April 1982.

69 Unpublished journal, 30 April [1pm—April 30—last day of April] 1982.

70 Bereano interview, 13 July 1999. Bereano could not recall the exact timing, but she believed this time frame was likely given her memory of subsequent details about their association.

71 *Chosen Poems: Old and New* was later revised and retitled *Undersong: Chosen Poems, Old and New* (New York: W. W. Norton, 1992).

72 Lorde, interview with Gaye Williams, "A Vision of Our Past," *Sojourner*, 18. Lesbian Herstory Archives, Brooklyn, NY.

73 Lorde, "The Evening News," *Chosen Poems*, 101.

74 Lorde, "Za Ki Tan Ke Parlay Lot," *Chosen Poems*, 101–02.

75 Explanation at foot of page, ibid., 101.

76 Lorde. "October," *Chosen Poems*, 108–09.

77 Ibid., 108.

78 bell hooks's essay, "Writing from the Darkness," was very helpful to me as I considered meanings of this poem. hooks explores her journey of coming to terms with a "shadow-self"—a wounded girlhood self that had to be "recovered" for her to be released from its shame and to embrace it. See hooks, "Writing from the Darkness," *Remembered Rapture: The Writer at Work* (New York: Henry Holt, 1999), 3–12.

79 Lorde, "October," *Chosen Poems*, 108.

80 Ibid., 108–09.

81 Lorde, *Zami*, 255–56. I am indebted to Professor Monica Jardine for helping me to construct this thinking after a conversation in May 2001.

82 The scholar Carole Boyce Davies's work was tremendously helpful in deepening my understanding of Afro-Caribbean women's literature and Lorde's particular location within that literature. See Carole Boyce Davies, *Black Women, Writing and Identity: Migrations of the Subject* (New York: Routledge, 1994).

83 Rosemary Daniell, "The Poet Who Found Her Own Way," review of *Zami* and *Chosen Poems* in *New York Times Book Review*, 87 (December 1982): 29.

84 Review of *Chosen Poems* in *Publishers Weekly*, 221 (May 1982): 214.

85 In his letter to Lorde dated 28 May 1982, John Benedict repeated and agreed with this comment.

86 See ibid. Audre Lorde Papers.

87 Sally Jo Sorenson, "A Poet You Can Trust," review of *Chosen Poems* in *Contact II*, 5:27/28/29 (Fall–Winter 1982; Winter–Spring 1983): 48.

88 Rochelle Ratner, review of *Chosen Poems* in *Library Journal*, 107 (15 June 1982): 1227.

89 Susan McHenry, "Audre Lorde's Biomythography," review of *Zami* in *Ms.* magazine, 11 (February 1983): 26.

90 Gloria I. Joseph. "A Bridge and Field of Women," review of *Zami* in *Sinister Wisdom*, 24 (Fall 1983): 163–67.

91 Regina Gagnier, "Feminist Autobiography in the 1980s," *Feminist Studies*, 17:1 (Spring 1991): 140.

92 Jewelle Gomez, review of *Zami* in *Conditions: Nine*, 3 (Spring 1983): 172.

93 Jonathan Rollins interview, 28 August 1999.

94 Unpublished journal, 10 and 24 August, 11 November 1982.

95 Bereano interview, 13 July 1999.

96 Copy of publishing contract between The Crossing Press and Audre Lorde, section II of Publisher's Agreement. Audre Lorde Papers.

97 Bereano interview, 13 July 1999. The title of this book of essays and speeches was also the title of a poem published in *The Black Unicorn*, 107.

98 Ibid.

99 Unpublished journal, 20 November 1982.

100 Unpublished journal, undated entry following entry dated 20 November 1982.

101 Unpublished journal, 20 November 1982.

102 Gloria Greenfield, memo to Michelle Cliff, Irena Klepfisz, Audre Lorde, and Barbara Smith, 28 September 1982. Audre Lorde Papers.

103 In her journal, Lorde dated her entry 20 November but the reading actually took place on 21 November.

104 *This Bridge Called My Back*, ed. by Cherrie Moraga and Gloria Anzaldua, was originally published by Persephone Press (1981), then reissued by Kitchen Table: Women of Color Press (1983). It was the first anthology of feminist writings by women of color.

105 Unpublished journal, 20 November 1982.

106 Unpublished journal, 2 January 1983.

107 Unpublished journal, entries for 2, 13, 19, 21 January 1983; also undated entries in the same journal.

108 Unpublished journal, 10 April 1982.

109 Nancy Bereano, letter to Audre Lorde, 23 January 1983. Audre Lorde Papers.

110 Unpublished journal, 13 January 1983.

111 Unpublished journal, undated, sequential entries, 1983.

112 Audre Lorde, WLIB, New York City, 6 January 1983, audiotape #18. Audre Lorde Papers.

113 Unpublished journal, 6 March 1983.

114 Audre Lorde, "Black Women's Anger," *Essence*, 14:6 (October 1983): 90ff; Lorde, *Sister Outsider*, 145–75.

115 Frances Clayton, letter to Audre Lorde, Monday AM, posted from Staten Island, 15 March 1983. Audre Lorde Papers. Gloria Joseph tells me that before Lorde died, she returned correspondence to several intimate people in her life. However, copies of a few of Frances Clayton's letters, notes, and cards were not returned to Clayton and were archived along with Lorde's own papers.

116 Unpublished journal, 20 March 1983.

117 Unpublished journal, undated, sequential entries at MacDowell, 1983.

118 Unpublished journal, second entry dated 20 March 1983.

119 Unpublished journal, 23 March 1981.

120 Unpublished journal, 9 April 1983.

121 Clayton, letter to Audre Lorde, Monday AM, posted from Staten Island, 15 March 1983. Audre Lorde Papers.

122 Unpublished journal, 26 November 1979.

123 Lorde, *Zami*, 255.

124 Gloria I. Joseph, telephone conversation with author, 28 June 2001.

125 Theodore N. Kaplan, letter to Persephone Press, 22 April 1983. Audre Lorde Papers.

126 Nancy Bereano, letter to Audre Lorde, 2 May 1983. Audre Lorde Papers.

127 Lorde's handwritten notes on letter from Nancy Bereano dated 25 July 1983. Audre Lorde Papers.

128 John Benedict, letter to Audre Lorde, 26 July 1983. Audre Lorde Papers.

129 When *Chosen Poems* was revised and published as *Undersong* in 1992, the jacket was changed.

130 Unpublished journal, 12 August 1983.

131 Official Program for the March on Washington for Jobs, Peace and Freedom, 27 August 1983, Audre Lorde Papers.

132 George DeStefano, "Audre Lorde Speaks and Gays Join March on D.C.," *New York Native*, 72 (Winter 1983): 12–13.

133 "Lesbian Addresses Civil Rights Rally," *The Body Politic*, 97 (October 1983): 17. Lesbian Herstory Archives, Brooklyn, NY.

134 DeStefano, "Audre Lorde Speaks and Gays Join March on D.C.," 12.

135 Unpublished journal, 28 August 1983.

136 Janice Irvine, "Jobs, Peace and Freedom: Activists Sit In, Lesbian Speaker Added to Program," *Gay Community News*, 10 September 1983, 1–2.

137 Ibid.

138 Ibid., 1

139 Unpublished journal, 28 August 1983.

140 DeStefano, "Audre Lorde Speaks and Gays Join March on D.C.," 12.

141 Unpublished journal, 28 August 1983.

142 "march for dream; words from lorde," *off our backs*, 13:9 (October 1983): 13.

143 DeStefano, "Audre Lorde Speaks and Gays Join March on D.C.," 12.

144 Ibid. 12.

145 Typed copy of Lorde's speech, Audre Lorde Papers.

146 DeStefano, "Audre Lorde Speaks and Gays Join March on D.C.," 12.

147 Unpublished journal, 28 August 1983.

148 The invasion was based on the argument that the September coup—which led to the collapse of the People's Revolutionary Government (PRG) and the executions of its leader, Prime Minister Maurice Bishop, and several of his supporters—had destabilized political conditions in Grenada. The Reagan administration contended it was concerned for the safety of U.S. students at the American-run St. Georges Medical School. In the end, the U.S. invasion helped to crush any sense of social democracy emerging in Grenada, if not

throughout the Caribbean. See Chris Searle, *Grenada. The Struggle Against Destabilization* (London: Writers & Readers Publishing Cooperative Society, 1983); Marable Manning, *African and Caribbean Politics from Kwame Nkrumah to the Grenada Revolution* (London: Verso Books, 1987); and Maurice Bishop, *Maurice Bishop Speaks: The Grenada Revolution*, ed. Bruce Marcus and Michael Taber (New York: Pathfinder Press, 1983).

149 Unpublished journal, 25 October 1983.

150 Unpublished journal, 1 November 1983.

151 Joseph, telephone conversation with the author, 28 June 2001

152 Unpublished journal, undated entry, 1983.

153 Joseph, telephone conversation with the author, 28 June 2001.

154 Unpublished journal, undated entry, 1983.

155 Joseph, audiotape to the author, 23–24 July 2001.

156 Editors' note, "Revolutionary Hope: A Conversation Between James Baldwin and Audre Lorde," *Essence*, 15:8 (December 1984): 133.

157 Joseph, audiotape to the author, 23–24 July 2001.

158 "Revolutionary Hope: A Conversation Between James Baldwin and Audre Lorde," *Essence*, 72–74. Gloria Joseph, who was at the event, remembers that Lorde and Baldwin did discuss sexuality. The conversation between Lorde and Baldwin was not published until a full year after it took place. According to Joseph, the rights to the piece were co-signed by Lorde and Baldwin and belong to their respective estates. Transcriptions of the entire conversation were provided by Charlotte Sheedy's literary agency. Sheedy gave the transcriptions to Joseph, who reedited them. The material has since been turned over to the Center for Lesbian and Gay Studies in New York for publication.

159 Editors' note, "Revolutionary Hope: A Conversation Between James Baldwin and Audre Lorde," 72.

160 Audre Lorde, ibid., 130.

161 James Baldwin, ibid., 133.

162 For examples of the magazine's outreach to lesbians especially, see Chirlane McCray, "Beyond Fear: A Lesbian Speaks" (September 1979) and Alexis De Veaux, "Sister Love" (October 1983).

163 Audre Lorde, *I Am Your Sister: Black Women Organizing Across Sexualities.* (New York: Kitchen Table: Women of Color Press, 1985), 7-8.

Chapter 15

1 The essay appeared first in *The Black Scholar*, 15:1 (January–February 1984): 21–29; and then in *Sister Outsider*, 176–89.

2 Audre Lorde, "Grenada: An Interim Report," in *Sister Outsider*, 181.

3 Audre Lorde, ibid., 179.

4 Ibid., 180–89.

5 Lorde, "Learning from the 60s," in *Sister Outsider*, 140.

6 Lorde, "Grenada: An Interim Report," in *Sister Outsider*, 189.

7 "Audre Lorde: 'I'm angry about the pretenses of America,'" interview with William Steif in *The Progressive*, 55 (January 1991): 32–33.

8 Lorde, "Grenada: An Interim Report," in *Sister Outsider*, 189.

9 Unpublished journal, 16 October 1986.

10 Unpublished journal, 18 March 1984.

11 Cliff interview, 18 July 1998.

12 Unpublished journal, 18 March 1984.

13 Unpublished journal, 4 March 1984.

14 Unpublished journal, 16 October 1986.

15 Unpublished journal, 18 March 1984.

16 Unpublished journal, 22 March 1984.

17 Mathew Williams, "Beam, Joseph Fairchild (1954–1988)," in George E. Haggerty, ed., *Gay Histories and Cultures: An Encyclopedia* (New York: Garland Publishing, 2000), 105.

18 Sidney Sylvester Brinkley, "The Point," *The Washington Blade*, 3 January 1997, 33. Before he died, Joseph Beam was working on a second anthology, *Brother to Brother: Collected Writings by Black Gay Men*. It was completed after his death by the poet-activist Essex Hemphill with the support of Beam's mother, Dorothy Beam, and Barbara Smith (Boston: Alyson Publications, 1991).

19 Audre Lorde, "Audre Lorde: So Like a Diamond," interview with Joseph Beam in *Au Courant*, 8 April 8 1985, 7.

20 Unpublished journal, undated entry between entries dated 28 December 1983 and 30 January 1984.

21 Audre Lorde, synopsis of unpublished novel. Courtesy of Gloria Joseph.

22 Unpublished journal, 25 March–1 May 1984.

23 Unpublished journal, 27 April [Berlin] 1984.

24 Unpublished journal, 27 April [Berlin], 9 and 17 May 1984.

25 Unpublished journal, undated entry following entry dated 22 April 1984.

26 Unpublished journal, undated entry between entries dated 28 December 1983 and 30 January 1984.

27 Cheryl Clarke, "Warrior for Black Women's Lives," *Eyeball*, 2 (January 1993): 17. I am indebted to Gloria Joseph for showing me Lorde's various passports.

28 Unpublished journal, 1 June [Friday] 1984.

29 Unpublished journal, 6 June 1984.

30 Review of *Sister Outsider* in *Booklist*, 80:20 (15 June 1984): 1432.

31 At first glance, these differing versions might seem contradictory. But they are explicable in context: the worlds Audre Lorde inhabited in her final

years were even more layered, complex, competing ones, in which the "private" and "public" were mediated by her consciousness of both living and dying, and by the responsibility she felt toward family and friends, history, her legacy, and her readers. These and other likely factors shaped "differing" accounts as authentic sources that are both self-contained and fluid.

32 Audre Lorde, "A Burst of Light: Living with Cancer," *A Burst of Light. Essays* (New York: Firebrand Books, 1988), 49–134.

33 Audre Lorde, "No, we never go out of fashion . . . for each other," interview with Dorothea, Jackie Kay, and Uma in *Spare Rib*, 149 (December 1984): 26–29.

34 Unpublished journal, 6 June 1984.

35 Unpublished journal, undated entry following entry dated 26 January 1984.

36 Lorde, "A Burst of Light: Living with Cancer," *A Burst of Light*, 59–62.

37 Unpublished journal, undated entry following entry dated 17 June 1984. In this entry, Lorde mentioned that Gloria Joseph was at a party with her where there was good food and dancing. Joseph confirms she was with Lorde in Europe at this time but Lorde failed to mention that in the appropriate published "journal excerpts" in *A Burst of Light*.

38 Ibid.

39 Unpublished journal, 29 July 1984.

40 Unpublished journal, undated entry following entry dated 4 October 1984.

41 The book, for which Lorde wrote the Introduction, was first published as *Farbe bekennen: Afro-deutsche Frauen auf den Suren ihrer Geschichte* (Berlin: Orlanda Frauenverlag, 1986); later, it was published in English: *Showing Our Colors: Afro-German Women Speak Out* (Amherst: University of Massachusetts Press, 1992). Both versions were edited by May Opitz, Katharine Oguntoye, and Dagmar Schultz.

42 Unpublished journal, undated entry following entry dated 4 October 1984.

43 Lorde, "A Burst of Light: Living with Cancer," *A Burst of Light*, 65.

44 Unpublished journal, 12 August 1984.

45 Unpublished journal, undated entries written while in Vermont, 1984.

46 Unpublished journal, 28 August 1984.

47 Review of *Sister Outsider* in *Publishers Weekly*, 225 (May 25, 1984): 58.

48 Thulani Davis and Cheryl Everette, "Books," review of Leon Forrest's *Two Wings to Veil My Face* and Lorde's *Sister Outsider* in *Essence*, 15 (August 1984): 48.

49 Barbara Christian. "Dynamics of Difference," review of *Sister Outsider* in *The Women's Review of Books*, 1:11 (August 1984): 6.

50 Kate Walter, "Outside In," review of *Sister Outsider* in the *Village Voice*, 4 September 1984, 52.

51 Tana Love, "Outsider Ends Silence," review of *Sister Outsider* in *New Directions for Women*, 13 (November 1984): 20.

52 Susan Hawthorne, letter to Audre Lorde, 14 November 1984. Audre Lorde Papers.

53 Brochure for "Women 150: Putting Women on the Map," Audre Lorde Papers.

54 Audre Lorde, letter to Susan Hawthorne, 1 January 1985. Audre Lorde Papers.

55 Lorde, "A Burst of Light: Living with Cancer," *A Burst of Light*, 68.

56 Unpublished journal, 7 January 1985.

57 Lorde, handwritten notes, Audre Lorde Papers.

58 Unpublished journal, 23 February 1985.

59 Unpublished journal, undated entry following entry dated 23 February and titled "M," 1985.

60 Unpublished journal, 3 March 1985.

61 Joseph, audiotape to the author, 23–24 July 2001.

62 Constructing the story in her journal, Lorde first named the two children Matthew and Joanna, but in her typed manuscript she changed the names to Ronald and Adrian.

63 Unpublished journal, undated entry, 1985.

64 Audre Lorde, "On My Way Out I Passed Over You and the Verrazano Bridge," *Our Dead Behind Us*, 54–57.

65 Unpublished journal, 12 April 1985.

66 Audre Lorde, "Sisters in Arms," *Our Dead Behind Us*, 3–5.

67 Lorde, "A Burst of Light: Living with Cancer," *A Burst of Light*, 68.

68 Unpublished journal, 16 June 1985.

69 Unpublished journal, 24 June 1985.

70 Unpublished journal, 29 May 1985.

71 Audre Lorde, letter to Donna Awatere, 10 July 1985. Audre Lorde Papers.

72 Unpublished journal, 20 July 1985.

73 See Hizikias Assefa and Paul Wahrhaftig, *The MOVE Crisis in Philadelphia: Extremist Groups and Conflict Resolution* (Pittsburgh: University of Pittsburgh Press, 1990).

74 Courtesy of Adrienne Rich.

75 Unpublished journal, 11 August [4pm EST-1pm PST] 1985.

76 After her return to the States, Lorde wrote to Sue Culling, one of the organizers of her activities in New Zealand. The letter was undated. Several other letters written upon her return were also undated, but the contents indicate they were sent within a month or so of her return. Lorde, letter to Sue

Culling, undated; Lorde, letter to Ngahuia Te Awekotuku, undated; Lorde, letter to "Beloved Women," 12 October 1985. All in Audre Lorde Papers.

77 Lorde, letter to "Beloved Women," 12 October 1985. This letter was sent to a group of young lesbian writers who shared a house at which Lorde was welcomed. During her stay with them, Lorde learned they'd read *Zami* and *Sister Outsider*. Their hospitality made her feel "so welcome as a Black sister." Audre Lorde Papers.

78 Unpublished journal, 31 August 1985.

79 Keynote address, 5 typed pp., Audre Lorde Papers.

80 Linda Ingram, letter to Audre Lorde, 8 September 1985. Audre Lorde Papers.

81 Ibid.

82 Unpublished journal, 3 September 1985.

83 Lorde, "A Burst of Light: Living with Cancer," *A Burst of Light*, 75.

84 Unpublished journal, 21 November [Day 3] 1985.

85 Lorde, "A Burst of Light: Living with Cancer," *A Burst of Light*, 75.

86 Unpublished journal, 21 November [Day 3] 1985.

87 Lorde, "A Burst of Light: Living with Cancer," *A Burst of Light*, 75–76.

88 Audre Lorde, letter to Gloria Joseph, 26 November 1985. Audre Lorde Papers.

89 Unpublished journal, 21 November 1986.

90 Unpublished journal, 11 and 21 November 1986.

91 Lorde, "A Burst of Light: Living with Cancer," *A Burst of Light*, 77.

92 Mabel Hampton had been an entertainer during the heyday of the Harlem Renaissance and knew such legendary figures as Gladys Bentley, Alberta Hunter, Bessie Smith, "Moms" Mabley, and Ethel Waters. When jobs for black performers became scarce during the depression, Hampton worked as a domestic. This shaped her lifelong friendship with Joan Nestle, a founder of the Lesbian Herstory Archives, whose family Hampton went to work for when Nestle was ten years old. A well-known fixture in New York's lesbian community as a gay activist, Hampton was an inspiration to younger lesbians and had long supported Lorde's work. See "Hampton, Mabel" (1902–1989), in *Completely Queer*, 265–67.

93 Lorde, "A Burst of Light: Living with Cancer," *A Burst of Light*, 78, 77.

94 Unpublished journal, 15 December 1985.

95 Lorde, "A Burst of Light: Living with Cancer," *A Burst of Light*, 84.

96 Ibid., 80.

97 Ibid., 82–83.

98 Unpublished journal, 19 December 1985; 20 December [7:30AM] 1985.

99 Lorde, "A Burst of Light: Living with Cancer," *A Burst of Light*, 79.

100 Unpublished journal, 15 December 1985, notes Lorde took from a book on meditation by Ernest Katz, MD, for which she did not record a title.

101 Lorde, "A Burst of Light: Living with Cancer," *A Burst of Light*, 79.

102 Ibid., 87.

103 Unpublished journal, 20 December [7:30AM] 1985.

104 Lorde, "A Burst of Light: Living with Cancer," *A Burst of Light*, 88, 86.

105 Ibid., 89.

106 Unpublished journal, [10:30AM], 23 December 1985.

107 Unpublished journal, 13 November 1986.

108 Unpublished journal, 6 May 1985.

109 Lorde-Rollins interview, 21 March 1999.

110 Unpublished journal, 25 December 1985.

111 Unpublished journal, 20 December [7:30AM] 1985.

112 Lorde, "A Burst of Light: Living with Cancer," *A Burst of Light*, 90.

113 Ibid.

114 Ibid.

115 Unpublished journal, 7 December 1985.

116 Unpublished journal, 3 January 1986.

117 Lorde, "A Burst of Light: Living with Cancer," *A Burst of Light*, 93.

118 Unpublished journal, entries for 7, 8, 9, and 15 January 1986; also several undated entries.

119 Unpublished journal, 7 January 1986.

120 Unpublished journal, 7 January [Dr. Charlotte said], 1986.

121 Unpublished journal, undated entry, 1986.

122 Invoice for Dr. Karnow's prescription dated 20 January 1986 found in Lorde's journal. The information specialists at Roswell Park Cancer Institute, Buffalo, NY, were very helpful in enabling me to distinguish between chelidonium and hepatodoron.

123 Unpublished journal, 15 January 1986.

124 Unpublished journal, 12 February 1986.

125 Unpublished journal, 21 October 1986.

126 Lorde, "A Burst of Light: Living with Cancer," *A Burst of Light*, 95.

127 Unpublished journal, 2 February 1986. The date of this entry is misleading since Lorde began it with the sentence, "The last day of 14 in Anguilla with Gloria," and the entry follows one dated 25 February.

128 Lorde, "A Burst of Light: Living with Cancer," *A Burst of Light*, 95.

129 Unpublished journal, 25 February 1986. The finished poem, "Making Love to Concrete," was later published in *The Marvelous Arithmetics of Distance*, 243.

130 Unpublished journal, 25 February 1986.

131 According to Lorde's journal, they went back to Anguilla in February 1987.

132 Unpublished journal, 10 and 12 February 1987.

133 Unpublished journal, 25 February 1986.

134 Lorde, "A Burst of Light: Living with Cancer," *A Burst of Light*, 96–97, and unpublished journal, undated entries, 1986.

135 Unpublished journal, undated entry, 1986.

136 Lorde, "A Burst of Light: Living with Cancer," *A Burst of Light*, 97, 96.

137 Unpublished journal, 16 April 1986.

138 Cliff and Rich interview, 18 July 1998.

139 Unpublished journal, 22 February 1987.

140 Ms of Lorde's unfinished novel. Courtesy of Gloria Joseph.

141 Audre Lorde, "Today Is Not the Day," *The Marvelous Arithmetics of Distance*, 57–59.

Epilogue

1 I am indebted to Gloria Joseph for telling me the story of the meeting between Lorde and her half sister, Mavis Jones. All subsequent details of their meeting are derived from Joseph's account.

2 Audre Lorde, "Inheritance—His," *The Marvelous Arithmetics of Distance*, 15.

3 In *The Marvelous Arithmetics of Distance*, Lorde dated the poem 23 January–10 September 1992.

4 For the full text of the poem, see ibid., pp. 15–19.

5 Lorde was designated New York State Poet, 1991–93, at an official ceremony in the Legislative Office Building in Albany, NY, on 13 November 1991. Governor Mario Cuomo presented her with the Walt Whitman Citation of Merit for Poets.

6 According to Gloria Joseph, the name was ultimately chosen by Lorde's daughter, with input from Joseph. Lorde accepted her new name at a communal naming ceremony in St. Croix in 1991. Such ceremonies are said to be rooted in the West African custom of naming as a ritual of renewal that links the individual to both the living and the ancestral worlds.

7 "Audre Lorde," interview with Alycee J. Lane, *BLK, The National Black Lesbian and Gay Newsmagazine*, 2:9 (September 1990): 17.

8 Hurricane Hugo touched down on St. Crois 17 September 1989. According to research on tropical cyclones by Monique M. Clendinen, the hurricane damaged 90 percent of the buildings. Many of the islanders were injured and the death toll was reported at seventeen. Some areas of the island experienced winds of 200 mph. See Gloria I. Joseph and Hortense M. Rowe, with Audre Lorde, *Hell Under God's Orders. Hurricane Hugo in St. Croix—Disaster and Survival* (St. Croix, VI: Winds of Change Press, 1990).

9 According to Gloria Joseph, the funeral home director, Jimmie Griffith, made this remark during their conversation.

10 Attributed to Jimmie Griffith, funeral home director.

11 A memorial for Audre Lorde was held at the Haus of the Cultures of the World in Berlin on 6 February 1993. Personal remarks by Manfred Kuno.

12 Lorde's essay, "I Am Your Sister: Black Women Organizing Across Sexualities," was used for the title of a "celeconference" honoring Lorde. "I Am Your Sister: Forging Global Connections Across Difference"—part celebration and part conference—was held at a number of sites in Boston and Cambridge, MA, 5–8 October 1990. It brought together thousands of people representing varied sexual, racial, class, and cultural communities from Central America, South America, Africa, Canada, Europe, and the United States.

13 Gloria T. Hull, "Living on the Line: Audre Lorde and Our Dead Behind Us," in Cheryl A. Wall, ed., *Changing Our Own Words: Essays on Criticism, Theory, and Writing by Black Women* (New Brunswick, NJ: Rutgers University Press, 1989), 156.

BIBLIOGRAPHY

Abel, Elizabeth, Barbara Christian, and Helene Moglen, eds. *Female Subjects in Black and White: Race, Psychoanalysis, Feminism*. Berkeley: University of California Press, 1997.

Adjake, Joseph K., and Adrianne R. Andrews, eds. *Language, Rhythm, and Sound: Black Popular Cultures into the Twenty-first Century*. Pittsburgh: University of Pittsburgh Press, 1997.

Albertson, Chris. *Bessie*. New York: Stein & Day, 1972.

Alderson, David, and Linda Anderson, eds. *Territories of Desire in Queer Culture: Refiguring Contemporary Boundaries*. Manchester and New York: Manchester University Press, 2000.

Alexander, Elizabeth. "Coming Out Blackened and Whole: Fragmentation and Reintegration in Audre Lorde's *Zami* and *The Cancer Journals*," *American Literary History*, 6:4 (1994): 695–715.

Allan, Tuzyline Jita. *Womanist and Feminist Aesthetics: A Comparative Review*. Athens, OH: Ohio University Press, 1995.

Allen, Robert L. *Black Awakening in Capitalist America: An Analytic History*. Trenton, NJ: Africa World Press, Inc., 1990.

———, and Pamela L. Allen. *Reluctant Reformers: The Impact of Racism on American Social Reform Movements*. Washington, DC: Howard University Press, 1974.

Andrews, William L. *To Tell a Free Story: The First Century of Afro-American Autobiography, 1760–1865.* Urbana and Chicago: University of Illinois Press, 1986.

Angelou, Maya. *I Know Why the Caged Bird Sings.* New York: Random House, 1969.

Annas, Pamela. "A Poetry of Survival: Unnaming and Renaming in the Poetry of Audre Lorde, Pat Parker, Sylvia Plath, and Adrienne Rich," *Colby Quarterly,* 18:1 (March 1982): 9–25.

Anzaldua, Gloria. *Borderlands/La Frontera: The New Mestiza.* San Francisco: Spinsters/Aunt Lute Book Company, 1987.

———, ed. *Making Face, Making Soul/Haciendo Caras: Creative and Critical Perspectives by Feminists of Color.* San Francisco: Aunt Lute Books, 1990.

Apetheker, Bettina. *Women's Legacy: Essays on Race, Sex, and Class in American History.* Amherst: University of Massachusetts Press, 1982.

Ashcroft, Bill, Gareth Griffiths, and Helen Tiffin. *The Empire Writes Back: Theory and Practice in Post-Colonial Literatures.* London and New York: Routledge, 1989.

Ashley, Kathleen, Leigh Gilmore, and Gerald Peters, eds. *Autobiography and Postmodernism.* Amherst: University of Massachusetts Press, 1994.

Avi-ram, Amitai F. "Apo Koinou in Audre Lorde and the Moderns: Defining the Differences," *Callaloo, A Journal of African-American and African Arts and Letters,* 9:1 (Winter 1986): 193–208.

Awkward, Michael. *Negotiating Difference: Race, Gender, and the Politics of Positionality.* Chicago: University of Chicago Press, 1995.

Baker, Houston A., Jr. *Workings of the Spirit: The Poetics of Afro-American Women's Writing.* Chicago: University of Chicago Press, 1991.

Baldwin, James. *Another Country.* New York: Dell Publishing Company, 1962.

———. *Giovanni's Room.* New York: Dell Publishing Company, 1965.

———. "The Outing," *Going to Meet the Man.* New York: Dell Publishing Company, 1965.

———. *Just Above My Head.* New York: Dial Press, 1979.

———. *The Evidence of Things Not Seen.* New York: Holt, Rinehart & Winston, 1985.

Bambara, Toni Cade, ed. *The Black Woman: An Anthology.* New York: New American Library, 1970.

Bambara, Toni Cade. *Those Bones Are Not My Child,* ed. Toni Morrison. New York: Pantheon Books, 1999.

———, ed. Toni Morrison. *Deep Sightings and Rescue Missions.* New York: Vintage Books, 1996.

Bannon, Ann. *Odd Girl Out.* Tallahassee, FL: Naid Press, 1983.

Barbour, Floyd B., ed. *The Black Power Revolt.* Boston: Extending Horizons Books, 1968.

Beale, Frances. "Slave of a Slave No More," *Black Scholar*, 6 (March 1975): 2–10.

Beckles, Hilary, and Verene Shepherd, eds. *Caribbean Slave Society and Economy*. New York: New Press, 1991.

Bell, Derrick. *Confronting Authority: Reflections of an Ardent Protestor*. Boston: Beacon Press, 1994.

Bell, Roseann P., Bettye J. Parker, and Beverly Guy-Sheftall, eds. *Sturdy Black Bridges: Visions of Black Women in Literature*. Garden City, NY: Anchor Books/Doubleday, 1979.

Bell Scott, Patricia. *Life Notes: Personal Writings by Contemporary Black Women*. New York: W. W. Norton, 1994.

———, with Juanita Johnson Bailey. *Flat-Footed Truths: Telling Black Women's Lives*. New York: Henry Holt & Company, 1998.

Bennett, Michael, and Vanessa D. Dickerson, eds. *Recovering the Black Female Body: Self-Representations by African American Women*. New Brunswick, NJ: Rutgers University Press, 2001.

Berry, Faith. *Langston Hughes: Before and Beyond Harlem*. Westport, CT: Lawrence Hill & Co., 1983.

Berry, Mary Frances, and John Blassingame. *Long Memory: The Black Experience in America*. New York and Oxford: Oxford University Press, 1982.

Bethel, Lorraine, and Barbara Smith, eds. *Conditions: Five; The Black Women's Issue*, 2:2. Brooklyn, NY: Conditions, 1979.

Blackwomon, Julie. *Revolutionary Blues and Other Fevers*. Philadelphia: self-published, 1984.

Blassingame, John. "Black Autobiographies as History and Literature," *Black Scholar*, 5:4 (1973–74): 2–9.

Bontemps, Arna, ed. *American Negro Poetry*. New York: Hill & Wang, 1963.

Boone, Sylvia Ardyn. *Radiance from the Waters: Ideals of Feminine Beauty in Mende Art*. New Haven and London: Yale University Press, 1986.

Bourne, Jenny. "Towards an Anti-Racist Feminism," *Race and Class*, 25 (Summer 1983): 1–22.

Bracey, John H., Jr., August Meier, and Elliott Rudwick, eds. *Black Nationalism in America*. Indianapolis and New York: Bobbs-Merrill Company, 1970.

Branch, Taylor. *Parting the Waters: America in the King Years, 1954–63*. New York: Simon & Schuster, 1988.

Braxton, Joanne M. *Black Women Writing Autobiography: A Tradition Within a Tradition*. Philadelphia: Temple University Press, 1989.

———, and Andree Nicola McLaughlin, eds. *Wild Women in the Whirlwind: Afra-American Culture and the Contemporary Literary Renaissance*. New Brunswick, NJ: Rutgers University Press, 1990.

Bristow, Joseph, ed. *Sexual Sameness: Textual Differences in Lesbian and Gay Writing*. New York: Routledge, 1992.

Brooks, Gwendolyn. *Selected Poems*. New York: Harper & Row, 1963.

Brown, Cynthia Stokes, ed. *Ready From Within: Septima Clark and the Civil Rights Movement*. Navarro, CA: Wild Trees Press, 1986.

Brown, Elaine. *A Taste of Power: A Black Woman's Story*. New York: Pantheon Books, 1992.

Butcher, Margaret Just. *The Negro in American Culture*. New York: New American Library, 1956.

Butler, Judith. *Gender Trouble: Feminism and the Subversion of Identity*. New York: Routledge, 1990.

Butterfield, Stephen. *Black Autobiography in America*. Amherst: University of Massachusetts Press, 1974.

Cannon, Katie S. *Black Womanist Ethics*. Atlanta: Scholars Press, 1988.

Carby, Hazel. *Reconstructing Womanhood: The Emergence of the Afro-American Woman Novelist*. New York: Oxford University Press, 1987.

Carmichael, Stokely, and Charles V. Hamilton. *Black Power: The Politics of Liberation in America*. New York: Vintage Books, 1967.

Carroll, Rebecca. *I Know What the Red Clay Looks Like: The Voice and Vision of Black Women Writers*. New York: Random House, 1994.

Cesaire, Aimé. *Discourse on Colonialism*, trans. Joan Pinkham. New York: Monthly Review Press, 1972.

Chapman, Abraham, ed. *Black Voices: An Anthology of Afro-American Literature*. New York: New American Library, 1968.

Christian, Barbara. *Black Feminist Criticism: Perspectives on Black Women Writers*. New York: Pergamon Press, 1985.

Churchill, Ward, and Jim Vander Wall. *Agents of Repression: The FBI's Secret Wars Against the Black Panther Party and the American Indian Movement*. Boston: South End Press, 1988.

Clark, Veve A., Ruth-Ellen B. Joeres, and Madelon Sprengnether, eds. *Revising the Word and the World: Essays in Feminist Literary Criticism*. Chicago: University of Chicago Press, 1993.

Clarke, Cheryl. *Narratives: Poems in the Tradition of Black Women*. New York: Kitchen Table: Women of Color Press, 1983.

———. *Living as a Lesbian*. Ithaca, NY: Firebrand Books, 1986.

———. *Humid Pitch: Narrative Poetry*. Ithaca, NY: Firebrand Books, 1989.

Cliff, Michelle. *Claiming an Identity They Taught Me to Despise*. Boston: Persephone Press, 1980.

———. *No Telephone to Heaven*. New York: E. P. Dutton, 1987.

———. "Sister Outsider: Audre Lorde's Fighting Words," *Village Voice Literary Supplement*, 114 (April 1993): 13–15.

Collins, Patricia Hill. *Black Feminist Thought: Knowledge, Consciousness, and the Politics of Empowerment*. Boston: Unwin Hyman, 1990.

Combahee River Collective. "A Black Feminist Statement," in Zillah R. Eisenstein, ed., *Capitalist Patriarchy and the Case for Socialist Feminism*. New York: Monthly Review Press, 1979.

Cook, Blanche Wiesen. "Women Alone Stir My Imagination: Lesbianism and the Cultural Tradition," *Signs: Journal of Women in Culture and Society*, 4:4 (Summer 1979): 60–65.

Cose, Ellis. *The Rage of a Privileged Class*. New York: Harper/Collins, 1993.

Coss, Clare, ed. *The Arc of Love: An Anthology of Lesbian Love Poems*. New York: Scribner, 1996.

Cosslett, Tess, Celia Lury, and Penny Summerfield, eds. *Feminism and Autobiography: Texts, Theories, Methods*. London and New York: Routledge, 2000.

Daly, Mary. *Beyond God the Father: Toward a Philosophy of Women's Liberation*. Boston: Beacon Press, 1973.

————. *Gyn/Ecology: The Metaethics of Radical Feminism*. Boston: Beacon Press, 1978.

Davies, Boyce Carole. *Black Women, Writing, and Identity: Migrations of the Subject*. New York: Routledge, 1994.

Davis, Angela Y. *Angela Davis: An Autobiography*. New York: Random House, 1974.

————. *Women, Race, and Class*. New York: Random House, 1981.

————. *Women, Culture, and Politics*. New York: Random House, 1989.

————. *Blues Legacies and Black Feminism*. New York: Vintage Books, 1999.

De Lauretis, Teresa. "Eccentric Subjects: Feminist Theory and Historical Consciousness," *Feminist Studies*, 16 (Spring 1990): 115–50.

Delgado, Richard, and Jean Stefancic, eds. *Critical White Studies: Looking Behind the Mirror*. Philadelphia: Temple University Press, 1997.

D'Emilio, John. *Sexual Politics, Sexual Communities: The Making of a Homosexual Minority in the United States, 1940–1970*. Chicago: University of Chicago Press, 1983.

De Veaux, Alexis. *Don't Explain: A Song of Billie Holiday*. New York: Harper & Row, 1980.

————. "Just Between Us: Remembering Audre Lorde," *Village Voice Literary Supplement*, 114 (April 1993): 14.

————. "Searching for Audre Lorde," *Gay, Lesbian, Bisexual, Transgender Literature and Culture*, ed. Charles Henry Rowell. Special issue of *Callaloo*, 23:1 (2000): 64–67.

————. " 'The Difficult Miracle of Biography': Reflections on Writing, Black Women's Stories, and Living Somebody Else's Life." College of Arts and Sciences Spring Lecture Series. State University of New York at Buffalo, NY, February 25, 2002.

Dhairyam, Sagri. "'Artifacts for Survival': Remapping the Contours of Poetry with Audre Lorde," *Feminist Studies*, 18:2 (Summer 1992): 229–56.

Diop, Cheikh Anta. *The African Origin of Civilization: Myth or Reality*, ed. and trans. Mercer Cook. New York: Lawrence Hill & Co., 1974.

Dill, Bonnie. "Race, Class, and Gender: Prospects for an All-Inclusive Sisterhood," *Feminist Studies*, 9 (Spring 1983): 131–50.

Duberman, Martin, Martha Vicinus, and George Chauncey, Jr., eds. *Hidden from History: Reclaiming the Gay and Lesbian Poet*. New York: New American Library, 1989.

Du Bois, William E. B. *The Souls of Black Folk* (1903). New York: New American Library, 1969.

Emanuel, James A., and Theodore L. Gross, eds. *Dark Symphony: Negro Literature in America*. New York: Fress Press, 1968.

Estes, Clarissa Pinkola. *Women Who Run with the Wolves: Myths and Stories of the Wild Woman Archetype*. New York: Ballantine Books, 1992.

Evans, Mari, ed. *Black Women Writers (1950–1980): A Critical Evaluation*. Garden City, NY: Anchor Books/Doubleday, 1984.

Evans, Mary. *Missing Persons: The Impossibility of Autobiography*. New York: Routledge, 1999.

Fanon, Frantz. *Black Skin, White Masks*, trans. Charles Lam Markmann. New York: Grove Press, 1967.

Foucault, Michel. *History of Sexuality*, trans. from the French by Robert Hurley. New York: Pantheon Books, 1978.

Freeman, Harold P. "The Meaning of Race in Science—Considerations for Cancer Research: Concerns of Special Populations in the National Cancer Program." President's Cancer Panel Meeting, National Cancer Institute, Bethesda, MD. 9 April 1997.

Gates, Henry Louis, Jr., ed. *Reading Black, Reading Feminist: A Critical Anthology*. New York: Meridian Books, 1990.

Gayle, Addison, Jr., ed. *The Black Aesthetic*. Garden City, NY: Doubleday, 1971.

Giddings, Paula. *When and Where I Enter: The Impact of Black Women on Race and Sex in America*. New York: William Morrow, 1984.

Gilroy, Paul. *The Black Atlantic: Modernity and Double Consciousness*. Cambridge, MA: Harvard University Press, 1993.

Ginzberg, Ruth. "Audre Lorde's (Nonessentialist) Lesbian Eros," *Hypatia*, 7:4 (Fall 1992): 73–90.

Glendinning, Victoria. "Lies and Silences," in Eric Homberger and John Charmley, eds., *The Troubled Face of Biography*. New York: The Macmillan Company, 1988.

Goldman, Anne E. "Autobiography, Ethnography, and History: A Model for Reading," in Sidonie Smith and Julia Watson, eds., *Women, Autobiography, Theory: A Reader*. Madison: University of Wisconsin Press, 1998.

Grahn, Judy. *The Work of a Common Woman*. New York: St. Martin's Press, 1978.

Griffin, Farah Jasmine. *"Who Set You Flowin'?": The African-American Migration Narrative*. New York and Oxford: Oxford University Press, 1995.

Guy-Sheftall, Beverly, ed. *Words of Fire: An Anthology of African-American Feminist Thought*. New York: New Press, 1995.

Heilbrun, Carolyn G. *Writing a Woman's Life*. New York and London: W. W. Norton, 1988.

Henderson, Mae G. "Speaking in Tongues: Dialogics, Dialectics, and the Black Woman Writer's Literary Tradition," in Smith and Watson, eds., *Women, Autobiography, Theory: A Reader*.

Henry, Paget. *Caliban's Reason: Introducing Afro-Caribbean Philosophy*. New York and London: Routledge, 2000.

Hernton, Calvin C. *The Sexual Mountain and Black Women Writers: Adventures in Sex, Literature and Real Life*. New York: Anchor Books/Doubleday, 1987.

Hill-Collins, Patricia. *Black Feminist Thought: Knowledge, Consciousness, and the Politics of Empowerment*. Boston: Unwin Hyman, 1990.

Hine, Darlene Clark. *Black Women in America: An Historical Encyclopedia*, 2 vols., Brooklyn, NY: Carlson, 1993.

Holland, Endesha Ida Mae. *From the Mississippi Delta: A Memoir*. New York: Simon & Schuster, 1997.

Holloway, Karla F. C. *Moorings and Metaphors: Figures of Culture and Gender in Black Women's Literature*. New Brunswick, NJ: Rutgers University Press, 1992.

hooks, bell. *Ain't I a Woman?: Black Women and Feminism*. Boston: South End Press, 1981.

———. *Talking Back: Thinking Feminist, Thinking Black*. Boston: South End Press, 1989.

———. *Yearning: Race, Gender, and Cultural Politics*. Boston: South End Press, 1990.

———. *Black Looks: Race and Representation*. Boston: South End Press, 1992.

———. *Sisters of the Yam: Black Women and Self-Recovery*. Boston: South End Press, 1993.

———. *Bone Black: Memories of Girlhood*. New York: Henry Holt & Company, 1996.

———. *Remembered Rapture: The Writer at Work*. New York: Henry Holt & Company, 1999.

Huggins, Nathan Irvin, ed. *Voices from the Harlem Renaissance*. New York and Oxford: Oxford University Press, 1995.

Hull, Gloria, Patricia Bell Scott, and Barbara Smith, eds. *All the Women Are White, All the Blacks Are Men, But Some of Us Are Brave: Black Women's Studies*. Old Westbury, NY: Feminist Press, 1982.

Jablon, Madelyn. *Black Meta-Fiction: Self-Consciousness in African American Literature*. Iowa City: University of Iowa Press, 1997.

James, Joy. *Shadow Boxing: Representations of Black Feminist Politics*. New York: St. Martin's Press, 1999.

———. "African Philosophy, Theory, and 'Living Thinkers,'" in Joy James and Ruth Farmer, eds., *Spirit, Space and Survival: African American Women in (White) Academe*. New York and London: Routledge, 1993.

James, Stanlie M., and Abena P. A. Busia, eds. *Theorizing Black Feminisms: The Visionary Pragmatism of Black Women*. London and New York: Routledge, 1993.

Jay, Karla, and Joanne Glasgow, eds. *Lesbian Texts and Contexts: Radical Revisions*. New York: New York University Press, 1990.

Jordan, June. *Passion: New Poems, 1977–1980*. Boston: Beacon Press, 1980.

———. *Civil Wars*. Boston: Beacon Press, 1981.

———. *On Call: Political Essays*. Boston: South End Press, 1985.

———. *Affirmative Acts: Political Essays*. New York: Anchor Books/Doubleday, 1995.

———. *Soldier: A Poet's Childhood*. New York: Basic Books, 2000.

Jordan, Sheila M., ed. *Broken Silences: Interviews with Black and White Women Writers*. New Brunswick, NJ: Rutgers University Press, 1993.

Joseph, Gloria I., and Jill Lewis. *Common Differences: Conflicts in Black and White Feminism*. New York: Anchor Books/Doubleday, 1981.

Kaplan, Carla. *The Erotics of Talk: Women's Writing and Feminist Paradigms*. New York: Oxford University Press, 1996.

Katz, Jonathan Ned. *Gay American History: Lesbians and Gay Men in the U.S.A.* Rev. ed. New York: Meridian Books, 1992.

Kelley, Robin D. G. *Race Rebels: Culture, Politics and the Black Working-class*. New York: Free Press, 1994.

———. *Freedom Dreams: The Black Radical Imagination*. Boston: Beacon Press, 2001.

Kennedy, Elizabeth Lapovsky, and Madeline D. Davis. *Boots of Leather, Slippers of Gold: The History of a Lesbian Community*. New York and London: Routledge, 1993.

King, Katie. "Audre Lorde's Lacquered Layerings: The Lesbian Bar as a Site of Literary Production," in Sally Munt, ed., *New Lesbian Criticism: Literary and Cultural Readings*. New York: Columbia University Press, 1992.

King, Woodie, ed. *Black Spirits: A Festival of New Black Poets in America*. New York: Vintage Books, 1972.

Klein, Herbert S. *African Slavery in Latin America and the Caribbean*. New York and Oxford: Oxford University Press, 1986.

Kuumba, Bahati M. *Gender and Social Movements*. Walnut Creek, CA: AltaMira Press, 2001.

Lee, Chana Kai. *For Freedom's Sake: The Life of Fannie Lou Hamer*. Urbana and Chicago: University of Illinois Press, 2000.

Lewis, David Levering. *When Harlem Was in Vogue*. New York: Vintage Books, 1979.

Lewis-Etter, Gwendolyn. "Black Women's Life Stories: Reclaiming Self in Narrative Texts," in Sherna Berger Gluck and Daphne Patai, eds., *Women's Words: The Feminist Practice of Oral History*. New York and London: Routledge, 1993.

Lorde, Audre: *The First Cities*. New York: The Poets Press, 1968.

———. *Cables to rage*. London: Paul Breman Ltd, 1970.

———. *From a Land Where Other People Live*. Detroit: Broadside Press, 1973.

———. *New York Head Shop and Museum*. Detroit: Broadside Press, 1974.

———. *Coal*. New York: W. W. Norton, 1976.

———. *Between Our Selves*. Point Reyes, CA: Eidolon Editions, 1976.

———. *The Black Unicorn: Poems*. New York: W. W. Norton, 1978.

———. *The Cancer Journals*. 2nd ed. San Francisco: Spinsters Ink, 1980.

——— *Zami: A New Spelling of My Name*. Boston: Persephone Press, 1982.

———. *Chosen Poems: Old and New*. New York: W. W. Norton, 1982.

———. *Sister Outsider: Essays and Speeches*. Trumansburg, NY: The Crossing Press, 1984.

———. *I Am Your Sister: Black Women Organizing Across Sexualities*. New York: Kitchen Table: Women of Color Press, 1985.

———. *Our Dead Behind Us: Poems*. New York: W. W. Norton, 1986.

———. *A Burst of Light: Essays*. Ithaca, NY: Firebrand Books, 1988.

———. *Undersong: Chosen Poems, Old and New*. New York: W. W. Norton, 1992.

———. *The Marvelous Arithmetics of Distance: Poems 1987–1992*. New York: W. W. Norton, 1993.

Martin, Joan M. "The Notion of Difference for Emerging Womanist Ethics: The Writings of Audre Lorde and bell hooks," *Journal of Feminist Studies in Religion*, 9:1–2 (Fall 1993): 39–51.

Mbiti, John S. *African Religions and Philosophy*. Garden City, NY: Anchor Books/Doubleday, 1969.

McKay, Nellie. "The Narrative Self: Race, Politics, and Culture in Black American Women's Autobiography," in Smith and Watson, eds., *Women, Autobiography, Theory: A Reader*.

McKinley, Catherine E., and L. Joyce DeLaney, eds. *Afrekete: An Anthology of Black Lesbian Writing*. New York: Anchor Books/Doubleday, 1995.

Mintz, Sidney W., and Richard Price. *The Birth of African-American Culture: An Anthropological Perspective*. Boston: Beacon Press, 1976.

Mitchell, Angelyn. *The Freedom to Remember: Narrative, Slavery, and Gender in Contemporary Black Women's Fiction*. New Brunswick, NJ: Rutgers University Press, 2002.

Moody, Anne. *Coming of Age in Mississippi: An Autobiography*. New York: Dell Publishing Company, 1968.

Moore, Lisa C., ed. *Does Your Mama Know?: An Anthology of Black Lesbian Coming Out Stories*. Decatur, GA: Redbone Press, 1997.

Moraga, Cherrie, and Gloria Anzaldua, eds. *This Bridge Called My Back*. 2nd ed. Latham, NY: Kitchen Table: Women of Color Press, 1984.

Morrison, Toni. "The Sight of Memory," in William Zinsser, ed., *Inventing the Truth: The Art and Craft of Memoir*. Boston: Houghton Mifflin Company, 1987.

Neal, Larry. *Visions of a Liberated Future: Black Arts Movement Writings*, ed. Michael Schultz. New York: Thunder's Mouth Press, 1989.

Neal, Mark Anthony. *What the Music Said: Black Popular Music and Black Popular Culture*. New York and London: Routledge, 1999.

————. Soul Babies: *Black Popular Culture and the Post-Soul Aesthetic*. New York and London: Routledge, 2002.

Neff, Heather. "Now That I Am Forever with Child: The Construction of Womanself in the Works of Audre Lorde." *Sage: A Scholarly Journal on Black Women*, 9:2 (Summer 1995): 72–75.

Nelson, Jill. *Volunteer Slavery. My Authentic Negro Experience*. New York: Penguin Books, 1993.

Omolade, Barbara. *The Rising Song of African American Women*. New York and London: Routledge, 1994.

Painter, Nell Irvin. *Sojourner Truth: A Life, a Symbol*. New York and London: W. W. Norton, 1996.

————. "Representing Truth: Sojourner Truth's Knowing and Becoming Known," in Patricia Bell-Scott with Juanita Johnson-Bailey. eds., *Flat-Footed Truths: Telling Black Women's Lives*. New York: Henry Holt & Company, 1998.

Parrinder, Geoffrey. *African Mythology*. London: Hamlyn Publishing Group, 1967.

Perkins, Margo V. *Autobiography as Activism: Three Black Women of the Sixties*. Jackson, MS: University Press of Mississippi, 2000.

Pryse, Marjorie, and Hortense J. Spillers, eds. *Conjuring: Black Women, Fiction, and Literary Tradition*. Bloomington: Indiana University Press, 1985.

Randall, Dudley, ed. *The Black Poets*. New York: Bantam Books, 1971.

Rich, Adrienne. "Compulsory Heterosexuality and Lesbian Existence," *Signs: Journal of Women in Culture and Society*, 5:4 (Summer 1980): 631–60.

Rosenblatt, Roger. "Black Autobiography: Life as the Death Weapon." in James Olney, ed., *Autobiography: Essays Theoretical and Critical*. Princeton: Princeton University Press, 1980.

Royster, Jacqueline Jones. *Traces of a Stream: Literacy and Social Change Among African American Women*. Pittsburgh: University of Pittsburgh Press, 2000.

Russell, Kathy, Midge Wilson, and Ronald Hall, eds. *The Color Complex: The Politics of Skin Color Among African Americans*. New York: Anchor Books/Doubleday, 1992.

Sandoval, Chela. "Dissident Globalizations, Emancipatory Methods, Social-Erotics," in Arnaldo Cruz-Malave and Martin F. Manalansan IV, eds., *Queer Globalizations, Citizenship and the Afterlife of Colonialism*. New York and London: New York University Press, 2002.

Scott, Kesho Yvonne. *The Habit of Surviving: Black Women's Strategies for Life*. New Brunswick, NJ: Rutgers University Press, 1991.

Shakur, Assata. *Assata: An Autobiography*. Westport, CT: Lawrence Hill & Co., 1987.

Shelly, Elaine. "Conceptualizing Images of Multiple Selves in the Poetry of Audre Lorde," *Lesbian Ethics* (Winter 1995): 88–98.

Smith, Barbara, ed. *Home Girls: A Black Feminist Anthology*. New York: Kitchen Table: Women of Color Press, 1983.

———. *The Truth That Never Hurts: Writings on Race, Gender, and Freedom*. New Brunswick, NJ: Rutgers University Press, 1998.

Smith, Charles Michael, ed. *Fighting Words, Personal Essays by Black Gay Men*. New York: Avon Books, 1999.

Smith, Sidonie. "Performativity, Autobiographical Practice, Resistance," in Smith and Watson, eds., *Women, Autobiography, Theory: A Reader*.

———, and Julia Watson, eds., *Women, Autobiography, Theory: A Reader*. Madison: University of Wisconsin Press, 1998.

Tate, Claudia, ed. *Black Women Writers at Work*. New York: Continuum, 1983.

Thompson, Robert Farris. *Flash of the Spirit: African and Afro-American Art and Philosophy*. New York: Vintage Books, 1983.

Townes, Emilie M., ed. *A Troubling in My Soul: Womanist Perspectives on Evil and Suffering*. Maryknoll, NY: Orbis Books, 1993.

Scales-Trent, Judy. *Notes of a White Black Woman: Race, Color, Community*. University Park, Philadelphia: Pennsylvania State University Press, 1995.

Walker, Alice. *In Search of Our Mothers' Gardens: Womanist Prose*. New York and London: Harcourt Brace Jovanovich, 1983.

———. *The Way Forward Is with a Broken Heart*. New York: Random House, 2000.

Walker, Rebecca. *Black, White, and Jewish: Autobiography of a Shifting Self*. New York: Riverhead Books, 2001.

Wall, Cheryl A., ed. *Changing Our Own Words: Essays on Criticism, Theory, and Writing by Black Women*. New Brunswick, NJ: Rutgers University Press, 1989.

Watkins-Owens, Irma. *Blood Relations: Caribbean Immigrants and the Harlem Community, 1900–1930*. Bloomington and Indianapolis: Indiana University Press, 1996.

Wilson, Anna. "Audre Lorde and the African-American Tradition," in Sally Munt, ed., *New Lesbian Criticism: Literary and Cultural Readings*. New York: Columbia University Press, 1992.

Wing, Adrien Katherine, ed. *Critical Race Feminism: A Reader*. New York and London: New York University Press, 1997.

Zinsser, William, ed. *Inventing the Truth: The Art and Craft of Memoir*. Boston: Houghton Mifflin, 1987.

INDEX

437